ISAAK-IGNAZ MOSCHELES

Dedicated to all forgotten composers

EMIL F. SMIDAK

Isaak-Ignaz Moscheles

THE LIFE OF THE COMPOSER
AND HIS ENCOUNTERS WITH
BEETHOVEN, LISZT, CHOPIN AND MENDELSSOHN

———

SCOLAR PRESS

First published in hardback 1988 by
J & V Edition Wien Verlagsges. m.b.H., Vienna – Austria

This translated edition published 1989 by
SCOLAR PRESS
Gower Publishing Company Limited
Gower House
Croft Road
Aldershot
Hampshire GU11 3HR
England.

Gower Publishing Company
Old Post Road, Brookfield
Vermont 05036
USA

© Copyright 1989 Avenira Stiftung für Gesellschaftsforschung, CH-6006 Lucerne

All rights reserved. No part of this publication may be reproduced, stored in a retrieval system, or transmitted in any form or by any means electronic, mechanical, photocopying, recording, or otherwise without the prior permission of the publisher.

British Library Cataloguing in Publication Data
Smidak, Emil F.
    Isaak-Ignaz Moscheles: the life of the composer and his encounters with Beethoven, Liszt, Chopin and Mendelssohn.
    1. Czechoslovak music. Moscheles, Ignaz, 1794–1870
    I. Title
    780′.92′4

    ISBN 0–85967–821–0

The portrait of the composer on the dust jacket was painted by his son Felix Moscheles in 1866 and his great-great-grandson Mr Paul G. A. Rosen was kind enough to lend it to us the publishers.

Printed and bound in Great Britain by Courier International Ltd, Tiptree, Essex

CONTENTS

CHAPTER 4 – LEIPZIG (1846–1870)

Introduction

This book is based on the written records and correspondence of Isaak-Ignaz Moscheles which were published by his wife Charlotte between 1872 and 1877 in two volumes entitled *Aus Moscheles' Leben* ('From the Life of Moscheles') and supplemented by her own additions and comments. As we shall read later, Moscheles himself had made preparations, together with his wife, to have his diaries and correspondence published. Thus, any reservations as to whether records such as these (sometimes of a highly personal nature) should be published at all, can be dismissed immediately, by virtue of the fact that they have already been published by Charlotte Moscheles.

As an introduction to the book, Charlotte wrote:

The last wishes of a loved one are sacred. They are above any personal feelings and petty considerations. I have undertaken this difficult task as a legacy of my husband's life, but not without some trepidation. Others might well have done the work better, but no one could have done it with such devotion. If its execution is to comply fully with Moscheles' wishes, my role must be that of an impartial and completely detached editor.

It was not my intention to write a biography of Moscheles the musician. Anyone who expects a complete account of his life would have to refer back to Charlotte Moscheles' original book. What guided me in the compilation of this volume was more the wish to offer today's reader an insight into a bygone world, to let him sense the atmosphere and, above all, to give him a deeper understanding of the great musicians of that time – Beethoven, Chopin, Liszt, Mendelssohn and others – in their human dimension, as seen through the eyes of one who knew them personally.

It was a deliberate decision not to present the book in such a way as to render its contents more exciting to the reader. This would have meant considerable amendments and alterations, and the testimony would thus have been deprived of both its authenticity and its immediacy. Consequently, the book itself does not present a fully-balanced, exhaustive and finely tuned narrative, which can be immediately 'consumed' by the reader. It does, however, allow plenty of scope for the reader to think and feel for himself, and he is invited to make his own creative contribution in the search for a forgotten epoque.

Countless books have been written about Beethoven, Mendelssohn, Chopin and other composers. But how many of them have been written by people who were contemporaries of these composers and actually met them? The majority of the books have been inspired by the beauty of the music, and the power it communicates to the listener. What would Beethoven, for example, have to say about all these books? The same Beethoven who has been acclaimed as one of the immortal greats, yet who, just before he died, was reduced to begging for a few pounds sterling?

Moscheles was not only one of the people who met Beethoven, Mendelssohn, Chopin and so on personally, but even more importantly, he was one of the very few who kept a diary. He is, therefore, a witness.

Obviously, Moscheles' account of the era in which he lived cannot claim to be objective and truthful in every detail. The words he penned upon the death of Chopin will serve as an example of this:

The musical world has suffered a great loss with the death of poor Chopin, for although he was not a truly great composer, and although he did not produce any great works of art, he possessed the rare qualities of warmth, sensitivity and originality.

It is hardly necessary to add today that 'poor Chopin' did take his place among the great composers and that his compositions now rank among the finest works of art. And who was forgotten? – Moscheles, of course.

On the subject of musical biographies he wrote the following in his diary in 1829:

When reading musical biographies we often come across lengthy dissertations about the music of the composer in question. Sometimes they even go as far as to mention his 'intentions', which reminds us of commentators on Shakespeare's work who, according to some learned authorities, have attributed thoughts to him which would have been quite alien to the great playwright. Great pains were taken to determine his most secret intentions while, all too often, the fact was overlooked that his inspirations were, quite simply, those of a genius. A similar fate seems to have befallen the works of Beethoven. Beethoven, of course, committed to paper only what and how he was thinking and feeling. However, his compositions have been subjected to widely differing interpretations ever since. No doubt the 'Moonlight' Sonata will never cease to be sentimental, and the 'Eroica' will always be majestic; but with a sonata such as 'Les adieux, l'absence et le retour', every performer will feel the piece differently and every listener will conjure up his own individual picture. 'And this is just how it should be,' Mendelssohn used to say. 'As long as the composer can stimulate the listener's imagination sufficiently to evoke some kind of image of thought, no matter what, then his purpose has been achieved.'

This is also my opinion. Music should be absorbed through every pore, it should penetrate right to the heart and strike a chord there. For this reason, it is impossible to describe a composition. The reader will forgive me, then, if I refrain from analysing Moscheles' music or discussing its merits or failings. It can, however, be reasonably assumed that a piece of music which was not only widely acclaimed when it first appeared, but which was also still played with enthusiasm and interest some thirty, forty or even fifty years later, must be of more than just passing worth.

In 1857 Moscheles wrote:

May the modernist composers never overthrow Beethoven, and never cease to follow Haydn and Mozart who have been our musical cornerstones up until now. We lesser mortals are, of course, destined to be buried under the rubble of these great men and I, for my part, consider it an honour. Who knows? Perhaps we shall one day be excavated in the same way as Pompeii and Herculaneum have been.

Ten years ago, more than one hundred years after his death, I began the task of excavating Moscheles from the rubble.

He may have found it painful rather than surprising that, by the middle of the nineteenth century, his music had lost favour with the public. In 1860, at the age of 66 he wrote:

I would willingly write larger scale works for my instrument if I were not convinced that they would be omitted from today's concert programmes. I pride myself on being more than someone who churns out waste paper which is destined to be stuffed in an old trunk for years to come. If the rats and mice insist on chewing this paper for their meals, then they shall certainly not be feasting on my music as long as I remain on this earth. I do still write the occasional piece for charitable institutions, or songs and small pieces for my family as well as for my grandchildren. However, restricting myself in this way is not a sign of incapacity on my part. It is merely a matter of pride.

If something has been 'excavated' like Pompeii and Herculaneum, the treasure should be displayed in all its glory. I have, therefore, brought out a record of two of Moscheles' works. Moscheles composed his G-minor Piano Concerto in 1820 when, at the age of 26, he saw the North Sea for the first time. His Sinfonia Concertante for flute and oboe was composed at the age of 74, just two years before his death.

I have also arranged for a film to be made about this symphony. The film is primarily dedicated to the place where Moscheles was born and to the spiritual environment which shaped him – the former ghetto in Prague. For European Jews, Prague represented 'Mother Israel'. According to legend, the Jews went there after the destruction of the temple in Jerusalem, and after they had been scattered by the Romans. They still pray there today in their place of worship, the early Gothic 'alt-neu' synagogue, which was built in the 13th century.

The synagogue and the ancient Jewish cemetery in Prague symbolize the continuous thread running through Moscheles' life – his deep religious belief. From this he received the strength to bear all the trials and tribula-tions of life and to follow his path without faltering. It was a path of constant seeking, alternating between light and shade, as shown in the dialogue between the flute and the oboe, and portrayed on the screen by a male and a female dancer.

Moscheles' path in life took him from Prague to Vienna, and then on to Paris, London and Leipzig, where he eventually died.

Who was this man Moscheles? For me, Moscheles was both a gifted musician as well as a deeply religious man. Belonging to one particular religious denomination was not of importance to him. He relied on God alone, and this trust helped him to live his life.

Dear Moscheles! I have now lived with you for more than ten years. The more time I have spent with you, the more my admiration for you has grown. I admire you for the courage with which you overcame the challenge of life in a strange city as a fatherless 14-year-old boy, and I admire you for the steadfastness which you managed to retain, even in life's most trying situations. When I found you in the rubble of time, I felt like someone who had just discovered a great treasure. Let this treasure now be revealed in your music. As you yourself said:

Music requires no explanation. It speaks to the heart. One merely needs to be human to understand it.

E. F. Smidak

Prague and Vienna (1794–1816)

THE BEGINNING IN PRAGUE

Moscheles compiled a description later in his life of the period from his birth until he embarked upon his diary in 1814:

I was born on May 30th, 1794 and my home town is Prague. I can remember as far back as the beginning of the century. From those early years I recall that there was much talk about the great and bloody revolution which had taken place in France. A preoccupation with military matters had even spread to the world of small boys, and we never seemed to stop playing at soldiers. I rarely missed an opportunity to go and hear the military band performing its show-pieces on the 'Ring' in front of the main police station. The wind players used to summon the small boys over to hold up their music sheets for them, and I was, of course, always at hand to perform this task for them. When returning home, full of enthusiasm, from these street concerts, I would announce to everybody that one day I was going to be a bandsman myself.

My mother was the epitome of kindness, love and cheerfulness, and she went out of her way to care for father, to whom she was a devoted wife, as well as for us, her five children. Father, who was a cloth merchant by profession, never allowed his business commitments to prevent him from indulging his love for music; he particularly enjoyed singing and playing his guitar. It is to my father that I owe my early desire to follow an artistic career. He often used to say: 'One of my children will receive proper musical training', which made me wish that I would be the one. Father did, however, start off with my elder sister. While she was having her piano lessons I would stand at the end, gawping and listening intently to the highest C that our little instrument reached. In so doing, I noticed that my sister derived little pleasure from the task, as she could never play any of her exercises correctly. When I was alone, I would try and figure out the exercises for myself. As I did not find them at all difficult, I became all the more frustrated with her for her clumsiness; so much so that I actually forgot myself sufficiently to call out in the middle of one of her lessons: 'Oh how stupid! I could do it better myself'. Her old tutor Zahradka made me climb onto the stool to play instead of my sister. He must have passed on a favourable report to my father, as I was told some days after the incident that I would be receiving lessons in place of my sister.

Nobody was more delighted than I was! Piano lessons started immediately and I made rapid progress. Perhaps my progress was too rapid for the old teacher whose lessons were no longer of interest to me. Using my pocket money I began subscribing to a musical lending library, taking out no less than six pieces at a time, by composers such as Kozeluch, Eberl and others, and going through them at great speed. Whether my actions were too much for the tutor or whether my father actually dismissed him, I shall never know. Whatever the case, he failed to appear again.

Friends of the family considered that they were doing father and me a great service by introducing me now and again to other families with whom they were acquainted and where I would be admired and pampered like some rare plant on account of my achieve-

ments, wretched as they may have been. I, of course, took great delight in the praise and kisses showered upon me by the ladies, not to mention the sweet meats they fed me with. Father, however, soon put a stop to all this nonsense by rebuking these foolish people. He rightly felt that such behaviour would be detrimental to my further development. The more my musical instinct stirred within me, the more solicitous he became towards me. If, however, I slipped away from those hateful finger exercises to play soldiers and to make cardboard scabbards and helmets to distribute among my 'company', there would be bitterness between us. I felt that as a Captain I had my duties to carry out, and it seemed unjust to me that I was not allowed to supply my troops with new equipment.

Meanwhile, under the guidance of my new music tutor, Horelsky, I had begun to study larger compositions, my practice being done in the free time not taken up by school work. This seven-year-old boy brazenly tackled even Beethoven's 'Pathétique Sonata'. Try to imagine how he played it, and try to imagine, too, the passion for Beethoven which had seized him and which spurred him on to try to get to grips with the master's other great works.

In 1792 Beethoven had moved from Bonn to Vienna where, sponsored by the aristocracy, he had reached the pinnacle of his first creative period by 1801. Moscheles writes about this time in the following extract:
My father put a stop to this nonsense by taking me to see Dionys Weber. 'As you are our leading musician', he told him, 'I have come to you for an honest opinion of my son, instead of all those gushing eulogies, and to find out whether he has sufficient talent for you to make a good musician out of him.'

I was, of course, expected to play for him and, conceited amateur that I was, I did so with a certain amount of pride. Mother had dressed me up in my best clothes and I played my best piece, Beethoven's 'Pathétique Sonata'. To my great surprise, I was neither interrupted by shouts of 'Bravo', nor was I showered with praise when I had finished. Instead, I was stunned to hear Weber's comment: 'To be perfectly honest, the boy is doing quite the wrong thing; he gallops through these great works, and has neither sufficient technique nor understanding for them. He does have talent though, and I could make something out of him if you were to leave him with me for three years, and if you follow my instructions to the letter. In the first year he must play Mozart, in the second Clementi, and in the third Bach, but not a single note of Beethoven. If, however, he continues with his visits to the lending library we shall have nothing more to do with each other.

My father readily agreed to all of this, and on our way home he delivered a homily concerning his resolve that my studies would henceforth would be a serious matter indeed. If I followed them through conscientiously, I would bring honour and glory to myself, to Father and to the whole family.

I would have been only too happy to exchange such distant horizons for the music of Beethoven and the ever changing delights of the lending library. I had, however, been chased out of my Garden of Eden, and I now had to begin to work in the sweat of my face.

Father kept a strict check on my progress with Weber, and he used to collect me from my lessons personally. If he received a good report about me, I would be rewarded with a visit to the cake shop.

Weber and his contemporary Tomasek did not see eye to eye, inasmuch as one of them preferred the musical ways of the Germans, while the other preferred those of the Italians. 'Who is there of any worth besides Mozart, Clementi and Bach?', Weber would say. 'None but mad fools who turn the young people's heads; even Beethoven, clever though he is, writes some weird things which lead our young pupils astray.' He would wax with youthful fervour on the beauties of Mozart, and he delighted in explaining Bach's ingenious inter-connections to me, drawing on his large store of theoretical knowledge. With his own compositions, however, he had no luck whatsoever, and he was never able to find a publisher for them. He had them printed at his own expense, and they would be left lying around in piles in his study.

One day, after Weber had repeatedly assured my father that he was optimistic about my prospects, the latter rewarded me by taking me to the theatre for the very first time. We went to see a performance of 'Achilles', an opera recently composed by Paër. I was particularly struck by the Funeral March and, on returning home, I was able to reproduce it correctly on the piano, bringing tears to Father's eyes. Thereafter, visits to the opera became a frequent occurrence, and I found them to be a source of great delight.

If only God had let me keep this splendid and understanding father for a while longer. It was not to be though, as he suddenly contracted typhoid, and was plucked from our midst. Thus, at the tender age of fourteen, I stood weeping at his coffin. As time passed, my grief at losing him gradually subsided, but I never forgot my gratitude and my deep affection for him. His wish to hear my first composition, which he had repeatedly uttered during his illness, was to remain unfulfilled. However, his death and the rather grim situation in which the family then found itself spurred me on to making my first public appearance in Prague.

Weber deemed that I was now quite capable of standing on my own two feet, and felt that I should be allowed to do so. He helped me to prepare the remaining part of the concerto on which I had been working. He then gave me permission to hold an evening entertainment which not only brought me a lot of praise, but also some financial reward, much to Mother's relief. An old uncle, however, predicted my ruin, since he could only envisage me playing dance music at society gatherings. On the other hand, if I were to follow a career of a merchant, and were lucky enough to make my way to one of the wealthy trading cities, such as Hamburg, I may well be able to gain the hand of a rich merchant's daughter! As it turned out, I did not become a 'pub musician', as the old man sometimes used to call me, nor did I end up as a wealthy merchant. The second of his aspirations for me was, however, fulfilled as I did go to Hamburg and led a native of that city up the aisle.

FURTHER TRAINING IN VIENNA

In 1808, not long after the death of his father, Moscheles was sent to Vienna on the advice of some of his mother's friends, in order to continue his education there.

It is not difficult to imagine what effect such a step must have had on the small Jewish boy, who was barely fourteen at the time. With the loss of his father still painfully fresh in his memory, he suddenly found himself torn from the warmth and comfort of his beloved family, alone in a strange and uncaring city. In this forlorn and lonely state, Moscheles found even greater solace in music and, determined to fulfil his father's expectations and pushing his personal grief firmly into the background, he gathered up all his courage and set about his studies.

His piano tuition was undertaken initially by J. A. Streicher, a composer and piano-maker. He also received lessons in musical theory from Albrechtsberger, the Director of Music at the cathedral. This entirely self-educated man had previously been Beethoven's teacher in 1794, and also counted C. Czerny, F. Ries, J. Eybler and J. N. Hummel among his pupils. When these studies came to an end, Moscheles received the following testimonial from his teacher:

ATTESTATION

I, the undersigned, hereby confirm that Ignaz Moscheles has achieved such a high standard in his study of musical theory with me in the course of the last few months that he is now able (by virtue also of his masterly skill on the fortepiano and the organ) to earn his living from either of these arts, wherever he should choose. Moreover, as he is now willing to travel, I find it right and proper that I should recommend him wholeheartedly to any city where he may decide to work.

Vienna, the 28th Day of September, 1808

(Seal) Georgius Albrechtsberger,
Director of Music,
The Cathedral Church of St. Stephen

Strangely enough, the name of Ignaz appears on the attestation, even though Moscheles can only have been given the name at his Christian baptism some years later. The original text presumably contained the name Isaak, which was subsequently altered by Charlotte and Moscheles himself when they were both working on the diaries. This baptism is, however, given no mention whatsoever in the revised diaries. As we shall see later though, it was not the formal aspect of religion which was so important to Moscheles, but rather his faith, and it was indeed this faith which helped him to overcome the tribulations of life.

Moscheles later became a pupil of Antonio Salieri, and mention is made of this in his diary:

It is only natural that the great Beethoven became the object of my most ardent admiration. My high opinion of him made it difficult for me to understand how the ladies of Viennese society could have the courage to invite him to their musical functions and perform his compositions in his presence. It would seem, however, that he quite enjoyed the experience, as he was often to be seen at one or other of their soirées. It may well be that his unfortunate hearing deficiency robbed him of the joy of performing, thus making it preferable for him to entrust his latest compositions to the lady pianists. I was even more astonished when, on calling to see Hofkapellmeister Salieri one day and not finding him at home, I happened to notice a piece of paper lying on the table upon which was written the following succinct message: 'Your pupil Beethoven called on you.' This made me think that if Beethoven considered he could still learn from Salieri, how much more could I benefit as his pupil? Salieri had been the pupil of Gluck and was his most fervent admirer, but he simply could not abide Mozart or his compositions. I went to him, nevertheless, and became his pupil, and for three years I was his assistant at the Opera, a post which allowed me to visit every theatre free of charge.

The diary begins on April 1st, 1814, and describes 'cheerful and bustling life in the good old Vienna' of that time. Attracted by the more splendid society gatherings and public entertainments, he now found favour for the first time as a virtuoso and composer. On April 8th, Meyerbeer, then aged 21 and known chiefly as a pianist, performed one of Moscheles' compositions, a Rondo. This is how Moscheles described the event:
Although I was quite convinced of his virtuosity, I was still curious to see what effect his

playing would have on a mixed audience. I noticed, though, that some parts which the audience may have found difficult to understand were received with amazement, mainly on account of their unusual boldness and the way in which the performer mastered the difficulties, seemingly without effort.

On April 11th, we have the following description of a piano recital given by Beethoven:

I listened to Beethoven playing his new B minor trio as part of a lunchtime musical entertainment at the 'Römischer Kaiser'. So many compositions are wrongly labelled as being 'new'. This is definitely not the case with Beethoven's work though, and least of all with this piece, which was, yet again, so full of originality. I was less enthusiastic about his playing which, though full of spirit, lacked purity and precision. Nevertheless, I noticed many touches of greatness which I had long since recognised in his compositions.

On April 10th, 1814, the news reached Vienna – ten days late – that Paris had been conquered by the allied troops and that Napoleon had subsequently been deposed. In their excitement, the Viennese took to the streets and celebrated by singing for joy.

The liberation of Germany from Napoleonic rule, the great event at that time, seemed to cast a magic spell on carefree Viennese high society. The poets and musicians of the city vied with each other in their expressions of jubilant relief. Spohr wrote his 'Befreites Deutschland' ('Liberated Germany'); Hummel celebrated the return of Kaiser Franz I by writing a song, and Moscheles composed his 'Entry into Paris' ('Einzug in Paris'), and later a sonata entitled 'Die Rückkunft des Kaisers' ('The Return of the Kaiser').

The Jewish community to which Moscheles still belonged at that time, commissioned a cantata from him to celebrate the

occasion. It was performed with great pomp and presented in a revised version to the public for a second time a year later at the Congress of Vienna.

During 1814, Moscheles also composed six scherzos, 'Variations on a Theme by Handel', his Rondo in A minor for piano duet, and minuets and trios for Artaria's collection of national dances. In addition, he wrote the Polonaise in E-flat – a sonata for piano and violin – as well as another one for piano and bassoon. The latter was especially written with the bassoonist Romberg in mind, with Moscheles himself playing the piano accompaniment, and lastly the theme of the 'Sonata mélancolique', which he himself, and also the musical experts of the period, described as one of his best works.

In spite of all this activity, he was constantly dissatisfied with his own performance, and the following remark recurs frequently in his diary:

Even though I received a great ovation today, I was not content with the way I played.

BEETHOVEN AND THE VIENNA CONGRESS

In the second half of 1814, we find this entry in the diary: *I have been asked (by Beethoven) to revise the piano score of his masterpiece 'Fidelio'. What more could anyone wish for?* Moscheles goes on to describe how he took the revised score back to Beethoven, two pieces at a time, to be checked and corrected. he notes in his diary that 'He changed hardly anything', alternating with 'He changed nothing at all', and sometimes 'He simplified . . .' or 'He reinforced what I had written'.

At one point it says:

When I went to see Beethoven in the morn-

ing, he was still in bed. He was in a particularly cheerful mood today and quickly jumped out of bed and stood, just as he was, at the window which looks out onto the Schottenbastei, and began to peruse the revised pieces. Quite naturally, a crowd of youngsters soon gathered underneath his window, and he shouted out: 'Those b . . . . y boys. What on earth do they want?' With a smile, I pointed to him in his indecent state. 'You're right', he cried and quickly snatched a dressing gown to cover himself. When we came to the great last duet in the work, 'Namenlose Freude', where the text I had submitted contained the phrase 'Ret-terin des Gat-ten', he crossed it out and substituted 'Rett-erin des Gatt-en', claiming that it was impossible to sing on the letter 't'. Underneath the last piece I had written 'Fine, with God's help'. He was not at home when I delivered it to his house, and when he returned it to me he had added 'O Mensch, hilf dir selber' (Help yourself, man!).

The entry on November 29th reads:

Attended Beethoven's midday concert at the Redoutensaal (Festival Hall). He was conducting his marvellous A major Symphony, the Seventh, Op. 92, as well as the cantata 'Der glorreiche Augenblick' (The glorious moment) and 'Die Schlacht bei Vittoria' (The Battle of Vittoria). All of them were worthy of him.

During this period, Moscheles regularly attended the concerts given by the Schuppanzigh Quartet at which Beethoven's string quartets were given their first performance. On each occasion he praised the excellence of the performance, and after one concert he wrote: I sat next to Spohr and we exchanged opinions about the music we had heard. Spohr was a fervent opponent of Beethoven and his imitators.

As the Congress of Vienna drew nearer, the diary describes the arrival of the foreign heads of state and the reception given to them by the Emperor and his court.

An enthusiastic crowd thronged the streets, and among that crowd were Moscheles and his young friends. First to arrive in Vienna was the King of Württemberg, Frederick I, followed by the King of Denmark, Frederick IV, and Frederick William III of Prussia, and finally, Alexander I, Tsar of Russia. The Hiller Regimental Band struck up to welcome them, with a march composed by Moscheles. A public festival was arranged in the Augarten to celebrate the event.

The most spectacular sight was a firework display recreating the spire of St. Stephen's Cathedral. After this a rainbow appeared, and later on there were imitations of the Brandenburg Gate and the Russian Obelisk. Among the gala performances were Spontini's 'Las Vestale' and Rossini's 'Mosé'. A public festival had also been arranged in Schönbrunn, and the visiting monarchs were treated to a performance of 'Johann von Paris' at the local theatre. The Orangerie was most tastefully illuminated, and the Temple of Flora looked exquisitely beautiful.

On October 16th, a performance of Handel's 'Samson' was given in the Spanish Riding School. Moscheles bubbled over with youthful enthusiasm about the piece. The first time I listened to it, I melted with delight. Since then, I have not missed a single rehearsal or performance of the masterpiece, and each has been an unforgettable experience.

As winter approached, Moscheles received a commission to write the music for an equestrian display in honour of the foreign monarchs.

With its festive illumination and embellishment with medieval ornaments, the Riding School had been transformed into a kind of arena. Twenty-four skilled horsemen, dressed as medieval knights, performed their manoeuvres admirably, and their ladies were *attired in magnificent costumes. I have never seen such glittering jewels.*

During the last few months of the year 1814, Moscheles spent a lot of time in Meyerbeer's company. He wrote in his diary: *His bravura is breathtaking and his playing is incomparable. I admire his very personal style of handling the instrument.*

They spent hours at a time sitting at the piano, inventing new tunes and improvising, which resulted amongst other compositions in the duet 'Punscheinladung'.

At that time, Meyerbeer was going through a period of transition. He started to devote himself more to dramatic compositions and, a short while later, he left for Paris where the direction his work was to take was finally settled.

An event of great importance for Moscheles was an invitation he received at the beginning of 1815 from Countess Hardegg, a lady much involved with charitable work.

She sent for me to ask whether I would be willing to play at a concert on Ash Wednesday in aid of some charitable institutions. I did not particularly relish the idea as I had no new compositions at hand, but she would not hear of my refusal. 'Write something quickly, Moscheles, and make it sound spectacular!' That was all well and good, but what? At last we agreed that I should write some variations on the march that was being played by the band of Tsar Alexander's own regiment at the time.

He began working on these variations on January 29th, and by February 5th they were finished. He named them the Alexander Variations, and for many years it was said that only Moscheles was able to play them. Both on tour and in Vienna they used to be the crowning glory of his concerts.

A few days after their completion, he and Hummel gave a concert together which was attended by Salieri. Moscheles was delighted that his teacher enthused so much about his achievements. Just how closely Moscheles was attached to his teacher is shown by a later entry in his diary:

My beloved teacher Salieri is in great danger at present, as he is suffering from pneumonia. May God grant that his illness takes a turn for the better!

It was during this period that Moscheles wrote the Polonaise in E-flat major, later to become the last movement of his E-flat major Concerto. As soon as rehearsals for the piece had begun though, Moscheles complained that the timpani were not in tune. This complaint was to be repeated at nearly every subsequent performance, prompting Mendelssohn to turn the matter into a joke when he exclaimed on one occasion: 'But they *are* in tune!)

The Polonaise was followed at once by another composition, a sextet. In later years Moscheles liked to tell people how hard he had tried to emulate the style of Hummel's septet. However, he always ended up with the remark: 'My endeavours never reached beyond a beginner's work, not to be compared with Hummel's Septet'.

Pianists at this time were divided into two camps – those preferring Hummel's style and those preferring Moscheles'. Competent contemporaries of them both maintained that Moscheles had not yet quite achieved Hummel's legato. Hummel, it was said, 'had velvet under his fingers from which the passages rolled off like strings of pearls', whereas Moscheles, by virtue of his dazzling bravura and youthful exuberance, tended to carry the audience away with him on a wave of irresistible emotion. There was, however, not a trace of rivalry between the two artists, as can be seen from the earlier comment about the septet, and other admiring references.

Of Carl Czerny he wrote:
No one was better qualified to strengthen

even the weakest fingers and to make easy work of the trickiest keyboard acrobatics which, though highly beneficial, might have spoiled one's taste for the instrument.

On another occasion, however, he added the following remark:

There is no denying the fact that we musicians, regardless of who we may be, are merely insignificant satellites orbiting around the one true heavenly light of Beethoven.

It was at about this time that Moscheles composed his sonata for piano duet in E-flat major which he dedicated to the Archduke Cardinal Rudolf.

In the spring of 1816 Moscheles returned to Prague for a reunion with his family, his old friends and his teachers. He was fated wherever he went, and found time to give a concert for the poor of the city which raised 2400 florins.

In his diary he wrote: *What a joy it is for me to be back with my mother and sisters, and how I love to play for them! Nobody listens to my playing with as much enthusiasm as they do.*

Nevertheless, Moscheles still had to play for his old teacher, Dionys Weber, whom he still held in high esteem, as well as for Weber's former rival Tomasek. There was now a close bond between them both, and they were eager to hear Moscheles performing again.

He spent the summer at Karlsbad as the guest of Count Wallis' family, and caused a sensation with his Alexander Variations and Fantasias.

One of these concerts was attended by a six-year-old boy who was deeply impressed by what he heard: Robert Schumann. It was not until three decades later that Moscheles came to know of the decisive influence his playing had had on the boy's development. In the late 1840s, Schumann wrote a letter to Moscheles:

You have given me much joy and done me a great honour by dedicating your sonata (Opus 121, for piano and cello) to me. In so doing, you provided me with fresh incentive for my own aspirations in which you have always taken a benevolent interest. More than thirty years ago in Karlsbad, when I was a stranger to you, I refused to part with a concert ticket for a long, long time because you had touched it, so I kept it as if it were a relic. Little did I dream that so famous an artist would one day do me such an honour. Please accept my deepest gratitude!

When he returned to Vienna, Moscheles began to make preparations for an extensive tour to which he had at last agreed, after his friends had persuaded him that it was time for him to try his luck in the world at large.

In the autumn of 1816 he left the city on the Danube, albeit with a feeling of regret.

Travels in Europe (1816–1825)

GERMANY, HOLLAND AND BELGIUM

The first stage of Moscheles' tour was a trip to Leipzig which he made via Prague. The journey was made in a hired coach and Moscheles complained bitterly about its laborious progress. He tried to pass the time by practising on a dummy keyboard that he had brought with him. When he finally arrived in Leipzig, he made straight for the theatre. 'As an Austrian, I was not prepared for the noisy interruptions from the students here; if they feel that the play is moving too slowly, they think nothing of tapping the ground with their sticks.' The play in question was a satire on artists' earthly hopes and aspirations, in which the author poured bitter scorn and ridicule on all the performers who had come to use the Leipzig Fair as a showcase for whatever spectacle they thought might bring in some profit. Somewhat taken aback, Moscheles asked himself: *What if the play was aimed at me?*

In those days, Leipzig was universally regarded as a highly civilized and cultured city; Goethe even liked to refer to it as 'Little Paris'. The town had an air of lively activity about it, and Moscheles was struck by the large crowds on the promenades, the exotic clothes that people wore, the Polish Jews in their strange attire, and the restaurants which were filled to overflowing. He was also surprised to see that the city gates were locked at night, a custom he had never previously encountered. He visited the fairground and mingled with all the weird and wonderful people to be found there. After this, he went to the site of the battlefield where Napoleon had been decisively defeated just three years previously.

Once he had found his feet in Leipzig, he called on Schicht, the director of music of that venerable Leipzig institution, the Choir of St. Thomas's (the Thomanerchor), which J. S. Bach had conducted from 1723 until 1750. They had a long conversation together in which they discussed the arts, artistic skill and artists in general, leading to a difference of opinion about Beethoven:

Schicht maintained, among other things, that 'Christus am Oelberg' (Christ on the Mount of Olives) was not written in the style of an oratorio. He told me that when Beethoven had sent the work to his publisher here in the city, the latter thought it right to omit the chorus 'Welchen Weg fliehen wir'. Apparently, this infuriated Beethoven, who called the action high-handed, and he wrote a letter to the publisher expressing his strongest disapproval. Schicht seemed to find this most peculiar, so I took it upon myself to explain to him the reason for Beethoven's attitude.

On October 8th, Moscheles gave his first concert in Leipzig, at the Gewandhaus.
I was very excited, so it was just as well that I was occupied with urgent business as early as 7 o'clock in the morning. In accordance with local custom, I paid the cashier in advance the sum of 66 thaler and 12 groschen for the use of the concert hall and the lighting. The rehearsal began at 9 o'clock, and my overture to the ballet 'Die Portraits' (The Portraits) went off perfectly the very first time. However, the orchestra wanted me to go through it once more, and this time it exceeded all my expectations. I cannot say enough in praise of the horns and trombones and, above all, the

excellent leadership given by Matthäi, the first violinist. The small audience in the hall gave me unstinted applause, and the Alexander Variations even lured some of the players in the orchestra away from their seats to the piano to watch me execute the difficult passages in the piece. Despite this gratifying success, I was in such a state of nerves about the evening's performance that I was unable to eat anything beforehand. In the afternoon I tested the pulse of my instrument once again, and found it to be well in tune; my own pulse was also normal. At five o'clock the hall was opened to the public and, with its splendid illumination, it had a truly magnificent appearance. Half an hour later, the first ladies arrived, most elegantly attired and eager to secure the best seats. It would be difficult to imagine a more beautiful or better equipped hall than this one. I found, too, that the seating was arranged in an entirely novel and very practical way. At half past six, after I had managed to drink a cup of tea laced with some rum, I gave the signal for the concert to begin. At my first entry on to the platform I was received with a warm welcome – a distinction not usually conferred. The orchestra gave of their best in the overture so that it came off better than I ever could have hoped. The audience was so enthusiastic and gave such tumultuous applause that these moments must rank as some of the happiest in my life.

There followed an invitation to give a second concert which took place on the 14th, and once again it earned Moscheles rapturous applause. His virtuosity had impressed the Leipzig public to such an extent that by now they wanted not only to hear him, but also to watch him play. When he opened the concert with his 'Fantasia', a piece in which he was able to show off his virtuosity to the full, members of the audience left their seats:

They pressed closer and closer, until they formed a close circle around me and, when I had finished playing, they expressed their satisfaction by giving me a rousing ovation.

Encouraged by his successes in Leipzig, Moscheles moved on to Dresden. During the first four weeks of his stay, however, he was confined to his lodgings as he had contracted a throat infection. To make good use of this enforced leisure, he settled down to orchestrate his four heroic marches. He then proceeded to write his Sonata in E major, which he dedicated to Beethoven, and he spent the remainder of the time reading Goethe.

He also began to study the work of the philosopher Moses Mendelssohn, a friend of Lessing's (and grandfather of Felix Mendelssohn-Bartholdy), who was the precursor of Jewish emancipation in Germany, and with whose family Moscheles was to forge such close ties in the years to come.

The following entry dates back to those weeks:

I must record an episode that has come to my notice, as it may serve to illustrate Haydn's sense of justice. Someone informed Haydn that Beethoven had made one or two disparaging comments about 'Die Schöpfung' ('The Creation'). 'That's hardly fair of him', Haydn replied. 'After all, what has he written himself? His Septet, for instance? Well, it must be said, it is certainly very beautiful, even magnificent!', he exclaimed, in genuine admiration, quite forgetting the bitterness which the criticism directed against him had caused.

Before being able to conclude arrangements for his first concert in Dresden, he had to overcome a number of obstacles that were put in his way by a scheming Director of Music, and also by certain aspects of court etiquette. *But at last I seem to have gained a foothold – nay a handhold! He played his* way up the ladder of the court hierarchy, as it were.

On December 20th, he was finally summoned to play before the court.

It seemed barbaric that the ladies and gentlemen carried on eating, and the members of the household listened from the galleries while the court orchestra and I were playing music for them; and it still seems barbaric to me now. For the sake of truth, however, I have to admit that the ladies and gentlemen and their lackeys did at least try to be as quiet as possible, and the former even condescended to engage me in polite conversation.

During the years 1817 to 1819 the diary was kept only sporadically. More regular entries appear again at the beginning of 1820 when Moscheles left Vienna once again, this time to go to Munich, where he played before King Maximilian. He then went on to Augsburg to give a concert at the invitation of ex-Queen Hortense and finally reached Amsterdam, where he gave four public performances.

At the Hague, Moscheles was overwhelmed by his first sight of the North Sea, and he recorded in his diary the powerful impact that this had had upon him. It was there that he wrote his Concerto in G minor, which was to become so popular in later years. Referring to this concerto, he says in his diary:

After listening every day to the melancholy sound of the bells from the nearby church, it seemed inevitable that I should choose a minor key, and give the first movement the title 'Malinconia'.

From Holland Moscheles returned to Germany once again, giving concerts in Aachen, Frankfurt, Mainz and Brussels. He then proceeded to Brussels, noted at that time for its flourishing musical life, where he had a number of opportunities to give concerts.

FIRST VISIT TO PARIS

On December 29th, 1820, Moscheles came at last to Paris, where he put up at the Hôtel de Bretagne.

I shall never forget my first impression as I drove through those crowded streets, with masses of shoppers surging everywhere, dashing from one luxurious store to another. While I was out on my morning stroll the next day, whom should I happen to meet but my old friend Spohr! A good omen indeed! We were both delighted to see each other again, and we stayed together for some while, strolling along the Boulevard des Italiens. Later on in the day we visited the Palais Royal, and in the evening we went to the Italian Opera to attend a performance of 'Don Giovanni', in the unabridged version, much to my amazement!

A few days later, at a morning entertainment given at a nobleman's house, Moscheles played the piano part in his friend's Quintet in E-flat for Piano and Wind Instruments. The warm ovation he received pleased him all the more when he noticed that Kreutzer and Reicha were in the audience and listening to him play for the first time.

He started to attend Reicha's Quintet entertainments with Spohr, as well as Sina's Quartets, and both men were happy to learn that Haydn, Mozart and Beethoven all had a large and devoted following in this cosmopolitan French city.

Moscheles spent his first few weeks in Paris exploring the city in every direction, delighting in seeing so much that he had never seen before. A somewhat less enjoyable aspect that Moscheles found about Paris was the reluctance of the Parisian audiences to acknowledge Spohr's status as a violinist:

Why is it that Spohr cannot arouse any general enthusiasm in this place? Does the

French national pride not allow them to give praise to any violinists other than their own? Or could it be that he is too uncommunicative, too detached for the cosmopolitan taste of the Parisians? Whatever the reason, today he had to cancel his evening entertainment because of a lack of public response, which I find very sad indeed.

As for Moscheles himself, he had no grounds for complaint. Parisian high society had accepted him into their midst, partly to benefit from the lessons he was willing to give them, and partly for the experience of watching him perform at the keyboard at one or other of their soirées.

In spite of his acceptance by these exclusive circles, however, Moscheles experienced some difficulty when he wanted to give a public concert. This was mainly due to the rivalry between the various instrument makers who were seeking preference for their own instruments at any such public performance. After lengthy negotiations, a date was at last fixed for a performance at the Théâtre Favart. Moscheles selected a Pape grand piano as its light touch most closely resembled the instruments to which he had become accustomed during his time in Vienna.

On the day of the concert, February 25th, 1821, he wrote in his diary
I spent the morning trying to find some additional trombones for my concert. In the afternoon I returned to the Théatre Favart to test Pape's instrument once more. Since the rehearsal it had been closely guarded in order to prevent envious rivals from tampering with it. The concert went very smoothly, and the attendance and receipts were just as pleasing as the standard of my artistry. One particular incident which occurred tonight made me aware of the risks to which artists expose themselves if they fail to observe the strict rules of etiquette in public. The singer

Bordogni was jeered off the stage when, either from forgetfulness or intentionally, he failed to extend his hand to Demoiselle Cinti to escort her backstage after their duet.

Some weeks later, on March 18th, 1821, Moscheles gave his second public concert at the Salle Favart, this time with Lafont. After this, they gave four more soirées together, the last of which was a benefit concert in aid of a poor family. It included a potpourri which Moscheles and Lafont had composed together. The duo also appeared at the court of Versailles, where they received a generous ovation, as well as a generous purse.

Moscheles wrote of Lafont:
He was a sweetly sentimental musician, and the sounds he produced, whether on his violin or from his throat had a similar effect on his audiences. His romance 'La larme' brought many a tear to beautiful eyes. His wife was also a singer of romantic ballads, although her looks were far superior to her voice. After one of her concerts, a mischievous critic penned the following words: 'Madame Lafont a chanté, elle a de beaux yeux.' (Madame Lafont sang; she certainly has nice eyes.)

Occasionally, Moscheles and his fellow artists would gather together at his lodgings, 'stimulated by plenty of food and drink', to make music until the small hours.
Anyone who could play, blow or sing was there, and everyone played, blew or sang to his heart's content. All in all, everyone had a marvellous time.

On another occasion he described how he and his fellow artists amused themselves:
I spent the evening at Ciceri's, the son-in-law of the famous painter, Isabey, who introduced me to an extremely interesting circle of artists. In the first room all the most famous painters were assembled, drawing and painting for their entertainment, and amongst them was Cherubini, drawing like the others.

As a newcomer, I had the honour of having a caricature drawn of myself. The task fell to Bécasse whose effort was highly successful. In an adjoining room, all those present were musicians and actors . . . I merely listened to the performance, but I was particularly taken with a quartet for voices, composed and conducted by Cherubini. Later on in the evening, everyone at the party was handed a reed pipe, and on these rather limited instruments, which are usually made of hardwood, but sometimes even of a sugary substance, the overture to 'Demophon' was performed in the manner of Russian horn music, with two frying pans taking the place of drums.

All during April, Paris was busy preparing for the christening of the young successor to the throne of the recently restored Bourbon dynasty, Henri de Bourbon, Duke of Bordeaux. Celebrations to mark this special event lasted for more than two weeks, and included a variety of concerts in which Moscheles took part.

When his stayed in the French capital was coming to an end, Moscheles was able to note with satisfaction:

As I look back upon my sojourn in Paris, I can tell my mother that it has been a successful venture, both artistically and materially, and that I wish her to enjoy with me the fruits of my success.

We have already mentioned how the early death of Moscheles' father had left his mother and her five children with inadequate means. Now that Moscheles' international career was firmly established, he occupied himself with the care of his mother and sisters, as well as looking after the needs of his sickly brother, and he devoted himself to this task with affection for the rest of his life.

On the morning of May 23rd he left Paris and headed for Calais where he boarded a ship to take him to Dover. Little did he

suspect at that time that England was soon to become his second home.

INTRODUCTION TO LONDON'S ARTISTIC COMMUNITY – FRIENDSHIP WITH KALKBRENNER

In the English Channel, on that 26th May, 1821, a howling gale was blowing, as if the island kingdom were determined not to admit the young musician, still eager for success, to its shores, at least not for the time being.

We spent fourteen whole hours on the turbulent sea, and most of the time I suffered badly from the effects of sea-sickness. When we finally approached Dover, at about midnight, and the steward came to ask me for my fare for the crossing, I had just about enough strength to point to my bulging pocket. 'For shame', the man exclaimed, 'a courier who gets sea-sick!' How on earth had I acquired the title of 'courier', I wondered. Then I remembered that the large box that contained my music had been given the Imperial seal and labelled 'Depeschen' (Dispatches) by the Austrian Embassy, to enable me to travel without paying any duty and with the least possible delay. That was the reason for the steward mistaking me for a courier, who would obviously be used to travelling to and fro.

Two days later, on the 28th May, the diary reports:

Yesterday evening I alighted at an inn called 'The Golden Cross', at Charing Cross. This morning I looked around the place and told the waiter how much I admired the surroundings, whereupon he informed me in a learned manner that this was a location of special historical interest. When the body of Queen Eleonore, the wife of Edward I, was carried to Westminster Abbey for burial, every stop on the route of the funeral procession was subsequently marked by the erection of a cross; thus the village of Charing, which in those days occupied this locality and the surrounding area, was renamed Charing Cross. I had never heard the story before, as I had previously taken very little interest in England's history.

As soon as he has arrived in London, Moscheles lost no time in submerging himself in the city's musical life, and he soon became a member of its drawing room society. He wanted to hear other musicians and to be heard himself, and England's capital city offered plenty of opportunity for both. As early on as the day after his arrival, he went to hear a performance of Beethoven's 'Pastoral Symphony' given by the Royal Philharmonic Society, and conducted by Kiesewetter. All in all a dignified performance, only the thundering timpani had a disturbing effect on me, he remarked. A visit to His Majesty's Theatre in the Haymarket introduced Moscheles to one of Britain's peculiar traditions: in order to gain admission to the theatre, patrons were required to wear shoes, stockings, a tailcoat and a white tie!

He made new friendships amongst the aristocracy and the artists, as well as renewing old ones, notably with Clementi and J. B. Cramer, the pianist. At that time, Clementi owned a piano building establishment, where Moscheles often used to visit him and play his compositions for him. However, he devoted most of his time to Kalkbrenner, a friend he had met in Vienna, now celebrated in London as one of the most brilliant virtuosi of the time.

We often play piano duets on the piano, show each other what we have written, and we like to share our artistic pleasures in a comradely fashion. I admire him, above all, for his unique skill in negotiating octaves, while at the same time condemning as detri-mental his habit of playing runs of octaves with a loose wrist.

There was also Ries, in whose company Moscheles spent many happy hours devoted to music.

I eagerly welcomed the chance of getting to know the man whose masterly C-sharp minor Concerto I had the pleasure of introducing to the public in Vienna.

The strongest bond between them was their wholehearted admiration for Beethoven, whose pupil Ries had been. Ries had now withdrawn from public performances and was concentrating instead on teaching and composition. Both of these occupations earned him sufficient financial reward and honour to enable him to retire in 1824 to some property close to Bonn, where he continued to compose music. While his piano pieces were immensely popular, his orchestral works were received less favourably. As was the case with Clementi's symphonies, the Royal Philharmonic Society audiences in London also disapproved of Ries's symphonic compositions, and they were, therefore, removed from the repertoire.

The diary also mentions another of Moscheles' colleagues, Cramer:

The way his silk-smooth fingers glide over his Mozart and his Mozart-like compositions could almost be interpreted as a direct challenge to my own style of bravura, but this is not so; instead he pays me the most unfeigned compliments, both in public and in private. He is witty and amusing and, like many very gifted people, given to sardonic humour. Not stopping short when it comes to his own weaknesses, he pokes fun at his well-known partiality for alcoholic beverages, to which a rather prominent vein of bluish hue on one side of his nose bears witness, saying 'C'est Bacchus qui a mis son pouce là, ce diable de Bacchus!' (It's that devil Bacchus who's left his mark there!) As it happens, he prefers to converse in French, having spent some of his early years in France and, in his manner and bearing, he reminds me of that country.

As to Cramer's pianistic qualities, Moscheles reported:

Those slender, well-shaped fingers (stained, alas, from excessive use of snuff) have come to prefer legato, to glide smoothly from one note to another, avoiding whenever possible any staccato runs or passages in octaves. He can make the piano sing, and he plays a Mozart andante as if it had been written for the human voice. I have to reprimand him, however, for taking the liberty of sneaking his own rather insignificant embellishments into Mozart's music.

On another occasion he extols Cramer's 'rare sensitivity' in interpreting Mozart.

At the beginning of June, Moscheles and Cramer attended the annual dinner of the Royal Society of Musicians. His description of the event is worthy of reproduction here:

The members of this society, a charitable institution for widows and orphans, dine together once a year and invite a large number of friends. The cost is 1 guinea per head, and some musical Lord or other presides. As soon as the meal has been cleared away, the tablecloth is removed and the beautifully polished mahogany dining table is covered with fresh dessert wine. In due course, ladies appear in the upper gallery; these being the wives and daughters of the most distinguished artists, accompanied by a few chosen friends. They are courteously received by some of the stewards, resplendent in their uniforms and white ribbons, and escorted to their seats up in the gallery. From down below, the 'Non nobis Domine' rings out, a four-part canon, precisely executed, of which every English artist knows his own part by heart; the text is taken from the prayer of thanksgiving 'Grace after meal'.

This is followed by a prescribed sequence of toasts, each called out in turn, at the top of his voice, by the Master of Ceremonies who has taken up his position behind the President's Chair. The King and his family, the President, the Navy, the Army, their leaders, all the guests at the dinner, and lastly even the ladies who are honouring the occasion with their presence – one by one, their good health and happiness are proposed by the speaker, and the assembled company responds to each toast by banging the table with their dinner knives, the degree of loudness depending on the extent to which the speaker's sentiments are shared by those present. The tinkle of glasses and bottles on the table adds to the general hubbub. The pattern changes when a specially invited artist steps forward to play a piece of music, or when the speaker makes the appropriate announcement, in which case, hand-clapping is considered to be the correct response. The main speech, which is the focal point of all such gatherings, encompasses the Annual Report about the financial state of affairs of the society, and moves on, with some well-turned phrases and an amusing anecdote or two, to call upon the assembled guests – their spirits by now warmed by wine and music – to dig deep into their pockets once again and give generously to the charitable work of the society. The House of Broadwood always seems to come top as far as these gifts are concerned. I must also mention the gallantry of the hosts, at whose behest the stewards conduct the ladies to a room, specially set aside for them, where they may regale themselves with wine, fruit and confectionery, placed on beautifully laid tables.

An entry on June 11th reports:

An important day. My first appearance at the last Philharmonic Concert of the season, good fortune indeed. I played my E-flat Concerto and the Alexander Variations. Because its theme bears a resemblance to the Marseillaise, the latter has been dubbed 'Fall of Paris' by the English.

This resulted in some unpleasant interpretations by French newspapers when he returned to Paris later on.

On July 4th, he wrote:

Today I was at last able to give a concert at the Argyll rooms, after all the trial and tribulation this has caused me. The concert, which included the Clair de lune variations, went well; but my fantasy on 'My lodging is on the cold ground' went best of all.

July 11th:

A grand musical soirée at the Rothschild country residence at Stamford Hill in honour of the foreign representatives who are in Britain for the coronation of George IV; I was introduced to most of them. They, as well as the old Prince Esterhazy, expressed a great satisfaction with my playing and improvisations.

Moscheles followed the coronation celebrations with great interest.

Early in the morning I took up a position near the Abbey, from where I watched the solemn procession in all its pomp and splendour as it made its way to Westminster Hall for the banquet.

Before leaving London, he wrote his Rondo for Piano and Horn.

TOURING FRANCE AND ENGLAND

Moscheles spent the summer of 1821 with Kalkbrenner at the Chateau Pralin, a country estate in Northern France. While there, he composed, among other works, the Allegri di Bravura, which he dedicated to Cramer, a Polonaise brillante in E-flat, as well as the Rondo 'La Tenerezza', in gratitude for the hospitality he had received from Kalkbrenner's companion.

In October he returned to Paris, where he wrote in his diary:

Young Erard visited me today and asked me to test his uncle Sebastian's new invention at the piano factory. Its purpose is the more rapid release of the hammers, and I judge it to be so important that I predict an entirely new era in the design of pianos. However, I still find the touch too heavy and prefer to play on a Pape or a Petzold. Of course I admired this latest improvement, but I also made some criticisms and urged him to try and make further innovations.

At the beginning of 1822, another important invention was presented in Paris, J. N. Mälzel's metronome, which had taken him years to perfect. It was originally produced in 1812 and had prompted Beethoven to write a canon, 'Ta ta ta . . . lieber Mälzel', which incidentally became the theme of the second movement of his 8th Symphony. It is clear from Moscheles' records that this gadget, which in the course of time became practically indispensable, brought its inventor very little money at first. Indeed, Mälzel found it so hard to launch his metronome that he produced mechanical trumpets and dolls that could speak 'Papa' and 'Mama', in order to make ends meet. From a later entry in Moscheles' diary we learn that this enterprise could not have been a great success either, because *Mälzel has forgotten to pay me back the 500 francs he borrowed from me in Paris in 1822.*

After a concert tour through Normandy with Lafont, Moscheles began preparing for a big concert in Paris at which he wanted to introduce a new work, Beethoven's 'Choral Fantasia'. It turned out to be an uphill struggle for him. Rehearsals with the choir almost drove him to desperation, and the French translation of the text was unsatisfactory, in spite of his efforts to have it improved.

Consequently, the concert was not a success, and Moscheles wrote in his diary afterwards: *I don't know whether the work was simply too long for a Paris audience, or whether the choir's poor intonation was at fault. Whatever the reason, the public did not like the work.*

There was also an annoying sequel to the concert: an ignorant journalist writing for the 'Miroir' put all the blame on Moscheles, and falsely accused him of having 'added the choral passages himself, thereby causing the "Fantasia" to become unbearably long'. This stung Moscheles into making a public denial.

In March he conducted Mozart's Requiem in Paris, and on Easter Sunday, at the 'Concert Spirituel', he was asked to perform his Potpourri, but he chose instead the following chorale tune for his improvization, as he deemed it 'more appropriate for the occasion'.

O ñ - li - i et fi - li - ac, rex coe - les - tis rex
glo - ri - ae mor - te sur - rex - it ho - di - e al - le - lu - ja.

After the performance he wrote in his diary: *I have managed once again to ignite the public with the fire of my own inspiration.*

When the Paris season was over, Moscheles decided to take up an invitation from some friends to go back to London.
I found J. B. Cramer in the middle of preparing for his annual concert. He showed me two movements of a sonata that he wanted to perform with me, and he asked me to write the Finale. He requested, however, that I should not include any of my difficult octave passages in his part, as he would not be able

to play them. Since I cannot refuse him anything, I shall have to write something that he, a disciple of Mozart and Handel, will find to his taste.

The work, composed in haste for Cramer's concert, was an Allegro which he later used as part of his famous 'Hommage à Handel', adding only an introduction. It was published in this form for two pianos, and later also for piano duet. But its originality even caused a sensation at its first performance, on May 9th, at Cramer's concert. The newspapers paid tribute to 'glorious John' (Cramer) and Moscheles, whose 'execution is most wonderful because he always makes the right use of his genius', and as for hearing them play together a composition on which they had both worked together, it was 'an unrivalled treat, an unprecedented attraction'.

For the occasion they had both chosen a Broadwood instrument, Cramer from habit, and Moscheles only for this particular event. *The strong metal plates Broadwood uses in the construction of his pianos make for a heavier touch but, at the same time, they give a fuller tone and better sonority, so admirably suited to Cramer's legato, to those fingers gliding gently from note to note. I, on the other hand, need the greater flexibility of Clementi's repeated mechanism for my repeated notes, jumps and intervals.*

Soon after, Moscheles performed his recently revised Concerto in G-minor; first at a Philharmonic Society event, and again at his own concert. For the latter, he had engaged the singer, Cinti, Kiesewetter, and the harpist Dizi. Their combined artistry earned them a warm response from the audience.

Moscheles made the following comment in his diary :
Our method of rehearsal was quite different from what they are used to here, where they

either dispense with rehearsals altogether, or half the orchestra turns up for a single run-through.

In addition to these public concerts, Moscheles was once again in demand for private soirées. He played for Chateaubriand, the French Ambassador in London, as well as for the Royal Family, although, as he had done before, he complained about engagements of this nature.

To make music in those stuffy, overcrowded rooms before a mostly ignorant audience affords nothing like the pleasure of the gatherings we artists enjoy! Thank God I never had to endure what happened to Lafont on one occasion; right in the middle of the piece he was tapped on the shoulder by the Duke of Devonshire who said 'c'est assez, mon cher!'. (That's enough old chap!) All I have to do is tickle their ears, and they'll applaud me!

There were, however, some agreeable sides to this kind of patronage, in that it was lucrative and likely to enhance the career prospects of the artist. After all, it was a privilege to be invited to the house of Chateaubriand; and it could not be denied that to take part in the soirées of high society held a certain fascination. Where else would one be able to rub shoulders with princes, statesmen, scientists and the like, and even meet such people and actually talk to them?

A particularly magnificent occasion, according to Moscheles, was a ball in aid of the suffering Irish, given by George IV at the Opera House. The grand auditorium was adorned with fabulous decorations, the diary tells us, and 3000 tickets were issued at two guineas each. As the ball drew nearer though, tickets were sold for up to 15 guineas a ticket, bringing in a profit which matched the grandeur of the event. Towards the end of the year, the London Academy of Music sent Moscheles an Honorary Membership Diploma, He promptly noted in his diary:

I feel more and more at home in England as it seems that people here wish to show me respect and friendship, for which I am enormously grateful.

A tireless worker, Moscheles continued to compose right through the winter of 1823; first the E major Concerto, followed by the Scottish Fantasy, the revised F major Concerto and, finally, the Sonata for piano duet. *I wrote a 'Gigue' as a contribution to the musical magazine 'Harmonicon'. Its editor, Mr. Walsh, who owns the Argyll rooms, has asked me to send him anything I choose, and he would pay 5 guineas for such a small thing. For the 'Charmes de Paris' I received 20 guineas, and the same amount for the first instalment of the Bonbonnière musicale. In spite of this, I withhold some of my manuscripts as the pecuniary advantages are not sufficient incentive for me. I have to feel that they represent progress on my part, as well as being worthwhile compositions.*

In his leisure hours he wrote a new arrangement of the Egmont Overture, as a sort of 'handmade article', as he himself used to call such things. Those who knew Moscheles intimately had occasion to observe the degree of precision with which he set down his compositions. His engravers were given detailed instructions as to where exactly a page could be turned. Every note had to be in its proper place, and every pause easy to read.

Only in this way shall we have precision in performance, and better understanding of the pieces, and if anyone has delusions of grandeur and feels entitled to write so badly that no engraver can read his score, which will be printed with mistakes in it, he would still have a long way to go before he is a Beethoven. He, of course, can do anything, but then he has an engraver who can read his writing! If everybody composed like Beetho-

ven, then they would doubtless be able to write as they wished!

Certain strange habits of the English never ceased to amaze Moscheles: for instance, when they expected some famous musician or other to conduct an orchestral concert while seated at the piano. After one of the Philharmonic concerts he mused:

What on earth can this mean, 'Conductor Mr Clementi'? he sits there turning over the pages of the score, but without his marshall's baton he is ill equipped to lead his army. That is done by the first violin, and the so-called conductor counts for nothing. But his astonishment does not stop there: Just look at this programme! Beethoven's C minor Symphony, performed for the first time; this sublime work of genius, this food of the Gods, to be followed immediately by a variation for flute, a violin concerto and several arias, not to mention Mozart's G minor Symphony and Romberg's Overture – I am committing the details to paper, just so that I never forget it.

The artists, on the whole, got along very well together, despite competition and the inevitable jealousy which crept in. There were, however, some embarrassing moments, such as one that occurred during a soirée at the house of one of Moscheles' pupils:

That was a nasty incident! After we had all played a lot of music together, Kiesewetter and I decided to finish with Mayseder's somewaht lengthy sonata. When Cramer called out 'Cela m'ennuie' (I find this boring), Kiesewetter jumped up as if he had been hit by a thunderbolt. He felt extremely insulted, and it took a great deal of trouble on our behalf to calm them both down.

As a music teacher, Moscheles was often asked for his opinion of talented young pupils. Some of them later made a name for themselves, such as Ferdinand Hiller, for whom Moscheles predicted a brilliant future the very first time he heard him play. Then there was the very young actress Maria Garcia, daughter of the singer Manuel Garcia, who, under the name Malibran rose to international fame, and whose musicality had delighted Moscheles from the very beginning.

The usual way to travel around in the London of 1823 was by carriage and pair, a costly and cumbersome conveyance. Moscheles welcomed the first appearance of one-horse cabs with great relief, and he praised them in his diary for their much greater mobility. As far as he was concerned, they could not have come upon the scene at a more opportune moment, as he had to dash to and fro to get everything ready for his concert on June 27th. Some of the preparations were in the hands of his friend Sir George Smart, who was always willing to act as his accompanist, to audition singers and soloists, and to relieve him of as many problems as possible. Moscheles wrote of him:

This most excellent man is responsible for practically every major music festival in London and the provinces. He is a painstaking and prudent organiser, and is one of that rare breed of men who, regardless of the pressures of work, always manage to keep their correspondence up to date. Moreover, he can be relied upon to come to the aid of his friends, and it is a result of his coaching that a number of foreign singers have acquired impeccable English accents for their parts in Haydn's and Handel's oratorios, and it is thanks to his guidance that they are able to follow an established tradition of style and presentation, without which they could hardly succeed before a British audience.

Moscheles left England at the end of the London season. Once again, his stay had brought him success, new friends, new ideas for compositions, and plenty of work. In August he set off for France, but he was once again affected by sea-sickness, and he went below deck, only re-emerging when the boat had docked in Calais. After only a few days in Paris, he started out on a tour of Belgium, stopping first at Spa, where his plans for a concert were eagerly received by a music-loving public. Some difficulty arose, however, when he tried to procure a suitable instrument. His efforts to borrow Lady Northland's celebrated grand piano were in vain. Moscheles had previously made her acquaintance at a ball, and he wrote of his frustration in his diary:

Her refusal is a considerable nuisance; she accuses me of treating her instrument too roughly, me of all people, since I despise nothing more than bashing into a piano. She actually had the audacity to say to one of her friends at the ball that I seem to be playing with my feet!

This may have been a misplaced allusion to one of Moscheles' often repeated jokes when he gave the appearance of playing with closed fists, when in fact he was using his hidden thumbs to play thirds, but without losing his usual gentle touch for a moment. In short, Lady Northland would not lend him her piano and he had to be content with another instrument.

From Belgium, Moscheles went to Aachen. Here he took the opportunity of indulging a peculiar inclination of his which he retained right up until his old age. He had a passion for listening to court cases and notwithstanding the lively artistic distractions to tempt him in Aachen, he hurried along to the court room to hear a case of murder being tried. He reported in his diary how the defendant's casualness had struck him as 'horrific', and the sobbing of his female accomplice as 'heart-rending'.

At the beginning of September he was on the move once again, leaving Aachen behind, which at that time belonged to France, and heading for Germany, and from there he proceeded to Vienna.

RETURN TO VIENNA AND PRAGUE – LAST MEETING WITH BEETHOVEN AND SALIERI

On his way to Vienna, Moscheles stopped at various German towns. His first destination was Frankfurt, from where he made the short trip to Offenbach to call on the music publisher André. While with André, he could wallow to his heart's content in the publisher's collection of Mozart's manuscripts. When he was rummaging through the papers, he noted down two bars which Mozart had crossed out in his overture to 'The Magic Flute':

And he recorded in his diary:

I was fascinated by the sight of the half-finished score of the opera 'L'oca del Cairo'; what a great pity that the last few numbers of this veritable treasure were scored only for voice and bass! Is there not someone who would like to complete the work that Mozart had started? I also came across a concerto written for the horn player Leitgeb, with an inscription that was typical of Mozart's roguish sense of humour: 'W. A. Mozart has taken pity on poor Leitgeb, that ass, idiot and whatever else he may be, and he has written a horn concerto for him'.

When André ventured a criticism of Mozart, Moscheles was livid:

What was I to say, worshipping every single note that Mozart ever composed as I do, and regarding him as the greatest musical genius of all time, when Hofrat André claimed that Mozart had no understanding of the libretto? He maintained that words with the opposite meaning to the texts he had used would fit his music just as well! I did not deem this accusation worthy of defending – I held my tongue!

Just at that time, a newly revised text of the opera 'Cosi fan tutte' appeared. It was given the title 'The Magic Mirror' (Der Zauberspiegel), and the opera was performed with Mozart's music unchanged. Moscheles was quite enchanted by the whole thing.

He listened to Mozart's Requiem in the Cathedral and also in the Cäcilien-Verein, where it was conducted exceedingly well by Schelbe. He also availed himself of every opportunity to hear Handel's music whenever it was performed.

After a successful concert in Frankfurt, Moscheles went on to Darmstadt, together with the flautist Böhm and the pianist Pixis, for a performance of Spontini's 'Olympia'.

But what an adventure it turned out to be! Our coach lost a wheel three times, and since there was no other vehicle to be found, apart from a handcart, and none of us was prepared to miss the opera at any price, we mounted this elegant equipage to make our ceremonial entry into Darmstadt, passing on the way many a luxurious coach with whose occupants we were well acquainted.

Of the performance itself he wrote: *Listening to 'Olympia' for the first time I noted a great many splendid and ingenious passages, while also being aware of one or two weaknesses from time to time.*

After Darmstadt, he next visited Munich where, very soon after his arrival, he was invited to Nymphenburg to take part in a concert of chamber music in honour of Friedrich Wilhelm, Prince of Prussia, who was a guest at court. King Maximilian was so impressed with Moscheles' performance that he asked him to play for the court a second time, and to postpone his public concert in Munich, so that they could all be present. Naturally Moscheles acceded to the royal request, and the concert took place on October 10th in the presence of the King's family, and was a triumphant success.

Shortly afterwards, Moscheles travelled to Vienna by the quickest possible mode of transport. Alas, there was nothing very glamorous about his return to the city he had once taken by storm. As soon as he arrived, he was taken seriously ill and, tormented by pain, he had to be nursed by friends who, alarmed by his condition, sent word to his brother in Prague requesting him to hurry to Vienna. A long convalescence ensued. But then something happened which gave him new life.

Carl Maria von Weber had come to Vienna to direct his opera 'Euryanthe'. As soon as the rehearsals were over, the most varied reactions and opinions were put forward by the two major parties, the devotees of the Italian and German schools respectively. Partisanship became so heated that serious clashes were expected at the première. Some malicious tongues went so far as to rechristen 'Euryanthe', calling it 'Ennuyante' (boring) instead. Moscheles made sure that he was present at the first performance, so that he could speak up in favour of Weber. After hearing the work performed by an outstanding cast, he wrote:

This opera is not meant for the uneducated listener. Its rhythms and harmonies are far too daring, and the text so contrived that the music really has to be in the same vein. It does, however, contain much that is beautiful, and the romances 'Glöcklein im Tale' (Little bell in the valley), 'Unter blüh'nden Mandelbäumen' (Under blossoming almond trees) and, above all, the finale of the first act, should win over any audience, both now and in the future!

After Moscheles was fully recovered and had played in his first public performance again, he set about paying some long-over-due visits, starting with Beethoven. This was to be his last encounter with the revered master.

Moscheles' brother, who was still with him at the time, had expressed a keen desire to meet the great man, so the two of them set out together. Moscheles recounted the visit in his diary:

Having arrived at the front door, I remembered with some degree of sadness how shy of people Beethoven was, so I asked my brother to wait downstairs until I had tested the water. However, as soon as I asked Beethoven, after greeting him briefly, whether he would be prepared to meet my brother, he enquired hastily, 'Where is he?' 'Downstairs', I replied. 'What? Downstairs?' he cried out even more hastily. He then rushed down the stairs, grabbed my astonished brother by the arm, and pulled him right into the middle of the room, demanding, 'Do you really think of me as a rough, unapproachable barbarian?' He then showed great kindness towards my brother, but unfortunately, on account of his deafness, we were able to converse with him only in writing.

Moscheles also wanted to visit Salieri, by now a poor and infirm man, who was in hospital on the threshold of death. First he had to obtain permission from Salieri's unmarried daughter, and also from the authorities, as hardly anyone was allowed to see him, since he did not like receiving visitors and made only very few exceptions.

Seeing him again was a sad affair, and his appearance alone horrified me. In disjointed sentences he spoke of his imminent death, and he added these words: 'This being my last illness, I can give you my word of honour that there is no truth in the absurd rumour; you know – Mozart, it was said that I had poisoned him. But it's not true, tell the world, dear Moscheles, that it's nothing but a malicious rumour; old Salieri told you on his deathbed.' I was deeply shaken, and when the old man thanked me yet again for visiting him, with tears in his eyes, having overwhelmed me with his gratitude when I arrived, I knew it was time for me to hurry away before I was overcome with grief in his presence. Concerning the rumour to which the dying man had alluded, I knew that it had been circulating, but it had never concerned me. In a moral sense he had certainly hurt Mozart by intriguing against him, and had doubtless poisoned many an hour for him.

During November and December, Moscheles gave two more concerts at the Kärntner-tor-Theater. For the second of these concerts, Beethoven had willingly agreed to lend him his Broadwood grand piano. Moscheles was keen to demonstrate the differences and good points of this English instrument and an Austrian piano by Graf by playing both in turn at the same concert. Beethoven, he said in his diary, was not the kind of player to treat a piano with care. His deafness caused him to bash mercilessly on his instrument most of the time. For this reason, Graf himself, fully anticipating a favourable outcome of the competition, magnanimously offered to restore Beethoven's damaged instrument to its former glory for the occasion. Moscheles wrote about the concert in his diary: *I tried to bring out the broad, full, albeit rather dull tone quality of the Broadwood piano during my Fantasy, but my attempts were in vain.*

On January 3rd 1824, Moscheles, now aged 30 returned to his native city of Prague again. Once there, he promptly suffered a serious relapse. An attack of peritonitis affected him so badly that the papers spoke of his imminent death. All his engagements, at Bath in the winter and in London in the spring, had to be cancelled. But his time had not yet come. After excellent medical treatment and four months of being nursed at his parental home, he was well again, but the final push towards a full recovery came once again through music.

Having spent most of his time between January and April reading Goethe's works and hardly touching the piano, he was asked in May whether he would like to give a concert, in the presence of the Emperor Franz I and the Empress, to celebrate the opening of the new Redoutensaal (festival hall). Moscheles accepted the invitation and noted in his diary: *It seems that I am to celebrate my recovery not just by thanking God and my family with all my heart, but also outwardly in a grand manner!*

And the concert did turn out to be a grand affair, for not only was the hall decorated most fabulously and the audience made up of personages of the highest rank, but he was also received afterwards by the Emperor in a private audience who paid him this compliment: *I liked you when you were still a boy, and since then I have always listened to you with renewed pleasure.*

After taking the waters in Karlsbad, he returned to Prague again in August. He paid a visit to his old teacher Dionys Weber, played for him and listened reverently to what he had to say about his, Moscheles', compositions. No matter how much Weber wished to treat him as a master, Moscheles still considered himself as a pupil.

But it strikes me as strange how the good man who once regarded Beethoven as more or less a madman and even warned me against him, has had to change his opinion gradually. He is, however, doing so carefully, for there are many things of which he still does not approve and, in order not to offend him, I find myself having to curb my own enthusiasm as best I can.

From Prague, Moscheles went to Dresden. Carl Maria von Weber, the city's court Kapellmeister, invited him to his house at Hosterwitz, near the Saxon capital. There Moscheles met the librettist of 'Der Freischütz', Friedrich Kind, and the three of them discussed in detail Weber's intention to follow a call to London.

I was, of course, able to supply him with information and advice as to the rules and regulations prevailing there. However, I was disturbed to see him in such poor health and feared that London would take its toll on him.

Unfortunately his fears proved to be justified.

Shortly after his arrival in Dresden, Moscheles was summoned to play for the Court at Pillnitz. As had been the case eight years previously, he was to give a musical entertainment while the Court was at table. This official dinner was attended, in addition to their Majesties Friedrich August I and the Queen, by the Princes Friedrich and Johann, and the Princesses Amalie and Auguste, Grand Prince Constantine and his Ambassador, von Reizenstein. Moscheles played his E major Concerto and 'Clair de lune'. When the concert was over, he and the other artists were given dinner and, a little later, presented with a golden trinket box and a thaler, the latter in accordance with an old custom to ensure that the artist could buy himself a pair of gloves. *This matches the vandalism of the dinner concert*, Moscheles commented in his diary.

Still accompanied by his brother, Moscheles went on to Leipzig, where he made the acquaintance of Johann Gottlob Friedrich Wieck, the music teacher. Moscheles recorded a visit to Wieck in his diary: *At Wieck's house I played his Stein grand piano and joined him and his family in eating potatoes.*

One of those present must have been Wieck's five-year-old daughter Clara, who was to achieve great fame as Clara Schumann, and who often used to share the platform with Moscheles at concerts.

In the second half of October, Moscheles gave two successful concerts in Leipzig. This city of commerce also yielded some other income for him: *Probst has bought my opus 62 and 63 for 35 kreutzer.* (The publisher Machetti had paid him 40 kreutzer for the G minor concerto.)

After a detour to Dessau, where Moscheles played before the Duke and Duchess, he proceeded to Berlin and arrived there on October 31st, 1824.

START OF FRIENDSHIP WITH MENDELSSOHN

One cannot fail to notice that Moscheles recorded the events of his stay in Berlin with a certain haste. It is almost as if he had dismissed everything else which he deemed unimportant so that he could speak only of his relationship with the Mendelssohn family. Page upon page is filled with details about the Mendelssohn household and its members.
This is a family, the like of which I have never known. There is fifteen-year-old Felix. What a unique appearance, indeed! What are all the other child prodigies compared to him?

Merely child prodigies, nothing more; whereas this Felix Mendelssohn is already a mature artist, and he's still only 15! We stayed together for several hours. I had to play a great deal when I really wanted only to listen and look at compositions, for Felix showed me his Concerto in C minor, a double concerto and a number of motets which were not only ingeniously conceived, but also correct in detail, and so tasteful! His elder sister Fanny, also immensely talented, played some of Bach's fugues and passacaglias by heart, and with admirable precision. I believe she can justifiably be called 'a good musician'. Both the parents seem to be highly educated people and are far from being proud of their children. They are concerned about Felix's future, and are unsure whether he has sufficient talent, or whether he will suddenly fade away like so many other talented children. I could not do enough to reassure them, convinced as I was of the prodigious gift which he possessed, that I had not the slightest doubt about his genius. I had to repeat this several times, however, before they believed me. They are quite different from the usual parents of child prodigies that I have come across so often.

The Mendelssohns repeatedly asked him to give lessons to Felix, but he always answered evasively. He did, however, confide to his diary: *He does not require lessons, and should he wish to glean something from me that is new to him, he can easily do so.*

On November 18th 1824, Mendelssohn's mother sent Moscheles a note in which she asked him once again:
'Have you been so kind as to give consideration to our request for lessons? We should be most obliged to you if it could be done without interfering with your stay here. Please do not think us immodest for repeating this request which you must ascribe solely to my desire that my child should

benefit from the presence in our midst of the 'prince des pianistes'.

Even then Moscheles could not bring himself to consent, so that yet another note reached him on November 22nd.

Would you permit me to renew my request for lessons for my two eldest children, dear Herr Moscheles, and to ask you to be so kind as to name your fee, in order that we may start very soon, and your pupils may gain as much benefit as possible from your stay here.

Moscheles must have given a verbal reply to this note, for on the same day, he wrote in his diary:

From two to three o'clock this afternoon, I gave Felix Mendelssohn his first lesson, never forgetting for a moment that I was sitting beside a master and not a pupil. I am proud that his excellent parents have entrusted their son to me after knowing me for such a short while, and I am happy to be allowed to pass on a few hints to him which, given his genius, he grasps and assimilates with ease.

Six days later he recorded:

Felix Mendelssohn's lessons take place every two days, with ever increasing interest on my part. By now, he has already played my Allegri di Bravura, my concerti, and other works, and how he played them! He guesses even my most subtly suggested ideas correctly.

Over the ensuing weeks, Moscheles' attachment to the Mendelssohn family grew steadily. He praised the spirit of the household, listened with enjoyment to the father's highly informed opinions on art, which he expressed at the table, and attended many of their morning and evening entertainments. All these events are carefully recorded:

November 23rd: Singakademie, Psalm by Naumann, then went to the Mendelssohn's. The brother and sister played Bach.

26th November: Went with the Mendelssohn-Bartholdy family to see his brother.

28th November (Sunday): Morning concert at the Mendelssohn's, C Minor quartet by Felix; D major Symphony, concerto by Bach; Duet in D minor for two pianos by Arnold.

December 3rd, 12 noon: Concert at Zelter's ; Fanny played the D minor Concerto by Bach, the one I had seen in manuscript; also Bach's mass for five voices.

December 5th: Accompanied Felix's playing at Geheimrat Crelle's ; Mozart's Requiem to honour the anniversary of his death, in the presence of Zelter and others.

December 11th: Birthday celebrations at the Mendelssohn's, much enhanced by a delightful theatrical entertainment, in which Felix distinguished himself every bit as much as E. Devrient, the actor.

December 12th: Sunday concert at the Mendelssohn's. Felix's E minor Quartet; also played my Duet in G for two Pianofortes with him. The young Schilling played Hummel's Trio in G.

A regular guest at these morning concerts was C. F. Zelter, at that time tutor in composition to Mendelssohn and his sister. He was more than a little proud of his pupils, even though, we are told, he was outwardly curt and dismissive. Moscheles accepted Zelter's invitation to supper, and wrote afterwards:

I found my musical conversations with Zelter most enlightening. He also mentioned his correspondence with Goethe on some rather amusing subjects, such as turnip-growing at Teltow!

December 13th: Returned Felix's visitors book to him after writing my Impromptu opus 77 in it yesterday. He played it magnificently at sight.

He played it magnificently at sight

Ten days later, Moscheles reluctantly took his leave of the Mendelssohn family and Berlin. Several concert engagements awaited him; the first being at Potsdam, where he played in the presence of the Court. After this, he proceeded to Magdeburg, Brunswick, Hanover, Celle and, finally, Hamburg.

MARRIAGE

Moscheles arrived in Hamburg on January 16th 1825, and it was here that part of what his elderly, well-meaning uncle had held up to him as the ideal in life twenty years earlier – marriage to a rich merchant's daughter – was to become reality. His meeting with Charlotte Embden had come about partly through the medium of music, and partly through his recent acquaintance with the banking family Jaques whom he had met in Hanover, and who had given him a letter of recommendation to their eldest son in Hamburg, as well as to his father-in-law, Adolf Embden. Charlotte, the daughter of the latter, first saw Moscheles at a concert in the Apollosaal in Hamburg. Later on in her life, she wrote of the event herself: *Being something of a pianist myself, I was positively entranced by his miraculous fingers.* In fact, the 'prince des pianistes' was quite unaware of this new admirer in the audience, but a few days later he met her at her father's house into which Jaques' recommendation had gained him entry.

There seems to have been no need on either side for a prolonged period of time to consider their joint destiny, since the engagement was announced as early as February 2nd, followed by the wedding ceremony on March 1st. This date is recorded in the diary: *My day of honour. Brimful of the happiest emotion, my heart filled with gratitude towards our Creator. I dedicated myself on this day to the solemn bond of marriage and affirmed my vow before God.*

Although both parties had embarked on marriage somewhat hastily, it turned out to be a happy one. Years later, Moscheles wrote in his diary: *We usually act in unison, and if ever there is any discord, there is always a sustained note which restores harmony between us again.*

Charlotte, for her part, described him in her book as *the most faithful and true-hearted husband a wife could wish for,* on whose personal qualities the happiness of her family, enriched in due course by four children, was founded. Before the children were born, however, they threw themselves into their new life together with all the zest and gaiety of unfettered youth. New horizons awaited the young wife who, never having previously been further than Berlin, now travelled everywhere by the side of her beloved husband.

After the wedding, Moscheles first took his wife to Bremen and Aachen, and then on to Paris to fulfil his concert engagements. There he met Felix Mendelssohn again who had come to the French capital with his father. Alexander von Humboldt and Hummel were also staying in Paris, and Moscheles was pleased to be reunited with them.

In April he took part in one of the Concerts spirituels again, after which he rushed off to London where his presence had been eagerly awaited for some time. On this occasion, crossing the Channel signified the beginning of a new chapter in his career, as he was to settle in the British metropolis for the next twenty years, and it was there that he would reach the peak of his professional life.

London (1825–1846)

SETTLING IN LONDON – TOURING THE PROVINCES – JOURNEY TO IRELAND

As soon as Moscheles had returned to England at the beginning of May 1825 – an event which hit the headlines in the British press – he resumed his concert activities. Together with his wife, he spent most of his weekends with Clementi at Elstree, not far from London.

Clementi is one of the most sprightly septuagenarians one could hope to meet. We often watch him from our window first thing in the morning as he potters about the garden, his bald head uncovered, in spite of the morning dew. His great vitality does not allow him to rest for one moment. At table he talks and jokes almost unceasingly, but he is also easily roused to anger; all part of his Italian effervescence, I suppose. It is a very rare achievement to get him to play the piano these days, as he claims to have been afflicted by a stiff hand ever since he fell from a sledge in Russia. Some people suspect him of avoiding the piano so as not to make it obvious that modern techniques have reached heights which he could no longer hope to attain. His wife (his second one), an Englishwoman is, in complete contrast to him, as quiet and reticent as he is bubbling and vivacious.

When the friends were together, the diary goes on to tell us, Clementi would call out: *Moscheles, play me something!* Obligingly, Moscheles would choose one or other of his host's sonatas, and the latter, with his hands folded behind his back and smiling benignly, his small, thickset body swaying in time with the music, would call out 'bravo' from time to time and, as soon as it had finished, he would pat Moscheles on the back and emit another chorus of bravos.

At that time, Clementi owned a flourishing piano manufacturing business, together with the Collard brothers. Moscheles preferred their pianos to the Broadwood instruments on account of their light touch and brighter tone, and for that reason he tended to choose them for his public concerts. The French company, Erard, which had a branch in London was also competing for his patronage. In the spring of the very same year, 1825, this company had obtained the patent for the new and improved version of a repetition mechanism which Moscheles had previously tried out in Paris. On June 1st, he wrote in his diary:

I have been asked to play the very first piano built with this latest innovation. As a result of this, a key will strike a note even if it is only half depressed. This is of inestimable value when playing repeated notes, as I had occasion to find out in Paris, where I first came across this invention. I do find, however, that a certain fullness and softness of tone is lacking, and I discussed this matter at great length with Pierre Erard.

Some time later, Pierre Erard, whose uncle Sebastian Erard had pioneered the new mechanism, tried to persuade Moscheles to enter into an agreement with the Erard company for the exclusive use of their pianos. However, although the conditions attached to this offer were very attractive, Moscheles refused, so that he could retain the right to use the instruments of his choice.

When the London season came to a close, Moscheles and Charlotte left London to be the guest of the Fleming family at their country residence, Stoneham Park, near Southampton. Their hostess was one of Moscheles' pupils, so music inevitably occupied a large part of their time during this visit which, combined with a rather hectic social life, proved to be rather exhausting.

We hardly find any time to enjoy the beautiful park since we don't get to sleep much before 1 or 2 o'clock in the morning and, consequently, we tend to get up late, so that we barely manage to make our toilet in time for breakfast at 11 o'clock. The only time I can set aside for composing or practising is between this meal and luncheon, which is served punctually at 2 o'clock. [During this time he managed to write the E-flat-major and A-minor Etudes.] Charlotte and Mrs. Fleming spend these few hours practising together in the magnificent music room where the piano sounds more like an organ, or they occupy themselves, reading or working, in Mrs. Fleming's boudoir. In this delightful room with its pale blue, silk-covered walls, all the latest literary publications are to be found, and those gathered there find their images reflected in eight large mirrors. At luncheon we are all asked which carriage and which horses we would like to order for the afternoon. Mrs. Fleming likes to claim Charlotte to accompany her pony carriage which she drives herself; I usually go riding with some of the gentlemen. Our second toilet has to be finished by 8 o'clock when dinner is served.

In a later entry, Moscheles wrote:
The visitors now include Lord Palmerston, his brother Mr. Temple, his sister Mrs. Sullivan, and her husband. I find it rather an interesting experience associating with a Lord, especially on account of the conversations at table which are centred exclusively around parliamentary matters, of course, and with everything based on unadulterated Toryism. It is just as well that the art which I represent is allowed to function on neutral ground.

Another entry reads:
New guests have arrived today. They live locally, but not in the immediate vicinity, as everything within a ten-mile radius of this place belongs to our host. He also owns an estate on the Isle of Wight. After dinner, the gentlemen remain at table and talk of nothing but politics; but towards midnight art gains the upper hand once again, and we make music in the drawing room until 1 or 2 o'clock in the morning.

The next destination of the young couple was Cheltenham, a spa town which had been recommended to Moscheles. Here he hoped to resume the cure he had taken at Karlsbad the previous year.

We thoroughly enjoyed the chance to be alone together in this place. Beautiful as it was at the palatial Fleming residence, the quiet life we lead here, the first restful time we have had since we married, is infinitely preferable. We can be in each other's company the whole time. When I am taking riding lessons, my wife watches me from the gallery; in the morning she walks with me to the fountain, and I accompany her to the market place when she buys fish or poultry for our meals. I am sure that London could never be as enjoyable as this.

And a little later:
Not only do I give my wife piano lessons, but I am also teaching her how to write notes, and while she is busy practising I am composing an Impromptu which has been commissioned by the Harmonic Institution. For the theme I have taken the march from Salieri's opera 'Tarare' currently being performed in London to much critical acclaim, after being adapted to suit the English taste.

There were other commissions for Moscheles, including three rondoes on the subject 'Wiener in Berlin' (Viennese in Berlin), 'La petite babillarde' for Cramer, and the Etude in B minor.

Moscheles and his wife went on excursions into the surrounding countryside and admired the many remainders from the Roman occupation, for which the area was famous. Finally, on October 1st, they set out for Oxford, where they visited the colleges of the famous university and stood underneath the huge bell named 'Great Tom'. They also attended a performance at the university theatre where the Tsar of Russia and the King of Prussia had received honorary degrees shortly before.

By the autumn they were back in London, where they took up residence at a small house in Norton Street. The focal point of their new home was a present from Clementi, a grand piano bearing the handwritten dedication: 'Muzio Clementi e Socii all'ingegniosissimo J. Moscheles ed alla sua amabilissima consorte' (Muzio Clementi and associates to the highly talented J. Moscheles and his most amiable wife.)

At the beginning of November, Moscheles gave concerts in Liverpool, Chester and Manchester. While in Liverpool, he paid a visit to the botanist Roscoe, whom he had very much wanted to meet.

I found him to be a most gracious and courteous old gentleman. He showed me a magnificent edition of the works of Lorenzo Medici, a gift with which the Duke of Tuscany had recently honoured him. He also allowed me to peruse his latest botanical work on plant life in the West Indies, giving me many interesting explanations at the same time.

The diary continues:

On November 8th, there was a concert rehearsal at midday. And what a rehearsal it was too! To say it was miserable would be an understatement. Mori, who had come to London, did do his best, but what could he do with a double quartet and four incapacitated wind players – instead of brass players – for an orchestra? The problem arose because the director of the theatre was playing a trick on the impresario, Mr. Wilson, by not putting members of the theatre's orchestra at his disposal. This meant that I had to play the first part of the E-flat major Concerto and the Alexander Variations accompanied only by a quartet. At the concert itself, the large and glittering audience was as pleased with my fantasy on 'Rule Britannia' as I was with the Clementi instrument which had been specially supplied for me.

A trip to Dublin had to be called off unexpectedly when Moscheles received news from London of the imminent confinement of his wife. He travelled back to London and on the same evening his son, a delicate and puny child, was born. The premature birth had a devastating effect on Charlotte. For four long weeks Moscheles lived in fear that she might not recover, and he cancelled all his engagements.

Towards the end of the year though, all was well again. Moscheles was able to concentrate on his own affairs and his joviality had returned to him.

A funny incident made us all laugh. At Christmas time, a brass band comes round to all the houses, usually at quite a late hour, to collect donations. I had already experienced this custom, and when I remembered the torture and disturbance they caused me with their badly played hymns, I ordered the maid to tell them that I would pay them only if they promised never to come back, whereupon the insulted band-leader replied: 'Tell your master, if he does not like music, he will not go to heaven!'

Moscheles was obliged to finish a fantasy

for the music publisher Collard by the end of the year. He refers to this in his diary: *Its only merit is that I will earn 25 guineas for it. It is one of these ephemeral pieces that don't even deserve an opus number.* On the last day of the year he wrote: *We end this year with a prayer of thanksgiving to divine providence for seeing us through a period of great danger.*

At the beginning of 1826, Moscheles set off for Ireland again. He crossed by boat from Holyhead in appalling weather conditions. He was never to forget the ordeal he had to endure before he finally reached the coast of Ireland, as it almost cost him his life.

No steamboat could be found to confront the raging storm, so Moscheles decided to board a mail boat, whose captain was keen to make full use of the easterly gale.

I was so affected by sea-sickness that after only a few hours I was utterly exhausted and suffered as a man does on his deathbed. The elements were raging even more furiously, and I counted the hours which dragged on and on. Night fell, but still we did not land. We asked our steward when we would be put out of our misery. He was heard to murmur: 'Who knows? Things aren't going too well'. It was all too obvious that he was speaking the truth, because the boat, tossed about by savage waves, was in real trouble. As I lay there, wrapped in blankets and coats, I had become increasingly aware of an icy numbness in my feet, for which I could find no explanation. I fought my weariness sufficiently to be able to feel that the water had already penetrated my bedding. There was now no doubt; the ship had sprung a leak for the water was pouring into my cabin. Outside, the howling gale was tearing into the sea unabated, and an impenetrable darkness enveloped the boat. All the captain could say to console his passengers was that we were not far from land, albeit not close enough to reach the harbour. If we did try to approach the harbour, there was every chance that our boat would be smashed to pieces by rocks and sandbanks. Unfortunately, we were not close enough for a distress signal to be seen by the coastguards, either. At long last, after a seemingly endless battle with the buffeting galewinds which had tortured our boat so badly, we succeeded in dropping anchor; the passengers still without help or comfort like sacrificial animals waiting our fate until daybreak. But even in this desperate situation my courage never deserted me, and my belief in the providence of the Almighty sustained me. I was able to think calmly of my wife and child. They would be sound asleep and, thanks be to God, they had been spared my terrible ordeal. We would either be happily reunited or, with God's help, they would be able to endure my loss. Likewise, my thoughts, tinged with sadness but nevertheless composed, went out to my other relatives and friends. It seemed a very short distance between this world and the next.

The long-awaited news came in the afternoon: 'We are shortly to be rescued. Another boat has come alongside and will take us aboard'. Gathering up our belongings, we were each hurled into the swaying vessel which, after struggling with the foaming surf for a short while, took us into harbour at Howth.

Poverty-stricken Ireland made a deep impression on Moscheles from the moment he arrived. In his diary he noted: *. . . the bleak, sandy soil, with deserted ruins pockmarking large stretches of land . . . wretched looking peasant folk.* The contrast with the sumptuous official gala evening, presided over by the Lord Governor, the Marquess of Wellesley, could not have been more stunning. This event took place on January 9th, at the Phoenix Park in Dublin, where the Marquess was to introduce his newly-wedded wife to the assembled nobility. Moscheles, who had been invited to attend, played a fantasy based on Irish melodies which earned him rapturous applause. This fantasy, in an extended form, was later to become one of his most successful compositions, bearing the title 'Souvenirs of Ireland'.

Several public concerts and invitations to private houses followed, prompting Moscheles to write the following observation in his diary at the end of his three-week stay in Dublin: *On the whole, I find the Irish nation more receptive to music than the English, although their leading composer, Sir John Stevenson, fails to arouse my interest.*

During this time, Charlotte kept him up to date about all his incoming correspondence. On one occasion she wrote:

Although this is a business matter, I have to laugh as I write it down. Just imagine; old Nägeli in Zürich is asking you to compose a sonata for his 'Portal of Honour', but he has laid down three conditions: no repeated notes, no tenths and no emotional annotations. Notwithstanding this, he goes on to drown you in a flood of compliments about your talent, saying what an honour it will be for his 'Portal of Honour' to be commemorated by your sonata. It is obvious that this man is not only a publisher, but also one of those who write in newspapers and who are, therefore, accustomed to extolling your gifts.

When Moscheles returned to London, he devoted the first few months of the year 1826 to writing more études, in E-flat minor, B minor and D minor (op. 70), as well as completing his 'Souvenirs of Ireland'.

THE LAST DAYS OF CARL MARIA VON WEBER

In March 1826, Carl Maria von Weber arrived in London. He stayed with Sir George Smart, and Moscheles often called on him there. In spite of his poor state of health, Weber gave several big concerts, the first of which took place at Covent Garden Theatre. Moscheles recorded the event in his diary:

His first appearance before an English audience last night at Covent Garden Theatre must have been exhausting for him. We were deeply moved by the thunderous applause that greeted him, but it must have affected him even more to be the celebrated object of all that enthusiasm! He conducted excerpts from his opera 'Der Freischütz', and the overture had to be repeated by popular demand. Braham, Miss Paton and Phillips sang the main arias of the opera with great gusto. The subsequent applause was deafening and, to show his appreciation, Weber shook each singer warmly by the hand. At the end of the performance, there was a standing ovation for Weber, and in their excitement, some members of the audience even climbed on to their seats to wave their hats and handkerchiefs high in the air, cheering the master for all they were worth. When I saw him a little later in the foyer of the theatre, he looked far too exhausted and ill to be able to savour this extraordinary triumph in a foreign country. We, his friends and compatriots, did it for him, however. In addition to myself, there were his librettist, Friedrich Kind (author of 'Der Freischütz'), the flautist Fürstenall, who had accompanied him on this trip, and good old Stumpff, the harp-maker, who had been resident in London for some time.

On March 12th, Moscheles attended a party given by the singer Braham.

Weber improvised at the piano and interwove some of the tunes from 'Der Freischütz' in a thoroughly ingenious manner, although he scarcely exerted himself physically. The state of his health, alas, no longer allowed him to do so. At 11 o'clock, however, he dashed off to another soirée given by Mrs. Coutts, because she was paying him well. After he had taken his leave of us, everyone expressed deep concern at his sad condition.

On March 13th, Weber was invited to the Moscheles' for dinner:

What a delight for us! But we could not help but feel compassion for him. He was completely out of breath after climbing the few steps leading to our drawing room, and sank straight away into the chair nearest the door. Thereafter, however, he soon recovered and proved to be a charming and intellectually stimulating companion. In the evening we drove with him to the Philharmonic Concert, the first he had attended. We heard a very pleasing rendering of two symphonies, one by Haydn and the other by Beethoven.

The next Philharmonic Concert was conducted by Weber himself, and the programme included, amongst other works, the overtures to 'Euryanthe' and 'Der Freischütz', as well as an aria by Weber, sung by Mme. Caradori.

On April 11th there was a dress rehearsal at Covent Garden for the première of 'Oberon'. Moscheles was present at this, and wrote the following account:

There were as many people in the audience as there would have been for a real performance; moreover there were no interruptions. Both the costumes and the beautiful sets, especially the movable moon for the Ocean-Aria, looked exquisite. This aria, which Weber wrote for Miss Paton, was extremely effective; so, too, was Hüon's great aria, specially composed for Braham. Both singers were given the chance to demonstrate the exceptional range of their powerful voices, calling upon all the necessary skill to delight the audience. As he stood there with his baton in his hand, Weber must have felt the whole of England was cheering him,

ensuring that his creations would live on in the country.

The première itself received nothing but complimentary notices. The poor master, however, whom Moscheles visited almost daily, was showing signs of increasing strain on his health, in spite of all his triumphs. Nevertheless, he still continued with his concert programmes.

On May 18th Weber was asked to conduct his own compositions once again. Unfortunately though, the concert turned out to be a far from glorious occasion. It had been organized by Braham and included Moscheles amongst the performers.

It was his (Braham's) own annual event at Covent Garden Theatre, and this most popular of English singers always knew just how to inspire his audience in the third gallery (nicknamed 'the gods', on account of its vertiginous height) by singing a string of sea-shanties. Today was no exception. The popular and coquettish Mme. Vestries was likewise greeted with loud cheers by these 'gods' who dominate the whole theatre. She sang various arias from the operetta 'The Slave', as well as some nursery rhymes, such as 'Goosie Goosie Gander, whither shall I wander? Upstairs and downstairs, and in my lady's chamber' etc. Up until then, everything was perfect. Braham miscalculated, however, by presenting a programme of good music to this type of audience in the second half of the concert, which he had called 'Apollo's Festival'. This started with the overture to 'Beherrscher der Geister' (Ruler of the Spirits), a complete contrast to the light-hearted mood of the first half. I don't know whether the audience were aware that it was Weber himself standing on the conductor's rostrum, but the shouting and general hubbub coming from the gallery prevented anyone from hearing the orchestra. I was incensed by this show of rudeness, and

42

when it was my turn to perform, I sat on the stage by my instrument, barely able to conceal my fury. I then signalled to the orchestra below me to begin playing my 'Souvenirs of Ireland'. Straight away, during the somewhat sombre introduction of the piece, the louts in the third gallery started whistling, hissing and yelling out things like: 'Are you comfortable Jack ?', and aiming whole salvos of sucked-out orange peel at the people below. All hell seemed to be let loose as I sat there listening to the noise washing over me in waves of crescendo and decrescendo. As the battle looked like going the other way, I stiffened my resolve not to give in. I quickly decided to turn the tables on my tormentors. Instead of breaking off, I said to the leader of the orchestra: 'I will carry on moving my hands as if I were playing, but without actually doing so. Tell your orchestra to do the same. After a while I'll give you a sign and we'll stop together'. No sooner said than done. When I stepped up to the front to take a bow, I was given tremendous applause. The 'gods' cheered madly because they had got rid of me, only to be faced with the immediate prospect of Miss Paton singing a serious aria. Needless to say, her fate was no different from mine. She broke off three times, but returned when the respectable members of the audience demanded 'Silence!' At last she left the stage, exclaiming tearfully 'I cannot sing'. This victory by the third gallery elicited another round of boisterous clapping and stamping from the 'gods', soon to be placated, however, by the resumption of popular melodies and sea-shanties, to which they now listened with contentment and attention.

The incident occupied the newspapers for a whole week, and Moscheles was praised for his calm behaviour, whereas poor Miss Paton was berated for breaking down in tears.

Weber's next concert, on May 26th, which was also his last, turned out to be even more disastrous. This is how Charlotte Moscheles described it:

The master, in a state of near exhaustion, had put considerable effort into arranging this event at the Argyll rooms but, in spite of it all, his concert took place in an empty hall! . . . With row upon row of empty seats stretching out behind him, Weber conducted his ever-successful overtures to 'Oberon' and 'Euryanthe', his hitherto unknown Cantata 'The Festival of Peace', and a new ballad, specially composed for, and sung by Miss Stevens. Braham gave a rendering of the Freischütz-Aria, Fürstenau produced a set of new variations on a theme from 'Oberon' on the flute, Kiesewetter performed his inevitable Mayseder-Variations in E major, and for his improvisations Moscheles took a theme from the Cantata, weaving into it melodies from 'Der Freischütz'. The solo parts in the Cantata were sung by Mme. Caradori and Braham.

Weber was so affected by the lack of support at the concert that he decided to forego his takings at the theatre where 'Der Freischütz' was about to be performed, with himself conducting. Instead, he turned his thoughts to travelling and preparations for leaving.

On June 4th Moscheles reported:

When I went to see Weber today, Sunday, he spoke confidently of his departure for Germany. Every so often, however, he would be overtaken by dreadful fits of coughing, leaving him weak and totally exhausted, and causing us the gravest anxiety on his account. He was able to speak only with the greatest difficulty, and when he told us he would be leaving in two days' time and that he would be pleased to take any letters we wished to have delivered, I felt an ache in my heart, even though I had no inkling then that I had seen him in the land of the living for the last time. I left him with his friends Fürstenau and Kind, and then exchanged a few sorrowful words downstairs with his kind host, Sir George Smart. He was in a state of some distress and informed me that Weber would not permit anyone to watch over him at night. Instead, he kept his door firmly locked, but today, as an exception, he had yielded to the combined pleading of his friends not to lock his door. However, he would still not consent to having his friends keep watch in his room, any more than he would agree to having a paid watchman sit with him.

On June 5th it finally happened, and Moscheles made the following entry:

Early this morning I received an urgent call from Sir George Smart, whose house is nearby. The night before, Fürstenau had put Weber to bed at 11 o'clock. Contrary to the promise he had made, his door was found next morning to be locked from the inside. Weber must have got up during the night to lock it and, as there was no response to repeated knocking and calling at the door, Sir George Smart sent for us, Weber's friends. When we were all present, the door was broken down, but the sleeping occupant of the room did not stir; he had already entered into his eternal sleep, his head supported by his left arm, gently resting on the pillow. . . . It would be profane to attempt to describe the pain I feel. I considered him to be one of the most individualistic composers, one whose art had led a public that vacillated between Mozart, Beethoven and Rossini back to our own German music – an immortal achievement indeed! I helped Sir George Smart and Fürstenau to gather up and seal Weber's papers, for which purpose the host, mindful of his great responsibility, sent for my own seal.

On June 6th Moscheles wrote:

This morning, with the master already lying in his lead coffin, we opened up and made a record of all his papers. There was £1000 which he must have earned in London, in addition to the £1000 which the publishers Walsh and Hawes had paid him for the piano score of 'Oberon'. We also found the manuscript of that opera, and a song, composed for a Mr. Ward for a fee of £25, which had an incomplete piano accompaniment. Sir George Smart implored me to finish it, which I later did. Moreover, I was allowed to keep some of the sketches from 'Oberon'.

A committee was set up to handle the funeral arrangements. It was decided that Mozart's Requiem would be performed at the Catholic Chapel in Moorfields. An entry fee would be charged and the money used to erect a monument in honour of the dead man. When the Catholic Bishop refused his permission on the grounds that the congregation should be allowed free entry into the church, the committee approached the authorities of the Anglican Church, seeking their consent for a performance of the Requiem at St. Paul's Cathedral, but they objected to a Catholic service being held in their church. So, after a lot of to-ings and fro-ings, the great man was finally laid to rest at the Catholic Chapel in Moorfields, on June 21st. No entry fee was charged, thus depriving him of his candidature for a monument.

We musicians all gathered for the funeral at nine o'clock in the morning at Sir George Smart's house, from where a procession of funeral coaches accompanied the body to the church. The usual service was followed by Mozart's Requiem. Afterwards, twelve pallbearers, consisting solely of musicians, including myself, carried the coffin down to the crypt accompanied by the funeral march from Handel's 'Saul'. The music resounded in all of our hearts, and there was not a dry eye to be seen in the place.

On June 12th the Philharmonic Society gave a concert in honour of the departed, and on the 17th of the same month, 'Oberon' was performed at Covent Garden for the benefit of Weber's family.

RETURN VISIT TO GERMANY AND AUSTRIA – REUNION WITH MENDELSSOHN

Late in the summer of 1826, Moscheles set out on another concert tour of Germany and Austria. His first engagement was in Leipzig, where he performed the C major Concerto, which he had only recently finished, the 'Souvernirs of Ireland', and the Rondo Brillant in D.

While in Leipzig, he renewed many old acquaintanceships, among them Grillparzer, whose play 'Medea' he went to see, accompanied by the author. After a short stop in Dresden he finally arrived in Vienna to be welcomed, as usual, with open arms. In October he gave two concerts at the Kärntnertor-Theater, and he also played music for his own pleasure with Czerny, Schindler – l'ami de Beethoven', as he chose to call himself on his visiting cards in Paris – and with other musician friends.

He had to refuse some very tempting offers to prolong his stay in Vienna, in order that he could attend his sister Nancy's wedding in Prague at the end of October. On the day after the wedding he played to a full house at the theatre in Prague, where the audience included his wife and mother who sat together in a box, delighting in the enthusiastic reception he was given and the repeated calls for encores. A second concert on November 2nd was equally well attended.

The way I combined, in my improvisation, the melody from Cherubini's 'Water Carrier'

with the Bohemian folk song

caused great excitement in the audience, and they gave me very appreciative applause.

By November 6th Moscheles was back in Dresden. He was invited to play at Court once again before the royal couple. This time, however, he did not have to play at dinner. as he had previously, and he was even presented with a royal gift. A few days later, on November 10th, Moscheles called on Weber's widow and promised her his loyal support in sorting out various matters connected with her husband's death in London.

He reached Berlin the following day, and went immediately to visit the Mendelssohn family. After listening to his 18-year-old friend's latest compositions, he wrote in his diary:

I was thrilled to hear him and his sister Fanny play his new overture to 'A Midsummer Night's Dream'. I also thought his Sonata in E major to be in perfect taste. Later on, he played his great Overture in C for me, with its main theme for trumpets, as well as a little Caprice which he called 'Absurdité'. This great genius, who is still so young, has made rapid progress since we were last together. This progress has, alas, been acknowledged by only very few outsiders, in addition to his teachers Zelter and Louis Berger. Like others before him, this prophet will have to seek glory in foreign lands.

During his stay in Berlin, Moscheles appeared in two public concerts, both attended by the Court. The first was conducted by Möser, who at that time was rehearsing Beethoven's Ninth Symphony. Moscheles attended all the rehearsals and the final performance of this colossal work with ever increasing admiration. Fifteen years later, he was to conduct the same work in London, being chiefly responsible for its breakthrough in England.

Moscheles and his wife returned to Hamburg to spend Christmas and New Year with her family. He found time to finish the second book of 24 Etudes (op. 70), as well as 'Anticipations of Scotland'. The new year, 1827, saw him continue his concert tour with performances in Hanover, Göttingen and Kassel, where his friend Spohr joined him in a big concert.

Seeing Spohr again gave me great pleasure; it is most agreeable to share one's thoughts with such a great man, and to be interested in each other's achievements. His garden is quite charming, even in winter.

Other entries in the diary reveal how much time Spohr devoted to Moscheles in these few days. On January 8th we read that Spohr helped Moscheles to prepare for a concert, and on the following day:

Spohr had invited a select band of musicians and music lovers. He played his latest Quartets in D minor and B major with his customary expertise, and I played the first movement of my C major Concerto and the first book of my Etudes, which seemed to arouse particular interest.

And a little later:

Went with Spohr to the Wilhelmshöhe and later dined with him. On the morning of the 11th of January he came with me to the rehearsal of my concert in the Stadtbausaal. To everyone's astonishment he was handed a note from the Kurfürst (Elector) informing him of his Highness's decision to change the venue of my concert from this hall to the theatre, intimating that the Court would be attending.

A letter from Charlotte fills in the remaining details:

The Elector does not enjoy attending concerts at the Saal, as it lacks a royal box. Moreover, he usually bans all concerts from the theatre (including one that Hummel wanted to give), and is said never to have attended any that did manage to get performed there. It is, therefore, the greatest honour for my husband to perform for the Elector.

Of the concert itself Moscheles reported:
With Spohr conducting so magnificently, I played my G minor Concerto and Clair de lune with the greatest affection.

At Elberfeld, where Moscheles wanted to break his journey for a rest, the local Director of Music refused to take 'no' for an answer when he pleaded with Moscheles to give a concert. The latter did finally relent, his thousand excuses having fallen on deaf ears and, much amused by it all, he wrote in his diary:

The Programme really should have read: Symphony by Beethoven, performed to the best of their ability by a ragbag of musicians calling themselves an orchestra; E-flat major Concerto, played with the utmost care, so as not to leave the orchestra behind; Aria, sung by a singer, if the town could produce such a singer; Male Voice Quartet, taking the place of the soloist; and to end with an Improvisation, after which I was allowed to depart without hindrance.

On the day of the concert, half the town was under water, so that only half of the orchestra turned up, which was 'rather like having a small piece of half an apple'. The public who did attend arrived in floods, in more ways than one, but enjoyed the evening nonetheless.

After engagements at Aachen and Brussels, Moscheles returned to London at the end of January 1827. In the ensuing months he composed his fifty Preludes for Piano (op. 73), 'Les charmes de Londres', and a second Rondo, which later appeared in the 'Album des Pianistes'. Several publishers managed to persuade him to write quite a number of purely fashionable pieces by offering him generous payment. These pieces cost him the minimum of effort, and he considered them to be of such little value that he did not even give them an opus number.

Considering the general public's predilection for melodious tunes and easily assimilated rhythms, it is small wonder that London responded warmly to the novelty of a recently arrived family from the Zillertal in Austria, comprising three brothers and a sister, by the name of Rainer. Like most musicians arriving from the Continent, they were recommended to contact Moscheles. He promptly negotiated on their behalf for a series of daily concerts to be given in the Egyptian Hall in which they presented their Tyrolean songs to the English public. Their charming manner, the purity of their voices, the distinctive character of their music, the genuine Tyrolean costumes – everything about them delighted the public and attracted more and more people to their performances which, despite the low-priced tickets, gave the group a handsome profit. Matters did not rest there, however. The Tyroleans became fashionable. At the most glittering soirées the leading society ladies would think nothing of expecting the greatest opera singer of the day to make way for the folksy Tyrolean melodies. King George IV himself became so fond of them that he presented them each with a brand-new national costume. They were regular visitors at Moscheles' home, asking and obtaining his advice, and chatting to him about their experiences in the English metropolis.

ILLNESS AND DEATH OF BEETHOVEN

Life had been running a smooth and pleasant course in the winter of 1827, when suddenly the news of Beethoven's grave illness struck Moscheles like a thunderbolt. The first reference in his diary to this read thus:

Today I received a dreadful shock when Stumpff told me that Beethoven was dangerously ill; he had a letter with him giving full details. What a terrible disaster for the musical world. And what a disgrace, for there is mention of his lacking proper nourishment; it is quite unthinkable!

Moscheles received the following, undated letter, via a third person, which had been written by Beethoven to Joseph von Warena in Graz, possibly as early as the end of 1826. In the letter he outlined the cause of his unfortunate financial state:

Dear Sir,

Rode must have been right in everything he told you about me. My health is far from good at the moment and, through no fault of my own, I find myself in circumstances more straitened than ever before. Neither this fact, however, nor indeed anything else in the world shall prevent me from trying, as best I can, to help your Convent ladies, whose suffering is as undeserved as my own, by contributing my modest work. –

I am, therefore, putting at your disposal two quite new symphonies, an aria for bass and chorus, several individual small chorales. Moreover, should you require the overture to 'Hungary's Benefactor' (Ungarns

Wohltäter), which you performed last year, I shall gladly put it at your disposal. –

The overture to the 'Ruins of Athens' is also at your disposal, although this is on a somewhat smaller scale. Amongst the choral compositions there is a Dervish song which should prove attractive to a mixed audience. In my opinion it would be a very good idea to choose a day on which you can perform the oratorio 'Christ on the Mount of Olives' (Chrisus am Oelberge). It has already been performed in a number of different places. I would suggest this for the first half of the programme, to be followed in the second half by a new symphony, the overtures and several choral works, as well as the above-mentioned bass aria and chorus. I feel that this would make for quite a varied evening, but it would be best if you were to discuss all this with the musical authorities there. You mention a possible financial reward for me from a third person, and I believe I can guess his identity. If times were as they used to be, I should reply at once: 'Beethoven never accepts anything when it is a question of helping his fellow men'. However, as it is this charitableness on my part that has brought about my present situation, of which I am, therefore, not ashamed, and as persons without honour and probity have had their share in my plight, I should not refuse such a reward from a wealthy person. – There is, of course, no question of my staking a claim to the reward, and if nothing were to come of this offer from a third person, you may rest assured that I should even now be as willing as I was last year to give comfort to my friends, the honourable ladies, as I should indeed be willing to offer my services to suffering humanity for as long as I live. –

And now I bid you farewell. Do write soon, and I for my part shall do everything that is necessary with all possible speed.

With my kind regards to the Convent,
your devoted friend
Ludwig van Beethoven
To His Honour
Herrn Joseph von Warena
in Graz.

While still recovering from the terrible shock, Moscheles wrote to his friend Lewinger in Vienna, asking for more information about Beethoven and the state of his affairs. Before he received a reply, however, the postal services being very sluggish and unreliable, particularly in winter, he received the following letter from Beethoven himself, leaving no possible doubt as to the misfortune that had befallen the great man:

Vienna, 22nd February 1827

My dear Moscheles,

I am sure that you will not be offended if I trouble you, as well as Sir George Smart, for whom a letter is also enclosed, to do me a favour. The matter is briefly as follows: A few years ago I received an offer from the Philharmonic Society in London to arrange a concert, the proceeds of which I was intended to keep. Fortunately, my circumstances at that time were such that I did not have to make use of this noble offer. Now, however, things are quite different, as I have been afflicted for the last three months by a long-drawn-out illness. I am suffering from dropsy. Schindler will tell you more about it in the enclosed note. You have known me for a long time now, and are also aware of how and where I live. There can be no question of my returning to composing for some time yet, and, I regret to say, it is quite possible that I may have to endure considerable hardship. You not only have a wide circle of friends in London, but you also have considerable influence with the Philharmonic Society. I am, therefore, asking you to use this influence as best you can to persuade the Philharmonic Society to repeat this generous offer to me, and to effect the same as soon as possible. The message contained in the enclosed letter to Sir George Smart is along similar lines, and so, too, is a letter which I have already sent to Herr Stumpff. I beg you to pass the letter on to Sir George and to get in touch with him and with all my other friends in London, in order that the matter can be resolved in the utmost haste. I am now so weak that it has even been difficult for me to dictate this letter to you. Please give my regards to your charming wife, and be assured that I shall ever remain,

Your friend
Beethoven

Please reply to this letter as soon as you can, so that I may know whether I have reason for optimism.

This letter was accompanied by a heart-rending enclosure from Schindler, Beethoven's friend and nurse:

Vienna, 22 February 1827

Dear Friend,

When you read this letter from our unfortunate Beethoven, you will see that I have reserved the right to send a few lines of my own. I would normally have much to tell you, but at the moment, there is no subject closer to my heart than Beethoven, so I shall confine myself to that. In his letter to you, he makes a request, and also tells you of his dearest wish. His letter to Sir George Smart is similar in content, as is an earlier letter also written by me on Beethoven's behalf, to Herr Stumpff, the harp builder.

Last time you were here I mentioned Beethoven's financial difficulties to you. However, I had no inkling then that the time had almost come when we would witness this great man reaching the end of his life in such troubled circumstances. Yes, it is true; he is coming to the end of his life for, as far as the current state of his illness is concerned, a recovery is quite out of the question, though he must know it himself, even though he probably guesses as much.

On December 3rd he arrived back here from the country with his despicable nephew. Bad weather on the way had forced him to seek shelter overnight in a miserable inn, where he contracted such a bad cold that it promptly turned into pneumonia, in which condition he returned here. He was barely cured of this complaint when all the signs pointed to dropsy. This spread through his body so quickly that he had to undergo an operation on December 18th, otherwise he might have burst. A second operation followed on January 8th, and a third on January 20th. After both the second and the third operation, the water was allowed to flow freely from the wound for eleven days. No sooner had the wound healed though, than the water began to accumulate again rapidly, causing me to fear that he would suffocate before it was possible to operate on him again. There are indications now, however, that the water is accumulating more slowly than before, which is just as well, as the fourth operation is not due for another 8 – 10 days.

My friend. Just try to imagine what it is like for Beethoven, struck down by such a terrible illness, especially with his impatience and, of course, with his temperamental disposition. Imagine him in this intolerable situation, brought about by his nephew, that most objectionable of men, and also to some extent by his brother, for, according to the two physicians, Herr Malfatti and Professor Wawruch, the illness has its roots in all those traumatic emotional upsets to which the nephew has subjected the good man over *such a long period of time. It seems, too from his lengthy stay in the country during the wet and cold season, an inevitable consequence of the fact that the young gentleman was not allowed to remain in Vienna on account of a police order. Moreover, it was not possible to secure him a place in one of the regiments. At the moment he is a cadet in the employ of the Archduke Ludwig, but he continues to behave towards his uncle as he always has done, although he is entirely dependent on his support, just as before. It is now a fortnight ago that Beethoven sent him his letter to Sir George Smart for translation into English, but there has been no reply to date, even though he is stationed only a few miles away in Iglau.*

Moscheles, my very dear fellow, if you could combine your efforts with those of Sir George to persuade the Philharmonic Society to agree to Beethoven's wish, you would be doing him the greatest favour. The expenses resulting from Beethoven's prolonged illness are exceedingly high, and the fear of having to suffer privation is torturing him day and night, because the thought of accepting assistance from his loathsome brother is enough to make him want to die immediately.

The indications are that the dropsy has led to emaciation, for he is now nothing more than skin and bones; only his constitution is strong enough to be able to stave off the terrible end for a while yet.

It also sickens him to think that no one here seems to care about him; this lack of compassion really is most remarkable. There have been times when one equipage after another would drive up if he happened to feel slightly unwell. Nowadays though, he is quite forgotten, as if he had never even lived in Vienna. This is a great trial for me, and I wish with all my heart for a change in his condition, one way or another for, as I am the only person he allows near him, I am sacrificing all my time for him, and it would, of course, be inhumane to leave him alone in his helpless state.

He now talks frequently of a trip to London once he is recovered, and calculates how the two of us could manage the journey with the minimum expense. But my God! I really hope that the journey will take him further than England. When he is alone, he reads the Greek classics for his entertainment and, lately, he has also enjoyed some of Walter Scott's novels.

As soon as you have obtained an assurance from the Philharmonic Society that they will carry out their previously stated proposal, please ensure that Beethoven is informed immediately, for such news would give him a new lease of life. If you could also persuade Sir George to write to him, it would reinforce this assurance.

May the Lord bless you! Please be good enough to convey to your excellent wife my deepest devotion. I remain, with the greatest respect,

Your zealous friend,
Ant. Schindler

P.S. If the matter with the Philharmonic Society should reach a successful conclusion, I suggest that the gentlemen in question make plain their wish that the money be used by Beethoven for his own benefit, and not for the benefit of his most abnormal relatives, least of all for his ungrateful nephew. This would be of great assistance, for otherwise he might give the money to his nephew once again, and he would merely squander it, leaving Beethoven himself to suffer hardship.

Sick and neglected in his hour of need – a Beethoven! Moscheles exclaimed. The news had caused a flurry in the household. Moscheles rushed off to see Smart straight away, and their first impulse was to send the great man £20 to enable him to meet his most immediate needs, and to make him feel that a Beethoven must never be allowed to have financial worries. On reflection, however, Moscheles remembered that Beethoven would probably look upon this as a kind of alms. He would consider that an insult to his pride and, worse still, would be extremely upset. So, instead of sending money, they lost no time in contacting the management of the Philharmonic Society. The latter, who were just as shocked by the matter, declared their willingness to help at once. They, of course, needed to call a meeting of their governing body, so that the question could be discussed in detail. Meanwhile, however, Moscheles received a second letter from Beethoven.

Vienna, 14th March 1827

My dear and good Moscheles,

I heard from Herr Lewinger that in a letter to him, dated February 10th, you enquired after the state of my health, about which the most diverse rumours seem to be circulating. Although I have no doubt whatsoever that you have received my letter of February 22nd by now, informing you of everything you should wish to know, I must nevertheless thank you most sincerely for your interest in my sad fate and also for your sympathy. I should also like to take the opportunity to implore you once again to promote my cause, of which I notified you in my first letter. I feel assured in advance that you, together with Sir George Smart, Herr Stumpff, Herr Neate and all my other friends, will succeed with the Philharmonic Society in securing a favourable outcome for me. I have already written to Sir George again after I found his address by chance, and I urged him once more to intervene on my behalf.

On February 27th I underwent a fourth operation, and there are signs that I may even have to undergo a fifth one. Where is all this going to end, and what will become of me if this state of affairs continues for much longer? Truly, a great disaster has befallen me! I nevertheless surrender to whatever Divine Providence may have in store for me. All I ask is that it may be the will of God to save me from hardship for as long as I have to endure this living death. This would give me enough strength to carry my burden, however hard and terrible, in devotion to the will of the Allmighty.

So, my dear Moscheles. Once again I entrust you with my concern, and remain, with the greatest respect,

Your friend,
Beethoven

Hummel is in Vienna at the moment and has been to visit me several times.

Schindler added the following note:

My dearest friend,

I must add a few lines myself. You will be able to see from Beethoven's letter how things are with him. It is now certain that he is nearer to the grave than to recovering, as the emaciation has now affected his whole body. This could continue for many months though, because of the iron constitution of his chest. If you could only ensure that, if or when the Philharmonic Society agrees to his request, the money be forwarded to a responsible agent here, such as a large commercial banking house, where he can draw enough for his needs at any time. The Philharmonic Society should explain quite categorically to him that such a stipulation will be solely to his advantage, as it was well known that his relatives were taking advantage of him. This may make him uneasy at first, but I, and the others whom he trusts, will make him under-

stand that this is a very beneficial ruling, and then he will accept our explanation. Whatever estate he may leave behind, will in any case go to the most undeserving recipients, and it would be far better if it were to go to a penal institution.

Hummel and his wife are in town, and he made every effort to see Beethoven before it is too late, since rumours are circulating in Germany that Beethoven is already on his deathbed. Their reunion last Thursday was a truly moving sight. I had warned Hummel beforehand to be prepared for Beethoven's changed appearance. Nevertheless, he was so taken aback that, despite his resolve to the contrary, he broke down in tears. Anticipating as much, Beethoven very quickly covered up for Hummel with this remark: 'Look here, my dear Hummel, the house in which Haydn was born was given to me today as a present, and I am simply beside myself. Can you imagine, a great man like that was born in a miserable peasant's cottage!' I thus saw two men, who had never been the best of friends, engaged in a heart-warming conversation, oblivious of any previous quarrels between them. Both have agreed to meet again in Carlsbad next summer. Oh dear! –

My most sincere regards
to your amiable wife!
Your ever devoted friend,
Ant. Schindler

By this time the Philharmonic Society had taken steps to come to Beethoven's assistance. During the discussions, which Moscheles attended, being a member himself, it was decided unanimously not to wait until a concert could be arranged, as this would require between four and six weeks in a large city like London. Moreover, this was not a good time of year for such an undertaking. Beethoven was to receive without delay the sum of £100, through the kind offices of Moscheles. However, in order not to hurt his feelings, he would be told that the money was an advance on the forthcoming concert. The following letter from Rau* (one of Beethoven's Viennese friends) proves that the money had reached Vienna fairly swiftly:

Vienna, 17th March 1827

Dear Friend,

After a very serious eye infection, which confined me to the four walls of my chamber for three whole weeks, I am, thank God, now well enough to hold a pen again, albeit with considerable effort. You will have to guess anything you cannot read, and you must forgive the illegibility of my writing.

Your letter, which has reached me together with £100 for Beethoven, has aroused as much astonishment as it has admiration. The great man, rightly honoured and acclaimed throughout Europe, the most noble and kind-hearted of men, is lying on his sick-bed, here in Vienna, suffering the greatest hardship and fighting for his life! And we have to learn this from London** where strenuous efforts are under way to alleviate his suffering and grief, and from where your generosity is reaching out to save him from despair. I went to see him at once, to see for myself how he was and to give him the news that help was forthcoming. It was heart-rending to see him fold his hands, barely able to repress his tears of joy and gratitude. How it would have gladdened the hearts of all you generous people if you had been able to witness this most moving scene!

*Rau was for many years tutor of the young Baron von Eskeles, whose parents had at one time shown great kindness towards Moscheles. It was to him that Moscheles sent the £100, asking Rau at the same time to enquire personally after Beethoven's condition.
**In the original letter we find the following hand-written comment by Moscheles:
It so happens that I have definite proof of concern for Beethoven's precarious condition on the part of the Viennese, and that many of his admirers would have gladly offered him help and consolation, had not his seclusion made access to him or to his immediate environment so very difficult.

I found poor Beethoven in a very sad state, more like a skeleton than a living human being. The dropsy has ravaged his body to such an extent that the doctor has already had to draw the water off four or five times. He is being treated by Dr. Malfatti, a competent physician. Malfatti holds out little hope for him, though. Nobody can say for certain how long his present state will continue, or indeed whether he can be saved. Meanwhile, the news that help has arrived at last has caused a strange reaction. One of the closed-up wounds reopened during the night, allowing all the water that had accumulated over the previous fortnight to flow out; no doubt as a result of all the excitement he had experienced. When I saw him again the following day, he was remarkably cheerful and felt wonderfully relieved. I rushed to tell the news to Malfatti. He feels very reassured by this incident. In order to keep the wound open and allow the accumulating water to flow away freely, it is intended to insert a hollow tube and keep it there for the time being. May God give his blessing!

Beethoven seems to be quite satisfied with his domestic arrangements and service, consisting of a cook and a maid. His friend, the dear and faithful Schindler, dines with him daily and, in this respect, takes good care of him as the honest friend that he is. Moreover, it is Schindler who looks after Beethoven's correspondence and pays his expenses, to the best of his ability.

I enclose herewith, dear friend, a receipt, made out by Beethoven for the £100 I handed to him. When I suggested to him that he keep only £50 and leave the rest, until such time as he needed the money, in the safe custody of Baron von Eskeles, he frankly confessed that at the very moment when the £100 arrived – like manna from heaven, as it were – he was facing the embarrassing prospect of having to borrow money. As he had expressed the urgent wish to have all the money at once, I yielded to him and handed it to him there and then.

Beethoven is going to write you a letter in which he will give details of how he intends to express his gratitude to the Philharmonic Society. If you can be of assistance to him in the future, and if you feel I can be of service to you in this endeavour, please count on my zeal and willingness. The whole Eskeles family sends its kindest regards to you, your wife and your little son, and I join them in sending you my warmest regards.

Your loyal friend,
Rau

As we can see from the comment Moscheles appended to Rau's letter, and also from entries in his diary, he contacted many friends in Vienna enquiring how it was that Beethoven, sick and in need of help, could be so neglected. He received the same explanation from all sides: Beethoven's repulsive manner, coupled with the jealousy of his brother and nephew, both of whom kept turning away his friends and suchlike. *I don't think they would have turned me away quite so easily.* Moscheles remarked, and probably with some justification.

Rau's letter of March 17th was followed by a most touching one from Beethoven himself. He had dictated it to Schindler, but signed it with his own hand.

Vienna, 18th March 1827

My dear, good Moscheles,
There are no words that could describe my feelings on reading your letter of March 1st. The Philharmonic Society's magnanimous gesture, almost anticipating my request, has moved me to the depths of my soul. I am asking you, dear Moscheles, to be the organ through which I may pass on my

warmest, most sincere thanks to the Philharmonic Society for their concern and support.

I found it necessary to take delivery of the £100 all at once, as just at that moment I was facing the distressing prospect of having to raise money by borrowing, which could have put me into an even more embarrassing position.

With regard to the concert which the Philharmonic Society has decided to arrange for my benefit, I beg the Society not to abandon their intention, and to subtract these £100, which they have already paid me as an advance, from the receipts of the concert. Furthermore, should the Society graciously decide to send me the remainder, I solemnly undertake to express my warm gratitude to the same by writing for them either a new symphony, sketches for which are lying in my desk, or a new overture, or whatever else the Society may wish me to write. If only heaven would grant that I may be well again soon, so that I can prove to the noble English how well I appreciate their concern for my sorry state.

I shall always remember your own noble conduct, and it still remains for me to send my special thanks to Sir George Smart and Herr Stumpf.

With all my best wishes and warmest thoughts, I remain,
Your very grateful friend,
Ludwig van Beethoven

P.S. Please remember me to your wife – I also have to thank you and the Philharmonic Society for a new friend, Herr Rau.

Would you please be so kind as to pass on to the Philharmonic Society the following metronome markings which you will find enclosed:

Metronome markings for Beethoven's last Symphony, Opus 125

Allegro ma non troppo e un poco maestoso	88 = ♩
Molto vivace	116 = ♩
Presto	116 = ♩
Adagio molto e cantabile	60 = ♩
Andante moderato	63 = ♩
Finale presto	96 = ♩
Allegro ma non troppo	88 = ♩
Allegro assai	80 = ♩
Alla Marcia	84 = ♩
Andante maestoso	72 = ♩
Adagio divoto	60 = ♩
Allegro energico	84 = ♩
Allegro ma non tanto	120 = ♩
Prestissimo	132 = ♩
Maestoso	60 = ♩

Attached to this letter from Beethoven was another one, written six days later by Schindler:

Vienna, 24th March 1827

My dear friend,

Please do not be confused by the different dates of the two letters. I deliberately held on to Beethoven's letter for a few days, as, on the very next day, the 19th, we had cause to fear that the great man's last hour had come. I thank God that this was not the case. However, by the time you read these lines, my good Moscheles, our friend will no longer be in the land of the living. His disappearance from this earth approaches ever more rapidly, and all of us here only wish that he may soon be delivered from his appalling suffering. For the past week he has lain there almost like a corpse, and only on rare occasions can he gather up sufficient strength to ask for something. He is in a most distressing condition, similar in fact to that of the Duke of York, about which we have been reading recently. His senses seem to be permanently dulled, while his head hangs down on his chest, his gaze fixed for hours on end on a particular spot in the room, and mostly he cannot identify even his closest acquaintances, unless he is told who they are. In short, it is a terrible sight. This state cannot continue for more than a few days, as all the functions of his body ceased to operate yesterday. God willing, he will soon be delivered from the suffering, and we with him. People have been coming here in droves to catch a last glimpse of him even though there is a strict rule to admit no one. In spite of this, some have the audacity to slip through and pester the dying man in his last hours.

The letter to you was dictated by him word for word, except for a few words at the beginning, and it may well be his last, although he did manage to whisper to me today 'Smart – Stumpff – write –'. If it were possible for him to write his name on paper, then he would surely do so. He can feel that his end is nigh, for yesterday I heard him say to Herr von Breuning and me: 'Plaudite amici, comoedia finita est!' (You may now applaud my friends; the comedy is over). It is just as well that we were able to sort out his will yesterday, although he leaves nothing but a few items of old furniture and manuscripts. He has been working on a Quintet for Strings, as well as on his tenth Symphony, to which he referred in his letter to you. Two movements of the Quintet are absolutely complete. It was intended for Diabelli. – For a few days following the arrival of your letter, he was extremely excited and spoke a great deal of his plans for the new symphony, deciding that it would be even grander than originally planned, now that he was writing it for the Philharmonic Society.

I only wish that in your letter to him you had pointed out to him quite firmly that he could have the £100 in instalments only. This is also what I had agreed with Herr Rau, but Beethoven stuck by the last words of the relevant sentences in your letter. In short, as soon as he had the money, all his grief and

worries disappeared, and he said quite cheerfully: 'Now we can have a good time again', for we had only the equivalent of £34 left in the kitty, and had for some time been limiting ourselves to boiled beef and vegetables, which grieved him more than anything else. The next day, he ordered his favourite fish dish straight away, just so that he could nibble at it. To cut a long story short, his joy at the noble gesture of the Philharmonic Society even went so far as to degenerate into childishness. He also ordered the purchase of a so-called Grandfather chair, at a cost of £5, in which he rests every day for about half an hour, so that his bed can be properly remade.

His stubbornness is still as trying as ever, and very hard to bear for me personally, as he will suffer no other person near him but myself. What choice did I have other than to give up all my students and devote all my free time to him? He insists that I taste every drink and every dish beforehand, in order to ensure that it will not harm him. – Devoted as I am to him, I regret to say, that for a poor devil such as I am, the whole business has gone on for far too long. – However, if I remain healthy, matters should resolve themselves after a time; at least, I hope to God that they do! – With the remainder of the £100 we want to make sure that he receives a decent burial, in the cemetery near Döbling where he always liked to go for walks.

Then there is the rent for his lodgings which is due shortly, and must be paid to cover the next six months. On top of this are other minor expenses (physicians), so that the £100 will just about be enough, with very little to spare.

Two days after your letter arrived we received a letter from the worthy Herr Stumpff, in which he spoke of you in glowing terms. It was altogether too much excitement for Beethoven, already much weakened by the outflow of water from the wound that was *thought to have healed a fortnight ago. Many times throughout the day I heard him say: 'May God bless them all a thousand times!'*

You can well imagine what a tremendous sensation this noble gesture of the Philharmonic Society has caused here. Just as the English are now widely praised for their generosity, so the behaviour of the rich people in Vienna is condemned by everyone. The 'Beobachter' published an article on the subject, as did the 'Wiener Zeitung'. I enclose them both.

Some hours later. –
I have just been to see Beethoven. He is already at death's door, and before this letter has left the city, the great light will have been extinguished for ever. Nevertheless, he is still fully conscious. I must hurry to the post, so that I can go back to him. I have cut these few hairs from his head to send to you. – May God be with you!

Your devoted friend,
Ant. Schindler

Only a few days later, a letter from Rau confirmed the sad news:

Vienna, 28th March 1827

Dear Friend,
Beethoven is no more. He passed away on the 26th March, in the evening between 5 and 6 o'clock, having spent his final hours in a terrible struggle against the inevitable. He had already lost all consciousness on the previous day.

Now a few words about his estate. In my last letter I told you, that, according to Beethoven's own words, he was without help, without funds and, consequently, in dire straits. However, when an inventory was made of his possessions, at which I was present, seven bank shares were found in an old decaying box.

Whether Beethoven had kept quiet about these shares deliberately (he was a distrustful man and hoped for a speedy recovery), or whether he had been unaware of their existence, is a problem that I cannot solve. – The £100 sent by the Philharmonic Society were found to be untouched. In accordance with your instructions, I reclaimed the money immediately but, until further directions are received from the Philharmonic Society, I have had to deposit the money with the Magistrate. Without the consent of the Philharmonic Society I could not give permission for this money to be used to cover the expenses of the burial. Provided the Philharmonic Society is in agreement, I should also like to request that this money be shared between the two poor servants who have nursed the sick man with endless patience, love and devotion, but who are not even mentioned in his will. Beethoven's only heir is his nephew. – Herr Schindler will write to you in due course concerning the gift Beethoven had intended to make to the Philharmonic Society. Please write soon and let me know exactly what you wish me to do. You can rely on my strict adherence to your instructions. Beethoven is to be buried on the 29th of this month, and invitations have been sent out to all artists, orchestras and theatres. Twenty solo instrumentalists and composers will walk beside the coffin carrying torches. Grillpanzer has written a most moving sermon, which is to be delivered by Anschütz at the graveside. Every possible effort has been made to arrange a funeral worthy of the deceased. –

The Eskeles send their regards to you and your family,
and kindest regards from me,
Your friend,
Rau

I wrote this in a hurry, and am still suffering from sore eyes.

Among Moscheles' papers were the following mementos of Beethoven's death:

EINLADUNG

zu

LUDWIG van BEETHOVEN's

LEICHENBEGÄNGNISS,

welches am 29. März um 3 Uhr Nachmittags Statt finden wird.

Man versammelt sich in der Wohnung des Verstorbenen im Schwarz-spanier-Hause Nr. 200 am Glacis vor dem Schottenthore.

Der Zug begiebt sich von da nach der Dreyfaltigkeits-Kirche bey den P. P. Minoriten in der Alsergasse.

Die musikalische Welt erlitt den unersetzlichen Verlust des berühmten Tondichters am 26. März 1827 Abends gegen 6 Uhr.

Beethoven starb an den Folgen der Wassersucht im 56. Jahre seines Alters, nach empfangenen heiligen Sacramenten.

Der Tag der Exequien wird nachträglich bekannt gemacht von

L. van BEETHOVEN's

Verehrern und Freunden.

(Diese Karte wird in Tob. Haslinger's Musikhandlung vertheilt.)

INVITATION

to

THE FUNERAL OF
LUDWIG VAN BEETHOVEN

on 29th March at 3 p.m.

Mourners are requested to assemble at the former lodgings of the deceased, Schwarzspanier-Hause 200 etc. – From there the cortège will make its way to the Dreyfaltigkeits-Kirche (Church of the Holy Trinity) etc. –

The world of music has suffered an irreplaceable loss as a result of the composer's death which occurred around 6 o'clock in the evening on March 26th 1827. – Beethoven dies from the effects of dropsy in the 56th year of his life, after receiving the Holy Sacrament. – The date of the exequies will be announced at a later date by

L. van BEETHOVEN'S

Admirers and friends.

(This invitation card will be available at Tob. Haslinger's music shop)

Bey
LUDWIG van BEETHOVEN's
Leichenbegängniss
am
29. Marz 1827
Von
J. F. CASTELLI

Achtung allen Thränen, welche fliessen,
Wenn ein Braver Mann zu Grabe ging
Wenn die Freunde Trauerreihen schliessen,
Die der Selige mit Lueb'umfing.

Doch der Trauerzug, der heute wallet,
Strecket sich, so weit das Himmelszelt
Erd'umspannt, so weit ein Ton erschallet,
Und um diesen Todten weint die Welt.

Doch um Euch allein nur müsst Ihr klagen!–
Wer so hoch im Heiligthume stand,
Kann den Staub nicht mehr – er ihn nicht tragen,
Und der Geist sehnt sich in's Heimathland.

Darum rief Muse ihn nach oben,
Und an ihrr Seite sitzt er dort,
Und an ihrem Throne hört er droben
Tönnen seinen eigenen Accord.

Aber hier sein Angedenken weilet,
Und sein Name lebt im Ruhmes-Licht,
Wer, wie er, der Zeit ist vorgeeilet,
den ereilt die Xeit zerstörend nicht.

For
LUDWIG van BEETHOVEN's
Funeral
on
29th March 1827
by
J. F. CASTELLI

Honoured be all tears that flow,
When a good man goes to his grave,
When his friends come together to follow his coffin,
Whom he had once surrounded with love

But the long line of mourners that we saw today
Stretched beyond the horizon, encircling the globe,
To wherever the sound of music is heard,
And for this dead man the whole world weeps.

But your grief must be for yourselves alone! –
For he who stood so high in God's grace
Had to shake himself free of the earthly dust,
Longing to reach his eternal home.

So the Muse called him to join her in Heaven,
To be with her and sit at her side,
And there by her throne he can still hear the sound
Of the melodies that once he wrote.

But here on earth his memory will endure,
And his name will live in a glorious light
For those, like him, whose earthly days are too soon passed,
Will never be destroyed in the passage of time.

Am Grabe BEETHOVEN's
(den 29. Marz 1827)

Es brach ein Quell vom hohen Felsen nieder,
Mit reicher Strömung über Wald und Flur,
Und wo er floss, erstand das Leben wieder,
Verjüngte sich die alternde Natur.
Ein jeder kam zur reitzgeschmückten Stelle,
Und suchte sich Erquickung an der Welle.

Nur wenige von richtigem Gefühle,
Empfanden seine Wunderkräfte ganz
Die übrigen erfreuten sich am Spiele
Der schönen Fluth und ihrem Demantglanz.
Die meisten aber fanden sein Gewässer
Dem Andern gleich, nicht edler und nicht besser.

Der Quell versank. Nun erst erkannte Jeder
Des Bornes Kraft, nun erst, da sie zerstob!
Und Pinsel, Klang, der Meissel und die Feder,
Vereinten sich zum längst verdienten Lob;
Jedoch kein Lied, nicht Sehnsucht, nicht die Klage
Erweckten ihn und brachten ihn zu Tage.

Du, der hier liegt, befreyt von Schmerz und Banden,
Du warst der Quell, den ich zuvor genannt!
Du grosser Mensch, von Wenigen verstanden,
Bewundert oft, doch öfter noch verkannt!
Jetzt werden Alle jubelnd Dich erheben:
Du musstest sterben, sterben, um zu leben!

At BEETHOVEN's grave
(29th March 1827)
by
Schlechta

A spring surged forth from the rock on high,
Pouring its waters on woods and fields,
And wherever it flowed, new life began,
And ageing nature was young again.
Everyone came to this beautiful place
Seeking refreshment from the cool well.

Only a few felt a deep response
To its wonderful, fortifying power,
The others enjoyed the majestic display
Of the beautiful spring with its glittering show:
But most of them thought this found of bright water
Was like any other, no nobler, no better

Yet when the spring vanished, they all were agreed
On its powerful lure, but – alas! – too late!
And brush, and melody, chisel and pen,
All vied with each other in overdue praise;
But neither song nor yearning, nor all their lament
Could awaken the spring to new life in their midst.

You, that lie there, from all pain and bonds delivered,
You were the spring of which I have spoken!
So few in this world, great man, have understood you
You were admired, misjudged more often still!
But now their praise will carry you on high:
You had to die, to die, so that you could live.

The following letters from Schindler, Rau etc. give further details of the circumstances surrounding Beethoven's death, but deal mainly with the £100 which Beethoven had received from the Philharmonic Society. After various factors had been taken into account, a solution was finally reached which could be approved by all concerned. Schindler wrote:

Vienna, 4th April 1827

My noble friend,

I am writing these lines to you in order to ensure that the attached letter reaches Sir George Smart without fail. It contains Beethoven's last message of thanks to Smart, Stumpff and the Philharmonic Society, as well as to the whole English nation, which he begged me to convey in the last moments of his life. I should be most grateful if you could pass this on in person at your earliest convenience. Mr. Lewisey from the British Embassy has been kind enough to translate the letter into English.

It was not until March 26th, at a quarter to

six in the afternoon that our immortal friend breathed his last. From the evening of the 24th until his death, he was in an almost continuous state of delirium. Even in his final struggle between life and death, however, in his more lucid moments, he did remember the great kindness shown to him by the Philharmonic Society. Moreover, he expressed his admiration for the English nation, which had shown such concern for him.

His suffering was indescribable, especially after the wound had reopened of its own accord, allowing the water to flow out all of a sudden. – During his last few days, he seemed to be undergoing a strange transformation, as if his great soul were entering the realm of death with true Socratic wisdom. I shall very probably write all this down so that it can be made known to the public, as I am sure his biographers will find it of inestimable value.

The funeral was only what a great man deserves. About 30,000 people lined the streets through which the funeral procession was to pass. I find it almost impossible to give a true picture of what it was like. The closest comparison I can imagine is to remind you of the Prater festivities during the Congress in 1814; it was similar to that. The pallbearers were made up of eight Kapellmeister, amongst them Eibler, Weigl, Gyrowetz, Hummel, Seyfried, etc. There were thirty-six torchbearers, including Grillpanzer, Castelli, Haslinger, Steiner etc.

Yesterday, Mozart's Requiem was performed in his honour at the Augustinerkirche. The huge church was not large enough to hold all the people fighting to get in. Lablache sang the bass part of the Requiem, and the committee of art dealers was responsible for arranging the memorial service.

You had the honour of receiving the very last letter that Beethoven wrote, the one dated 18th March, and Schott in Mainz has his last signature.

His liquid assets consisted of seven bank shares and several hundred Gulden. They are now proclaiming publicly here in Vienna that he had not been in need of assistance from a foreign nation etc., never bearing in mind that Beethoven, at fifty-six years of age and nervous as he was, could be expected to live to the age of seventy. If what his physicians had told him was true, that he would not be able to work for years to come, he would have been left with no option other than to sell those shares one by one; and for how many years could he have lived off seven shares, without suffering deprivation? In short, dear friend, Herr Hofrath von Breuning and I would be greatly obliged if you could see to it, if such despicable sentiments are broadcast as far afield as England – for the love of Beethoven's memory, that the letters Beethoven wrote to you on these matters are published in one of the most widely read German newspapers, such as the 'Augburger Allgemeine'. In fact, the Philharmonic Society could even instigate such an action themselves. If this were to happen, his critics here would be taught a well-deserved lesson. The Philharmonic Society has the honour of having financed the great man's funeral, for without their money, we could never have done him justice.

Everyone screamed 'What shame for Austria! We must not allow this to happen. Surely everyone will contribute!' But screams were all they gave. The Musikverein decided on the day after his funeral – – – – to hold a Requiem Mass in his honour, and that is all. However, all of us from the Kärrterthor are determined to organise a large concert and to put the proceeds towards a decent tombstone for him.

I also have to inform you that we received

a visit yesterday from the gravedigger at Währing, where Beethoven was buried. He reported to us that he had received a note, which he showed to us, offering him 1000 Gulden (£100) for depositing Beethoven's severed head at a certain location. The police are already looking into the matter. The funeral cost a little over 300 Gulden. Your friend will have mentioned this to you in his letter. If the Philharmonic Society should decide to leave the money here and, for instance, decide to make me a small present of part of the money, I shall regard this as a legacy from my friend Beethoven; as neither I myself, nor indeed any of us, have even the smallest keepsake from him. His death was, in fact, just as much a surprise to him as it was to those of us close to him.

Please do let me know whether you have received the letters dated 22nd February, 14th March, and 18th March, and whether Sir George Smart has received his letter. Beethoven's relatives behaved despicably towards the end; he was barely dead when his brother arrived, ready to take everything away, including the £100 from London. However, needless to say, we threw him out immediately. Such scenes also occurred at Beethoven's deathbed. I suggest that you draw the Philharmonic Society's attention to the Gold Medal which Ludwig XVIII presented to Beethoven ; it weighs 50 grams and would be the most perfect token of remembrance from the great man. May God be with you!

A. Schindler.

Hummel will be playing at the Kärrtnerthor-theater tomorrow. Mr. Lewisey sends his regards to H. Neate.

Shortly afterwards there was another letter from Schindler:

Vienna, 11th April 1827

My noble friend,

You will doubtless be shocked to receive yet another letter, and also to see how bulky they all are. But you must read on, my friend, and see for yourself! – In order to save your honour, as well as Beethoven's and that of the Philharmonic Society, we had no choice but to relate to you in detail all the circumstances. – In my last letter I told you how everyone here screams and scribbles about the noble action of the Society. Now, however, the 'Allgemeine Zeitung' has published an article set to cause the utmost consternation. We considered it our duty to reply to it, and Hofrath Breuning took it upon himself to write the enclosed article, setting out the facts. Pilat is going to send it today to the Editor of the 'Allgemeine Zeitung'. You do not need to know the contents or purpose of the original article to guess what it was by reading our reply. It now remains for you and Smart to publish your own letters in the 'Allgemeine Zeitung', to make absolutely sure that these evil-doers are properly humiliated. Rau and Pilat are of the opinion that what we wrote is too polite; however, neither Breuning nor I can be quite as blunt as we should like to be. We feel though, that we owe it to the world, and in spite of having made many enemies already, as Beethoven's defender and friend, it would be despicable of me not to speak out when his memory is being defiled, and his well-meaning friends are being attacked for their noble efforts on his behalf.

I suggested in my last letter to you that the Philharmonic Society should intervene in the affray by publishing your letters and Smart's. Now everyone has agreed with me and expressed the same wish. – The Philharmonic Society should make a statement to the effect that it was a well-known fact in London that, following his first benefit concert at the Kärtnerthor-Theater two years ago, after deduction of all expenses, including the 1000 Gulden payable to the administrators of the theatre, Beethoven was left with a mere 300 Gulden, as none of the season ticket-holders paid him a penny for their boxes, and not one member of the Court deigned to make an appearance, although Beethoven had, in my presence, personally invited every member of the Imperial House. They had all promised to attend but, not only did none of them turn up, but they did not even send the slightest contribution either, something quite unheard-of, even in the case of the most ordinary beneficiary.

When at his second concert at the Redoutensaal in the same month, the administrators, having arranged it on their own account, lost out by as much as 300 Gulden, I had to use all my powers of persuasion to prevent Beethoven from refunding the deficit to the administrators out of the 500 Gulden which were his guaranteed fee. He was deeply distressed, thinking that through him they had suffered such a loss.

When subscriptions were invited for his last great Mass, nobody came forward to subscribe, not even the Court. There were, I should add, innumerable other instances of malicious behaviour and humiliations which the poor man had to endure, and the time has come to bring all this out into the open, because we now have the best reason for doing so.

Everyone in Vienna knew that Beethoven was ill for two, even three months, but nobody came to enquire how he was, or what his financial situation was. After he had undergone such terrible experiences at the hands of the Viennese people, could he really be expected to seek help here? By God! If the Philharmonic Society had not, by virtue of their noble action, instigated the action and got the Viennese so excited, then Beethoven would have died and received a burial similar to Haydn's, with no more than fifteen mourners walking behind his coffin.

The concert which is to be given by all members of our theatre to raise money for a tombstone will be arranged thus: The Norma-Day after Easter has been put forward to this week; consequently more people would be able to come this month. Weigl is not in favour of the concert being held at midday, and even suggests postponing the whole project until the autumn. But what little enthusiasm there is will have certainly evaporated by then, and no one will be prepared to do anything any more.

I must also tell you somthing about the medical treatment received by Beethoven. He asked the doctors who usually looked after him to do so during his illness. Dr Braunhofer asked to be relieved of the task on the grounds that he lived too far away, and Dr Staudenheim paid one call, three days after we had first sent him a message, but he never returned. Beethoven, therefore, had to put himself into the care of a Professor from the general hospital, whose services he was able to secure in a most peculiar fashion. It so happened that a coffee house proprietor called Gehringer, whose premises are in the Kohlmarkt, had a sick servant whom he wished to send to the Professor's clinic. He therefore wrote to this Professor Wawruch, asking him to accept the servant. In the same letter he suggested that the Professor should go and see Beethoven who was in need of medical attention. It took some time before I discovered that it was the amiable nephew, Karl v. Beethoven, who had given Gehringer this commission while playing billiards at the coffee house one day. The Professor was not acquainted with Beethoven, nor was he familiar with his particular temperament, and he treated him strictly according to the book. During the first four weeks, Beethoven was required to take no fewer than seventy-two bottles of medicine, with up to three varieties on some days. The result of all this was that Beethoven was more dead than alive by as early as the first few days of January. Eventually I could bear this deplorable state of affairs no longer and, without further ado, I went to see Dr Malfatti who used to be his friend. A long time elapsed before he consented to come, and at the first consultation Beethoven himself begged the doctor to take on his case. Malfatti pointed out, however, that courtesy towards the other doctor would prevent him from doing so, and he visited Beethoven at the most only once or twice a week. It was only during Beethoven's final week that he came every day.

In short, I may tell you this much: Beethoven was a victim of outrageous behaviour and ignorance, and he has gone to his grave at least ten years before his time. I shall have more to say about this at a later date.

Hummel returned to Weimar on the 9th. He came here with his wife and his pupil, a Herr Hiller from Frankfurt. The latter sends you his regards, as does Hummel.

The funeral expenses have now all been added up, and they amount to 330 Gulden.

There is a lot more I should like to [tell] you, but I most close there. Lewinger asks to be remembered to you both; he has kindly agreed to dispatch this letter via Rothschild. Rau also sends his regards. Do write as soon as you can. Our very best wishes to Herr Stumpff. Please tell him that it was Beethoven's wish to dedicate one of his new works to him. This shall be done, provided we can find something that is complete.

With kindest regards from
Your old friend,
Schindler

Some months later Moscheles received the following letter from Rau:

Vienna, 17th June 1827

Do not accuse me of neglect, my friend, just because I have not given you any news of Beethoven's affairs for such a long time. I have already mentioned that I put in a claim for the £100 which Beethoven had received from the Philharmonic Society. However, the executor of the will, Herr Hofrath Breuning, had no authority to dispose of the money until a convocation of Beethoven's debtors had been announced in the papers, as is the usual custom. This convocation took place on June 5th. On the advice of Baron von Eskeles I sent a lawyer to the meeting to make representations on my behalf for the return of the money. But Dr Bach, the Public Curator, raised objections. In order to expedite this matter and bring it to a successful conclusion, I need a written authority from the Philharmonic Society, certified by the Austrian Embassy, entitling me to ask for the return of the money, in accordance with the law. I also need to appoint a legal representative, and for this I propose to ask Dr Eltz to deal with the case.

After the meeting on June 5th I went to see Dr Bach for a confidential discussion, as I failed to see why our legitimate claim had met with such difficulties. He told me honestly and openly that he was duty-bound to object to any claim for as long as possible, in the interests of the nephew who was still a minor. In his opinion one could best avoid legal proceedings and the considerable expenses often incurred, if the Philharmonic Society graciously consented to make a contribution out of the sum in question towards Beethoven's monument, and to ask either the House of Eskeles or Rothschild to forward the remainder to the Society. Provided this plan is accepted, Dr Bach promised to do everything in his power to ensure that the money is returned to the Society. Baron

Eskeles and several other experienced legal experts find this proposal highly acceptable, especially as one of the key figures in this matter, Herr Hofrath von Breuning, has since passed away. The good man caught a cold at the auction of Beethoven's personal effects and died three days later. He was the only witness who could attest that the £100 had originally been sent by the Society. I trust that you will let me know in your next letter how I should proceed from here.

Kindest regards from the Eskeles family and from Wimpffen to you and your dear wife, and the same from me,

Your friend,
Rau

Schindler gave the following version of the events:

Vienna, 14th September 1827

My dearest friend!

I am taking the opportunity of having this letter forwarded to you by the English Cabinet Courier Lewisley and, thanks to his kindness, I am also sending the enclosed memento of our friend Beethoven. In your last letter you asked for something in his hand-writing and, if possible, something well-known. Here is the finale of the Scherzo from the last symphony. Also enclosed is one of those distinctive pocket note books in which Beethoven used to jot down his musical ideas, usually when he was out in the open air, so that he could work them out in detail when he returned home. I was so pleased that I was able to rescue several such items, which are of the greatest interest to me. However, unless one is familiar with the children of which these are the embryos, it is impossible to make any sense of those jottings. The one enclosed here contains the draft for one of his last quartets, and when you come to hear the quartets, I am sure that you will know to which one it belongs. Some of the ideas are written down quite clearly. – I trust that you will accept these as a proof of my friendship for you, and even more so when I assure you that no one, apart from you, has received, or is even likely to receive, a relic like this – unless he is willing to pay a large sum of money for it. Beethoven's portrait has already been forwarded to you via Lewinger. Yesterday he said to me: 'I only hope it is the lithograph depicting Beethoven with pen in hand; it is by far the best; all the others are worthless'. The heading on the sheet of paper in front of him reads 'Missa Solemnis'. I had intended to send you everything via Herr Clementi, whose acquaintance I made in London, but unfortunately I missed him, not having been told previously of his departure.

Pixis has been here from Paris. He stayed for a fortnight and left yesterday to return to Paris, with a stop in Prague en route. Spontini also left yesterday. He is engaged on a recruiting mission. While he was here, he enlisted my sister, and I shall probably accompany her to Berlin in the spring, since the Kärntnerthor-Theater is going to close again anyway. It is at least definite that Barbaja's term of office as administrator will end in April, and then we shall have to wait and see what becomes of the theatre. It is strongly rumoured that Madame Pasta will do a season here in the winter. I should be very much obliged if you could find out if there is any truth in this rumour, which should not be too difficult for you. If it were the case, you see, I should welcome an opportunity for my sister to sing for Madame Pasta before she leaves for Berlin. Perhaps you would be kind enough to enclose a note for me in a letter to Lewinger or Rau, as well as confirmation that you have received these papers. I also look forward to hearing that all is well with you and your family.

Several obstacles have delayed the winding up of Beethoven's affairs. In June Hofrath von Breuning, that most worthy of men, passed away, and for the last six weeks the Curator has been ill. I am really curious to know what will happen with the English money. The tombstone should be erected soon, but I have neither heard nor seen anything of it. The matter is being dealt with behind a veil of secrecy, presumably so that the final glory does not have to be shared with anyone else. A certain Herr Schlosser in Prague has published a most inadequate biography of Beethoven, and it is rumoured here that Herr Gräffer has already received an advance payment on another biography. However, Beethoven's chosen biographer is Hofrath Rochlitz in Leipzig, and Beethoven entrusted Breuning and me with important documents for him. Notwithstanding this, the newly appointed legal guardian for Beethoven's nephew has handed the papers that were in Breuning's possession over to Herr Gräffer. Although it was an objectionable thing to do, it cannot do much harm, because they were, for the most part, only family papers. I have held on to the most important papers.

This is all for today. May God be with you!
Your devoted friend
Ant Schindler

The eventual outcome of the affair in which Moscheles had become involved, by virtue of the fact that he rendered a service of friendship to the great man before his death, was not entirely satisfactory. In February 1828, Moscheles received the following letter:

Vienna, 10th February 1828
To Ignaz Moscheles Esquire, Composer of Music and Member of the Philharmonic Society of London.

Noble Sir,

Following the death on June 4th 1827, here in Vienna, of Herr Hofrath von Breuning, the municipal authorities have appointed me to be the legal guardian of Carl v. Beethoven, a minor, the nephew and heir of the composer Ludwig v. Beethoven, whose death on the 26th March deprived the musical world of one of its greatest artists. I have assumed this heavy responsibility only because the nephew of the great man, who has from childhood enjoyed his uncle's unstinted support – despite straying repeatedly from the path of virtue, as I am ready to admit, albeit with an ache in my heart – has let it be known that he has every confidence in me. I have set myself the task of guiding this talented young man back to a decent way of life, hoping that I may be more successful in my choice of methods than was his uncle. In his military career to date (he is currently a cadet in one of the Imperial infantry regiments), his behaviour has been quite exemplary.

With regard to Beethoven's somewhat meagre estate which, according to the evidence (after deduction of the more significant debts and the high expenses of his illness and funeral) will probably amount to no more than 8000 Gulden of Austrian paper money, I am now waiting for the legal processes to finish and then I will put before the authorities a deposition according to which my ward, under the testator's will, is entitled only to interest payments for life accruing from the capital, while the capital itself will, after his death, pass to his natural heirs, or such heirs as are named in his will, whereupon the courts will take due notice of the substitution.

In addition to several other debts brought to the notice of the authorities at the Convocation, there was a demand for £100 from the Viennese lawyer Dr. Eltz, representing Herr Rau and, through him, the Philharmonic Society in London, claiming that this money *was sent as a gift by the Philharmonic Society for Beethoven's support just before he died.*

Before probate can be granted in respect of Beethoven's estate, the above claim, which Dr. Eltz has taken the precaution to lodge, has either to receive legal backing or be invalidated. It is incumbent upon me as guardian to ensure that the legal processes are brought to a swift conclusion. I therefore beg you in all humility, as one of Beethoven's best and most highly respected friends, and as agent for the generous and magnanimous Philharmonic Society of London, and no less as our fellow countryman, highly esteemed and revered, albeit from a great distance, and lastly in the name of an orphaned young man, talented and hopeful (twenty-one years of age), and through the death of his uncle deprived of his only support and thus facing the prospect of imminent hardship, to have the kindness to persuade the Philharmonic Society, having given such proof of their generosity in the past, to desist from pursuing the claim provisionally put forward by Herr Rau, represented by Dr. Eltz, and to authorise Herr Rau to notify the authorities that the claim will not be upheld.

Inasmuch as I am deeply concerned with the welfare of a most promising young man who, as a result of the death of his uncle and guardian, Ludwig, v. Beethoven, has lost his only support, and whose favourite he had been; and since I have every confidence that the noble Philharmonic Society will refrain from claiming back a present to the deceased, made long before his death and intended for his support, even though the law would accord them this right, and provided, of course, that the sum exists 'in natura', I turn to you, Sir, begging you to ask the illustrious Society not to reduce the further scant means, amounting annually to 400 Gulden at most, out of which I am supposed to pay for the support of my ward. The matter has

become the more urgent since I have had to settle bills far in excess of 1000 Gulden for physicians, and for funeral expenses and other debts, and since, you may rest assured, I shall be very hard pressed to find a way of protecting my ward from future hardships, or until such time as he is fortunate enough to attain the rank of commissioned officer when, in order not to go short, he would still need additional means of support.

It is for this reason that I trust it will not be taken amiss if I dare to ask the most illustrious Philharmonic Society and Beethoven's old friends and admirers to consider honouring the memory of the famous man by pledging their support for his nephew and wretched heir, to save him from future want. I would take personal responsibility for the legal and fruitful investment of any such funds.

I can hardly bring myself to consider the possibility of the Philharmonic Society's continuing in the pursuit of their claim, but I must point out that the law does not permit the gift under discussion to be revoked, even if it were possible to establish the identity, and I am certain that the judge would only embarrass me further in view of the very modest size of the estate, especially since I still have to meet the not inconsiderable costs already incurred, such as legal fees and death duties.

I think I can at last explain to the Philharmonic Society why the late Ludwig v. Beethoven complained of his wretchedness before his death, and sought help from the generous Philharmonic Society. I believe it was because Beethoven looked upon his nephew as his son and ward, for whose support he felt himself responsible. There can be no doubt that this was why he no longer regarded the seven shares of the Austrian National Bank as his own property, designating them in his will for the support of his dear nephew. He was an honourable and religious man, and was fully aware that the burden of caring for his poor nephew, for whom he would have given his life, rested upon him.

I can say with absolute certainty that nothing would appease the ghost of Beethoven more, or correspond more closely to his most ardent desire to which he had devoted himself wholeheartedly during his lifetime, than if help and support were forthcoming for his deserted nephew, protecting him from future hardship. I would gladly take the duty upon myself if I found myself in more fortunate circumstances, and if I were not obliged to care for my dependents.

I trust, Sir, that my good, and certainly honest, intention will not be misunderstood, and that I may be excused all the more, since I can assure you that I have accepted the guardianship of the great man's nephew for no other reason than pure affection, to which fact, as well as to my character, Herr Rau can easily testify.

I hope that I shall soon receive favourable news, either directly, or through Herr Rau. Meanwhile, I am honoured to be able to commend myself and my ward to your benevolent attention, and to remain, with all my respect,

Your most obedient servant,
Jacob Hotschebar
K. Hofconcipist
Am alten Fleischmarkte, No. 695

Rau added the following letter:

Vienna, 10th February 1828

Dear Friend,

I enclose herewith a letter from the trustee of Beethoven's estate. You will see from it that the legal proceedings are drawing to a close. I was asked by the authorities to make a statement regarding the £100 sent by the Philharmonic Society. However, since I have received no further news from you, and since I did not wish to make a legally binding statement without further instructions, I requested an adjournment until I had received your answer and solution. The letter from the trustee will put you fully in the picture.

I should like to tell you the following in confidence: If you could manage to have the claim for the £100 withdrawn, it would do away with much unpleasantness and possibly even a court case. Dr Eltz and Baron Eskeles also feel that it would be very difficult to prove that the £100 found after Beethoven's death were those sent by the Society, all the more so since Hofrath Breuning, who was entrusted with the inventory, is now dead. – If, however, contrary to all expectations, the money should be claimed back, the Philharmonic Society will have to grant Dr Eltz power of attorney, in order that he can pursue their claim through the courts, at the expense of the Society. – It is quite possible, though, that all the money could be swallowed up if this course of action were pursued. – Please let me have your reply and definite instructions as soon as possible.

All the Eskeles family, Wimpffen, Ephraim etc. are well, and send their regards to you and your dear wife. I do likewise.

Your friend,
Rau

As a result of all this correspondence, which showed Beethoven's nephew in a somewhat different light from that communicated in Schindler's letters, Moscheles conferred with the directors of the Philharmonic Society and obtained their agreement to withdraw their claim for the return of the £100 quietly, thereby bringing to a conclusion this rather unpleasant aftermath of Beethoven's demise.

In London, the master was commemorated

in a whole series of performances of his works by the Philharmonic Society.

PLAYING TO PRINCESS VICTORIA AND MAKING THE ACQUAINTANCE OF HEINRICH HEINE AND SIR WALTER SCOTT

Moscheles' involvement with Beethoven's affairs has taken us right up to the year 1828, thus omitting everything else that happened in 1827. We now return to the first few months of 1827, where we find the following entry:

We artists gave a dinner party for old Clementi, enlivened with music and speeches in his honour. There were ninety of us altogether, and each had paid a guinea, but Clementi was to be our guest. Cramer and I welcomed him in a separate room and, after everybody had arrived, we led him to the assembled company where he was greeted with tumultuous applause. He was seated between the head of the table, Sir George Smart, and myself. After dinner there were speeches, interwoven with music, and after some of us had said our piece, a toast to the memory of Handel seemed an opportune moment to ask Clementi, the father of piano playing, to grace the keyboard with his presence on this auspicious occasion. Thunderous applause. Clementi rose, and Smart, Cramer and I led him to the piano. Everyone was full of eager anticipation, as Clementi had not been heard in public for years. He improvised on a theme by Handel, and enraptured us all. His eyes shone with the fire of youth; while those of the audience moistened with tears. After much handshaking and enthusiastic applause he returned to his table. Clementi had been famous in his youth for his beautiful legato playing, the delicacy of his touch in fast passages, and the most accomplished technique. Even now we were able to admire what still remained of these attributes. However, we were delighted in particular by the youthful and ingenious elements in his improvisation.

Clementi was at that time 75 years of age.

Cramer, the other veteran of the pianist's art resident in the British capital, was at that time writing his 'Reminiscences of England', a fantasy based on English folk melodies. Moscheles described it as *a sound piece of work, but neither new nor inspired.*

Hummel was trying to have his new piano tutor published in England, and Moscheles undertook to negotiate a contract on his behalf. The whole thing came to nothing, however, when Hummel insisted on a fee of £150, whereas the publisher was not prepared to pay him more than £100.

We read in the diary that Mozart's 'Die Entführung aus dem Serail' (The Abduction from the Seraglio) was being performed that season but, as Moscheles reported:

not in the unadulterated Mozart version, as we Germans know it. No! They have cut out whole sections and substituted popular English tunes – a horrifying desecration! The person who has this crime on his conscience is Kramer from Brighton, the Director of the Royal Band.

The English predilection for light music is stressed on another occasion in an entry in the diary about an invitation from the Duchess of Kent to Kensington Palace, where Moscheles played for the royal guests:

The little Princess Victoria was present, and the Duchess asked me to play at once so that the Princess, who had to go to bed early, could hear me play. After my second piece she did indeed retire . . . . The ladies and gentlemen took a friendly interest in my playing, but I think they enjoyed most of all my improvisation on some of the now very fashionable Tyrolean songs, since the

Duchess had already invited the Tyrolean singers to her home on two occasions.

In the early summer, Heinrich Heine appeared in London. While studying in Hamburg he had become acquainted with Charlotte Moscheles' family, and later this bond was reinforced by ties of kinship. No one in the Hanseatic city had any inkling, so Mocheles' wife tells us, what great fame lay in store for this rebellious youth. There were many who held it against him that he was not one of those who were satisfied by the easy option of a rich uncle's offer of a desk job as a safe ladder to the pinnacle of success. Heine was a poet, and could not be anything else, thus all he was left with after his office job was a loathing for this type of work, as well as the ability to write beautifully by hand. In this very same handwriting he wrote down a few stanzas in Charlotte's album, showing what he thought of those Hamburg circles:

'Dass ich bequem verbluten kann,
Gebt mir ein weites edles Feld!
O lasst mich nicht ersticken hier,
In dieser engen Krämerwelt!

Sie essen gut, sie trinken gut,
Erfreu'n sich ihres Maulwurfglücks;
Und ihre Grossmuth ist so gross,
Als wie das Loch der Armenbüchs'.

Cigarren tragen sie im Maul,
Und in der Hosentasch' die Händ'.
Auch die Verdauungskraft ist gut –
Wer sie nur selbst verdauen könnt

O dass ich grosse Laster säh',
Verbrechen blutig, colossal –
Nur diese satte Tugend nicht,
Und zahlungsfähige Moral!

Ihr Wolken droben, nehmt mich mit,
Gleichviel, nach welchem fernen Ort –
Nach Lappland oder Afrika,
Und sei es nach Pommern, immer fort!

O nehmt mich mit ! – Sie hören nicht –

Die Wolken droben sind so klug !
Vorrüberreisend dieser Stadt
Aengstlich beschleun'gen sie den Flug.

H. Heine.

So that I may bleed to death in comfort,
Give me an open, noble field!
Oh do not let me suffocate here
In this narrow, petty world!

They eat well, they drink well,
They enjoy their mole-like good fortune;
And their generosity is as immense
As the opening in an alms box.

Cigars they hold between their lips,
And their hands they hold deep in their
                                        pockets,
Their digestion also seems to function well –
If only they were digestible themselves!

Would that I could see some nasty vices,
Bloody and colossal crimes –
Anything but this self-satisfied virtue,
And solvent morality!

You clouds up there, take me with you,
It matters not to which far-off land –
To Lapland or to Africa,
Or even to Pomerania, just take me away!

Oh take me with you – They hear me not –
Those clouds up there, they are so clever!
Rolling across the city's sky,
They anxiously speed up their flight.

The reputation of the poet, who had just published his 'Buch der Lieder' (Book of Songs) in 1827, had reached England, and it was not surprising, therefore, that his appearance in London society life caused some excitement. He was a frequent guest at Moscheles' home, causing the mistress of the house to have certain misgivings about him. She wrote:

Even during his first visit to us, he and I had a funny conversation. I don't know what gave me the courage, but when he told me what he wanted to see, I replied: 'I can obtain entry tickets for you for that and for all private galleries and parks, and all public buildings. Moreover, it will be my pleasure to do so; I must, however, ask for something in return, and I should like you to give me your word on it'. Naturally he asked me to explain, and I did so at once. 'I should be pleased if you did not mention Moscheles in the book you are currently writing about England'. He was really astonished by this, so I continued: 'Moscheles' speciality is music, which may possibly interest you, but you don't have any special understanding for it. You are, there-fore, not qualified to write about it in detail. On the other hand, it would be easy for you to make him the butt for your ingenious satire, and I should not like that to happen'. He laughed, or rather smiled, and we shook hands, agreeing that he would omit our names from the book and I would obtain the entry tickets for him.

In the winter of 1827–28, Moscheles went with his family, including his baby daughter, on a concert tour which took them to Liverpool, Chester, and then up to Scotland. On January 2nd 1828, they reached Edinburgh, which at that time was experiencing an upswing, thanks to the effects of industrialization. Moscheles recorded his impressions in his diary:

Walking through the city gave me one surprise after another. At night, the old houses, overcrowded with poor and noisy families living in every room, look rather like illuminations on account of their numerous dimly-lit windows. As I stood on the viaduct that connects the old town with the new, I could see these old houses on my right, and on my left there was Princes Street in all its splendour, and all around it the new part of the town which is still being developed, and which has been designed to include elegant crescents and streets with many fine, palatial residences, built of square stone blocks. Many such buildings can be found in other cities, but Princes Street seems to be unique in its way. The whole way along there are houses on one side and landscaped gardens on the other. This is not an uncommon feature, and can also be found in London, but here the row of houses is intersected at right angles by ascending streets, from the top of which one can look out over the Firth of Forth and, in the middle of the landscaped gardens, is Edinburgh Castle, standing high up on a rock, an original, impressive and somewhat surprising edifice. During my evening stroll I saw a detachment of one of the Highland regiments, just relieved from guard duty, marching down from the illuminated castle. They were clad in their full dress uniform, the Scottish national costume, and as they passed just by me, I was able to enjoy some real Scottish music played on the fife and drum.

Moscheles gave several concerts in the Scottish capital, and he was particularly successful with his 'Anticipations of Scotland'. He met Sir Walter Scott, author of *Ivanhoe* and *Kenilworth*, who, as the 'great and unknown' author of the time, was read avidly by the public. He was the first novelist to base his stories around historically interesting characters and to give them the immediacy of living men and women. He chose most of his material from Scottish history, weaving its figures into his novels, without feeling any compulsion to adhere to historical accuracy. Walter Scott was at that time regarded as the foremost writer of fiction in the English language.

Moscheles' first meeting with Scott, then aged 57 and housebound owing to gout, occurred when Scott asked him and his wife to his home for breakfast.

He opened the door himself, supported on a

crutch, and bade us welcome in a most heart-warming and friendly manner. Even before we had removed our coats, my wife's fear of the great man had left her, and we both felt quite at home. Breakfast was served straight away, a real Scottish meal brought in on the most elegant silver dishes by two servants wearing powdered wigs. Each dish was spiced by the amusing conversation with our amiable and cheerful host. He understands German and is well versed in German literature, being a fervent admirer of Goethe in particular. He told a few anecdotes about how his lack of musical understanding had caused him embarrassment on some occasions. 'And how do you like my cousin the piper?' he asked me. 'You know, we Scots are all cousins'. I, of course, could not pretend to have much enthusiasm for bagpipers, and he had suspected as much. He, however, thought that this music had a most wonderful effect on the native Scottish Highlanders, so much so that they would waylay any piper wandering round the streets of Edinburgh, and in a war the tunes of the bagpipes would arouse courage even unto death. 'You should hear my cousin the piper play and sing the Pibroch o'Donald Dhu, but with the Gaelic words'. These words were necessary to make the blood course like fire through one's veins, but the melody alone was stirring enough. He started to sing it for us, tapping its rhythm on the carpet with his stick, which he never put down. He soon gave up though, saying that he was not doing it very well; a newly arrived cousin would have to play it for me upstairs. We went with her and, after hearing her play the melody, I extemporised on it, thus winning the ever youthful heart of my host. More and more Scottish tunes had to be played to me, and I had to play them myself, and then work out variations for them, as well as weaving them into other pieces. We finally took our leave, having spent many

happy hours together. They were all the more pleasant, not just because they had been interesting, but also because every word the man utters confirms the good-heartedness that is written all over his face. He treated my wife like a little daughter and kissed her on the cheek when we said good-bye, saying that he would soon come and see our children and would bring them a book. The book in question was 'Tales of a grandfather', written for his grandson, John Lockhart. The copy he gave to our children had the following dedication inside: 'To Adolphus and Emily Moscheles, from the Grandfather'.

Shortly after this meeting, Scott was confined to his bed, suffering from yet another attack of gout. By the time Moscheles gave his third public concert though, he was up and about again and, to the amazement of the fashionable assembly, he entered the crowded concert hall shortly before the performance started.

As usual, my wife was sitting in a hidden corner of the hall. He soon spotted her, however, and went to sit next to her, thus making her the centre of attention and the envy of all the ladies present. Their excitement was increased when he shouted 'Bravo' at the top of his voice, and gave other audible signs of appreciation, which reached their culmination point during the 'Scottish Airs'. During the interval he asked Charlotte whether she had read G. A. Bürger's 'Der Dichter liebt den guten Wein' (The poet loves good wine), and when she answered in the affirmative, he said how much he liked the poem and mentioned that he had translated it into English, adding: 'Would you like a copy? I shall send it to you'. And when she asked him to recite the poem in German, he did so quite willingly with people on all sides listening to him.

The fact that Scott had a very thorough

knowledge of German is shown by the following episode. As was the custom, Moscheles had sent him his album, asking for an entry. On leafing through the album Scott had come across this poem by Grillparzer:

'Tonkunst, dich preis' ich vor Allen,
Höchstes Los ist dir gefallen,
Aus der Schwesterkünste drei,
Du die frei'ste, einzig frei.

Denn das Wort, es lässt sich fangen,
Deuten lässt sich die Gestalt ;
Unter Ketten, Riegeiln , Stangen
Hält sie menschliche Gewalt.

Aber du sprichst höhere Sprachen,
Die kein Häschenchor versteht,
Ungreifbar durch ihre Wachen
Gehst due, wie ein Cherub geht.

Darum preis' ich dich vor Allen
In so ängstlich schwerer Zeit;
Höchstes Los ist dir gefallen,
Dir, und wer sich dir geweiht.'

This 'cri de coeur' from the poet, who was oppressed by Austrian censorship must have awakened Scott's sympathy, for when he returned the album after only a few hours, it contained the following translation of Grillparzer's verse, together with this comment: 'I am afraid that Mr. Grillparzer's verse and Mr. Moscheles' valuable album are only disgraced by the following rude attempt at translation:

Of the nine the loveliest three
Are painting, music, poetry
But thou art freest of the free
Matchless muse of harmony.

Gags can stop the poet's tongue,
Chains on painter's arms are flung,
Fetter, bolts and dungeon tower
O'er pen and pencil have their power.

But music speaks a loftier tone

To tyrant and to spy unknown
And free as angels walk with men
Can pass unscathed the gaoler's ken.

Then hail thee freest of the free
'Mid times of wrong and tyranny
Music, the proudest lot is thine
And those who bend at music's shrine.'

Moscheles remarked afterwards that:
His signature looked like 'Waller Scoll' as he did not cross his t's or dot his i's, but in spite of this he was Clerk of the Court, and we had fun watching him on the day before our departure, sitting at a green table behind a huge pile of documents.

Their friendship lasted until Scott's death four years later.

Moscheles had more to say about his stay in Edinburgh:
I found it strange that organ music was not allowed during the church service. A four-voice choir chants the psalms, and the congregation follow. But how? The baritones sing in unison with the sopranos instead of supporting the basses! The sermon, preached by a Dr Thomson, was not bad in itself but, as a result of the preacher's lilting Scottish accent and the gestures he used to stress his points, it was more bizarre than uplifting. I also find the excessive piousness of the Sunday ritual somewhat of a burden. Praying at church two or three times, praying again at home, or at least folding one's hands in one's lap, not being allowed to make music, or to work or pay visits – we have to put up with all of it. At least letter-writing in the privacy of one's own room, where no one can see you, is allowed. It is also permitted to read books of a secular nature! And that is as far as one may go.

Winter and deep snow limited any excursions to the city itself or to its immediate surroundings, but there were days on which it was possible to go further afield.

Today we went to Carlton Hill; marvellous view; on one side is the blue ribbon of the sea, on the other Holyrood House, the ancient royal castle; above us the rock, Arthur's Seat, on which stands Nelson's monument. It is of clumsy dimensions and looks as though it is too heavy for the rock. The gusting wind, which blows twice as strongly at this height, hardly allowed us to keep a firm footing. Excursions to Roslyn Castle and Salisbury Craigs were less satisfying, on account of the severe weather. Holyrood House is always interesting. The interior furnishings date back to the time of Mary Stuart; although the curtains on her bed, the chair covers and tapestries, which she made herself, are yellow with age. In fact, the whole place has suffered from the ravages of time. One cannot help remembering in these rooms the fate of that beautiful and perhaps guilty, yet unhappy woman. The suit of armour that once belonged to Darnley is here, as well as his boots and gloves. We are shown a little window through which the newborn James I was handed, because his royal mother inside the room was under arrest. Next to her bedchamber there is a concealed door leading to an underground passage. When the Queen's husband took her and her royal favourite, the lute player Rizzio, by surprise, it is said that Rizzio was dragged to this very door after being mortally wounded by a dagger. The dark stains by the door are said to be his blood. As proof of this assertion, which seemed rather mythical to us, Mr. Ballantyne, a friend of Scott's and printer of all his books, presented me with a note from Scott referring to these frequently challenged blood stains which said: 'I have no doubt of Rizzio's blood being genuine. I will look at a plan of the place, but think I am right'. This is important coming from the pen of Walter Scott.

On another occasion, Moscheles was taken to see the Great Hall of the High Court. *Members of the legal profession, many wearing their official garb of black gowns and powdered wigs, were milling about. The noise seemed deafening, and yet the judges, in their respective sections of the hall, were listening to evidence from learned counsel representing both sides of the cases being heard. How they managed to hear anything – let alone understand – is beyond my comprehension. I stood next to Mr Murray, one of Scotland's greatest advocates, who was just presenting a case. The noise was such that I could not understand a word. All I could make out were the movements of his hands and lips, as though he were performing a mime. I asked myself whether these judges were qualified to pronounce judgement based on such inaudible evidence. This question remained unanswered.*

Moscheles had more to say about the High Court of Justice in Edinburgh:
From the back of the court there is a staircase leading into a maze of courtyards, narrow passages and secluded corners, finishing at the edge of the Firth. Having walked down those backstairs and through the maze, one can easily understand how Jeanie Deans' seducer was able to make his escape.

In February 1828, Moscheles returned to London. The subsequent concert season was dominated by a young singer, Henriette Sonntag, a devotee of Italian opera whom Moscheles had befriended during his time in Vienna. He often accompanied her on the piano at her recitals, and even dedicated some of his compositions to her, such as 'Gems à la Sonntag.' In July she sang in 'Donna del Lago', based on Sir Walter Scott's epic novel 'The Lady of the Lake', and Scott himself was present at the performance. Afterwards Moscheles was host at a soirée at which, to their mutual delight, the poet was introduced to the prima donna. When Clementi joined the company, he was so taken with the singer and his meeting with Scott that he went to the piano without being prompted to play for the assembled guests. Moscheles wrote afterwards:

He extemporised with the vigour of youth, and the very fact that he never plays in public lent extra charm to his performance. It was a real pleasure to see the two old men, Scott and Clementi, enjoying each other's company, shaking each other by the hand, not in the least jealous of each other's admiration for Henriette Sonntag to whom they were both paying court in equal measure, each acknowledging the eminence of the other. It was inevitable that the two great men should be the focus of everyone's attention, and all those present were delighted to be able to observe them and their intercourse at such close quarters!

The Moscheles family spent the month of September in Hastings, a delightful and most agreeable resort, where they were joined by Charlotte's father. They went on long walks together or went to the beach to swim and sunbathe.

It was there that I composed a piece of light music for which I had been commissioned called 'Strains of the Scottish bards'; I gave it some sort of significance by later dedicating it to Sir Walter Scott.

Scott replied:

My dear Sir!

I regret that my absence upon short journeys from home should have caused your obliging proposal to inscribe the music of Donald Dhu to me, to remain some time unanswered. Believe me, I feel obliged by the proposal and will accept it with great pleasure. Tell my fair friend Mrs Moscheles that I send my best compliments and beg to retain a place in her recollection, and when you see

the fine old gentlemen, Mr. Clementi, will you oblige me by remembering me to him.

I am always, dear Sir,
Your obliged humble servant,
Walter Scott
Abbotsford, Melrose
October 18

In the published diary we find the following passages written by Charlotte to supplement the entries relating to the early part of 1829:

When reading musical biographies we often come across lengthy dissertations about the music of the composer in question. Sometimes they even go as far as to mention his 'intentions', which reminds us of those commentators on Shakespeare's work who, according to some learned authorities, have attributed thoughts to him which would have been quite alien to the great playwright. Great pains were taken to determine his most secret intentions while, all too often, the fact was overlooked that his inspirations were, quite simply, those of a genius.

A similar fate seems to have befallen the works of Beethoven. Naturally Beethoven himself committed to paper only what and how he was thinking and feeling. However, his compositions have been subjected to widely differing interpretations ever since. No doubt the 'Moonlight' Sonata will never cease to be sentimental, and the 'Eroica' will always be majestic, but with a sonata such as 'Les adieuz, l'absence et le retour', every performer will feel the piece differently and every listener will conjure up his own individual picture. 'And this is how it should be', Mendelssohn used to say. 'As long as the composer can stimulate the listener's imagination to evoke a vision, a thought, or any kind of reaction, then his purpose has been achieved.'

And this is also our view. Music is meant to be absorbed through every pore, to penetrate to the heart and to strike a chord there. For this reason it is useless to describe a composition. The reader will forgive us then, when we refrain from analysing Moscheles' music or discussing its merits or failings. It can, however, be reasonably assumed that a piece of music that was not only widely acclaimed on its first public performance, but which was also still played with enthusiasm and interest some thirty, forty or even fifty years later, must be of more than just passing merit. Of Moscheles' works we include in that category his G minor Concerto (1820), the 24 Etudes (1825 and 1826), the 'Hommage à Haendel', the Rondo in A, the E-flat major Sonata, the 'Sonate mélancolique', the 'Souvenirs of Ireland', and the three Allegri di Bravura: 'La force, la légèreté et le Caprice'.

From the time when Moscheles played less often in public (from about 1840), his latest concertos (C major, fantastique, pathétique and pastoral) received less attention than the earlier ones which he performed himself with the perception of authorship. He often complained that the G minor Concerto was played over and over again, while he considered the other seven to be equally worthy of attention. By the same token, he would have liked to see his 12 great Etudes caractéristiques performed only by artists capable of surmounting the inherent difficulties, rather than seeing preference being given to the 'Kindermärchen' (Children's Tale) contained therein. Moreover, he considered the sentimental 'Traum' (Dream) or the brilliant 'Terpsichore' to be just as well suited to the concert hall.

During the winter of 1828–29, Moscheles wrote a G minor Sonata for Piano and Flute, and subsequently the Symphony in C. As far as the smaller pieces requested by various publishers were concerned, he wrote:
I regard them as my poor-box to help support some poor devil or other in Germany who can write, but does not get paid enough for doing so. I have now increased my fee to thirty guineas per piece.

From about this time we have an account that gives us an idea of the value placed upon art and culture by a leading London hostess. *I paid out the following sums, received from Mme. v. Rothschild, after one of her soirées which I had arranged:*

Mme Stockhausen	£ 35 for 2 soirées
Mr de Bériot	£ 5 for 1 soirée
Mr Mori (Violin)	£ 7 for 1 soirée
Mme Pisaroni	£ 20 for 1 soirée
Donzelli	£ 10 for 1 soirée
Curioni	£ 10 for 1 soirée
Mr & Mrs Schütz	£ 15 for 1 soirée
De Begnis	£ 25 for 2 soirées
Myself	£ 40 for 4 soirées
	£167

A tidy sum of money for those days.

In January, Moscheles played in Bath as usual, after which he wrote the following comment: *I really did not expect the concert to be a success as I felt I had insufficient rehearsal beforehand; the audience, however, thought otherwise.*

When he arrived back in London he decided to acquire a carriage to enable him to travel with greater ease to the large number of professional engagements he had now to fulfil.

Meanwhile his teaching commitments had undergone a change, in so far as he retained only a handful of private pupils. Instead, he taught for nine hours a day at the Royal Academy of Music, where he held the post of professor. On the whole, however, he derived little pleasure from being director of this institution which, in his opinion, put too little stress on musicality.

MENDELSSOHN IN LONDON

In March 1829, Moscheles' house was suddenly plunged into grief. Both children contracted severe whooping cough, and the three-year old son succumbed to the illness. Moscheles poured out his sorrow in his diary:

His poor mother knows nothing but fear, sorrow and sleepless nights, having nursed one of her darlings into the grave, she is now trying, with God's help, to snatch the other from a similar fate. Despite my profound suffering, as a man and as an artist, I belong to the public.

Nevertheless, his appearances at concerts and in society had become irksome to him . . .

listening to those awful amateurish attempts at singing, and Herz or Czerny rattling off a few pieces at the piano, while devouring jellies and cakes at the same time. And if that were not bad enough, to be asked after all this to go to the piano to play an improvisation!

It was a great relief when in the middle of this sad and gloomy period of Moscheles' life, Mendelssohn, by now aged nineteen, arrived in London.

Felix's father wrote to me last winter to ask whether I thought it a good idea for his son to come to London with some of his compositions, amongst them the Overture to 'A Midsummer Night's Dream'. I wrote back saying that I believed his son to be a genius, and I invited him to come to us at Easter. I promised wholeheartedly that I would introduce him to this strange world.

Moscheles, who at that time was spending most of his time in the country away from London, where Charlotte had taken up temporary residence, so that her little daughter could recuperate more quickly, rented lodgings for Mendelssohn at 203 Portland Street. In his diary he noted the following:

Since his arrival, I have taken the keenest pleasure in his dealings and in his artistic work. As a human being, he is most precious to us. He is always cheerful, and yet he shows compassion for the grief we suffer on account of our lost child, as well as appreciating the concern we feel for our other frail child. He is always willing to share our rural seclusion and forego the pleasures of London. Moreover, he has a healing effect upon our wounded spirits and seems to have set himself the task of making up as best he can for all our suffering.

Nothing gave Moscheles greater pleasure than when Mendelssohn brought along his latest compositions.

Anyone else would have realised even then that I acknowledged him as my master, and that I was enraptured by his work when he expected only criticism; but he still considers himself as my pupil, no matter how much I try to convince that the contrary is in fact the case. The enthusiasm which greeted his Overture to 'A Midsummer Night's Dream' did not go to his head at all. 'But I must be able to do better than that!' he told us. When I praised the work, he replied, almost child-like: 'Did you like it? Ah, that makes me very happy'.

Mendelssohn showed Moscheles his manuscript of the Cantata on a Chorale in A minor, a sixteen part anthem 'Hora est', as yet unpublished, and a Violin Quartet, also in A minor. He was always willing to perform impromptu musical favours, and he wrote a charming tune in Moscheles' Album entitled 'Perpetuum mobile', in C major.

During Mendelssohn's stay in London, a pupil of Haydn, by the name of Neukomm, arrived in the British capital. Moscheles thought highly of him on account of his noble character and gentle manners. Indeed they were to remain friends until Neukomm died. He was less complimentary about his music, however, and said that 'it suffered from a regrettable lack of vigorous imagination'. Neukomm and Mendelssohn often met at Moscheles' house, and Charlotte wrote of their relationship:

They were extremely fond of each other, each finding in the other an exceptional human being; but as a musician, the gentle Neukomm looked upon the spirited Mendelssohn as being too impetuous, too emphatic, too extravagant in his use of brass instruments, too excessive in his tempi, and too restless in his playing, while Mendelssohn was wont to give way to youthful impatience now and again: 'If only our splendid Neukomm would make better music! He can express himself so eruditely in words and in letters, but as for writing music, he writes such clichés!'

At about the same time, a Belgian musical theorist by the name of Fétis was lecturing in London. He found no more favour with Moscheles than he did with Mendelssohn.

What is the point of talking so much about it? he commented to Moscheles. *It is much better to be able to write well. Why listen to a lecture on 'musique mise à la portée de tout le monde', delivered in French to an English audience who probably understand only about half of the technical terms, and perhaps as a result pay only a half as much into the lecturer's money box as he would hope?*

Moscheles and Fétis did, however, collaborate on the publication of the 'Méthode des méthodes', the latter's linguistic ability proving very useful to Moscheles whose principles on the study of music Fétis was able to translate into perfect French.

In the early summer of 1829, Mendelssohn's Overture to 'A Midsummer Night's Dream' was performed twice, each time with great success. The English public also praised his Concerto for Two Pianos in C major, which he played together with Moscheles. The proceeds from the concert amounted to £500.

The most popular violinist of the season was undoubtedly de Bériot, then at the peak of his virtuosity. His latest composition, the B minor Concerto, a more interesting work than his previous piece – on account, perhaps, of his wife's influence or even help! (he was married to the highly talented Malibran) – was also received with much acclaim.

Of Maria Malibran, Moscheles wrote the following:

She always sings beautifully, and always with the highest degree of dedication. Every time she performs, she is not merely a singer, but a musical genius . . . She dominates the orchestra and its conductor with the greatest ease, and even the most cold-blooded orchestral player cannot help catching a little of the fire of which she has such an abundance that it is hard to imagine that the flame will ever be extinguished. She has managed to ignite even de Bériot's smooth, accomplished, but not always appealing performance, and I recognise her dynamic touch especially in his B minor Concerto.

Of his own compositions Moscheles dedicated to her the 'Gems à la Malibran', an arrangement of her favourite songs and arias into which he had managed to introduce faithful echoes of her inimitable coloratura voice.

At about the same time, Moscheles complained about the difficulties which composers like himself experienced when organizing their annual London concerts.

We're not just out to make a vile profit for ourselves; we also consider these concerts as the means of having our latest works judged by a large music-loving audience, and its inevitable quota of art critics. However, the Director of the Opera, Laporte, proves to be a considerable obstacle for us with his tiresome demands.

According to Moscheles, the situation was as follows: in order to attract as large an audience as possible, those composers who could rely on substantial takings frequently tried to induce the most popular opera singers to appear at these concerts, and, of course, they were paid no mean fee for doing so. Laporte, who had become Director of Her Majesty's Theatre in 1828, was opposed to this practice, however. The artists who tried to engage his singers were presented with an alternative from which he would not budge: either they had to hire his theatre for their concerts, or they had to do without his singers. Like many others in his position, Moscheles was obliged to pay an exorbitant fee in order to put on his annual concert in Laporte's theatre.

In July, when the season was over, Moscheles, his wife and his family boarded a boat for Hamburg to visit their relatives. He wrote in his diary:

Nobody could be happier than we are to leave behind the chronic vexation of the concerts and all the problems involved. Once we are with our relatives again, all the pent-up grief and tears over our lost child can be allowed to flow freely, and we hope to find solace and comfort there.

They remained with Charlotte's relatives, the Embdens, on their country estate near Hamburg until the end of September. During these weeks of leisure, Moscheles sketched out new ideas for later compositions. The pure country air brought the colour back to the little girl's cheeks, and on September 10th the whole family celebrated her second birthday, as well as the 100th birthday of Moses

Mendelssohn, about which Moscheles wrote the following comment: *There was loud rejoicing on his behalf in the Jewish community, but for us there is only quiet thanksgiving for the precious child that was spared.*

SCANDINAVIAN TRAVELS

From Hamburg, Moscheles started out at the end of September on a journey to Scandinavia. He arrived at Copenhagen on October 2nd and began immediately to explore the musical scene.

He wrote this letter to his wife:

First I heard Weyse, who is idolised here as a theoretician, playing a fugue on the organ of the Frauenkirche. Afterwards I went home with him and was shown many of his interesting compositions. I also met Kuhlau, the highly skilled architect of puzzle canons. He forges artistic musical locks which are incredibly difficult to work out but, in order that I could gain some practice, I persuaded both of them to show me the puzzle canons by means of which they correspond with each other from house to house. I first met them both at the home of a Herr W., at whose soirées all foreign and local artists make music before an audience of devotees and art critics. Oehlenschläger was also present. Kuhlau opened with his Quartet in G minor. It has great style and is very well put together, but it is not free of reminiscences. Some of the more difficult passages were, unfortunately, beyond him. Then Funcke and I followed with my Caprice, which he accompanied very well on the cello, and after us came the Anderson brothers with a Caprice for Three Horns. Then everybody wanted me to play a solo, but I requested that Weyse should do so first. Even though I urged him with the full support of everyone present, he would not oblige. I had to go to the piano, therefore, and in next

*to no time I was completely surrounded.
There was a deathly hush while I collected
my thoughts for a while. I wanted to be
learned like Kuhlau and Weyse, but at the
same time harmonically interesting, then
soulful, and then I wanted to finish with a
dashing display of virtuoso flourishes. I seem
to have been successful in all of these. As you
have never experienced anything like it for
my performances, you cannot imagine the
ecstatic cheering that erupted all around me,
and the way people looked at each other,
speechless with amazement. Old Professor
Schall seized me and kissed me (for shame –
as the English would say), and Kuhlau and
Weyse rushed at me, so that I was barely able
to get my breath back. For shame, I say to
myself, to write such things about oneself!
But then, who am I writing to? . . .*

Not long after his arrival, Moscheles was
invited to the Danish Court, where he found
the circle surrounding the royal household
'exceptionally brilliant' and their Majesties
'very kind'. As usual, the concert ended with
an improvization by Moscheles. What this
entailed can best be imagined from the
following description:

*I let myself go like a racehorse, using all my
power and all my fire, even adding a dash of
coquetry to make an impression on the royal
senses. First I improvised some Rossini, as I
know that this composer has taken the people by storm here as well, then I became a
Dane and played variations on folksongs
and, spurred on to bold heights by the loud
calls of 'Bravo!', I concluded with the Danish
equivalent of 'God save the King': 'Kong
Christian'. When I had finished – well you
can just imagine. . . . There was one novelty
for me, though: The King went to all the
musical experts in the room to voice his
amazement and to seek confirmation of his
opinion.*

Moscheles' public concert in Copenhagen

was not until a fortnight later, which made
him decide to use the interim period for a
quick trip to Sweden.

*The journey from Copenhagen to Elsinör
took six and a half hours, and from there
across the Sund, in the afternoon, another
threequarters of an hour. I was advised to
hire a coach and a so-called hussar, who acts
as my coach-driver and valet for the journey
to Gothenburg. I can count myself as lucky
once again, as the weather is fine and clear.*

The journey went well, but was not without a certain amount of strain.

*The so-called coach I had hired consisted of a
small chaise fixed to a four-wheel cart, and
my suitcase and nightbag were held between
my legs. There was also a great deal of
bumping around. I was unable to understand
my loquacious hussar, so instead I profited
from the natural beauty all around me, a
breathtaking panorama, here at the banks of
the Kattegat, of romantic rock formations
and natural woodlands. The roads were, for
the most part, tolerably good, and a messenger who was sent ahead twelve hours
before our own departure, had ordered fresh
horses at every coaching station. Unfortunately, however, we caught up with him three
hours outside Gothenburg, at Kungsbacka,
and we were then told to wait for two hours!
– The local inn had nothing to offer apart
from some grey rusks and a tallow candle, to
which I added the smoke of my cigar. At last
we were off again into the night, but in the
meantime it had started to rain. At 11 o'clock
we made a stop, still outside Gothenburg
though, but it was just to change horses again
to enable us to negotiate a difficult mountain
pass ahead. A 1 o'clock we finally saw the
welcome light of the Gothenburg customs
house.*

The light proved more welcome than the
visit itself, for which he first had to alight.
What followed was certainly less agreeable:

Some loud knocking on the door of Blone's Hus (an inn) awakened a maid from deepest slumber but, despite having ordered accommodation beforehand, I had to make do with a chamber in the attic, where I knocked my head against the ceiling. When I asked why I could not have one of the empty rooms we passed on the way up, I was answered with a Swedish shrug of the shoulders. So I asked for a fire to be lit up in my garret; the smoke filled the room, and I went to bed wrapped in my fur. . . . This morning I was assigned the pretty rooms I saw last night; they are the ones that had been reserved for me.

Moscheles' concert in Gothenburg was fixed for October 27th. This left him with three days to get to know the town and its musical pastures.

In a strange town like this I usually climb the rampart first, in order to get a good view. How romantic and eerie are these cliffs and torn-off rocks, all around and in the harbour itself! The gently winding river Gôta-Elf reminded me of our own River Elbe, and I no longer felt alone.

He then gave an account of the two great families who dominated the musical life of the town, naturally not without some rivalry, for one of them owned a Clementi instrument and the other a piano made by Graf. Which of the two would he choose for the concert? This was the burning question for the two competing houses. Diplomatically, Moscheles picked both instruments, playing on each in turn. Before the concert he was the guest of honour at a typically Swedish dinner party.

My host, a real character, presided over a table of twenty-five in a most eccentric Hogarthian fashion. Before the guests sat down, the gentlemen stood at one of the side tables drinking schnapps and eating herrings; three glasses had to suffice for all of them.

This was followed by a ragout of veal, then a pike dish, soup (at last), roast goose, plum pudding and delicious fresh fruit to finish. My host is a stockily built sixty-year-old, whose twinkling eyes look out from under a greyish-brown wig; his upper teeth are missing, and four lower teeth form a sort of palisade to protect his very large, drooping, and always moist lower lip. He knows how to dominate the conversation, regardless of which dignitaries may be present. His wife, by contrast, seems to have signed a pledge of silence in her marriage contract.

The good man was so overcome by the great honour of having Professor Moscheles in Gothenburg and, what is more, at his own house, that he never stopped lavishing praise upon the visitor, who allowed the flood of words to wash over him with mock seriousness.

Gentlemen! May I have the privilege, as your host, of saying a few words? So help me God, I do enjoy this honour – as all of the esteemed company here know me as a modest man – and the coincidence! The coincidence, I say; what is coincidence? So help me God, without wishing to put this man's modesty to the test – the coincidence, I say, that has brought this man to us – quite apart from the admiration – will certainly leave a lasting impression – Three cheers for the Master of sound in the realm of the beautiful.

Moscheles recorded all this in his diary:
So much incoherent drivel coming from the head of the table, and yet the Governor, the Councillors, the local Commandant, and all the other guests don't seem in the least surprised; they obviously know him. . . . 'Long live the Master!'. The glasses clinked, and I got up to thank everyone, but no sooner had I uttered the words that it was not coincidence which had brought me here, but rather the desire to share my art with the music-loving people of Gothenburg, than Herr S.,

our host, interrupted me and, with suitable modesty, announced: 'God forbid that the Professor should think that I meant that coincidence (for coincidence is everything in this world) was responsible for our, not his, happiness at seeing a man in our midst whose modesty – God forbid! – I would not wish to offend!' There followed more toasts; then the ladies got up, and the gentlemen remained to consume an enormous bowl of some alcoholic concoction, and all the while, our host never stopped his inane babble. Some people began to sing, but I steered well clear of it. At last everyone filed out of the spacious dining room, through several elegant salons to the one in which the Clementi stood. I was asked to extemporise, which I did, giving due consideration to my surroundings. You may guess the result. The piano teacher Schwarz and the organist of the cathedral, Bärnroth, suggested that I should play the organ. This I did, the following day at noon, in the presence of the same company. Once again I let myself go and worked on the pedals as if I had Vestris's feet.

Moscheles' public concert attracted a capacity audience; with his fantasies on Swedish folksongs, which were handed to him from the stalls, he conquered the hearts of all those present. He refused an invitation to give a concert in Stockholm, however, and hurriedly returned to Copenhagen. From there, he wrote to Charlotte:

I have been to the theatre to see the popular lyrical drama, 'Elverhoy'; it is based on an old Danish legend, with characteristic songs and choruses by Kuhlau, all very tastefully arranged. I enjoyed the overture immensely, which consists of a compendium of the whole. I have paid another two-hour visit to Weyse, whom I regard as the most interesting person here. He entertained me with a learned discourse on art, dealing with the technical and the aesthetic aspects; his fugues and especially his puzzle canons are masterly creations. He is coming to see me tomorrow, and I am sure we shall visit each other a good few more times.

On the day of his concert, Guillou received 150 Danish thaler from the King (who did not attend), and 20 louis d'or from Prince Christian; I hear that Mme. Milder and I are to be rewarded along similar lines, 'to avoid any feelings of envy'. This means that my nose will have do without a snuff box, my finger without a ring, my chest without a tie-pin, and I shall not be able to set the longed-for hour of my departure by a court watch – no matter! it will come all the same.

November 10th was the day of Moscheles' public concert in Copenhagen.
What a strange day it was yesterday! I was besieged from eight o'clock in the morning until six o'clock in the evening. People fought to get hold of the most expensive boxes at the theatre, and they were almost begging for single tickets; many had to go away disappointed, as there were none left. And this happened despite ticket prices being doubled. My net takings were 1500 thaler. . . . Notwithstanding my having been unfaithful to the Alexander Variations, I had to play them, as you may see from the enclosed programme; and the Fantasy – well it is impossible to write about that! Guillou, who announced his second concert at the usual prices, suggested that I should join forces with him at double the price. As this would entail a delay of only three days, I accepted the offer.

Later he wrote:
After the concert was announced, there was a repeat of the scenes which preceded my first concert. All the tickets were sold at double the price. My share amounted to 641 thaler. Incidentally, I shall have to take snuff after all, as his Majesty honoured me with the gift of a gold enamelled box. Prince Christian

also sent a diamond ring, Madame – a gold watch chain but, more important still, the Court passed on its charming compliments via the Lord Chamberlain.

After his success, Moscheles returned to Hamburg at the end of November, where he stayed for six weeks before going back to London in February 1830.

SIGN OF THE TIMES

The year 1830 was one of revolutions and upheavals in Europe. In France, Charles X was ousted by the 'Citizen King', Louis Philippe ('July Revolution'), and he fled with his family to England. In Brussels and Warsaw, national governments were formed after public rebellions against the Netherlands and Russia respectively. In Germany, a revolutionary movement called 'Junges Deutschland' came to the fore, one of its supporters being Heinrich Heine; and in England, under William IV and the new Grey-Palmerston cabinet, a period of liberal reforms was introduced with the aim of mitigating the widespread misery caused by industrialization and the resulting urbanization and proletarianism of vast sections of the population.

These events also had an effect on Moscheles' life. His planned journey to France at the end of the 1830 season was thwarted on account of the radical changes which that country had undergone; and in Southern England where he had retired for the summer to write, among other things, his Trio in C minor, dedicated to Cherubini, and his 'Recollections of England', dedicated to Queen Adelaide, labour unrest took on such proportions that he felt himself compelled to return prematurely to London, together with his family.

Some months later, the Reform Bill was rejected. Its purpose was to change the ossi-

fied system of elections to the House of Commons and to allow for a more democratic share in political power. As a countermeasure to the bill's failure to get through the Lower House, the King dissolved parliament. Moscheles gave an account of events in the streets of London on the eve of the dissolution of parliament as he witnessed them on his way to Camberwell:

You have read in the newspapers that many people illuminated their houses on account of the dissolution of parliament. Many others, however, were against it and they suffered badly, as their windows were smashed. On the way to Camberwell, all of seven miles away, nearly every house was lit up, and scores of banners were to be seen in the windows with the most ridiculous slogans, such as: 'The bill, the whole bill and nothing but the bill!' A patriotic butcher walked up and down carrying a placard with the words in flaming red letters: 'The enemies of reform to be sent to the dominions of Don Miguel'. 'William the Restorer' and 'William the Patriot King' could also be seen on hundreds of banners, while some of the houses remained dark and locked up. A huge crowd such as I have never seen thronged the main road and blocked the traffic.

On April 13th the Reform Bill was finally passed.

In the winter of 1831, on a trip to the North of England, Moscheles had his first encounter with one of the most spectacular achievements of the dawning age of the machine: the steam train. This is how he described his first journey by rail:

On February 18th, at six o'clock in the morning, I left for Manchester, and arrived at half past twelve. I had gone there to see the famous railway and to make the thirty-six mile trip to Liverpool in one and a half to two hours. A seat on the train cost 5 shillings. At half past one I got on one of the buses which take all the passengers free of charge to the starting point of the railway in one of the suburbs. There one had to walk through a large building where the offices are located. The train consists of between eight and ten wagons, each the length of an omnibus, closely linked together, with twelve comfortable easy chairs in each wagon. At a given signal, each passenger has to take his seat, which bears the same number as his ticket. The locomotive is not joined to the leading wagon until the guards have closed the wagons. The movement of the train, although as swift as an arrow, is barely noticeable and only surprising when one looks out of the window to see the remotest object approach with incredible speed and then fly past in the twinkling of an eye. I cannot describe in words the impression my journey on the first English railway has made upon me, nor the ecstasy I felt over this new invention which is nothing short of magic. The man responsible, the famous English engineer, George Stephenson, has brought about this miracle only after overcoming the most fearsome obstacles and difficulties.

In the world of music at about the same time, there were some not inconsiderable technical innovations. The grand pianos built by Erard in 1830 were then so superior to all other makes in their quality of tone, power and touch that Moscheles made as little effort to disguise his preference for such an instrument as he had previously done to hide his dissatisfaction with Erard's pianos, criticizing them for being slow and dull. For his annual concert in 1831 he used one of Erard's instruments for the first time instead of the usual Clementi, and at his new house in Chester Place, Regent's Park, the Clementi piano had to make way for one presented to him by the House of Erard.

The organ-like sound produced by the new Erard pianos found so much favour with Moscheles that he no doubt felt inspired to use every possible advantage it offered him when playing adagio passages. 'Truly like a cello', he exclaimed, praising the sound that could be sustained without soft-pedalling. All his life he abhorred the excessive use of pedals: *A competent pianist should use these aids only very rarely, or else he may misuse them.* Often, after listening to a good player, he would praise him for this or that, but he would always add:

If only he did not always put his feet down on the pedals! What are his hands for if all the effects are to be achieved by using the pedals? It would be like a good horseman always riding with his spurs.

One event stood out during the London concert season of 1830, if only in a negative sense: the failure of Beethoven's Ninth Symphony at the Philharmonic Concerts. In the diary it says:

Beethoven's Ninth Symphony, a failure! What am I to make of that? Is it the fault of the conductor, the performers or the audience? I really don't know, but something has to be done about it!

And something was done about it, for when the Directors of the Philharmonic Society decided, after the second unsuccessful attempt (the first having been in 1824), never to perform the Ninth Symphony again, convincing themselves that 'the deaf composer wrote such weird stuff because he could not hear it', the German press took umbrage and was so vociferous in its condemnation of those who scorned Beethoven's great work that it became a question of honour for England to learn to appreciate it and to perform it. Admittedly it did take a few more years before this came about.

In the late autumn the Moscheles family moved to their new house at 3 Chester Place, Regent's Park, where they were to stay for the next sixteen years until they went to live in Leipzig. During that time, their home became a focal point of musical activity, as well as a neutral meeting-place for the artistic community.

As the Philharmonic Concert Season got under way, Moscheles once again found himself in disagreement with some of the time-honoured customs. For example, there was the conductor, still seated at the piano, without a baton, turning the pages of his score, and having absolutely no effect on the performance, his rôle being performed unaided by the leader of the orchestra. This strange practice, Moscheles concluded, must be to blame for the unevenness which frequently marred the performances of great orchestral works.

PAGANINI

In the spring of 1831, Nicollò Paganini made his first appearance in London. The news of his arrival was greeted with enormous excitement. In England, as on the Continent, this most intriguing and most fascinating of all living violin virtuosi had for some time been the subject of many rumours. It was said, for example, that when he was imprisoned for the supposed murder of his wife, he spent the three years of his captivity practising on the one remaining string of his violin, the G-string, and that was how he acquired the consummate artistry with which he had since been dazzling his audiences all over Europe. While his physical appearance was supposed to remind one of a fairy-tale character, his miserliness was reputed to be beyond belief.

That was approximately the reputation that preceded him as far as the English were concerned. For Moscheles there was a special message of introduction from Charlotte's father, who had met Paganini in Hamburg, and helped him to an advantageous engage-ment through the kind offices of a friend of his, the director of one of the theatres.

The generous financial returns, and the even more generous applause prompted Paganini to heap all his gratitude upon my father-in-law in the typically Italian manner, and to extend this feeling to us, the children of his honoured friend, when he came to visit us. We had ample leisure to examine those distinctive features, the glowing eyes, the olive-skin, the long strands of thinning black hair, the sunken cheeks, the whole gaunt figure on which his clothes hung loosely and, lastly, those long fingers that seem to be covered with nothing but skin.

They talked about Paganini's plans while in London. His intention to charge twice the usual ticket price for a concert at the Italian Opera had been thwarted.

It is rumoured that the Duke of Devonshire has been campaigning against the idea. Regardless of that, only two boxes were sold and the concert had to be cancelled. He now informed us of his decision to play at the Opera charging the usual prices.

Some days later, Moscheles wrote: *My assistance which is useful to him here and there, earned me similar grateful compliments to those previously received by my father-in-law.*

Moscheles penned the following entry after Paganini's first concert:

The first impression was simply overwhelming, even stunning. A thoroughly excited audience demanded that he play almost everything twice. Not only did they applaud rapturously every time, but the ladies lent forward over the edge of their boxes, waving dainty handkerchiefs, and everyone in the stalls climbed up on their seats shouting 'Hurrah!' and 'Bravo!' at the top of their voices. Not even Mesdames Sonntag and Pasta caused such a stir as this, let alone any other artists. . . . Those long, sustained notes that penetrate one's very soul would, if held for a fraction longer, degenerate into meowing. He never crosses the line though, and the notes retain their unique quality that we associate with Paganini. In any other violinist's hands, those thin strings on which it was possible to produce the millions of notes, and more besides, of his bravura passages and cadenzas, would have proved fatal, but he manipulated them with indescribable charm. Above all, however, his compositions were ultra-original and, for that reason, so completely in keeping with his fantastic appearance, and the manner of his performance was so bewitching that neither lack of depth, nor lack of serious application, nor any other flaw intruded on one's attention.

The general enthusiasm did not subside, and Moscheles was entranced to hear Paganini at private gatherings, where he would play either the violin or the viola part of the quartets he had composed himself. At that time Moscheles wrote his 'Gems à la Paganini', in the short space of a day and a half, for the publisher and violinist Mori. As a precaution, Moscheles sought to obtain Paganini's approval prior to publication. Together with Mori he went to see him and played his 'musical portrait' for him. Paganini threw his arms around Moscheles' neck and showered him with compliments.

He thought that my understanding of his style and my way of reproducing his cadenzas were stupendous. At that moment there was only one Moscheles. What was Hummel in comparison? Hummel and others like him might also have written fantasies à la Paganini, but he would have disliked them and protested. My conception was the only correct one, an honour for him.

All of a sudden, however, Moscheles' opinion of Paganini changed, as he recorded in his diary in July:

My attitude towards him is somewhat peculiar. At first I was brimful of surprise and admiration. The sheer wealth of the most daring passages, his newly discovered source of 'sons harmoniques', the ingenuity with which he knows how to combine the most heterogeneous material and reproduce it to full effect . . . all of these had overwhelmed my musical perceptions to such a degree that for days after my head seemed to smoulder like a recently extinguished conflagration. Besides, the ravishingly tender, melting sound, so much like that of an Italian singer, produced by him with seductive ease on the strings of his violin, held an immeasurable charm for me. . . . Suffice it to say that my admiration for this phenomenon, where nature and art seemed to walk hand in hand, knew no bounds. Now that I have listened to him more often, however, everything has changed. In all his compositions he goes for the same effect; in his style and manner of playing I have discovered monotony. His concerts are beautiful and have their outstanding moments, but they remind me of a summer's evening and brilliant fireworks on a green meadow: the individual bursts of incandescent glory, which are indeed effective and admirable, but one is unfortunately very much like the rest.

At this time, and also on other occasions later on, Moscheles used extremely strong words against Paganini, with which we need not concern ourselves here. What is the explanation? What had happened? There would seem to be two possible reasons. Firstly, as we shall read later, Moscheles complained on the occasion of a Handel concert that he was mentally too exhausted to enjoy the full beauty of the music. It may well be that this exhaustion was partly responsible for his harsh verdict on Paganini. Secondly, Moscheles had been steadily drifting away from the generally accepted trends into a sort of isolation. He found it very hard to accept the fact that certain composers whose music he greatly admired did not find favour with the public and, conversely, that composers whose work he regarded as mediocre were very popular. Mendelssohn first drew attention to this when he commented to Moscheles: 'Du wolle, ich solle' (you wish it, I must do it), by which he meant: You cannot tell people what they should and should not like.

We know that Paganini has gone down as one of the greats in the history of music. As a violinist he possessed all the attributes of which only a few would have been sufficient to make him a great virtuoso: ingenious interpretation, a magical tone, stupendous technique for double-stopping, staccato and flautando playing, not to mention his pizzicato with the left hand. A number of composers were sufficiently inspired by him to produce virtuoso pieces – Robert Schumann wrote his 'Paganini Etudes', Brahms his 'Paganini Variations', Liszt produced six concerts études and Rachmaninov a 'Rhapsody on a Theme of Paganini'.

It is possible that Moscheles' rejection of Paganini was due in part to the generation gap between them. In his younger days, Moscheles had failed to understand why his teacher in Prague, Dyonis Weber, would have nothing to do with Beethoven. Now, as a grown man, he felt an increasing reluctance to go along with anything new, all the more so since, in his opinion, his own works no longer elicited the same strong response as previously. In music, however, as in every other branch of the arts, one epoch gives way to another. Every era has produced its own music, and it is unjust to apply labels such as 'beautiful' and 'good' or 'unpleasant' and 'bad'.

The second and third volume of Moscheles' 'Gems à la Paganini' even became the subject of a court case which Paganini had instigated against the publisher Mori, accusing him of plagiarism. This brought to an end the personal relationship between the two musicians. In later years Moscheles attended concerts given by Paganini on several occasions, but he never changed his negative attitude. Paganini is last mentioned in the diary in 1833 in connection with his visit to London to undergo an operation on his lower jaw: *for which he prepared himself with enormous courage; he was completely restored to health.*

THE ARTIST'S SORROW AND JOY

In 1832 Moscheles was voted unanimously on to the Board of Directors of the Philharmonic Society; however he had no illusions as far as this honourable appointment was concerned:
There are seven of us on the Board and the other six share the same ideas. They are conservative and traditional, whereas I am alone in striving for musical reform, and I just cannot bring them around to my way of thinking. They put on symphonic works together with quartets at the same concert, and they allow mediocre singers to perform. The antiquated Trio by Corelli, which has been a compulsory item on the programme for many years, continues to be performed by the old matadors Cramer, Lindley and Dragonetti, while the rest of us run out of patience. . . . None of them would dare to tackle Beethoven's last quartets.

Moscheles judged his own compositions with the same degree of severity. The success of his latest symphony and of the C major Concerto at the Philharmonic Society concerts prompted him to write: *The success I achieve with my new works certainly never goes to my head, as I am convinced that the public will applaud even the mediocre.*

Although the symphony was performed several times, Moscheles was well aware that some of his contemporaries would surpass him in orchestral composition, and that his beloved Mendelssohn had outstripped him long ago. Admittedly, the instrumentation of his G minor Concerto had led to widespread belief at the time that the young composer, as he then was, would go from strength to strength. Indeed, one of his earliest compositions from his time in Vienna, the ballet 'Les deux portraits' had likewise been hailed as very promising by the critics of the day. In spite of his later attempts at composition though, he himself felt that his real vocation was as a pianist.

On March 10th Muzio Clementi died at the age of 84. He was buried at Westminster Abbey, where Handel had also found his last resting place. A few months later Sir Walter Scott followed Clementi to the grave. On March 31st a large banquet took place to commemorate the 100th anniversary of the birth of Haydn. The diary reports: *Ninety-two men were present, mainly professors of music. The ladies observed the banquet from the gallery.*

In the course of the season Moscheles was once again a frequent guest at the houses of well-known politicians, which he described thus:
Every time I am applauded at such soirées, I think it is because they are relieved that I have finished playing, and that the thing is over and done with. We sacrifice as little time as possible for such evenings and hurry home as soon as the rules of etiquette permit.

It was at about this time that Moscheles first felt a desire to withdraw from the concert scene, but the state of his finances would not allow him to do so just yet. It was in fact his relationship with the other artists that gave him the incentive to continue. At the end of April Mendelssohn came over from Paris, where he had just been fortunate to survive an attack of cholera. Moscheles wrote: *Now I can look forward to some marvellous times again.* Mendelssohn immediately played his so-called 'Songs for Instruments', later to be renamed 'Songs without Words', as well as the Capriccio in B minor, causing Moscheles to note: *Everything is suffused with spirituality and animation.*

We can now follow other more detailed entries from that time:
April 30th: Today Mendelssohn played his cantata 'Die erste Walpurgisnacht' (The First Walpurgis Night) for us. I had previously heard and admired it while in Berlin. However, since he has revised it and made quite a number of significant changes, during his stay in Italy, the whole thing is far more terse than before. He also played his operetta 'Die Heimkekr aus der Fremde' (Son and Stranger), which he composed in celebration of his parents' Silver Wedding, an enchanting musical comedy, and his 'Hebrides' overture (Fingal's Cave). He insisted that I should play for him as well, and when invited for the evening, he replied with these lines: 'I am much obliged to Herr Moscheles for wishing to see some of my work, and if he promises that he will tell me when he has had enough, I shall bring along a cab-full of manuscripts and play you all to sleep.'

May 1st: Mendelssohn and Klingemann were already here at one o'clock. The former presented me with the score of his 'Hebrides' overture which he had finished writing in Rome on December 16th, but which he had later revised for publication. For the most part, I thought his pieces beautiful and polished, even in their first version and could not imagine any changes being able to improve them. We talked about this point again today. Nevertheless, he stuck to his principle of alteration.

May 28th: In the morning rehearsal for my concert (the Mozart Concerto for Two Pianos) with Mendelssohn at Erard's factory. He joined us for dinner at our home, and in the evening we went to the Philharmonic Concert together. He performed his new G minor Concerto, which was an absolute success. Invention, form, instrumentation and performance – all were to my entire satisfaction; a piece of scintillating genius.

May 29th: Mendelssohn came for dinner and, without telling me, my wife had assembled the German artists as a surprise for me. . . . . A parcel I was handed contained a sheet of paper on which Mendelssohn had compiled a subject index of my works with humorous drawings in the margins.

June also had all manner of artistic delights in store, thanks to Mendelssohn's continued presence in London. He and Moscheles played together at the latter's own concert, and at St. Paul's Cathedral he gave a masterly recital of organ fugues. Later in the month, at one of the Philharmonic Society's Concerts, he repeated his Concerto in G minor, once again to tumultuous applause. Moscheles wrote in the highest terms of their time together:

Those quiet evenings at home, when we talk and make music together, are precious beyond measure. Today we went through his arrangement for piano duet of 'A Midsummer Night's Dream' in great detail; it is shortly to be published.

On June 22nd Mendelssohn returned to Berlin, where Moscheles, accompanied by his family, was to see him again in the October of the same year. Here, too, they spent happy days of music-making together. Moscheles wrote:

I practise daily on Felix's magnificent Erard piano which he has kindly offered to lend me for my concert. We often extemporise on it together, each trying to pick up the other's harmonies at lightning speed, and to develop them further. Every time I start with a theme from one of his compositions, he derives tremendous pleasure by cutting in as quickly as possible with one of my own, usually ending in bursts of laughter on both sides. It often turns out to be like a musical version of blind man's buff where the players, as they grope about uncertainly, sometimes bang their heads together.

On October 17th Moscheles gave a brilliant recital at the Berlin Opera and, after a farewell party at Mendelssohn's house, he moved on to Leipzig. There he visited his old friend Wieck and made a point of hearing Wieck's daughter Clara, now aged thirteen, play the piano. Her obvious talent made a profound impression on him. A few days later he was the guest of Frau von Goethe in Weimar.

It was a glittering company of starred and titled persons who seemed to be very taken with me and my performance. My wife and I, on the other hand, were lamenting the death a few months earlier of Weimar's great genius, Goethe. Here we were at his house, but unable to look inside any of his own rooms, as nothing had been tidied up yet, thus preventing anyone from entering. The only mementos of the great man that we could procure were some facsimiles, his last medal and a lock of his hair which Frau von Goethe gave to us.

From Weimar Moscheles proceeded to Frankfurt from where he paid another visit to Hofrath A., of whom he said:

He heaped the fruits of his erudition upon me and tried to prove with every line of his recently published textbook that no one had ever understood the art of printing music, except of course himself, let alone the ability to write it. He then showed me the unfinished score of an opera by Mozart, 'Bettula Liberata', for which, according to the textbook, Gassmann wrote some additional music in 1786. A. has taken it upon himself to complete the work. He also showed me the score of his overture which I played and deemed to have a certain value.

After further recitals and concerts in Frankfurt and Cologne, Moscheles refused all subsequent offers and headed back to London with his wife and children. His diary reflects his feelings of relief at their safe return.

True to my custom of composing something for my wife's birthday, I started out this year – not, as before, on some trifle or other, but on my septet for which I received a commission from the Philharmonic Society. For two years it shall remain her exclusive property, thereafter I may hand it over to a publisher.

As he was in the habit of working most evenings, it came as a rather unwelcome interruption when he was asked suddenly to go to Brighton: the Court, so he was told, was in residence, a friend there had prepared everything, and Moscheles would be playing for Their Majesties, who wished to hear him as soon as he arrived.

December 11th, 8 o'clock in the morning, to Brighton, thinking only of Goethe's Götz! – Arrived at 2 o'clock, handed in letter, met no one. Large crowds in the streets on account of imminent elections. Groups of supporters of the various parties marching through the streets, accompanied by music and shouts of 'hurray'. Went to the theatre alone; it was empty and cold.

December 12th. Was given an appointment at 10 o'clock this morning at the Pavilion (Royal residence) by the Director of Music, Sir Andrew Barnard, but he failed to keep it. The same applied for Dr Davis, who had sent me a card asking me to come and see him at 2 o'clock. When I complained to my great friend, Lady C., she agreed with me that Sir Andrew's hostility may be due to his preference for Italians. In any case, she wrote to him requesting an explanation. As a result, I had the honour of being allowed to see him. He told me that I ought to have known that I was playing for the Court that evening. 'How was I supposed to know that?' I asked. – 'Did Dr Davis not tell you anything?' – 'No!' – Whereupon he muttered some polite phrases and asked me to try out the Erard at the Pavilion. I found it creaky and stiff, as a result of standing too long in an unheated salon, but I had to prepare hurriedly so that I knew how I was going to play it, and I did not even find time to rehearse with the royal orchestra. We met in the evening in the music room of the Pavilion, with its magic lighting and fantastic decorations, which give the whole setting a fairytale quality. King William IV and Queen Adelaide arrived with the royal family and sat down at the far end of the room away from the piano; the royal household followed suit. I was not introduced. I played my new fantasy on English national songs, which I had dedicated to the Queen; while I was playing, the King approached the piano by himself and seemed to listen; he inclined his head rather condescendingly when I got up, but he remained silent. All the while there were lively conversations going on amongst the guests. Then Sir Andrew intimated to me that I should play the organ, and a little later on, I had to accompany the royal band (a badly trained double quartet) in parts of the 'Creation'. In the general hubbub of conversation, the Princess Augusta and the Marchioness of Cornwallis alone showed any interest in my Alexander Variations and subsequent improvisation. Extracts from 'Robert le Diable', played by the band, and a rendering of 'God save the King' brought the evening to a close.

The Court retired after Sir Andrew had presented a copy of my English Fantasy to the Queen, having refused my request to be granted the honour of presenting it to the Queen myself. With a few polite, courtly phrases imparting their Majesties' satisfaction, I was dismissed. Not a word was addressed to me by anyone else.

It is hardly surprising that Moscheles left Brighton somewhat annoyed.

FIRST APPOINTMENT AS A CONDUCTOR: 'MISSA SOLEMNIS' – WORKING WITH MENDELSSOHN

Towards the end of 1832 a great music lover by the name of Grimal brought Moscheles the score of Beethoven's Mass, Op. 123, which the latter had not seen before. Grimal asked him to conduct a performance at the home of a certain Mr Alsager. Alsager, the arts correspondent of the 'Times', was a passionate admirer of Beethoven's and enjoyed arranging for a full orchestra to play Beethoven's works in his own, very large music room. The 'Missa Solemnis' had not been performed in London before, and Moscheles accepted the offer. Thus, on December 23rd, he took up his baton for the first time to conduct an orchestra consisting mainly of amateurs, as was to be expected, but who nonetheless played reasonably well together. He was to conduct the Alsager orchestra on a number of subsequent occasions.

On the subject of the 'Missa Solemnis' he wrote in his diary:

I spent much time engrossed in the study of this colossal work. Now and again I came across phrases that seemed to me to be somewhat below the best in church music; but compared with the spirit that suffused the whole work, they are of trifling importance. The enthusiasm of my English friends made me eager to do justice to the composition. The 'Benedictus' with its divine violin solo (played by Mori) enraptured everyone.

Moscheles devoted the Christmas holidays and the first few weeks of 1833 to further work on his septet, of which only two movements had so far been completed. With his usual meticulousness he set about copying the parts. Over the years he was to grow particularly fond of this piece, as it had found favour with Mendelssohn.

Charlotte wrote the following account of this:

With childlike modesty that was typical of him [Mendelssohn], he asked; 'Would you permit me to arrange this for piano duet?' And then again, while he was actually doing it: 'Do you really like it? You would have made a much better job of it yourself' . . . . Whenever he talked like this we used to call it his 'sinful modesty', but always remained convinced that the great artist, underestimating his own worth, truly meant what he said.

In February 1833, Charlotte Moscheles was delivered of a son, their second, the first having fallen a victim to whooping cough. As soon as the child was born there was never any doubt that Felix Mendelssohn would be his godfather, and the child was named after him. In reply to the birth announcement, Mendelssohn wrote the following letter accompanied by a pen drawing:

Here you have the brass instruments to go with the violins, for the son and heir must not be made to wait until I come; he must have his lullaby now, with drums and trumpets and Turkish music; the violins by themselves would not be nearly jolly enough. Good fortune and happiness and every blessing for the new child; may he enjoy a good life, and whatever he may choose to do, may he do it well, and may he always be cheerful and light-hearted!

So he is to be called Felix. It is very kind and wonderful of you that he is to become my proper godchild, and my first present as his godfather is the entire orchestra above; it is to accompany him through life: the trumpets, in case he should wish to become famous, the flutes, if he should fall in love, the cymbals if he grows a beard, the piano is self-explanatory, and if he meets the occasional villain, which happens to the best of us, there are the timpani and a large drum in the background. Oh Lord, forgive all this stupid nonsense, but I feel so happy when I think how pleased you must be, and how I will be able to share in your joy when the time comes. I want to be in London by the end of April, at the latest, and then we shall give the boy a proper name and his entry into the world; it will be such a delight.

I am very much looking forward to your septet. Klingemann has written me eleven notes from it, namely:

and I like them very much.

I imagine that it is probably a lively, jolly piece. He also described the B-flat major Andante to me, but it will be even better when I can hear it myself. Don't expect too much of my own pieces which I shall be bringing along. You will notice traces of ill humour which I am only now beginning to shake off, slowly and with some difficulty. I have often had the feeling that I have never composed before and had to start all over again, learning everything from scratch. Now I feel a little better, and my more recent compositions should not sound too bad. It was such a pleasure to receive your letter while I was busy composing, alone and peaceful in my room, as you had hoped, and for that reason I hope that my reply finds you in a happy frame of mind, at home in the evening among your family, who I trust are all well. We shall now have to see whether I am as lucky with my hope as you were. I am in a hurry and have to close now; I had only half an hour in which to write, and the pretty drawing has taken up most of that. I have no other news to tell you, and just want to say 'good luck!' and 'Auf Wiedersehen'. My family are all well and send you their regards. They are also very happy for you. Only my father is suffering constantly with his eyes, which makes us all rather unhappy because it very often puts him in a bad mood; if only he would get better soon. My sister and I play a lot of music together, and every Sunday morning friends come and join in the music-making. At this very moment I have just received a whole green volume of Moscheles from the bookbinder, as we shall be playing your trio next time. But now farewell, farewell, and all the best.

Yours,
Felix Mendelssohn-Bartholdy
Berlin, February 27th 1833

There was a separate letter for Charlotte Moscheles:

Dear Madame Moscheles,

I can only manage a few lines today, but I send my congratulations on the happy event and tell you how happy I feel for you. How I look forward to meeting the new arrival in person very soon, and how pleased I am that he will bear my name! I bet you to wait until I come, so that I can accept your earlier invitation to the christening; I shall hurry as best I can, and be with you as soon as possible. I am glad that it's a boy; he will have to become a musician, and may everything we want to do and are not able to, be possible for him one day, or maybe not. It's all the same, for he will become a good man, and that is the most important thing. I can already imagine how his two elder sisters, the grown-up Misses Emily and Serena, will tyrannise him; of course, once he reaches fourteen, he will have to suffer their sidelong glances at his long arms and short coat and erratic voice; but thereafter he will be a man, ready to protect his two sisters and render himself useful to them. Moreover, he will have to suffer boredom on their account as their escort to many a soirée. – I expect that you have been slightly annoyed with me, or perhaps even very annoyed, as a result of my very infrequent letter-writing, but please forgive me, and I'll promise to improve – particularly, of course, when I'm in London and free to bring my questions and answers and improvisations to you in person; but I shall also improve in other respects. My sisters send a thousand good wishes and greetings, as do my parents; we are all very happy for you and congratulate you on your first son. I must now start on the last part of my symphony, and that is really what preoccupies me at the moment, ruining my style and taking up all my time. Please excuse the hurried words, but you know what they are intended to convey.

Respectfully yours,
Felix Mendelssohn-Bartholdy.

The symphony Mendelssohn mentioned in his letter is the one in A major. It received its first performance on May 13th in London at a Philharmonic Concert, about which Moscheles wrote the following in his diary:
Mendelssohn was the outstanding success of the concert; he conducted his magnificent A major symphony and received rapturous applause.

In the same concert series Moscheles performed his recently finished septet that he had written for the Philharmonic Society. With him were Dragonetti, Lindley, Mori et al. This is the work that Mendelssohn later arranged for piano duet.

Moscheles' participation was also in demand again at various private functions. At Mr Alsager's concerts, for example, he played Beethoven's Sonatas, Op. 109 and 111, before an audience of admirers of the great composer.
They were devoted listeners, very different from the musicians at my own house with whom I achieve very little success. On the one hand, they are moved, of course, but on the other they are really happy only when I play the D minor Sonata which they can understand more easily.

In the spring, the Royal Society of Musicians put on a rather unusual function. *Old Parry, his Welsh harp in his arms, sang Welsh songs with a kind of pathos that made them appealing for me. We musicians had organised a musical dinner in honour of the dear old man and had presented him with a silver dinner set in recognition of his many years of faithful service in our guild and of his work on behalf of impoverished musicians. His gratitude and emotion touched us all.*

Mendelssohn's arrival in London at the end of April came just in time to help Moscheles out of a predicament in which he then found himself. A fearful influenza epidemic was gripping London in that spring of 1833, and when Moscheles contracted the illness, he was quite incapable of working. To make matters worse, he had not even started on the new composition that was required of him for his annual concert on May 1st. He seriously considered calling the concert off, but then Mendelssohn appeared on the scene, and the two friends rapidly agreed to chance a joint composition for two pianos. It had to be a brilliant piece, if possible with variations on a popular theme. But which one? At last they decided on the Gypsy March from Weber's 'Preciosa'.

Mendelssohn told Moscheles: *I'll do a variation in a minor key that rumbles down in the bass, and you do a brilliant one in a major key at the top, don't you think?'* And so it was decided that the introduction and the first and second variation would be Mendelssohn's, while the third and fourth variations, as well as a tutti linking them, would fall to Moscheles. *We agreed to share the work on the finale; he began with the allegro section, which I then interrupted with a più lento.*

In two days they were finished, and despite the late hour at which they went to Erard's piano factory for a first rehearsal. *. . . We found two pianos, and our somewhat rushed creation found favour with our only listener, my wife.* This nocturnal rehearsal was only slightly hurried compared with the subsequent orchestral rehearsal on the morning of April 30th, when an extended opera rehearsal detained the brass players, so that only a few overtired members could be prevailed upon to skim through the piece once.

In spite of it all, the concert on May 1st went extremely well, and nobody noticed that the whole thing had been fleetingly sketched and that we had left ourselves free to improvise in our respective solos until we reached a previously agreed juncture when we would once again join up with our partner, both gently and harmoniously. This seemingly unsafe enterprise turned out to be a great success after all.

Shortly afterwards, Mendelssohn returned to Germany, albeit only temporarily, to take charge of the Düsseldorf Music Festival. He soon returned, this time accompanied by his father. And now there was time to celebrate the christening of little Felix Moscheles. From his godfather he received an album containing a new composition, 'Schlumm're und träume' (Sleep and dream), a lullaby with words by Klingemann which, in due course, became widely known and very popular. Moscheles wrote warmly about the event in his diary: *There can never have been a happier christening party than this one.*

The relationship with Mendelssohn figured in many of the subsequent entries in the diary. This is how Mendelssohn replied on one occasion to an invitation for dinner: *Oh God! What a pity that we cannot come! We are giving a dinner of our own this evening, and I have just ordered salmon and lobster for five. Alas, we have to say how sorry we are! As a matter of fact, Rosen and Stenzler and Klingemann promised to spend the evening with us, and that is why we cannot come. My father hopes to see you this morning, nonetheless, to thank you in person.*

And in a note to Charlotte, he wrote:

Dear Frau Moscheles,
It is two o'clock, and I have just returned from the country to find your note telling me that I should have been at Grosvenor Place at ten o'clock. I would gladly have been there, but you must admit that fate does not seem to

*want me either to be or to appear fashion-
able. You were kind enough the other day to
ask the three of us for lunch today (Dr Franck
has indeed arrived), but now I should like to
know whether you were in earnest, or
whether it is no longer convenient for you, or
whether we are still in fact expected to come.
Please – pass your decision on to me via the
bearer of this note by word of mouth.*

It goes without saying that the decision
was in the affirmative.

During the season Moscheles and Mendelssohn joined forces at several more concerts,
and at the last of the Philharmonic series,
Mendelssohn's overture to 'Ruy Blas' had its
première. As we see from the diary, however,
they played together more often in private.
*We made so much music, the two of us!
Again and again he had to play his pieces for
me while I read them from the score. He
would also indicate some brass instrument or
other in the music or, in his attractive tenor
voice, sing where the chorus would come in.
And if he happened to arrange one of his
overtures for piano duet, we would try it out
until it seemed playable to us!*

Their music-making was by no means
always as serious as that. When the mood
took them, they would improvise musical
caricatures or, much to the delight of the
Moscheles children, play around with the
nursery rhyme 'Polly put the kettle on'.

So far, we have seen that Moscheles and
Mendelssohn spent mostly happy and carefree hours together. However, their friendship also stood the test of those inevitable
moments of dejection. When Mendelssohn
heard that his old teacher Zelter had died, he
rushed to Moscheles' house at once, in spite
of the early morning hour, begging to be
allowed in. *I cannot work, I want to spend
the day with you.* Tired and exhausted from
the exertions demanded of him by London's

musical hustle and bustle, he could be sure of
a soothing reception at the Moscheles' household. Charlotte would make him sit down in
a dark corner of the sofa, where . . .
*he would rest for a few minutes during which
even our noisy children would remain as
quiet as mice; a little refreshment would
restore him completely and, with his usual
high spirits, he would tell us all about some
difficult musical rehearsal or a morning
concert, or one of the political meetings he
was in the habit of frequenting.*

Charlotte was even allowed to berate him
for having disturbed the domestic harmony
on the previous day when he came to see
them, by *twisting and turning impatiently on
his heel and behaving rather ungraciously to
one of their visitors* – to which he replied:
*Yes, but why did he have to come when I was
so looking forward to making music with
Moscheles?*

Those frequent meetings with Mendelssohn continued until his departure in August;
they helped to break up the relentless pattern
of Moscheles' work programme. Thus he
wrote in his diary at the end of 1833: *According to my calculations, I have given 1457
lessons this year.*

Those endless lessons on top of the hectic
pressure of the London concert scene could
not fail to have an effect on the artist's state of
mind. Following a performance of Handel's
much-loved 'Messiah', Moscheles had this to
say:
*I had gulped down my lunch in order not to
miss a single note of this masterpiece. However, after listening attentively for a while, I
came to the painful conclusion that what
little mental freshness I had retained from the
bustle of the season was insufficient to do
justice artistically to such a gigantic work. It
is reflections such as this that always bring
me back to the idea of returning to Germany,
when the times comes, to enjoy the fruits of*

my independence gained as a result of my activities in England.

It was in 1833 that Moscheles first began to occupy himself with the works of Chopin. He wrote:

I like to spend a few hours in the evening, when I am free, getting to know Chopin's Etudes and his other compositions. Their originality and the national colouring of their themes hold great attraction for me; but every so often my thoughts, and through them my fingers, stumble over certain harsh, inartistic and incomprehensible modulations, while the music as a whole at times seems too sweet to me, and it hardly seems worthy of the man and educated musician.

This ambivalent attitude to Chopin's music remained with Moscheles to the end, even after he had met the composer in Paris, and the two had played together on many occasions, to their mutual satisfaction.

With the intention of becoming better acquainted with the British system of government, Moscheles and his wife decided one day in the autumn to visit the House of Commons. Moscheles was shown to a good seat in the Stranger's Gallery, whereas Charlotte, like all the other lady visitors, had to watch the proceedings through a ventilation flap above the chandelier. The air that met their faces from below was hot and stifling, the result of so many gaslights illuminating the Chamber, while from behind they had to endure cold draughts blowing through the lattice-work from outside. There were no better places to be had for ladies who wished to visit Parliament. There were, however, some interesting debates in progress. One member held forth complaining about the British Post Office which, he maintained, not only opened letters, but also read them. One of his fellow members on the other side then took up the cudget on behalf of the Post-master General and silenced the accuser.

There followed a long discussion in favour of a proposal by Murray to revoke the law on armed service on behalf of foreign powers. A certain Captain Napier, it was alleged, was about to be expelled from the Navy for fighting a victorious battle in the service of Don Pedro. The debate on this proposal lasted for four whole hours.

Towards the end of the year a number of visits to the theatre were recorded in the diary. The entry for November 11th reads: *At one point during yesterday's performance of 'Hamlet' at Drury Lane, I was vividly reminded of what I have been trying to instil into my pupils: to remain resolutely in control of oneself, however trying the task. The great poet speaks through the mouth of Hamlet: 'Nor do not saw the air too much with your hand thus, but use all gently, for in the very torrent, tempest and, as I may say, whirlwind of your passion, you must acquire and beget a temperance that may give it smoothness.'*

On attending the first performance of Auber's 'Le bal masqué' Moscheles remarked: *The music is often intoxicating, but also often piquant, and the ball quite overwhelmingly brilliant.*

LONDON MUSIC FESTIVAL 1834

Moscheles devoted what little time was left in his very busy schedule to composition.

1834 saw the completion, despite many disturbances and disruptions, of his Concert fantastique in B-flat major, an Impromptu in E-flat, the Overture to 'Jungfrau von Orleans' (The Maid of Orleans) based on Schiller's play, several songs, setting to music poems by Byron and Ludwig Uhland, as well as a first draft of the Concert pathétique. The B-flat major concerto had its première in the spring of the same year at the Philharmonic

Society concert, and on the same evening Moscheles conducted Mendelssohn's previously unknown overture to 'Die schöne Melusine' (Melusina). Both pieces were given rather a cool reception, to which Mendelssohn, apprised of the outcome of the concert in a letter from Charlotte, reacted rather philosophically:

So the people in the Philharmonic did not like my 'Melusine'? So what, it won't kill me. I was, of course, sorry to read what you wrote, and I quickly played the whole overture right through to see whether I would not like it any more either – but I found it still gave me pleasure, and so I am not too sad about it. . . . In any case, my chief delight in everything I write is to see it finished on paper, and if I have the good fortune to be praised for it by you and Moscheles, then it has been well received as far as I am concerned, and I can go on working quite happily. However, when you write that the same fate has befallen Moscheles' new concerto, it concerns me greatly, because I cannot understand it. I took it for granted that they would like it, especially when he played it himself. When is it going to be published? Just watch how people will snap it up then!

The most important event in the music season of 1834 was without doubt the London Music Festival in June. It took up a lot of space in the newspapers, and in one of them we read:

Handel was responsible for introducing the oratorio to England. It is small wonder, therefore, that the Festival is named after him, and that its venue is Westminster Abbey where his earthly remains lie buried and his ghost can give it its proper blessing.

In the press we also find reference to earlier London music festivals which were held annually from 1784 to 1791 under King George III to aid charitable institutions, and which brought in a total of £50,000. The present monarch, King William IV, and his wife, Queen Adelaide, are praised for their resolve to revive this tradition after a lapse of 43 years and, by donating a handsome gift, to ensure that the country's aristocracy would follow their example. Handel's legacy to the 'Society of Decayed Musicians and their Families' is also mentioned.

In a letter to relatives, Moscheles described the four-day event as follows:

The Festival took place in the nave of the church which was covered with a sturdy wooden floor. At one end of the Abbey could be seen the royal enclosure bearing the royal coat of arms, the rose and other emblems and decorations artistically carved on a field of blue. The enclosure with its weighty cerise damask curtains, rich ornamentation, sumptuous carpets and velvet cushions, was illuminated from above. Immediately below the royal enclosure, underneath a canopy, sat the Directors of the Festival. As in 1784, the public occupied rising tiers of seats reaching right up to the capitals of the stone columns. There was enough room for 2700 people; there were some seats for 2 guineas, the rest cost 1 guinea. These seats, adorned with yellow and red ornaments, together with so many white and gold lyres on a background of red cloth all around the walls, looked tasteful and picturesque. Also following precedent, the orchestra was placed directly opposite the royal enclosure and its component parts arranged thus: the solo singers in front, behind them the small chorus, only forty strong, and immediately next to the chorus, a grand piano for the conductor, Sir George Smart. Behind him was the orchestra in a semi-circle of rising tiers, in the centre the violins with the cellos on either side, then came the brass, and lastly the magnificent organ, built specially for this occasion by Gray, who had also decorated its case with richly carved gothic motifs. The console was placed in such a way that the organist, instead of facing the organ, sat right opposite the conductor. The large chorus was located in the transept and aisles of the Abbey, thus considerably reducing its impact on the public; not only were its members partially obscured by some of the instruments, but their singing was only heard by a section of the audience, while in some seats the effect was exactly the opposite, so that only a small part of the mighty building guaranteed perfect listening.

The following list offers a comparison of the number of participants at the Music Festivals of 1784 and 1834 (the statistics from the earlier festival are taken from the records of the music chronicler Dr Barney):

Instrumental	1834	1784
Violins	80	95
Violas	32	26
Violoncelli	18	21
Double basses	18	15
Flutes	10	6
Oboes	12	26
Clarinets	8	
Bassoons	12	27
Horns	10	12
Trumpets	8	12
Trombones	8	12
Ophicleides	2	
Serpents	2	
Drums	3	4
	223	250

Vocal	1834	1784
Sopranos	113	47
Trebles	32	47
Altos	74	48
Tenors	70	83
Basses	103	84
Opera singers	5	2
The above instruments	223	250
Total	625	525

Moscheles reported:

On June 20th, at 12.00 noon, Sir George Smart raised his baton for the first time to conduct one of Handel's 'Coronation Anthems' which, given the acoustics of the abbey and massive presence of choir and orchestra, made for an overwhelming, unforgettable effect. The ladies, so the papers tell us, had tears streaming down their faces; some were even said to have fainted. As for myself, I was deeply moved by those sounds; I must admit that I have never heard anything like it. The programme also included the whole of the 'Creation' and part of 'Samson' . . .

On the second day the first item was another of Handel's 'Coronation Anthems', of which the closing 'Hallelujah' was electrifying. In an attempt to achieve less of a grandiose whole and more of certain special effects, a selection of arias from the sacred repertoire had been included to give singers and brass soloists an opportunity to display their artistry. Even the audience was encouraged to participate, to add to the sparkle. . . . Then followed what is, in my opinion, Handel's most beautiful oratorio, 'Israel in Egypt', executed to great effect. The newspapers revelled in ecstatic praise. Referring to the final recitative sections, when the choir interrupts here and there with some glorious singing, the 'Athenaeum' said that one felt so elated by this music that it was like being transported back to those great days when the Lord appeared to his people as a cloud or column of fire, but as soon as the heavenly sounds have died away, one is returned to bleak reality and our shadow-like everyday life. For me personally it was a great, almost undreamt-of experience, and I feel almost certain that my impression was shared by most of the people around me.

On the third day there was unfortunately

yet another mixture of arias, choruses and ensembles, and a jumping back and forth between the ancient and the modern.

For the fourth day, the Queen had specifically requested the 'Messiah' (just as Queen Charlotte had done in 1784). For a German musician it was only natural that everyone's interest should be focused on this magnificent work. Tickets for the performance and for the rehearsals were soon sold out, and some changed hands at ever more exorbitant prices to satisfy demand. The Abbey was filled to capacity and an atmosphere of rapturous attention prevailed. The 'Times', which had seen fit not to criticise the somewhat tasteless fragmentation of great works to which we had been exposed over the previous few days, now considered it right, as the Festival was drawing to a close, to give some good advice: 'To enhance the effect of such performances even further, oratorios should in future adhere to the spirit of the composer, that is to say, they should not be fragmented'. The advice came too late for the current presentation, however. For a German musician these programmes were by no means beyond criticism, but at the same time their total effect has been such that it would seem ungracious if one were to pick out details for disapproval. The religious feeling that is so much part of the English character certainly came into its own, in this sacred place and in this kind of music, much of which was inspired by this national inclination; everyone came away with a sense of exultation. The Abbey had donned its festive raiment, and the ladies their jewels, but more festive than either was what the people felt inside; a kind of reverence had gripped this heterogeneous mass of people, more eloquent by far than shouts of 'bravo' and applause. The King and Queen, who attended every performance, were seen as embodying this great charitable undertaking, amply supported by the nation. I don't know why it is so, but I have deduced all this from the way people behaved; if you wish, you may put it down to my imagination.

When the festival was over, Moscheles took his family for a holiday to Broadstairs, a popular seaside resort. Back in London, feeling very much better for this pleasant interlude, he threw himself straight away into preparations for yet another musical festival, this time in Birmingham. On the programme were works by Handel, Haydn, Beethoven Neukomm and Spohr but, as the 'Spectator' pointed out disapprovingly, quite inexplicably only the best-known and most hackneyed music. The new oratorio by Neukomm, 'David', had well written vocal parts, so it claimed, but in terms of style and development it was stale and out of date. It went on to say:
All that Neukomm has absorbed of the spirit of the time is the conspicuous use of horns and trombones, to which he has added for good measure, two ophicleides and even a tam-tam. The latter was used to create a certain effect that he would have done better to reject. The performance as such, conducted by the composer, was satisfactory and left a good impression with the great multitude that had come to listen. The oratorio was promptly followed by a selection of Handel's music. – At one of these concerts, when Neukomm played the organ, he had arranged for someone to drop wooden planks and other objects to imitate thunder, which cannot have done his reputation a lot of good, for this kind of thing should be left to suburban theatres. The third morning brought us the whole 'Messiah', albeit without the additional Mozartian wind instruments, and for that reason it was sharply criticised. On the

fourth morning we heard 'Israel in Egypt', not in its original form but much mutilated by deletions and insertions. To have preceded this most splendid of oratorios with a selection of other pieces from religious works can only be compared with the Scandinavian custom of inviting guests to a sumptuous meal and filling their stomachs with stimulating tit-bits before sitting down to a phalanx of dishes.

In addition to these performances of church music every morning, there was a decidedly secular emphasis in the concerts that took place in the evening. For one of these evenings Moscheles was engaged to play his 'Recollections of Ireland' and the 'Alexander March'. The mighty sound of the Erard triumphed over the colossal size of the abbey, more suited to massive pieces than to a solo instrument. Indeed, the 'Spectator' observed that not only the vast interior was filled with sound, but a grateful audience of ordinary citizens had gathered outside in the precinct to enjoy the music. The concert made a profit of £14,000.

During the quiet summer holiday at Broadstairs, Moscheles had collected a great number of sketches to his overture to 'The Maid of Orleans' so that he could work on them in the autumn. The diary refers to a number of interruptions which interfered with the work, one of them being of more general interest:

On October 16th in the evening I was deeply engrossed in my work when the news spread suddenly that the House of Lords was on fire. From our house, which is some distance away from the Houses of Parliament, we were soon able to make out a pall of smoke to confirm the sad news.

The old House of Lords was completely gutted, being a far less durable structure than the new one. Desite this interruption, and many others besides, the overture was soon finished, and Moscheles himself arranged it for piano duet. Instead of a noisy bravura finale, he let the piece die away in a tender, melting melody which he deemed more in keeping with Joan of Arc's manner of death. In a letter he referred to it thus:

In this overture I strove to achieve momentum, style and integration of ideas; the work will give pleasure to the right listener; on the other hand those who seek easily assimilated, Italian-style dilly-dallying will be disappointed. Moreover, it will have little to offer to those who find the interweaving of ideas and the appearance of a comparatively unheralded modulation excessively demanding, whereas to initiates of counterpoint these are musical delicacies. In my opinion, a clear melodic line and the integrity and ingenious handling of the main themes are the most important ingredients of a composition, and I shall never cease to strive for these. . . . Mendelssohn's Octet, where you have a scarcity of 'tunes', inclines more towards artificiality, but it is well worth listening to this magnificent work several times, giving it one's full attention until one has learned to understand and appreciate its originality, which at no time degenerates into absurdity . . .

The year 1835 began with the routine annual trip to Bath. As in previous years, Moscheles reaped a rich harvest of both praise and guineas during his three-day stay. Back in London, the Philharmonic Society started rehearsals for new compositions, as it did every year. Spohr's 'Weihe der Töne' (The Consecration of Sound) was conducted by Sir George Smart. Moscheles wrote the following account:

He [Sir George] thought he could overcome the chronic shortcomings of English orchestras, resulting from inadequate rehearsal time, by addressing his army of musicians, baton in hand. 'The Germans', he said, 'needed innumerable rehearsals before they could perform this beautiful work; let's see what we can do in one rehearsal'. Whereupon the English national pride erupted into the traditional shouts of 'Hear! Hear!', and the music began. Sure enough, the work was played correctly, but certain nuances were sadly missing. I followed by reading the score and enjoyed the high quality of the work as a whole, in particular some very beautiful passages. However, for my enthusiasm to be kindled properly, I found the characteristic style and colouring of Spohr's music too predominant. Nothing but inventive genius can succeed in igniting the imagination of the listener. The Andante, with its mixed time signatures – 3/8 and 9/16 – presented serious problems. As it turned out, the combination of one rehearsal and British pride were not sufficient to prevent the performance from appearing rigid and uneven, though it was better than the rehearsal. By contrast, Mozart's Symphony in D was delightful in its classical unity. Mendelssohn 'Hebrides' Overture suffered as a result of being played too slowly; but I greatly enjoyed the sixty-four-year-old J. B. Cramer's sensitive touch and brilliant fingerwork, although I missed a pithy element in his performance. There was another example of bad taste, however, when he combined the first part and Andante of his own C minor Concerto with the last movement of Mozart's concerto in the same key. . . . I played my G minor Concerto, but had much trouble with Erard's sticky keyboard.

Moscheles conducted the third concert himself; his Overture to 'The Maid of Orleans' was well received. The newspapers were unanimous in saying that in his performance of Beethoven's B-flat major Symphony he managed to reveal its full beauty as never before.

Just as Bath in the south demanded a visit from its favourite pianist, so, too, did Manchester in the north. Moscheles described this trip in his letters to Charlotte; as always, they disliked being apart from each other, and their correspondence was a lively one.

The first of Moscheles' accounts of his journey came from Leicester, where he stopped en route:
My travelling companions were three silent, scrawny, self-sufficient Englishmen. I slept exceptionally well, and every time I awoke I thought of you, but I also thought of you in my dreams. Kiss the children for me, and be reassured and happy.

From Manchester he wrote:
I am writing this note in the company of the Beale family who are caring for my every need. If it turns out to be short, it will be for three reasons: the hubbub of conversation in the room, my tiredness and your exhortation not to write late at night and only to let you know whether I am well. This I certainly am. I trust that you have received my letter from Leicester. We arrived here at 5 o'clock in fine but frosty weather, and after dinner we all went to rehearsal; I played 'Recollections of Ireland' on a Broadwood.

And the following evening:
The first concert is over – excellent, to my entire satisfaction. This letter has to be posted before 7 o'clock tomorrow morning, consequently I am writing at night again, at the Beales', while supper is being served and everybody is talking about the concert. . . . My time before dinner (4 o'clock) was taken up by the many visits I had to make. By that time I was impatient to get your reply and, therefore, indifferent to the taste of the food. I must have enquired at least ten times whether there was still a chance of letters being delivered that day. 'It's too late now', Mr Beale said. I swallowed the bitter pill, and five minutes later your wonderful letter

arrived to save me. I read it straight away at table and felt very happy. After that we all went to the concert. The overcrowded hall was very impressive, and the 'Recollections' were well received. I should have liked to follow the plan you proposed for my fantasy, if only one of the Directors had not given me Rubini's 'vivi tu', which had just been sung, and another Beethoven Andante in A minor as themes, to which I added:

To begin with, it was one of those calm, structured fantasies that gradually worked itself up into a frenzy. Deafening applause.

The next day he wrote:
The most pleasurable finale to my day's work is writing to you. I was unable to do so earlier as I had as busy a day as I would have in London. Just imagine, I gave seven lessons today, and tomorrow I shall be teaching the same pupils again. . . . Yet again, the highlight of the day was your letter. It arrived while we were at table, and the way I reached out for it must have prompted all those present to grant me permission, – nay, to exhort me – to read it immediately over dinner, so that I had no compunction to do so, and to amuse myself immensely in the process. Everything you write – your bulletin, how you pass your time, the report on the children – gives me pleasure. I feel perfectly well, as fit as a fiddle, even though the weather is awful. I hope you're faring better in that respect. It's getting late and I can hear you say: 'Are you going to stay up half the night?', to which I reply: 'No, but I should like to talk to you for a little while, since I am writing this letter in my comfor-table bedroom in front of a roaring fire of which even you would approve. But reason prevails, and I can hear you repeat your warning, so I will bid you "good night" and, while you're reading this, "good day!".'

Before leaving Manchester he wrote:
4 o'clock in the afternoon. I'm starting this letter now, as there will not be much time after the concert. This is the last letter before my return, but despite many enquiries I cannot tell you yet how and by which coach I shall be returning. I have given more lessons today, and just now I have tried out the instrument at the concert hall.
11 o'clock at night. The concert was a great personal success; I received tumultuous applause and had to repeat my fantasy. At one point I wove in a little 'badinage à la Paganini' which was very effective. The continuous rain and scarcity of coachmen in this city gave rise to a series of adventures after the concert, some serious and some amusing; I shall have to tell you about those in person, though. I also want to convey to you in person my thanks for your exquisite letter which I received yesterday. If only I knew by which coach I would be travelling back to London. You know how much I would have liked to meet you at Islington, but with all this uncertainty, we shall just have to resign ourselves that it cannot be. A pity, too, that I shan't be able to write to you again from Sheffield tomorrow, because the letter would not be delivered in London until Monday, but I am looking forward to reading yours which should be awaiting me in Sheffield. By the time you read these lines I shall be on my way to you. Au revoir.

Back in London he could allow himself only a few hours of rest, as the pressure of work was on him almost at once. Since the only form of communication in London was by letter, a great pile of mail had accumulated during his five days' absence. In the words of Figaro in 'The Barber of Seville', Moscheles' complaint was 'Tutti mi chiedeno, tutti mi vogliono', with a lesson to give here, an invitation to accept there, and a gift to receive with gratitude somewhere else etc. As he was accustomed to a great deal of attention, he did not take kindly to any show of disregard, and it is hardly surprising that he complained about a particular incident in one of his letters (we should like to pass it on to readers, without comment, as a piece of cultural history):

During the past season I had to teach two young ladies, the daughters of Lord L. As it happened I never felt comfortable either with the daughters, with their mother, or with their powdered and braided servants. The girls showed no interest in learning to play and, like their mother, they were arrogant. the servants copied them in their condescension as I came and went, and I had to conduct myself with an air of determination to preserve my rights as a gentleman. After nearly nine months I sent in my bill for £35. It took some time before a steward appeared at my house and, finding me absent, he talked to my wife and showed her the back of my invoice where the Lord had scribbled these words: 'Pay this man £15 on account of bill'. My wife, justifiably indignant, refused to accept the money, whereupon the steward said to her sympathetically: 'Well, ma'am, I advise you to take them while you can get them.' Then she recalled that this family was notoriously bad when it came to paying debts, and so she accepted the money. Soon afterwards, her Ladyship sent for me and asked me to resume giving lessons to her daughters. I refused. Then came an extremely courteous enquiry from his Lordship wishing to know the reasons for my refusal, and whether there was something I was complaining about. I went in person to voice my complaint, only to be overwhelmed with kindness by both Lord and Lady L., causing me to resume the four lessons a week.

From that time on, and for a number of years, he was treated with consideration and paid punctually. *That's the way to teach these people a lesson*, Charlotte added.

Towards the end of March 1835, Moscheles gave a morning concert at the Italian Opera in which he played his Overture to 'The Maid of Orleans' and the first movement of his Concert pathétique for the first time. Referring to the latter, the 'Times' criticized his use of drums and trumpets, judging them to be unsuitable in a work of this nature. Also included in the programme were Beethoven's Triple Concerto, where he was joined by Mori and Lindley, and the inevitable free fantasy which was expected of him at all his concerts.

Moscheles wrote about his work in a letter at that time:

The urge to compose is ever present; but where shall I find the time? I have spawned a few songs, such as Byron's 'There be none of beauty's daughters' and Uhland's 'Im Herbste' (Autumn), but there is never enough peace and quiet for me to finish my Concert pathétique. Besides, I want to give a new introduction to 'Hommage à Handel', which I composed in 1822.

The latter was composed shortly afterwards and became a popular item in his programmes.

At around the same time, Kalkbrenner had his 'Etudes préparatoires' published, but they never gained a wide following. Also at this time, Chopin's Scherzo gracioso and his 24 Etudes appeared, prompting this response from Moscheles:

I am a genuine admirer of his originality. He has presented pianists with the latest and most attractive novelties. I personally dislike his contrived, often forced modulations. My fingers trip and stumble over such passages, no matter how much I practise them; I simply cannot bring them off without mistakes.

Referring to Berlioz's 'Symphonie Fantastique', of which he had received a piano score from the publisher, he wrote:

I am reluctant to pass judgement until I have seen the orchestral score, but I cannot reconcile myself to the eternal unison passages, the consecutive octaves and the tremulandos. I fail to find the basis for a sound sequence of harmonies; instead I can see evidence of an ailing imagination in the 'Dies Irae' and in the 'Witches' Sabbath'. Besides, Berlioz tends to pack his musical ideas so closely together that, as he tries to develop them, they often end up in a Gordian knot; and who is supposed to unravel it? But there is no doubt that the young man has warmth and poetry, and some parts of his music possess grandeur reminiscent of an ancient torso.

In order to give a better insight into the cosmopolitan atmosphere that permeated the musical life of London and the life of its musicians in those days, here is a quotation from one of Moscheles' letters:

In a true account of our musical sorrows as well as our musical joys, I would have to admit that the horizon is darkened at times by the influx of foreign musicians, just as the sky of Egypt was darkened by a plague of locusts. One of these musicians takes German simple-mindedness to such an extreme that he will not speak a word in any foreign language. This, however, did not prevent him from coming here so that he could be recognised by the English; he is the spitting image of Dominie Sampson and even speaks in the same pedantic manner. Moreover, every time he comes, he is accompanied by his pupil, a boring young Dutchman. Whenever the two of them run into the Frenchified German, the perfumed H., or the arch-English H., a composer who speaks only his own native tongue, conversation becomes some-
what strained. At table the German enjoys his food, my wife tells me, while the Frenchified German turns up his nose at every peppercorn, and the Englishman arranges portions of mustard, cayenne and other strong spices around the rim of his plate, like a painter's palette, before he has even tasted the dish in front of him. With so much interpreting to be done, and having to suppress repeated fits of laughter when dining with them, we hardly ate anything ourselves. In the end, the German and the Englishman tried to resolve their communication difficulties by talking to each other in Latin. Unfortunately though, they had miscalculated the discrepancy in each other's pronunciation, which soon got them hopelessly entangled in the tortuous paths of a labyrinth, from which it was difficult to extricate themselves.

LEIPZIG ONCE AGAIN – MEETING ROBERT SCHUMANN

In the spring of 1835, another prominent veteran of London's musical life decided to retire: J. B. Cramer, now aged 64, wanted to spend his remaining years in Munich. However, he did not stay there for very long, for he was soon back in England where he spent his days in strict seclusion and in very modest circumstances, as the publishing house of Cramer, Beale & Co., to whom his name represented an extremely valuable asset, paid him only a very small pension.

Moscheles and his family again spent the summer months with relatives in Hamburg. From there he journeyed on his own to Leipzig, where his mother came from Prague to visit him and where Mendelssohn had just become conductor of the famous Gewandhaus concerts. He stayed for two enjoyable weeks in Leipzig, to which his letters to Charlotte bear witness.

Leipzig, October 1st 1835,
10 o'clock in the evening.

My dear wife!
I began my day's work at half past four this morning by writing you a few lines; let me now bring this day to a close by giving you an account of everything I have done. At 8 o'clock in the morning I went to see my mother and my dear sister-in-law at their lodgings; there were hot tears of joy all around. We talked a great deal about the circumstances which had made it impossible for you to accompany me on this trip; this upset them a great deal. Kistner, who has already been very active on my behalf, accompanied me to Mendelssohn's place, a very agreeable location outside the city, at Reichelsgarten. Felix welcomed me with his usual childlike friendliness and asked after you with great warmth and respect and, I would like to say, with love. He was delighted with your present. . . . I found that he was no more beautiful than before (half youth, half man), nor did he appear to be bursting with good health, but he was in better spirits, more amusing and brighter than ever. He played three new songs without words for me, which were worthy additions to the others; he has not heard any of my latest pieces yet. – I returned to mother's lodgings to see some of the furnishings. There I was given presents for all of us, including a splendid gateau, of which I hope to save you a piece. Mother is looking well, and although everyone calls her a beautiful old lady, to me she seems much younger than her years. I also went to see Wieck and had the pleasure of listening to Clara play the piano. Among other pieces, she played a manuscript sonata by Schumann which I thought was rather contrived, difficult, and somewhat involved, but interesting nonetheless. The girl is an outstanding, very accomplished pianist. She appears to have less fire than Mme Pleyel, because she plays without any affectation; her childlike modesty is the absolute opposite of that tempestuous and vivacious young artist of whom Felix spoke in great detail while we were having dinner at Kistner's. According to Chopin, who passed through here recently on his way back to Paris from one of the spas, Mme. Pleyel is suffering from hepatitis. After dinner I went back to mother's and then with Felix to Hauser for coffee. We had a serious and amusing discussion, standing round his Streicher grand piano which I assume I shall ask him to lend me for my concert, even though Felix has offered me his piano. The latter took me to Dr Härtel's new villa in the country, situated near the Wall. It is quite a curiosity for Leipzig as the owner, an admirer of all things Italian, had it designed entirely in the Italian style. How beautiful, rich, and yet simple this villa has turned out to be, but I had better tell you about it in person rather than write about it. In the evening I was at Wieck's again until 9 o'clock in order to meet Schumann, a quiet but interesting young man. I asked Clara to play for me once more, which she did beautifully, as I said before. I then gave them a little taste of my improvisations.

Clara Wieck was 16 years old at that time, and had already made a name for herself on concert tours. Four years later she was to marry Robert Schumann, who had become one of her father's pupils in 1828, and had since been a regular visitor to their home. As he was prevented by some paralysis in his fingers from following his intended career as a concert pianist, he turned to composition as his main occupation, in addition to writing on musical matters and becoming the editor of 'Neue Zeitschrift für Musik'.

On October 3rd Moscheles wrote:
Yesterday evening I went to see my mother

again; she had just finished her prayers from the family bible which I remember so well. I kept her company for an hour and amused her with stories about our life. Then I went to Felix who has asked me to come to tea today and every day. His place has a very informal and friendly atmosphere reminiscent of my own bachelor days. In the middle of the room stands his Erard; in a bookcase he keeps his beautifully bound Handel editions, as well as a multitude of other scores; on a table stands his silver inkstand, a present from the Philharmonic Society, on the wall hang two delightful engravings, Titian's daughter and the portrait of Schätzel. The piano is also strewn with a profusion of scores and new publications – but everything looks clean and tidy. We drank tea and talked until Schrey, an advocate, (and one of the directors of the Gewandhaus) joined us. He is a music enthusiast and has a beautiful tenor voice; he sang some of Felix's new songs which are quite excellent. I hope to be able to bring you copies. I played my Concert fantastique and the pathétique, and was complimented on both. I then played the Ronda which Felix had dedicated to me. Together with him I played my Overture and his Octet; it went off without a hitch as you can imagine. – Soon it was 11 o'clock, and he lent me his overcoat so that I would not catch cold on my way home, after playing all those hot notes. He is a wonderful human being. Incidentally, Felix has agreed most willingly to my playing my latest duet with me at my concert, but he has to inform the board of directors of the Gewandhaus beforehand. Yesterday he expressed a wish to visit Mother and Regina. We went there, and they were delighted to see him and, of course, offered him some of the gateau they had brought from Prague. In their room there is a grand piano from Vienna, and at Mother's request I had to play something. Regina would have liked to hear Felix play, but he refused – his ultra-capricious humility would not let him. He did, however, promise to come again and play for them.

A little later:

Felix came to fetch me this morning for rehearsal. The marvellous way in which he conducts the orchestra, his manner of addressing its members, in short his entire demeanour makes one love and respect him. His Overture to 'Calm Sea and Prosperous Voyage', of whose glory the piano score does not give the least idea, as well as Beethoven's Symphony in B-flat major went off superbly. The rehearsal lasted until half past twelve. Afterwards I went to see Mother, as arranged, and found her in good spirits. Felix came to dine with me at the table d'hôte, as usual. After that we were invited to the Wiecks, together with Schumann, Banck, Hofrath, Wendt and others. Clara Wieck played Beethoven's great Trio exceptionally well, and then I played mine, accompanied by Gerke and Knecht, to the satisfaction of all present.

11 o'clock at night. It is necessary for me to write to you every day to tell you what has happened. That is why I choose this late hour, the only free time I have. Early in the morning I went to see Mother to take her some fresh pastries as I noticed that her landlord and his wife never offer her any for breakfast. Then Kistner and I made arrangements for my concert. My next engagement was to see Felix, with whom I tried out the 'Hommage à Handel' from the proof copy. We had to do this in rather a funny way. You see, he only has the Erard, but he remembered that he had heard the sound of a piano at various times coming from behind a door in his room. A more or less immovable wardrobe stands in front of this door which divided him from his neighbour, an elderly lady. He went to ask her permission to play

in her room which she granted with pleasure, while I played in his room. The door was opened but the wardrobe remained where it was; luckily the two instruments were in tune, and the whole thing was a great success. Kistner and Reichard, an organist, were present and seemed very impressed. We are now firmly decided to play this piece at my concert. Amongst the new things Felix showed me are two piano caprices and a fugue in F minor, all excellent in their way. For our midday meal we went to Hauser (the bass singer at the theatre and Felix's intimate friend); the after-dinner conversation was, once again, partly serious and partly amusing as we grouped around his Streicher, which he is lending me for my concert. From Hauser's beautiful collection, Felix played a concerto by J. S. Bach for me.

October 5th, 10.30 at night: I have just entered my room which I have not seen since this morning. It was impossible for me to have a piano installed in here on account of the great scarcity of good instruments in Leipzig! I received your letter this morning. Felix and I are very glad to hear that you have been playing his octet. He told me he felt embarrassed at not having written, and also to thank you and to place himself in black and white at your feet; in short, he talks just like his letters about this subject. First thing this morning I called on Mother and found her in excellent spirits, cheerful and contented.

October 6th: Between 12 noon and 1 o'clock, that pregnant hour when all social intercourse in Leipzig comes to a standstill so that the locals can indulge their stomachs, I have carried on writing these lines. I had intended to go through the piano score of Bach's Concerto for Three Pianos this afternoon, having just received it, but every piano warehouse I went to was shut. There was no time to go to Felix before dinner at 1 o'clock.

Five o'clock in the afternoon: I have just returned from Wieck's place where I had gone with Regina. Clara played a trio by Schubert very well indeed. Then she joined Felix and me in playing the Bach Concerto for Three Pianos; it was very interesting. I shall have it copied for London. Madame V. sang again, and Felix accompanied her in an aria from 'Macbeth' and the variations on 'nel cor'. Alas, she could only manage some pretty pathetic caterwauling! You should have seen poor Felix as he sat there surrounded by about 30 people, looking as though the world was about to end. There was a dangerous sparkle in his eyes, reminding me of a tiger about to pounce, and his cheeks burned enough to set a match alight. – At this moment I am supposed to sign my newly-printed concert tickets. I miss your helping hand, but every time I sign my name I can think of you, and that is a very pleasant feeling. Felix informed me today that the board of directors would like me to take part in the second subscription concert on Sunday. He advised me that instead of accepting the usual honorarium of 5 – 6 louis d'or, I should get them to agree to exempt me from paying for the hall, lighting etc., and I think he is right. As far as my departure is concerned, I am plagued by uncertainty. The express coach leaves either at 5 o'clock on the Monday morning or at 9 o'clock on the Tuesday evening; one of them is too soon after the concert and the other too late for my impatience.

October 9th: I am writing this letter one hour before my concert . . . Ticket sales are going very well; 750 have already been sold, and it looks as though some people will be disappointed at the box office.

October 10th: I wish I could give this letter a pair of wings so that it would bring you the news without delay that my concert in Leipzig yesterday was a brilliant success. The demand for tickets was overwhelming and the hall was crowded. My mother looked younger than ever. My overture was superbly played, and the Concert pathétique and Concert fantastique received rapturous applause. But above all, my duet with Felix caused a sensation: the applause went on and on, the audience wanted an encore; but the heat stopped us, and all we did was to step forward once more to take a bow. My fantasy on the theme of the aria from 'Titus', sung by Fräulein Gruber, and a chorus in D from 'Euryanthe', also seemed to give the audience a great deal of pleaure, as I was rewarded with loud applause. The gross takings were 497 Thaler. After deduction of expenses of 70 Thaler, there remains a profit of 427 Thaler. Any other expenses are paid for by my playing at the subscription concert.

In addition to the G minor Concerto which went extremely well at rehearsal today, my overture will also be repeated, as will the duet with Felix, for which we have received a special request. Felix behaves towards me with the same kindness and consideration that he has always shown, and with a rare modesty. He told me that before I came he had been pondering the question whether I should like to play a duet with him; he was on the point of writing to me about it. He is idolised here and seems to be on friendly terms with several musicians and local dignitaries, but is intimate with only a few and rather distant with many others. He behaves towards my mother with a very special kind of attentiveness. You are right when you say that being with him lifts up my spirits and gives me much pleasure.

Sunday morning, 7 o'clock: Together with Felix and Hauser, I was invited to dinner at – yesterday . . . I spent part of the evening with the family, and the remainder with Felix tête à tête. We drank tea and talked amicably for a while, and then he played some of his excellent fugues and songs without words for me (from the manuscript). Tomorrow morning my mother will be leaving; her departure will affect me a great deal, but I will try to be courageous!

The next letter came from Berlin and is dated October 14th:

I received your letter in Leipzig on Monday, and it made me very happy. What you wrote was balm for my soul after my parting with Mother who left on Monday morning. You have succeeded in convincing me that it was your desire that I should allow myself the pleasure of making the detour to Berlin. All my doubts on that score now having been laid to rest, Felix and I accompanied his sister here. On Monday we went to a soirée at Härtel's where we stayed until after midnight. First I played alone, and then together with Felix. Afterwards I started packing (without John) and finished at 1.30, and by 6 o'clock we were already seated in the coach. We had a very lively conversation all the way, and you were frequently the subject. Felix's sister is a very charming young lady. – Felix had sent a letter to his parents announcing our imminent arrival. But when we arrived there at half past one in the morning, we realised that the letter could not have arrived in time as the house lay in deathly silence. We were very careful not to awaken any of the family as the servants rushed to prepare our quarters. By then we were, of course, ravenously hungry and, not being able to lay our hands on anything to eat, we had to make do with the gateau from Prague which I was carrying in my luggage; it served us splendidly! The reunion this morning of parents and children was a family celebration, a truly blissful occasion which I witnessed with immense pleasure, heightened still further by the welcome I received, not merely as an onlooker, but one that would befit a son of the family. I am being urged by everyone to abandon my decision to continue my journey this evening. They say on no account must I leave Berlin before tomorrow evening. The many late nights I have had recently, the warm reception I have had here and, last but not least, your encouraging words will all probably make me change my mind in favour of tomorrow.

Felix Mendelssohn added his own plea:

If you have to be angry with somebody for having to do without Moscheles' company for one more day, then you must be angry with everyone at No. 3 Leipzigerstrasse; for they are all guilty: he wanted to depart in spite of his late arrival yesteray (or rather this morning) at half past one; so we went down on our knees to him, figuratively speaking, and the police would not give him a pass. Besides, you will have him again in Hamburg and Holland and London, while he and I must go our separate ways tomorrow and we won't be able to talk together for a very long time. In short, I joined wholeheartedly in the effort to persuade him, and I hope you will put yourself in my place, where I know you would have done the same. When you see him again he will convey my greetings to you, as well as those of the family. I must not miss the post, so farewell, and do not be angry with

Your devoted
Felix Mendelssohn-Bartholdy

Felix's father dictated these lines :
May I also send you my best regards and tell you of our great joy at having Felix's excellent friend staying with us, albeit for such a short time. We have to thank you for the pleasure of his company, which we owe to your persuasion. I trust that you, in your turn, will thank me for inducing Moscheles not to leave this evening in an ordinary carriage, after spending a night travelling, but instead to leave tomorrow night by the proper mail coach. Best wishes for your welfare – and please do not be angry.

During this short stay in Berlin, Moscheles was able to witness Felix's carefree exuberance and his intense happiness at being with his family. In a letter, written at bedtime, as usual, Moscheles wrote to his wife:
Today we indulged in a musical romp. First I played with Felix the Duet in D for two pianos by Mozart and my 'Hommage à Handel'. Then we abandoned ourselves to all manner of musical extravaganza; we extemporised, both together and then on separate pianos – a sort of conquest of each other's minds! I followed with Felix's Rondo brillant in E-flat and my Concert fantastique, with Felix playing the orchestral accompaniment. After that we took turns playing his 'Songs without Words', and we finished with a medley of musical jokes. I very much enjoyed listening to Fanny Hensel playing her compositions for me. Felix and I also spent a long time leafing through his collection of old music. In short, these hours will remain forever engrained on my memory, and it is only with reluctance that I leave my kind and attentive hosts to pay a visit here and there.

Very soon after his return to Hamburg, Moscheles set out on a concert tour of Holland and Belgium, this time accompanied by his wife and children. While on this tour, he experienced certain difficulties with poorly rehearsed orchestras:
The conductors are trying their best, and I myself hardly sit at the piano at all when I am playing a concerto; it is more probable that I can be found scurrying back and forth between the first violin and the timpanist whispering instructions into their ears. When even that fails to achieve the desired result, I may take the extreme measure of omitting a

difficult adagio and playing only the first and last movement. In Rotterdam, where I had to battle with an inferior instrument in addition to everything else, I improvised on the theme of Mozart's 'Ich kann nichts tun als Dich beklagen' (I cannot help but pity you), meaning myself, and would not allow myself to be lured into a second battle with that sticky keyboard, however much the audience tried to get me to do so.

In November 1835 Felix Mendelssohn's father died, plunging Felix into a state of deep melancholy. He withdrew completely from any social intercourse and communicated with no one, not even his friend Moscheles. At the beginning of 1836 Moscheles wrote in his diary:

Still our Felix remains silent. He has still not got over the pain of losing his father, or else he would surely write. What little news there is from him is not reassuring. He is said to have lost his best support; he also feels an indescribable emptiness and is unable to work. Something has to be done about this. I can understand his grief only too well, however, when I think back on those few autumn days I spent at his parents' house. Although frail and almost blind, the venerable old man had such an active mind and such clever judgement that, not only can I understand Felix's adoration of his father but, more than that, I can share it with him.

Just how deeply his loss was felt by the other members of the family becomes apparent in the following letters. The first is from Felix's mother:

Berlin, January 12th 1836

Amidst this great and wholly unexpected disaster that has befallen me, your compassionate heart, my beloved Madame Moscheles, will find solace in the knowledge that those two days when the excellent Herr Moscheles stayed with us last October must rank among the happiest, most enjoyable times that graced the twilight of my late husband's life. They left him with a feeling of profound satisfaction. When I look back, everything seemed set to fulfil every one of his expectations, and our circumstances were exactly as he had wished them to be. He was aware of this and deeply grateful. How noble and understanding he was, how kind and spiritual his nature; becoming even more perfect, more remarkable, more all-embracing as the days went by! How unforgettable the remarks with which he accompanied our reading session the evening before the parting (the profession de foi du vicaire savoyard', from Rousseau's Emile)! How friendly and serene our last evening together was, before he went to sleep – for ever! I never thought that death could come in this painless ethereal guise, and that is why I was unable to grasp the thought or the terrible inevitability of it all. Unaware of my misfortune, I was already irrevocably alone and miserable!

My children – all of them – have behaved like angels, and it would be ungrateful of me, despite the searing pain I feel, not to be deeply thankful for what I still possess. The way Felix bore his grief moved me greatly and made me anxious on his account at the beginning. In the company of us women he found tears, as well as the courage to carry on living. The fact that he now lives nearby is very reassuring – he has already visited us twice since then. . . . Please accept my warmest thanks, kindest Lady, for all the kindness you showed to the deceased when he was in London. He often spoke about it with deep emotion and appreciation. Lately, when he found himself unoccupied on account of his failing eyesight, he would say, more often than not, 'I am not bored; I have had so many wonderful and interesting experiences !' Amongst these, London took pride of place, and especially meeting you. But he also remembered the kindness he was shown by your excellent friends, and never ceased to be grateful for it. Please tell everyone how moved and grateful I am.

L. Mendelssohn-Bartholdy.

Next came a letter from Mendelssohn's eldest sister, Fanny Hensel:

. . . Do you remember, dear Herr Moscheles, Felix played the beautiful Adagio in F-sharp major from Haydn's Quartet on one of the evenings when you were staying with us in the autumn. Father loved Haydn above all others, and this particular piece was new to him and moved him strangely. He cried while listening to it and said afterwards that he found it immeasurably sad. This struck Felix as very odd, because the piece had 'mesto' written above, and to the rest of us it sounded cheerful enough. His verdict on music was at times remarkably clearsighted for one to whom the technical aspect was a closed book. You, dear Herr Moscheles, ranked very high in his estimation; he loved you dearly. As far as Felix is concerned, I am no longer worried about him; he is quite composed now, although still stricken with the sense of his grievous loss. This is a natural feeling however, and no longer of that painful nature which had filled us all with such concern for him and had doubled our suffering at the beginning. With the better weather approaching, and once he resumes his travelling, we trust that he will recapture the frame of mind at which he must aim if he wishes to go on living the way Father would have wished him to do – the way he did when Father was alive. There was a special understanding between the two of them that must be all too rare in this world. . . . And now I send you both my very best regards.

Fanny Hensel

MARIA MALIBRAN – 'UNTIL MY VOICE FAILS ME'

For the 1836 season, Maria Malibran, the great artist and prima donna, was engaged to sing at the Drury Lane Theatre. This brought her into very close contact with Moscheles at whose house she was a frequent visitor. From the following passages there emerges the picture of a woman which runs counter to everything one associates with the cliché of a prima donna. The first description was written by Charlotte.

Married to . . . de Bériot and mostly seen and heard in his company, she stood out because of her effervescent genius, here tireless energy and her cheerfulness and sense of humour. Unlike other great singers, she did not claim attention by virtue of her artistry, nor was it her gentle manner and conversational talents that attracted people to her, as was the case with other intellectually stimulating and charming women. Instead, she captured all one's senses at once, including one's heart and mind. Every time she appeared at Moscheles' house, she was the centre of attention. The children quite naturally looked upon her as one of their friends, for she had such marvellous ways of playing with their dolls' house, and besides, did any other visitor carry such an irresistible black silk pouch as Madame Milibran did? The purse did not contain the usual games or sweetmeats, but a paintbox, paper and brush. She would sit down on the carpet straight away, surrounded by the children; they would turn out the black silk pouch, look at everything, and then the painting would begin. It was all done with great enthusiasm, devotion, and energy.

On June 12th Moscheles wrote in his diary: *Early this Sunday morning I started setting Goethe's 'Meeresstille und glückliche Fahrt'*

(Calm Sea and Prosperous Voyage) to music, as a song for Malibran. . . . At 3 o'clock she arrived, along with Thalberg, Benedict and Klingemann. We dined early, and as soon as the meal was over, Mme Malibran sat down at the piano to sing for the children. They were songs from her father's* repertoire to which she added the missing guitar accompaniment by tapping rhythmically on the front panel of the piano. Next came some French and Italian romances that she had composed herself – all very attractive and executed with grace, charm and virtuosity. She was followed by Thalberg, who entertained us with all manner of musical jokes at the piano – Viennese songs and waltzes garnished with the obligatory tricks; then I came with my twisted hand and fisticuffs**, at which no one laughed more than Mme Malibran. At 5 o'clock we all set out for the Zoological Garden to mingle for an hour or so with the fashionable strollers whose Sunday promenade ground it is. When we had seen all we wanted to see of people and animals, we went for a walk in the park. But no sooner had we arrived back home than Mme Malibran sat down at the piano to sing for one whole hour. Finally, she called out to Thalberg: 'Venez jouer quelque chose, j'ai besoin de me reposer.' Not surprisingly her 'repos' consisted of painting an exquisite landscape in watercolours, something she has never studied. Meanwhile Thalberg played a number of his études, fragments of his recently composed Rondo, and then my études, Allegri di Bravura, G minor Concerto, all by heart, with consummate mastery. We then sat down to dinner, but even during the meal it was Mme Malibran who entertained us. She parodied with deadly accuracy Sir George

*the singer Manuel Garcia
**A trick Moscheles frequently used to amuse his guests: to play seemingly with a clenched fist, while in fact using his thumbs that were hidden from view to play thirds.

Smart, several singers – who had all been her fellow guests at the Duchess of C.'s soirée – and lastly the fat duchess herself as she spoke condescendingly with the artists. At the very end she sang 'Home, sweet home' in the manner of Lady ***, her voice quivering and infinitely nasal. All of a sudden, however, she put comedy to one side and started some serious singing. In the authentic German interpretation she sang scenes from 'Der Freischütz' in the original German, as well as a large number of songs by Mendelssohn, Schubert, Weber and myself. To end with, she chose 'Don Giovanni'. Not only does she know her own vocal part, that of Zerlina, but every other part in the opera and every note of the entire score, all by heart. And so she played and sang without a break until 11 o'clock, always in good voice and supremely in control, both mentally and physically. When she had left us, we talked in amazement about her musical and linguistic gifts and her obvious talent for painting, but most of all we admired her unassuming nature and feminine charm.

Another time, when she and de Bériot came for an early dinner with Moscheles and the children, he wrote afterwards:
We had enormous fun. The conversation turned to that well-known comical duet by Gnecco, which she and Lablache had sung together so many times. In it, a man and his wife mock each other's physical shortcomings; he sings: 'la tua bocca è fatta apposta pe'l servizio della posta' (your mouth is tailor-made to be a letter box). 'Just like my mouth', insisted Mme Malibran, 'and to prove it I shall put this orange inside!' Anyone who knows de Bériot can imagine his dismay, expressed in gesture and word, as she opened her mouth wide, showing her beautiful teeth, to shove in the orange, which was none too small, after which she burst out laughing, bubbling over with high spirits.

Moscheles composed a song for her by Klingemann, 'Steigt der Mond auf' (When the moon rises); and she would frequently ask him to play for her.

Often in those years, Moscheles would invite a large number of guests to his house to attend one of his musical soirées. He wrote about one such soirée in a letter.

Mme Malibran arrived around 11 o'clock, accompanied by de Bériot, after our 80 guests had already digested some English songs, solos by Lipinsky and Servais, and my Concerto fantastique. One could easily see how tired she was, and when she began to sing, her voice seemed unrecognisably feeble. We learned only later that a few hours before, during a ride in the park, she had fallen from her horse, and although uninjured, she had not yet got over the severe shock of the accident. But it was not long before she was her old self again, singing the 'Freischütz' aria in German, then a comical duet with John Parry in English, then Spanish, Italian and French songs; and as a finale she and de Bériot gave us the 'Cadence du Diable' in which she prefaced is spirited and often hair-raising passages on the violin with the words 'Voyez comme le diable prélude'. The proper title of this piece is 'Le songe de Tartini' (Devil's Trill Sonata), and as it tells the story of a maestro who has a dream in which the devil plays the violin for him, there is room for every kind of eccentricity. When my wife enquired gently whether Mme Malibran might not be overtaxing herself, the latter replied: 'Ma chère je chanterais pour vous jusqu'a l'extinction de la voix'.

A little later we read:

On July 16th, the day of her departure from London, we had agreed that we would call on her for an hour or so. She was sitting at the piano, with Costa by her side. She sang a funny song for us that she had just finished composing: a sick man, tired of life, implores

death to come to him. But when his wish becomes reality and death knocks at his door in the guise of a doctor, the patient turns him away in no uncertain terms. Mme Malibran had set this text to music so delightfully, and sang it with so much honour, that we were barely able to contain our laughter, eager as we were not to miss a single note. Then she wrote a charming French romance in my album, and sang it into the bargain, and my wife received a watercolour landscape that Mme Malibran had painted herself. The time had come to say goodbye.

Mme Malibran went first to Brussels, where she spent the next few weeks, and from there on to Manchester for the music festival. She sang there on September 20th, taking the audience by storm. She sang so beautifully that they urged her to encore after encore. The promise she had once made then became reality. Charlotte reported it thus:

Already tired to death and in urgent need of rest and respite, she gathered up her remaining strength to go on singing, even to produce one of her inimitable trills on a high C; then she collapsed and fainted. They carried her to her hotel and bled her, and she seemed to revive, only to depart this life for ever on the 23rd September.

Moscheles wrote:

It would be futile to try and pour out one's grief in a few inadequate phrases, when her loss has shaken the musical world to its very foundation and placed the saddest burden upon the circle of her friends. I for one felt impelled to express my sorrow in music, and so I composed a fantasy commemorating her death.

It was his opus 94, 'Hommage caractéristique à la mémoire de Mme Malibran de Bériot en forme de fantaisie'.

Maria Malibran's death, at the early age of 28, also found an echo in Germany a little later. In October, Felix Mendelssohn's mother wrote to Moscheles and his wife: *I feel deeply shocked and saddened by the death of Maria Malibran. Felix has always ranked her talent amongst the most outstanding of our time.*

The great artist had been scheduled to sing at the première of Mendelssohn's oratorio 'St. Paul' on October 3rd. The performance had to be postponed. It did take place some time later, however, and brought Mendelssohn one of his greatest triumphs. Moscheles, who did the corrections for the English edition, wrote in his diary:

I derive great pleasure from the fact that by working on the wonderful 'St. Paul', I have the chance to become quite engrossed in it. Its chief qualities are, in my view, its sublimity, noble simplicity, deep feeling and its antique form. In this work, Mendelssohn has given stunning proof of his acknowledged mastery.

During the first days of October 1836, Moscheles received the unexpected news of Mendelssohn's engagement. Four years previously he [Mendelssohn] had written to Charlotte:

Klingemann intends to remain a Knight of the Order of Bachelors, and I shall be keeping him company; and when in about thirty years from now the two of us want to get married, no girl will have us. You may burn this letter, but do remember my prophecy very carefully; in 30 years' time we shall see whether it has been a true one.

However, a letter from his mother arrived, telling quite a different story:

Berlin, October 6th 1836

Now that rumour travels faster than people, by railway and steamship, I may assume that the news of Felix's engagement has already reached you, dearest Madame Moscheles. Be that as it may, I cannot forego the pleasure of being the bearer of these glad tidings. As an affectionate mother yourself, you can imagine how I feel not knowing either his bride or any of her numerous family, nay more than that, not having heard her name mentioned before now. In addition to that, I shall have to wait a long while yet before I can meet this precious stranger, which is hard to bear for someone like me, who takes far too keen an interest in such matters for one so old! But you also know how unselfish the feelings of a mother are, and this will give you the true measure of the joy we all feel, especially since Felix seems so blissfully happy. There is, however, one bitter thought which keeps returning to me: if only his dear father had lived to partake of this happiness! He had wished for it with all his heart, but never expected his wish to come true. – Of course, the sad shock of his death may have been the prime cause of Felix's resolve. When he came to us last Christman he was unspeakably sad, so inwardly torn apart, so silent and, therefore, all the more dejected. He even experienced great difficulty in making plans for his art and was so lacking in purpose that his sisters pleaded with him to make a fresh start.

His mood of despair was finally conquered when he met a girl in Frankfurt; and now he is happily engaged to his Cécile. Her mother is Mme Jeanrenaud, whose parents' name is Souchays; they in turn are related to the Benekes.

May I ask you and your dear husband, and all Felix's friends in London for not having written for a long time; even I, as you will understand, have to do without his letters these days. Rebekka, who has just returned from a two-week stay with her brother on her way back from Eger, writes in his defence that his place is like a beehive. Please forgive him, and may I presume even further on your generosity by asking you, in his name and mine, to give the news of his engagement to his friends in London.

Ever your devoted friend,
L. Mendelssohn-Bartholdy.

The season of 1836 had other gratifying events in store for Moscheles, not least the successes of his former pupil Thalberg, now a master in his own right. Moscheles wrote about him in his diary:
I find it very clever the way he renders those harp-like effects on the piano. If, for instance, the middle part carries the main theme, he brings it out very clearly, while playing an accompaniment of intricate arpeggios, and it is those ones which remind me of the harp. The public is always impressed, while he sits there quite unperturbed, with lips tightly closed, his coat buttoned right up to the neck like a soldier, with an extremely military posture. This he learned, so he tells me, when he used to practise the piano smoking a Turkish pipe whose length made this upright position a necessity!

Another diversion was caused when H. Herz brought a piano on to the market with seven octaves. However, on account of its weak tone, it was not a great success. By contrast, Broadwood's first trials with their Bichorda baby grand pianos proved that even two-stringed instruments could produce a powerful tone. These baby grands soon became very popular, and Moscheles himself greatly enjoyed playing them.

RETURN TO THE SOURCES – BACH, SCARLATTI, BEETHOVEN (NINTH SYMPHONY)

While on holiday in Ramsgate on the southeast coast of England in the late summer of 1836, Moscheles wrote to a friend:
When my wife asks me why it is that I don't use all this peace and quiet to compose, I tell her that my conscience would not allow it.

After the stresses of London, my mind and fingers are paralysed, and the former can be healed only by the latter, that is to say I have an urge to play a lot of good, nay the best, music before I permit myself to have thoughts of my own, let alone write them down, because the result would be superficial and hackneyed; just as an exhausted body that has just survived a serious illness requires strong medicine before it is fit to resume its normal duties.

The medicine seems to have done the trick, for after his return to London in the autumn, Moscheles began work on his 'Charakteristische Etüden', which he described thus:
These are not intended for pupils; they contain difficulties which only a master of his craft can conquer. Thalberg, Liszt – they will all have their work cut out with them.

By the end of the year he had finished 'Juno', 'The Dream', 'Bacchanal' and 'Children's Fairy Tale'. He also wrote some contributions to musical journals which he had been requested to do. He wrote on this subject in his diary:
Manual skill finds its outlets in Thalberg's new compositions. For the mind I have Schumann. His romanticism is so different from all that has gone before, his inventiveness is so great that I feel it necessary to immerse myself ever more deeply in his works in order to be able to arrive at a proper assessment of the qualities and weaknesses of this new school. He has just sent me his newly published sonata 'Florestan and Eusebius' with the flattering remark that no one but myself could do it justice in a review, and would I please do one for the new 'Zeitschrift der Musik', published in Leipzig.

This he did, and Schumann later included the review in his 'Gesammelte Schriften' (Collected Writings). At that time, Moscheles and Schumann were keeping up a lively correspondence. Schumann dedicated his 'Konzert ohne Orchester' (Concerto without orchestra) to Moscheles, and the latter, in his turn, sent Schumann the Fugue in E-flat contained in his 'Charakteristische Etüden'. During the same period, the publishing house of Cramer commissioned Moscheles to prepare the English edition of Beethoven's piano works. This assignment was to occupy Moscheles for over two years.

In the course of the winter of 1837, Moscheles gave three soirées for early piano works. Amongst others, he played pieces by Scarlatti and his contemporaries on a harpsichord (spinet) built in 1771 by Broadwood. In its outward appearance, the instrument resembled an old Viennese grand piano; when it was played with the lid open, one could see that at the touch of the pedal a kind of louvred arrangement of slats (similar to a Venetian blind) would open, giving the rather thin and not very pleasant tone of the instrument more fullness and warmth, in other words a more muted sound. Moscheles had studied this effect very carefully and was able to make full use of it. The two manuals of this instrument undoubtedly served the purpose of enabling the pianist to play those passages by Scarlatti and other masters which, on a modern grand piano, could be achieved only by crossing hands. By playing alternately on the upper and lower manual, one two-stringed and the other three-stringed, certain nuances of tone could be produced that were not otherwise possible.

Johann Sebastian Bach's Concerto in D minor with Quartet accompaniment received its first performance by Moscheles. Everyone agreed that true musical appreciation could only be enhanced by closer acquaintance with works of this nature. The newspapers expressed the hope that the 'crowded rooms' of these soirées would persuade Moscheles to repeat them the following winter and, if possible, to include even older composers in his programme.

But the diary and letters of that winter also reveal how assiduously Moscheles, in his capacity as co-director of the Philharmonic Society, tried to organize another performance of Beethoven's Ninth Symphony, which had been rejected by the critics in 1824 and dismissed as impossible. In the face of strong opposition on the part of his colleagues, the decision was taken at last to put him in charge of this venture. No one believed that it would be a success. There were many weeks of hard work ahead of him. Instead of one orchestral rehearsal, they granted him two, and that was all. So he decided to rehearse the finer points with every single player in turn. Both singers and instrumentalists knew their parts; even before the first orchestral rehearsal, Moscheles had gone through their parts with them and explained to them all the details of this gigantic work. He then used the second rehearsal to touch up some of the nuances and more subtle distinctions. Although a lot was still missing, and the soloists were not quite up to their task, the performance turned out to be a brilliant success.

Moscheles wrote about it to his relatives: *You can imagine my excitement, both before and during the concert on April 17th – not to mention the work that had gone into it beforehand, and you can see from the enclosed article in the 'Atlas' how worthwhile it has all been. I am sending this particular one because it is short and concise and touches on the main points; I don't know who the critic is. As for the other papers, they are unanimous in their praise, and all demand that this gigantic work should remain in the repertoire, and that it should be performed at the larger venues, such as Exeter Hall and the Birmingham Music Festival. In short, prosperous England has enriched herself by one more treasure, and I am so pleased that it was left to me to unearth it.*

It is significant that the article referred to above made the point that conductors who do not understand a work cannot possibly perform it successfully, and that musicians who are not themselves overwhelmed by its beauty can only succeed in producing insufferable boredom in the listener. Thus Beethoven's honour was restored and he was cleared of the blame for the earlier failures.

In the course of the following season, Moscheles conducted the 9th Symphony three more times. In a letter dated 1838, he made some rather interesting remarks regarding the score of this work which he had been using. The letter refers to a small volume on Beethoven by Ries and Wegeler, published shortly before by Bädeker of Koblenz:

It gives a very good insight into Beethoven's life and work, and I believe everything in it is quite authentic. It is a pity, though, that his last letters have not been included. It closes with the letters to Ries, which is when my correspondence with Beethoven started. I must also draw your attention to page 50, where Beethoven is reported to have said that he had also sent him the manuscript. All I can say is that I have conducted all three performances of the Ninth Symphony this year from a score corrected in Beethoven's own hand, and the title inscribed by himself. It reads: 'Ninth Symphony, composed for the Philharmonic Society of London by Beethoven'.

The appearance of Chopin in London in the winter of 1837 was like distant sheet lightning on the musical horizon.

Chopin, who has spent a few days in London, was the only foreign artist who neither paid visits himself nor encouraged anyone to visit him, as his bad chest would only be made worse by conversation. He went to a few concerts and then promptly disappeared.

Moscheles' tendency to return to the sources of contemporary music, which had become increasingly noticeable of late, found expression in his active participation in the Ancient Concerts. This concert series owed its inception in 1776 to the Earl of Sandwich, whose aim was to bring to the British public old and even very old music, regardless of whether it came from England, Italy, Germany or France. He also promoted the use of period instruments which had been housed for many years in antique showrooms. Thus the viola da gamba and the viola d'amore were heard once again.

The summer holidays, nine weeks in all, were again spent with Charlotte's relations, this time at Flottbeck, one of the beauty spots on the River Elbe. It was there that Moscheles composed two more of his twelve great études which were to be published the following winter.

Meanwhile negotiations were continuing with the house of Cramer on the English edition of Beethoven's works. Cramer also agreed to grant Moscheles a 20 per cent share in the profit on his new compositions, which he preferred to an honorarium.

The autumn was devoted mainly to the preparations for the forthcoming soirées for historical piano music which Moscheles had been invited to repeat again during the winter. Week after week he played through the old pieces and, in view of the wealth of material, the process of selection was a difficult one. On January 1st he wrote in his diary:

My fingers are in good shape, and I have decided on the programmes for the forthcoming soirées. As before, I have been digging amongst the buried treasures of musical Pompeii and have unearthed some rare beauties. Beethoven is great; indeed, who could be greater than he? But since the public is used to little else but his music, with modern bravura pieces for the rest, I have decided to introduce the public first to those composers from whose shoulders Beethoven launched himself on his eagle's flight. The background to his art must not be forgotten if one is to pay homage to his music now. But having begun with the old masters, I wish to take the listeners gradually into the present, so that they may draw comparisons and make up their own minds.

The concerts were a great success with the public, and the papers reflected the general reaction. Charlotte wrote the following account:

The tone at these soirées was set by the Duke of Cambridge. He wanted to hear everything twice over. . . . He is extremely kind to Moscheles and asks after each soirée, 'Pray, when is the next?'

At about this time the death occurred of Ferdinand Ries, and in his honour the annual Philharmonic Concerts started with a funeral march.

LONDON POTPOURRI – JOHANN STRAUSS, CORONATION CELEBRATIONS, LOUIS NAPOLEON

The year 1838 brought a number of musicians into the Moscheles household, and among them was Johann Strauss, whom Charlotte described thus in a letter:

Everybody dances, in fact everybody feels compelled to dance whenever he plays. In the concerts which he gives with his small orchestra, people even find themselves dancing in their seats. He has played at Almacks, the most fashionable of all the society subscription balls and he had all the aristocracy skipping around to his melodies. We, too, were fortunate enough to be able to dance to

this same music at a soirée we attended, and all the married couples present felt decidedly rejuvenated by the experience. What is more, Strauss himself dances 'corps et âme' while he plays; not with his feet, however, but with his violin, which keeps bobbing up and down. Meanwhile, his whole body marks every beat of the fine music, thus showing that he is a true, easy-going Viennese at heart; not possessed of the poise and manners of a worldly-wise traveller but, instead he is amusing and always cheerful. So much the better, as there are more than enough miserable people in the world.

However, the outstanding event of that season was the coronation of Queen Victoria.

Sir George Smart found a cassock and surplice to fit Moscheles and allowed him to sing bass in the Westminster Abbey choir, so that he could observe the marvellous spectacle at first hand without having to pay the exorbitantly high fee demanded for entry into the Abbey. Moscheles recorded the event in his diary:

What a spectacular sight! This festively adorned temple filled with row upon row of festively adorned ladies in their finest attire. And what a fine impression the eighteen-year-old queen made as she entered in her regalia, surrounded by the dignitaries of her realm. Everything was impressive and thoroughly moving. However, the most impressive thing of all was the Handel Coronation Anthem 'Zadok the Priest', with its closing 'Hallelujah' passages. It was absolutely breathtaking, as indeed was the moment when His Grace The Archbishop of York placed the crown on the maiden queen's head.

Charlotte, who had viewed the festivities from a balcony, wrote her own account:

Shortly after nine o'clock, the city started to bustle with activity. Everybody was out on the streets; devoted mothers with babes in their arms, fathers supporting sons on their shoulders, and older boys who had climbed on to lampposts, railings and posts in order to get a better view. There was absolute chaos, the like of which you could hardly imagine. Finally, though, the hour drew nigh when the Coronation procession would leave St James's Palace, from whence it was to drive up Piccadilly. An orderly line of people was formed at last; but do you know how? Two horseguards rode at walking pace through the throng , which forced the people to withdraw. This operation was repeated until the width of the street had been cleared for the procession. The newspapers will obviously give you a better account, but I must tell you that the golden coach of state, drawn by eight Isabella horses, looked resplendent with its mediaeval-style adornment, and the Queen, a girl of merely eighteen years, was a picture to behold. It must be said, though, that her senior lady-in-waiting, the Duchess of Sutherland, who sat opposite her in the coach, is a veritable beauty indeed.

In his compositions at this time, Moscheles was striving more and more to get away from the old style virtuoso pieces. He described his own works, such as the 'Alexander Variations', as being 'lost and gone for ever', and he sought to achieve a more classical approach in his writing. In the autumn of 1838, he composed the Pastoral Concerto and wrote the following in his diary:
I play the latest works of all four of today's heroes, Thalberg, Chopin, Henselt and Liszt, and find that their chief attraction lies in those passages requiring a wide spread of the hands, this being made easier for the composers themselves because of the shape and size of their hands. I am not so enamoured of the pieces myself, having been brought up on what I deem to be less pretentious music. Notwithstanding my great admiration for

Beethoven, I am unable to neglect Mozart, Cramer and Hummel. Did they not write noble pieces in their day as well, those very same pieces on which I was weaned? The new style is certainly finding increasing favour now, and I am attempting to find a compromise between the two schools. I am, however, not afraid to spurn these new effects in favour of the best of the tried and tested traditional methods. The Pastoral Concerto, which I am currently writing, consists of the shorter, modern form with three connecting movements, and it is livelier and even lighter than my previous concertos. It is my aim to try and avoid plagiarising ideas from the works I have written up until now.

Moscheles played the Pastoral Concerto for the first time to his friends at a Mendelssohn evening, which he described in his diary:
My friends enjoyed the work, but now and again I have doubts about it myself. It has crossed my mind that the music I am now writing, according to fixed principles, somehow lacks the lightness and freshness which characterised my early works and made them popular with the public. Nevertheless, I am pleased to show the musical world that I am making more serious and more profound efforts with my work, even though my current successes fail to meet the standard I myself wish to achieve.

The winter of 1838 to 1839 saw the composition of the Etudes in A, written in 6/8 time, as well as the song 'Liebesfrühling' (Spring of Love). In addition to these Moscheles worked on the complete edition of Beethoven's works. He also played the master's Op. 102 piano sonata, but noted the following reservation: *I cannot find myself entirely in agreement with the very scholarly fugue in this piece; I must say I consider Beethoven's genius to be of greater worth than his scholarliness.*

At the same time Moscheles undertook the corrections of Mendelssohn's Andante and Presto in B-major and B-minor, as well as those of Liszt's nine Etudes.

On account of vast differences of opinion with his colleagues on the board of directors of the Philharmonic Society, Moscheles decided not to seek re-election to the committee for 1839.

A sad happening in Germany then presented Moscheles with an unexpected offer. J. H. Hummel had died in 1837 and Moscheles was asked whether he would be willing to fill the now vacant post of Kapellmeister in Weimar. Charlotte wrote this account of his decision:

He hesitated for a moment and then decided that he preferred the freedom of his position in London to the tight rein which would be imposed on him by working for a Court and a theatre. He did add, however, that he would remain their devoted servant and was convinced that they wanted only the best for him.

The Moscheles family spent the beginning of 1839 at a country house in Hampshire owned by their friends the Flemings. Everyone was in high spirits and the clement weather enabled them to undertake various excursions and to go out riding in the surrounding countryside. When the weather was bad, they stayed indoors and danced or played charades. Whatever the weather though, there was a great deal of music-making.

When Moscheles gave his annual concert many prominent figures attended, including Napoleon's nephew, Prince Louis Napoleon, son of King Louis of Holland and Queen Hortense. Thirteen years later, after several attempted coups and a bloody takeover, he was to be instated as Napoleon III, the Emperor over all France. Moscheles met him after the concert and found him to be a 'civil

and fine young man'. A year later, following his abortive landing at Boulogne, he wrote that one would never have deemed him capable of such political scheming.

The Prince courteously mentioned to Moscheles how much his mother, Queen Hortense, had enjoyed Moscheles' playing on a previous occasion. The Prince himself had been a boy at the time and the occasion had left a lasting impression with him. In a letter Charlotte disclosed her own opinion about the Prince: *When he attends soirées and stands quietly in the corner, he gives the impression of wishing to be merely a passive observer, rather than someone who would plot against his own country.*

At this time Thalberg was becoming increasingly famous and popular. Moscheles had this to say about him in a letter written in the early part of 1839:

Thalberg continues to amaze me in his concerts. He is a veritable Jupiter when it comes to power and bravura in his playing, and the techniques employed in his latest Etudes are of herculean proportions. I correspond frequently with Mendelssohn on all the latest musical matters, and he shares my opinion on this.

One of the main talking points of the summer of 1839 was that Moscheles – who was 45 at the time – had expressed the desire to retire from performing in public. His audiences had not cast any disapproving looks in his direction, nor, indeed, had he given any disastrous performances. However, as he wrote in his diary:

How pleasant it is to be able to retire, basking in the admiration of the public, fully aware of one's powers, and in a position to make way for others. In so doing, one avoids those all too often heard comments that this person or that still plays beautifully, even though he is not what he was ten years ago, that he has become complacent in his playing or that he complacent in his playing or that he has lost the wealth of imagination that he once enjoyed in his improvisations etc.

I am thinking in particular of Clementi who bequeathed an immortal treasure both to his art and to his disciples, but who gave up playing while the up and coming generation of pianists flourished by using the same methods as he had done, altering them slightly and, thereby, establishing a new school. The disciples of this school, while supposedly taking its guidelines as their basis, actually despise them on principle, and their strength is derived only from the enormous power of their hands. While enthusing in their unbelievably sickly manner, they seek their most piquant effects by the swiftest alternation between the sustaining pedal and the soft pedal, or in the use of rhythms and modulations which, although not entirely frowned upon, were previously permitted only in the rarest of cases. It goes without saying that I have not joined these innovators; I do not like much of what they do, and I would be unable to emulate the power they employ in their playing. Moreover, I still feel very much at home with my own school of playing and neither too old, nor unnerved by these new developments. In my school, use of power such as this was quite unheard of. The less interest the world takes in my performances in the future, the greater I shall feel the desire and need to devote myself to my compositions in accorance with my own wishes and convictions. How and what I shall compose henceforth is still concealed by the mists of the future. Up until now I have always introduced my new works to the public by performing them myself. Will the musical world still show the same enthusiasm if this is no longer the case? Nous verrons.

PARIS – 'LA SONATE' MOSCHELES-CHOPIN

After spending a few weeks of the summer of 1839 at the French resort of Boulogne, Moscheles arrived in Paris at the beginning of September. For the first time on a visit to the French capital, he did not have the burden of having to give public concerts, and, therefore, none of the various obligations which these entailed. During his stay, one of his long cherished wishes was fulfilled – he was finally able to meet Chopin, an encounter which prompted the following letter:

We are enjoying our freedom and independence to the full, the most enjoyable aspect for me being the temporary cessation of my teaching. When I am at Leo's, I enjoy making music most of all, and it was there, in fact, that I first made the acquaintance of Chopin, who had just returned from the country. I could hardly wait for our meeting. His appearance matches his music perfectly, both being tender and passionate. At my request he played for me, and it is only after hearing him play that I am now able to understand his music. I was also able to grasp why he has such an enthusiastic following among the ladies. The ad libitum passages adjoining his works, which become mere displays of tactlessness when attempted by other interpreters of his music, are the essence of charming originality in his own performances. His hard modulations, which I cannot get over when I play his pieces, are a sign of his dilettantism, and no longer shock me, after having seen his elfin fingers gliding over the keyboard to execute them with such skill. His piano is tuned in such a way that he does not need to play with much forte in order to produce the contrasts he desires. Thus one does not miss the orchestra-like effects which the German school demands of its pianists, but instead one is enraptured by the playing, as if it were a singer who does not worry about his accompaniment, but follows his own intuition and feelings completely. Suffice it to say, he is unique among pianists. Moreover, he professes to have a great admiration for my compositions and even if this is not the truth, he does have a thorough knowledge of them. He played me some Etudes he had written, as well as his latest work 'Preludes', and I returned the compliment by performing a number of my own pieces for him.

Who would have believed that Chopin also possessed a talent for amusement? However, among repeated entries describing his playing in Parisian artistic and dilettante circles, we also find the following accounts: *Chopin was in a lively and amusing mood today when he performed his imitations of Pixis, Liszt and a hunchbacked piano enthusiast whom he knew. All were hilarious.* And a few days later. . . . *Chopin once again appeared as a quite different person from what he had been the last time we met.*

Moscheles and Chopin were often to be heard together at the Parisian society soirées. The E major sonata for piano duet by Moscheles, performed together by the two master exponents, became so successful that they had to give a repeat performance at almost all the functions they attended. As a result of their frequent renditions of the work, they finally earned themselves the nickname of 'La sonate'.

After some time, as the diary reports, the French Court decided that it would like to hear them both play together:
Today I received a note from Count Perthuis, King Louis Philippe's Adjudant. He had heard Chopin and I performing my E major sonata on a number of occasions, and must have praised it highly to the Court, for it now desired to share the same thoroughly pleasurable experience which he himself had recently enjoyed.

Chopin and Moscheles were thus summoned to St-Cloud on October 29th, and we find the following account in the diary:

Yesterday was a remarkable day indeed. Kalkbrenner came round to shake hands and make his peace with me. He had previously arranged for an intermediary to ask me whether I would be willing to accept this gesture of reconciliation, and my answer had been in the affirmative. He embraced me and indeed embarrassed me by his show of love and admiration for me – all in earnest, I might add. When I told him that I would be playing on one of his instruments again, my presence having been requested at St-Cloud, he jumped up out of his seat, quite startled, and said that there was not a moment to lose. He would have to check whether the instrument was in good working order. He also told me that the Duchess of Orleans was well versed in good music, having received tuition in playing and composition from him. At nine o'clock Chopin and I were collected by P. and his charming wife, and we drove out together in the torrential rain. We all began to feel decidedly cosy as we saw the bright lights of the castle shimmering in the distance. On arrival, we passed through several magnificent chambers before reaching a square salon where the royal family had gathered en petit comité. The Queen sat at a round table with an elegant work basket in front of her (was she perhaps embroidering a purse for me?). Next to her sat Madame Adelaide, the Duchess of Orleans and their ladies-in-waiting. These distinguished ladies were all extremely affable, as though we were old friends. The Queen and Madame Adelaide both wished to express their gratitude for the pleasure I had given them with my playing in the Tuileries, after which the King came up to me to express the same sentiment. He said that he thought the concert must have been 15 or 16 years previously, and I confirmed this. I also noticed the poor Count of Armois who was present as well. The Queen then enquired whether the instru-

ment, a Pleyel, was situated where he wished it to be, whether we would require any special lighting, and whether the seats were at the correct height, all manner of meticulous details in fact, such as befitted this Queen of the people. First of all, Chopin played a collection of Nocturnes and Etudes, making him the much adored and mollycoddled darling of the Court. After I had played a selection of old and new Etudes, and had received the same enthusiastic applause, we both sat at the instrument again with Chopin playing at the lower end, something he always insists on. The feeling of tense expectancy among those in the room was broken only by cries of 'divin, délicieus'. At the end of the Andante, the Queen whispered to one of her ladies-in-waiting: 'Ne serait-il pas indiscret de leur redemander?' (Would it be too indiscreet to ask them to play it again?), which was, of course, tantamount to ordering it to be played again. We did so, but this time with even greater abandon, and in the Finale we were both taken over by a musical delirium.

The enthusiasm which Chopin exuded must have been thoroughly infectious for our audience, who proceeded to heap praise on both of us. Chopin then played on his own again with the same charm and compassion as before, and I followed him by playing an improvisation on some well-loved pieces by Mozart, which finished in a flourish of energy and power on my part with the 'Magic Flute' Overture. The King listened attentively throughout the evening, which was far more rewarding for us that any royal words of praise which performers like us hear so often. Chopin and I celebrated our mutual triumph like true brothers; each of us had been able to demonstrate his individual talent, but there had been absolutely no sign of either one trying to outdo the other. We were finally able to partake of the refresh-

ments graciously offered to us, after which we took our leave from the castle at 11.30 pm. This time, however, we were showered only with compliments, as the earlier rain storm had made way for a beautifully clear night.

Shortly after this, Moscheles was approached in confidence and asked whether the King could reward him with the légion d'honneur, or another similar award, as a token of appreciation for his playing. Instead, Moscheles opted for something different from this frequently presented order and received an expensive travel case with an inscribed dedication from the King.

During his visit, Moscheles also met some of the other musicians working in Paris at the time, such as Hector Berlioz, Auber and Cherubini. He penned the following accounts in his diary:
I have now come to the end of my great tour of artists, and am left with the most varied impressions. Berlioz, whom I had eagerly wanted to meet, proved to be cold and indifferent. On his table lay his elegantly handwritten score of Romeo and Juliet. I leafed through it but it is so complicated and the noise, which I could hear just by looking at it, is so overpowering that I find myself unable to pass further judgement. However, one thing is certain, there are bound to be some new effects in the work. When I called on Auber he greeted me in a most friendly manner, and I was extremely interested to be able to have a look at the square piano on which he has composed his operas. I also had to try out his Erard grand piano, and I was even requested to play for him and for Zimmermann, a professor at the Conservatory who had joined us. Cherubini, who was usually not the most affable of men, turned out to be exceptionally friendly, and we remained engrossed in discussions about the arts for a good hour. He informed me that he had

nothing more to do with music, apart from his position as Director of the Conservatory; he no longer wrote a note and was unable to tolerate or enjoy musical impressions. I believe that I could have assured him without flattering him that he was one of the very few who had achieved immortality in his own lifetime.

Moscheles also renewed a number of old acquaintanceships while in Paris. There was Meyerbeer, his artistic companion from his days in Vienna, who said of Moscheles that he was the only one who could play Beethoven perfectly. He also saw Peter Pixis, 'the same trusty friend as ever', and Heine, the 'génie par excellence'. His stay in the French capital was, however, tinged with sadness:
Alas, I was only able to see poor Lafont lying in his coffin at the funeral service which was held for him in the Church of St Roch. The music was by Cherubini, but with no organ accompaniment, which I felt left a gap in the ceremony. Just as Lafont had joined me on my travels in earlier years, so he had wished to do the same thing with Herz. Unfortunately though, the coach collapsed and the unlucky Lafont, who had been perched high up on the roof, was killed by the sudden fall.

Thalberg was in Paris at the time as well, and Moscheles wrote the following comment about him:
After giving a number of concerts to overfull houses, he is receiving just as much criticism as he is acclaim. However, when one of the critics goes so far as to compare him with Van Amburgh the lion tamer, as was recently the case, it does at least give him something to laugh at.

Moscheles' eventful stay in Paris was prolonged until well into November. Following his return to the London smog, he worked on the 'Méthode des méthodes', which he wanted to publish with Fetis, as well as writing the songs 'Mit Gott' (With God) and 'Liebeslauschen' (Eavesdropping on Love). Mendelssohn also sent Moscheles one of his own songs with an old German text: 'Es ist in den Wald gesungen'.

At this time Moscheles was asked by one of his pupils whether it was beneficial to continue piano tuition with a teacher, once a certain level had been reached in the instruction. Moscheles replied thus:
Anyone who has heard and studied good music in abundance should not require a teacher to spur him on to greater things. He should press on boldly, bearing in mind all that his mentor has told him, striving to achieve the very best. He should be accompanied in his playing whenever possible, and should become acquainted with more and more of the great masterpieces, attempting earnestly to penetrate their hidden beauties. In so doing, the technique he has previously acquired will go far beyond the usual dilettantism of so many pianists.

WITHDRAWAL FROM PUBLIC CONCERTS – LISZT IN LONDON

From 1840 onwards, the general public was to hear Moscheles playing on rare occasions only, although he did continue to play for various admirers in private. By withdrawing from public concerts he was turning the remarks he had made in the summer of 1839 about retiring into reality: *. . . basking in the admiration of the public, fully aware of one's powers, and in a position to make way for others.* One of those for whom he did make way was Thalberg, once one of his own pupils. He comments on this in the following letter, dated January 8th 1840, which he wrote to friends in Vienna:
Thalberg is using all his youthful power and talent to earn himself both laurels and guineas while he is in Britain. I see a great deal of

him whenever he is in London, but he has just recently given his farewell concert before departing for Scotland.

Among others for whom Moscheles had made way was the 29-year-old Franz Liszt, who had likewise made his way to London for the concert season. Although it would be all too tempting to connect Liszt's arrival with Moscheles' retirement, and to look for a rivalry between the older maestro and his youthful counterpart (which many a malicious tongue did, and has continued to do over the years), contemporary accounts of Moscheles' father-in-law, Alfred Embden, who was staying in London at the time, wrote the following letter on the subject:

Liszt is often a welcome guest at the house, and we never cease to be amazed at his exceptional playing. You know already that Moscheles likes to treat everyone with due respect and fairness. Well, Liszt is no exception, even though many would deem him a redoubtable rival for Moscheles. This is, however, not the case at all – they are, and will continue to be, artistic brothers, despite the fact that they are now pursuing different paths.

Liszt's presence in London did prove to be a thorn in Thalberg's flesh, however. Moscheles remarked upon this in his diary:

Thalberg is back in London, but he intends to move on to Paris and thence to America. The fierce competition with Liszt is becoming too much for him and, as a result, it seems that he will be avoiding London in the future.

Unlike the up and coming pianists who were struggling to establish themselves, Moscheles could afford to marvel at Liszt's performances quite openly. At one of the Philharmonic Concerts Liszt played three Etudes by Moscheles, and the latter wrote the following words of praise in his diary:

Truly magnificent. His technique was faultless, but his genius absolutely transformed the pieces, so much so that they have now become his Etudes rather than mine. Nevertheless, I enjoyed them thoroughly and would not have him play them in any other way. His Paganini Etudes, which I had heard previously at a Sunday matinée concert, were also of immense interest to me, and the technique surpassed anything I had ever heard. Not only is he able to do anything he wishes, but he also brings it off so splendidly. Moreover, it is only rarely, remarkably rarely in fact, that his hands, which he throws high into the air when he is playing, land on a wrong note.

On another occasion, Moscheles called him *a rare artistic phenomenon, a vital link in the chain of artistic development.*

Liszt also returned to London for the following season in 1841. He played a great deal and was rewarded with tumultuous applause. However, he failed to take Britain by storm in the same way as he had France and Germany beforehand. When he gave his first performance at the Philharmonic Concerts, Moscheles was also present. The audience awaited this performer, whose reputation promised so much, with great anticipation, and when he finally took the stage to play the Septet by Hummel, everyone was expecting something tremendous. But, as the diary reports, all they heard was:

. . . the well-known piece played with consummate mastery and the occasional moment which would have taken even the heavens by storm. By and large though, he played without extravagance but with outstanding execution nonetheless, for it is there that Liszt's great intellect and genius lie; he knows precisely where, for whom, and what he is playing, and how to use his skills, which allow him to do anything he chooses, to produce the most varied effects.

In that same year, Liszt contemplated the idea of accepting a professorship at the Conservatory in Brussels and, while pondering over his decision, he undertook a tour of England – accompanied by the music publisher Lavenu – with the hope that his name alone would be sufficient to fill the concert halls. It was not a successful venture, however, and Lavenu had to return to London with an empty cash box. In spite of this though, Liszt made an extremely magnanimous gesture and waived his entire fees for the tour. Moscheles recalled the incident in his diary: *He told me the story as if the whole thing were a joke and called him [Lavenu] a 'pauvre diable'.*

In the series of concerts that Liszt gave in London, he played many of his most brilliant and outrageously difficult works. Occasionally he and Moscheles could be heard playing the Preciosa Variations together. Moscheles said afterwards: *It felt as though we were both sitting on Pegasus together.* And when he showed Liszt his recently completed F-major and D-minor Etudes, which he had written for Mechetti's Beethoven Album, Liszt played them superbly at sight, in spite of the enormous difficulties they presented. He called on the Moscheles on many occasions, sometimes without invitation, but his visits were always interesting, thanks to his exceptional skill as a musician and his intellectually stimulating and often exuberant conversation.

On one occasion he recalled the time when he had played together with old Cramer, in whose company he had toured the English provinces the previous year: *'J'ai joué un duo avec Cramer, j'étais le champignon empoisonné et j'avais à côté de moi mon antidote, le lait.' (I played a duet with Cramer; I was the poisoned mushroom and next to me I had my antidote, milk.)*

They often enjoyed a laugh together, but there were also some serious discussions. As a result of one such discussion about educa-

tion for women, Liszt presented Charlotte with a book written by Mme Necker de Saussure, claiming that it was an excellent work and that it would dispel any doubts she may have on the subject.

When Liszt left England, he gave Moscheles a walking stick with a marvellous gold tip. The two of them were to meet again frequently over the next two decades, and during that time they remained the closest of friends.

In spite of ceasing his concert performances, Moscheles was still kept extremely busy. He had a large number of pupils, and these took up the lion's share of his time. The remainder of his time was spent fostering the varied musical contacts he had made over the years, both with artist friends as well as with visitors from abroad. He also gave private performances of old and new compositions, and was involved in a variety of editing work.

In 1840, Moscheles had been appointed as H.R.H. Prince Albert's official pianist. Unfortunately though, much as he would have enjoyed the opportunity of meeting this highly musical Prince to perform and discuss music with him, Moscheles was never once summoned to play for him. It was well known that the Prince both played and composed, but Moscheles neither taught him nor advised him in either activity.

TRAVELS WITH MENDELSSOHN

On September 18th 1840, Mendelssohn returned to England. Among other things, he had come to direct his new work 'Lobgesang' (Hymn of Praise), which had been rehearsed by Moscheles in the Hanover Square Rooms prior to his arrival.

On September 20th, Moscheles and Mendelssohn set off for Birmingham, where Mendelssohn heralded his arrival with a magnificent organ recital. This was followed later on by the first British performance of the 'Lobgesang'. While in Birmingham, Moscheles wrote this letter to Charlotte:

When you read these lines you may take new courage when you embark on your journey to Birmingham, as my own journey which passed so pleasantly is a sure sign for me that yours will be just as enjoyable. We travelled remarkably quickly and arrived in just four and a half hours. My discussions with Mendelssohn en route were always lively and interesting. You were often the subject of the conversation, and we thought of you a great deal. Upon arrival, I put up immediately at the very pleasant Stork Hotel and subsequently dined with Mendelssohn and Ayrton at Moore's residence (he is one of the Festival Committee), where Mendelssohn is staying. I wrote the first part of the letter in his bedroom, from where we were summoned to dinner. And now, instead of taking my siesta, I am continuing the letter to tell you that there will be a rehearsal for the choir this evening. Before that, however, I am going with Mendelssohn to the concert hall, where he wishes to play the organ. I shall be at the station to meet you when you arrive. . . .

Mendelssohn added the following message to the letter:

Will you permit me to pen my greetings to you, and to tell you in Moscheles' letter how very kind, friendly and generous he was to me on the journey here, and how quickly the hours flew by in his company, as if they were minutes, and also how it constantly occupies my thoughts in what way I could express my gratitude for such kindnesses. It is, however, simply not possible for me, not even in writing, but my gratitude is heartfelt nevertheless. – I look forward to seeing you again

soon – tomorrow, in fact! Please give my very best wishes to the children.

Ever yours,
Felix Mendelssohn Bartholdy.

A few days later Moscheles wrote again:

With Mendelssohn's arrival I have gained an extra pleasure in life and, apart from his family, he devotes himself entirely to me. He seems to alternate between being a brother, a son, a lover and, above all, a passionate music enthusiast, who hardly seems aware of what heights he has already scaled. Even though his genius is far beyond anything in our mundane world, he is able to live with it so well. While the people of Birmingham were boasting about temporarily possessing this highly talented man and about performing his latest work in their concert hall, he managed to detach himself and find both the time and the inclination to sketch a picture of Birmingham (with pen and ink) for our children.

It was of great architectural interest for us both to view this city, as we sat in our steam wagon, with its chimneys, its factories, and its Town Hall. The Town Hall also afforded an impressive spectacle yesterday with its great wealth and elegance and, added to this, the masses of performers from both chorus and orchestra. The first part of the concert was taken up with music by Handel, Fasch, Palestrina and Mozart, given in a somewhat confused sequence. Lablache was marvellous as usual. Then came the second half, which was devoted to works by Mendelssohn. He was greeted with warm and heartfelt applause but, unfortunately for him, he was obliged to thank all those present. This he did with almost childlike haste, as if he, in his modesty, was keen to get the whole thing over with. When he came to conduct the orchestra, they played with a rare quality of ensemble and precision. 'Lobgesang' is in fact a symphony followed by a sacred cantata. The symphony part, which incorporates severe, fiery passages, as well as more relaxed and uplifting ones, is a masterpiece throughout. The hymn which follows this is also written in a very strict style.

Braham sang his recitative part with great pathos, his voice sounding considerably rejuvenated. Then came a duet for two sopranos which made way for the massed choirs breaking into jubilant song.

The powerful fugue was received triumphantly, with the organ booming majestically and the drums, doubled for the occasion, marking the rhythm like the pulse of an excited man. The chorus which came next was of such power and dignity that all those assembled in the hall stood up spontaneously, such as they would normally do only for the Halleluiah Chorus. The fugue in the closing chorus is extremely grandiose with its main stress being on the words 'Lobet den Herrn' (Praise the Lord), as is the case throughout the whole work. Of all those present, it was the magnificent composer of this work who deserved the loudest applause.

At 3 o'clock in the afternoon, when the hall had been cleared, Mendelssohn played the organ for a select few people for 3/4 of an hour. He did not play as though he had already been listening to and conducting music for most of the day, however, but more as though his day was just beginning.

When the Birmingham Music Festival was finished, Moscheles decided to accompany his friend back to Germany, and from there he would travel on to Prague to visit his aged and ailing mother. Chorley joined them to make a threesome, and at midnight on October 2nd, they all left for Dover in the mailcoach.

(For today's readers who are accustomed to high-speed travel by air, it may be of interest to know that the journey from London to Leipzig took up to a week in Moscheles' day.)

After crossing the Channel, which took eight hours, the three friends arrived safe and sound in Ostend. They continued the journey in Mendelssohn's coach which was pulled by post horses. Just as they were approaching Liège, though, an axle broke on the coach, forcing them to spend a night in the Belgian town, much against their will.

The next day they were able to continue their journey to Aachen:

We were unexpectedly fortunate when we reached the Prussian border. We were asked whether we had anything to declare, and when we replied that we had nothing, he immediately told us to drive on. Obviously we looked suitably gentlemanly!

On October 9th they finally arrived in Leipzig, where Moscheles stayed as a guest of the Mendelssohns and met Mendelssohn's wife and children for the first time. Once in Leipzig he wrote to Charlotte:

Leipzig, Saturday, 10th October 1840.
4 o'clock in the afternoon.

Since I arrived here at 11 o'clock yesterday evening, I haven't been able to find a spare moment to write to you, and now my head is on fire when I think how much my heart has to pour out to you and how little time I have before the post is collected. (By the way Felix's son is in the next room singing at the piano.) I should also like to write to Mother, as well as replying to your father's letter – but everything has to be done in such a hurry. I have been given a splendid reception here at Mendelssohn's pleasant little house; his wife is full of charm, unpretentiousness and is possessed of a childlike manner. As far as I am concerned, however, she cannot be classed as a true beauty, on account of her being a blonde. Her mouth and nose look very similar to Sonntag's. Her manner of speech is simple, her German being Frankfurt German and, consequently, not particularly pure. She told me at table somewhat ingenuously: 'I speak too slowly for my Felix, and he speaks so quickly that I sometimes have difficulty in understanding what he is saying'.

Mendelssohn pressed Moscheles to stay for a whole week and to give at least one concert. Moscheles hesitated over this, having decided never to perform in public again.

On October 12th, he wrote in his diary:
I spent yesterday afternoon alone with Mendelssohn. Much of the time was spent at the piano, and he played some pieces to me which were intended for use in his oratorio 'St. Paul', but which were deemed to be worthy neither of performance nor of publication. They are absolutely splendid, although possibly somewhat too dramatic to be heard with the oratorio. I think, therefore, that they would perhaps be more suitable if played as individual pieces in the concert hall . . . At 5.30 we hurried to the Gewandhaussaal, which was already bursting with people. Mendelssohn had taken me up to sit with the orchestra, but the directors of the Gewandhaus insisted that I join them in their box. The thunderous applause which Mendelssohn received was no less than he deserved following his performance of the Overture to 'Euryanthe' and Beethoven's B flat Symphony. The tremendous influence he had over his orchestra caused them to play with fire, mellifluousness and great nuances, so much so that I felt exhilarated by the whole performance.

The concert finished at 8 o'clock (!!), but the hall emptied slowly as it was raining heavily outside, and there are no cabs to be had in Leipzig! As a result of this, Mendelssohn and I stayed a while longer and chatted with Schuncks, before finally walking home in the rain. The warm room and the tea we drank on our return were both very cosy and pleasant, as was our discussion at the piano, where Mendelssohn played me some of his most recently published songs which I shall be bringing back to England with me. He then turned to his wife and said: 'Cécile, you should also have the courage to sing a little song for Moscheles and to allow him to accompany you.' She made the usual excuses that some people do, but then started to sing the following old German song:

as well as one or two others in her soft voice. Her singing was, nonetheless, perfectly in tune. She also sang a particularly attractive song by Hensel. . . .'

The entry for October 18th reads as follows:
Yesterday we all went to the Schumann's who were holding a soirée in their own house. She played my Trio, as well as one by Mendelssohn, giving a masterly performance of beauty and power. David accompanied, and at the end I was requested to play a selection of Etudes.

As Moscheles had made a definite decision not to give a concert on his own, and as it would be impossible for him to take part in a subscription concert owing to the limited time available for preparation, Mendelssohn arranged a similar celebration on October 19th to the one he had previously put on for Liszt. Three hundred guests attended the private concert by invitation, and Charlotte, who had remained in London, received the following invitation:

Mrs. Moscheles is cordially invited by

Felix Mendelssohn-Bartholdy

to a private musical party on Monday, the 19th day of this month, in the Gewandhaus Hall at precisely 6 o'clock, in order to hear his setting of Psalm 42 with orchestra and a large choir, as well as the Hebrides Overture and the Overture to the Maid of Orleans. The patriarch of pianists (as Fink describes him in the Music Journal), Moscheles, will play his G-minor Concerto himself, and the Bach Triple Concerto with Madame Schumann and Dr. F. Mendelssohn. Some characteristic Etudes will also be heard.

You are kindly requested to show this invitation at the door.

If this invitation is not shown, Professor Moscheles will be sent back to London to receive the applause due to him which he was not able to receive here.

R.S.V.P. by return of post.

After the concert, Moscheles wrote the following to Charlotte:

With Felix conducting the orchestra, everything went superbly. There were absolutely no flaws whatsoever, and I played with great enthusiasm; Chorley claims that I have never played better. The applause was thunderous. Can you imagine it? Sebastian Bach's Triple Concerto played by Mme Schumann, Felix and myself. And to round the evening off, I performed some of my Etudes.

Before leaving Leipzig, Moscheles wrote very little. Then came the following lengthy letter:

Prague, 21st October 1840. 10 o'clock in the morning.
(One hour after arrival)

Sunshine! The heavens resound with the sound of violins! I hugged Mother warmly, as well as hugging all our brothers, sisters, *brothers-in-law and sisters-in-law! My joy would not have been complete, though, if your letter, dated October 10th, had not been given to me upon my arrival. When I greeted Mother and embraced her, I found her to be much stronger and more composed than I had expected her to be. It seems to me that she only gets older so that her spirit can become stronger and so that she can become even more lovable than ever. She is in good health, apart from the slight cough which usually troubles her at this time of the year. It gives me great comfort to feel her looking at me, to see her smile and to experience her liveliness. All this pleasure is doubled, however, whenever I have to tell her about you, and when she asks me to pass her love and warmest admiration on to you. While I am here, she is for ever wandering about the four adjoining rooms which she has, doing her utmost to make my stay as comfortable as possible . . .*

During this visit to Prague, Moscheles devoted all his attention to his elderly mother. He took her for walks, played to her and, as a result of all the affection he had shown, she felt so rejuvenated that she even danced along with all the young people at a family soirée when Moscheles played some Strauss waltzes. After he had repeatedly turned down invitations from the people of Prague to give a concert, he did finally yield and decided that he could not leave his home city without at least playing for some charitable institution. The concert took place on October 31st, and the proceeds were donated to two hospitals. During the congratulatory reception after the concert, Moscheles's old teacher, Dionys Weber, arrived and promised his own special tribute, which Moscheles described in his diary:

He arranged an orchestral concert for me, given by the students at the Conservatory, after which he took me into the library where, all at Weber's instigation, a marble bust of Mozart had been erected and his complete works had been assembled. As you see, he has stuck by his beliefs ever since my childhood. . . .

Moscheles started on his return journey to London at the beginning of November. This letter was sent en route from Hof:

I managed to endure the most critical moment of my departure from Prague the day before yesterday; everything had been so well prepared and was so contrived that the whole thing seemed to pass off without too much difficulty. I was able to distract Mother's attention for several hours before I left, so that she barely had the opportunity to think of my imminent departure. I allowed her to assist me with my packing, and I played so many pranks and cracked all sorts of jokes that she could not stop herself laughing; I even had to suppress my own tears! Finally the moment arrived when I had to leave. We hugged one another for a long while and the floodgates were opened. My last words to her were 'Auf Wiedersehen', and I then hurried down the steps. It was easier for me than for those I had left behind, as I was able to think of you and the fact that I would soon be seeing you again.

Shortly after Moscheles had returned, a letter arrived from Mendelssohn, in which he reminisced about their journey together:

Dear Madame Moscheles,

I imagine that Moscheles is with you once again and comfortable by the fireside. I am now writing to you to send my best wishes, and to tell you how often I look back to the time that I have recently spent with you all and how grateful I am for everything. After you and I parted company, the three of us spent a thoroughly enjoyable time together, which Moscheles and Chorley des-

cribed in their letters to you some time ago. Now, however, times are quiet again, ever since Moscheles left on the train and Chorley took the express mail coach back to England. These times do not even seem to be worthy of description; even happiness itself has temporarily deserted us. And yet I really should not need to ask for any more than I have, when I see that I am constantly busy with my work, and that my wife and children are happy and healthy. Nevertheless, it was with much sorrow that we received the news from Moscheles that he would definitely not be paying us a visit on his return journey to England. In those few days that he did stay with us, he was just like one of the family, and we were all saddened by his departure. Moreover, he seems to have won my wife's affection, and this appears to have been mutual. I noticed it with her on the very first day that they met, in fact. I wonder when my old prophecy will finally come true, and the time will come when you, too, will have the opportunity to admire my Cécile and the two of you will be intimate friends, entirely at home in one another's company. I fear that the chance for this will not present itself in the early part of the New Year, and it remains to be seen whether Germany has made a sufficiently favourable impression on Moscheles for him to want to return to repeat the experience in the immediate future. I sincerely hope, however, that he was able to sense how we all felt when he stayed with us; these were feelings that everyone would have dearly loved to show and express to him (if only expressing and showing one's feelings was not so difficult for us in this part of the world!). Indeed, he would not find a stronger affection for him anywhere else. We feel the deepest admiration and love for him as a person and for his skill as a musician, as well as a profound gratitude for the great pleasure and enjoyment he has given us. It is still a daily topic of conversation in our household, and even young Carl will not allow a day to pass without asking 'Daddy, how does Uncle Moscheles play?' I then attempt to imitate him in a rendition of a certain E-minor piece in 6/8 time, but the result is pitiful!

I have enclosed the following song for you. . . .*

I shall now hand the quill to my wife, and close by sending my kindest regards to Emily, Serena, Felix and Clara. Please remember me to your dear children from time to time. You will also find a letter to Moscheles accompanying this one. I do not need to tell you how delighted I was to learn of his successes in Prague. I trust that he will think of us with affection whenever he has the time. We hope, too, that he will not keep us waiting too long with the news of his safe return. Farewell Mme Moscheles!

Respectfully yours,
Felix Mendelssohn-Bartholdy

FURTHER TRIUMPH AS A CONDUCTOR

During the winter of 1841 more and more people in the Philharmonic Society were demanding that Beethoven's Ninth Symphony should be performed again in England. At that time, Moscheles was at loggerheads with the directors of the Society, as they had continually re-elected each other on to the Board, whereas Moscheles, who was constantly pressing for innovation, was completely neglected. Nevertheless, when he was approached and offered the opportunity to direct the Ninth Symphony at one of the Philharmonic Concerts, he managed to cast aside any grudges he had previously harboured against the leaders of the Society. He

*(The song he sent was the Shepherds' Winter Song 'O Winter, schlimmer Winter).

now had the chance to perform the great work again and had no intention of turning the offer down. As he wrote in his diary at the time... *If it is at all possible for me to make this work more popular with the public, then that is what I must do.*

We can read just how successful Moscheles was in his attempt to give the masterpiece a worthy performance in *The Times* of May 4th 1841, which published the following review:

Both artists and music enthusiasts alike are now quite willing to admit that Beethoven's Ninth Symphony is not distinguished merely on account of its greatness and its sublimity, but also on account of its simplicity. We are particularly grateful to Moscheles for allowing us to appreciate these qualities, as a result of his carefully prepared interpretation and well directed performance. With his special talent in this field, he is able to surpass nearly every other musician, for, unlike many conductors, when he wields his baton he actually leads the orchestra, while all the performers allow themselves to be led by him. Indeed, nothing could enhance these concerts more than the appointment of Moscheles as the permanent conductor. He always gains the necessary respect of the orchestra and, consequently, would be in a position to lead them on to new triumphs.

In that same year, 1841, Moscheles and Mendelssohn each received a commission from a wealthy pupil to set a psalm to music using orchestral accompaniment. For his setting Moscheles chose Psalm 93: 'The Lord is King', while Mendelssohn opted for Psalm 13: 'How long wilt thou forget me, O Lord?'. Moreover, their wealthy patron arranged for both pieces to be carefully printed and bound.

At the end of July, the Moscheles family went to stay in Boulogne once again; these summer visits to the French resort had by now become almost an institution for them. In those peaceful weeks spent by the sea, Moscheles spent a lot of his time making music with his children. His eldest daughter, Emily, was already able to play some of her father's more difficult works, while Clara, who was just five at the time, was practising scales. Moscheles commented thus on the musical ability of his children: *I am very pleased to watch their musical development as I cannot envisage much further musical development in myself.*

And when asked about teaching children the piano, he wrote the following reply:
When giving young children piano tuition, special attention should be paid to strengthening the fingers, as the fourth and fifth fingers are naturally weaker and, therefore, need to be brought up to the same strength as the others. In my opinion, the hand support is superfluous. The pupil should first be encouraged to hold his hands and arms in a natural way – thus, the elbows and wrists should be held neither too high, nor should they be allowed to hang down. An attentive teacher will do his utmost to ensure that his pupil achieves this. Furthermore, the child must endeavour to develop a good sense of timing and expression in his playing, albeit at a somewhat later stage. Variations and fantasies on themes from operas are not particularly suitable for developing a particular style in the pupil, as the ear tends to concentrate too much on forms that it already knows. It is more beneficial to use original works by good composers. However, if all these exercises need to be practised with a hand support (as is recommended by Kalkbrenner, who still uses one every day), the pupil's feeling tends to go to sleep, while his hands move stiffly, although in a correct and admirable fashion. I sometimes wonder what would have become of us older players, and also of Liszt and Thalberg, had we been made
to use hand supports! Would our art have been any the better for it?

And on another occasion, he wrote:
They [children] should also be made to play in front of other people. This dilettantish shyness, which almost borders on coyness, cannot be driven out of them soon enough. They have to be taught not to think of their own little egos, but rather of the greatness of the work of art they have to perform.

While in Boulogne, Moscheles composed the 'Tarantella', which he dedicated to his daughter Emily, as well as a 'Sérénade', a piece called 'Romanesca', two difficult Études and a short 'Barcarole' in D-major, so that, in his own words, *I remember why I come to stay by the sea.* In addition to all of these, he arranged Beethoven's Septet for piano duet.

Moscheles still continued a lively correspondence with Mendelssohn and received some of his latest compositions, prompting him to write the following:
It is indeed manna for both my heart and my mind that I have been asked to undertake the corrections of the fourth book of 'Songs without words'. I find myself playing them and the 'Variations sérieuses' unceasingly, and on each occasion I am able to enjoy their beauty afresh.

The two friends often used to ask each other for constructive criticism of their compositions, and on occasions they did not mince their words. Apart from this, Moscheles and Charlotte kept Mendelssohn informed of all the latest developments on the British musical scene. In the course of this correspondence, Charlotte wrote to Mendelssohn and told him about the comparisons being made between himself and Spohr, all of which had caused a stir in the press. Mendelssohn replied to this in a letter:
The only thing that really upset me in your charming letter was the fact that you did not

intervene in these peculiar comparisons and in all the 'cockfighting' which, much to my astonishment and regret, have been started between Spohr and myself. Moreover, I have not the slightest idea who could have dreamed up such odious comparisons and competition between us. I know that you will either laugh at me or be furious that I have taken such a frivolous argument so seriously, but I feel that it is a serious matter, and that as a result of the continued competition and squabbling between us, of which only God knows the perpetrator, neither of us will do himself any good but, on the contrary, untold harm will be done to us both. Apart from the fact that I could never compete, and indeed would never wish to compete, with a man from Spohr's time and of Spohr's ability, I have always respected him far too much as a human being and a person ever since I was a boy, and my increasing years have done nothing to diminish this respect in any way.

On January 1st 1842 he wrote this entry in his diary: *I start this year happy and content in the knowledge that I am with my wife and children, and look forward with great confidence to the continued education and tuition of the latter.* However, this year was to bring its share of grief and hardship.

An epidemic of scarlet fever broke out and Moscheles' son Felix became critically ill. The rest of the family also contracted the disease, but to a lesser extent. The only one who escaped was Moscheles, and he was obliged to isolate himself from his family in case he infected any of his pupils. Moreover, in the middle of this trying time, Moscheles' mother died in Prague. The following entry describes his profound emotion at the time:

I am deeply shaken by this tragedy. Never could a mother have shown so much love to her son, and no son could ever have loved a mother as much as I did. This is a gap in our lives which cannot be filled. Nevertheless, God has spared my wife and children with his wondrous mercy. I must likewise be grateful to him that I was able to fulfil my engagement I had promised in York. During the three days that I was there, I spent much time fighting against my mental state, but fortunately the public was not aware of it.

While the scarlet fever continued to threaten London, Moscheles received permission, via Bunsen, to dedicate his large piano school to Prince Albert. Thus, on a day previously fixed by the Prince, Moscheles found himself at Buckingham Palace so that he could present a special dedication copy. While he was there, he wrote a letter to his wife:

Antichamber Buckingham Palace. It is a quarter past one o'clock and I have been sitting completely alone since noon in an antichamber of the Palace. I am holding my own audience for my thoughts, but without keeping them waiting as long as the Prince has kept me waiting or I, in turn, some of my female pupils, who are also waiting. The sun is shining through the windows and warming me from one side, while on the other side I am receiving the heat from a large open coal fire. Is that not a delight? But what about my freedom, my precious freedom? I wish I could be with you again, sitting at home and looking at you, rather than staring at these blank walls. Fortunately, I managed to find myself a writing implement and am now able to prove to you in black and white that I think of you at every possible opportunity. 2 am. Dr Schenck finally came to visit me in my prison and informed me with considerable embarrassment that the Prince had not been notified of my presence for the second time, as a result of the absent-mindedness of one of the pages. And all this, after I was told as soon as I arrived at the Palace that the Prince was otherwise engaged. The Prince will doubtless not allow this neglect on the part of the page to pass without some form of reprimand. 5 o'clock. I have now returned to my place of exile and must tell you the conclusion of my visit to the Court. Dr Schenck came in to the chamber, closely followed by the Prince, who apologised profusely and told me how sorry he was that he had taken up so much of my time. He turned out to be exceptionally kind, and my impatience was soon forgotten. I handed him the piano tutor, which he leafed through at great length. He told me that he thought he would probably have to be content with playing the easier Etudes, whereupon I replied that he would only have to give the word and I would be pleased to play the more difficult ones to him. He gave a friendly reply but without stipulating a time when I should come. In other words, he wished to hear neither my Etudes nor me. A page then entered the room and announced: 'H.M. the Queen is ready', after which the Prince hurriedly took his leave of me and Dr Schenck, who was also present, and I rushed off to give my lessons.

Just as the family was beginning to enjoy good health again and the pain of losing Moscheles' mother had subsided somewhat, more bad tidings arrived in May – Hamburg was on fire. Even though their immediate relatives were spared the catastrophe, the number of homeless people was enormous. Moscheles decided to give a concert for the benefit of all the needy of the city. Mendelssohn arrived in London at the eleventh hour, and immediately offered his services for this special function. The public scrambled to buy tickets, so that in the end the area reserved for the orchestra was converted into stalls. The boxes were occupied by members of the Court, and for anybody who had not been able to obtain a seat, scaffolding was erected by piling up tables just in front of the entrance to the concert hall. A lot of music

was played, including an Etude composed by Moscheles especially for the occasion, and there were also a lot of guineas collected. The following list shows the receipts and the expenditure for the concert:

Theatre Manager Lumley	£ 50.	–		
Refreshments for the artists	£ 2.	10.	9.	
Extra seats	£ 2.	3.	6.	
Police	£ 1.	8.	6.	
Advertising posters and poster holders	£ 4.	7.	–	
Carpenters and decorators	£ 8.	8.	–	
Announcements	£ 23.	–	–	
	£120.	14.	9.	

Net receipts	764.	
Surplus	£643.	5. 3.

After the concert, Moscheles wrote the following:

I requested that the senate should give me 1000 marks of this sum, so that I could deliver it in person. The city later sent me a medal which had been struck from the melted ore of the bell tower with the following inscription: 'Hamburg dankt' (From Hamburg with thanks). . . .

Up until July 10th, Moscheles spent a marvellous time with Mendelssohn and his wife. Charlotte described these days spent together:

At last, my most ardent wish has been fulfilled, and I have had the chance to meet the angelically beautiful and lovable Cécile. Mendelssohn was quite justified in saying that the two of us would get on with each other well and eventually come to love one other. As far I was concerned, the affection I felt for her was immediate for, as soon as I saw her, I felt attracted to her at once. We spent some wonderful Sundays at her aunt's, Mrs B., and as the weather was so heavenly, we organised running races in the garden. In the course of these games, Mendelssohn proved to be just as nimble of foot as he is when he plays the pedals on the organ. We also played charades and in one game Mendelssohn acted out the concert director, Moscheles and the orchestra. The mime we had guessed was 'being serious, and playing music with great skill'. After this, we listened to a lot of beautiful music, and the usual daring improvisation, which must never be missing on such occasions and which usually turns out to be highly successful. Afterwards, the two performers would say to each other: 'It was marvellous how you managed to weave my lively Scherzo into the theme of your subdued A-minor Etude, which I myself had intended to play in a most sentimental way'. Or 'How could it possibly have gone so well? We were almost too boisterous today'.

When the Mendelssohns spent a few days with the Moscheles family, Moscheles wrote the following in a letter:

One can but wish this excited and effervescent man the greatest happiness and good fortune, as he has chosen for his companion in life a woman of such feminine and soft nature.

On another occasion he wrote:

He played me his Antigone choruses, accompanied by his own singing or humming. Just that was sufficient for me to realise how great and noble this work is; the Bacchus chorus is so much in keeping with the spirit of the piece.

In 1842, Moscheles devoted a great deal of attention to Spohr's Double Symphony. He had been expressly requested by Spohr to direct the work and went to a great deal of trouble over it, as he was once again having differences of opinion with the Directors of the Philharmonic Society, this time on account of the membership of the orchestra. The entry in the diary for this time reads as follows:

This work contains all those great qualities which one knows and loves in Spohr's music: beautiful treatment of his themes, ingenious modulations and superb instrumentation. My main complaint, however, is that it lacks innovation, and I wish that there were more episodes and contrasts, as the music is so similar throughout that it almosts borders on monotony. It may well please the harmonists but, in my opinion, the ear has to put up with too many identical sounding impressions. Even though the orchestra performed the piece with love and zeal, the applause at the end was only moderate.

In the same year, Moscheles joined the Handel Society which had just been founded with the aim of publishing an improved edition of Handel's works. He commented on the progress of the Society in his diary:

I had expected great things of the Handel Society, but alas it is proving to be most unsatisfactory. Instead of sensible debates, such as one would expect at the conferences, we see nothing more than personal vanity among the members.

Some while later, the following entry is to be found in the diary:

The Society has at last been properly organised so that it can achieve its original purpose, and we are starting with the publication of three of the Coronation Anthems. I have been entrusted with the Edition of 'L'Allegro, il Pensiero ed il Moderato', which is to be brought out at a later date . . . .

At Christmas of that year, the children were not only able to enjoy the delights of a Christmas tree, but also of Jullien's new Promenade Concerts, described as follows:

The whole of Drury Lane Theatre was converted into a large salon, draped, and decorated with flowers. A fidgety public dressed in hats and coats sat downstairs, while up above people sat resplendent in their evening outfits. Entrance to the lower salon cost 1 *shilling, whereas the boxes were somewhat more expensive. But now to the main attraction, the music. All the music was played by a good orchestra on an elevated platform and was for the most part directed by Jullien with his baton. All the while, however, he played on a piccolo flute with a piercing tone which marked the time in the music. At the end of every piece he threw himself, as if throughly exhausted, into a red velvet chair, which had been placed in the middle of the podium. Moreover, he always showed the public his evening suit, consisting of half a mile of white waistcoat! His dancing act, which was given a spicy accompaniment on drums, timpani and trumpets, was also a source of great entertainment for the audience. I would say without hesitation that no schoolboy should miss the chance of attending Jullien's Promenade Concerts during his school holidays.*

FINAL YEARS IN LONDON

The last few years that Moscheles spent in London were particularly tranquil ones for him. Any traces of depression which had been discernible from time to time in the previous decade seemed to have vanished, and he appeared to have finally accepted the interplay of light and shade as an intrinsic part of human existence, having previously described it as the essence of real music. He disarmed his critics by swallowing their remarks calmly without retaliation, and when one of them, as was often the case, saw his own negative remarks unexpectedly turned into praise from Moscheles, the latter was able to reply: *You see, I am for ever the happy prince. Those people who envy me can do nothing to harm me, and eventually we are obliged to become friends again!*

During the winter of 1843, Moscheles was chiefly occupied with his scale book, the aim of which was to enable pupils to practise their scales with both hands and, more importantly, to do it with enjoyment and affection. The idea for the book came to him while he was working with his daughter Clara:

Ever since I have been accompanying my five-year-old daughter while she plays a C-major scale using various time signatures, I have entertained the idea of writing a scale book with harmonies. It should make the mechanical dryness of practising scales much more enjoyable for the pupil, as well as developing his taste. Thus he is able to hear a melody, and is given the essential strength in the rhythm. This method could prove useful throughout the piano-playing world for, the sooner the purely mechanical side of learning can be overcome, the easier it is to develop the really artistic element.

The diary goes on to say:

It is also my wish that the teacher, who has the difficult task of teaching a beginner to play scales and of listening to him practising them, should not become bored with the whole thing, as is so often the case. Both teacher and pupil should enjoy what they are doing: the teacher by reading his own part and attending to what the pupil does, and the pupil by hearing a rhythmical piece and a melody, instead of mere scales, thereby becoming more accustomed to counting.

As well as working on this book, Moscheles also revised three pieces to be played with Fidelio for Cramer. These had been published after Beethoven's death, and Moscheles derived a great deal of pleasure from the work.

In the 1843 season, Moscheles was once again asked to direct Beethoven's Ninth Symphony for the Philharmonic Society. After the performance he wrote the following succinct comment in his diary: *A great deal of effort, but an enormous pleasure for me.*

When asked his opinion of Hector Berlioz's great symphony, Moscheles wrote the following reply:

I have seen only the piano score of this work, so I would be unable to pass judgement competently on it. Nevertheless, I think that it would be hard for me to come to like it, as its lack of melody, rhythm, phraseology and contrapuntal proportions were all too apparent to me. I have previously heard his Overtures to 'Francs Juges' and 'Benvenuto Cellini' with a full orchestra: however, his effective instrumentation was, in my opinion, no compensation for the shortcomings I have just mentioned, particularly in some passages where he sought to introduce melodically poetical innovations, but instead produced nothing but stale and prosaic ideas. Moreover, I am quite happy to prove to the world and to my friends that I do not cling stubbornly to old and traditional music, but that I am also able to admire the modern composers. At the moment, for instance, I am playing a great deal of Chopin, and am endeavouring to delve deeper into the music to gain greater understanding, even though it is not exactly my genre. The pianist Hallé, who has been in London for a short while, plays a lot of Chopin, and he plays it well to boot. He has just come from Paris and has definitely brought the true tradition of these Nocturnes and Mazurkas with him.

This last entry serves as a further illustration of the point made in the introduction to the book: while Moscheles' testimony was extremely subjective, it was also candid and honest. Can we hold it against him that he could not fully acknowledge the genius of someone like Berlioz or Chopin? Hardly, since the history of the arts abounds with similar examples of an inability to perceive true originality in a genius but, in spite of this, the world will doubtless continue to find room for such people.

One of the most important events in early 1843 was the opening of the Conservatory in Leipzig. We read the following description in the diary:

The Leipzig Conservatory was officially declared open on April 10th with the first intake of students. With Mendelssohn as Director, one can expect great things from this new institute. It would be a marvellous post for me to be able to work together with him and to be relieved of the burden of my teaching in London and all the dilettantism here, in order that I could devote myself to training the artists of the future!

Moscheles' wish was to be fulfilled just three years later.

Meanwhile, Charlotte reported on a different kind of opening:

The successes and failures of the Thames Tunnel have kept the world occupied for some time now, but it has finally been officially opened, and with great success. We were all the more pleased to be able to attend the ceremony, as we are on friendly terms with the builder's family. It was a somewhat eery experience to go underneath the constant roaring of the water down into the damp depths of the tunnel. Nobody was left with any illusions, however, with the mighty Thames rolling inexorably on overhead. My imagination started to wander, and I found myself wondering how soon the moment would come when the bright illumination and these happy hordes of people would be swallowed up and destroyed by the power of that swishing element up above. The shouts of joy which greeted Sir Isambard Kingdom Brunel and his fellow workers as they made their way through the tunnel, accompanied by music from a band, were, thank God, the only answer that I received to my question, as everything went off without a hitch.

In the early part of the summer, Spohr came to London. This great violinist was received with great appreciation by the British, both as a composer and as a conductor. His work 'Die Weihe der Töne' (The Power of Sound) was performed under his own baton in one of the Philharmonic Concerts, during which he played his Concertino as well. Later on, the Philharmonic Society arranged a special concert in his honour, which was also attended by Queen Victoria.

The Sacred Harmonic Society, for their part, honoured the master by holding a performance of his 'Fall of Babylon' in the Exeter hall, at which Moscheles was present:
The highly theatrical nature of the work did much to increase his popularity with the mixed crowd of people which filled this large hall. Moreover, the audience took great delight in the military drums and the various dance rhythms which appear throughout.

The artists in London laid on a spectacular banquet for him in Greenwich. Moscheles was also present, of course, and was able to translate his eulogies, which were given in English, into German for his friend. Finally, Moscheles entertained the assembled gathering by playing an improvisation on themes from Spohr's 'Weihe der Töne' as a special tribute to him. Afterwards, the press described it as *one of those fantasies for which he stands unrivalled.* Moscheles also arranged a soirée for Spohr at his own house, to which over one hundred guests were invited.

After his customary stay in Boulogne in the summer of that year, Moscheles travelled on to Paris where, once again, he stayed for a few weeks. This is an extract from a letter he wrote while there:
Yet again we have had the chance to see and admire many different things. We have spent many enjoyable times with Meyerbeer, St. Heller, Benedict, Ernst and Hallé. But we have also heard the young Kalkbrenner playing one of his own compositions, with his

arms resting on his hand support as if he were suffering from the palsy.

On October 3rd he wrote:
It was a great delight for me to go and visit Halévy in prison. He had committed a small offence during his service as a garde nationale and had received a forty-eight-hour prison sentence as a result. A number of painters had obviously suffered the same fate before him in that very same cell, since the walls were covered with highly imaginative paintings and drawings, and occasionally there were some particularly eccentric collections. We were able to converse just as well 'aux haricots' (the derisive nickname of the prison) as if we had been in his own house, all the more so in fact, as his young wife was also there.

Towards the beginning of 1844, Mendelssohn returned to London, this time for a much longer stay. He had been engaged to conduct five of the Philharmonic Concerts, as well as rehearsing various new works with the orchestra. Moscheles accompanied him to the first rehearsal and later commented:
When Mendelssohn appeared before the orchestra, they showed the greatest enthusiasm and affection for him, just as one would expect. The concerts could only gain in quality with him as the permanent conductor. . . . In the first half we heard Mozart's E-major Symphony, followed by the C-minor Concerto by Sterndale Bennett, which proved to be a particularly interesting composition in the style of Mozart. . . . The second part of the concert was devoted to Mendelssohn's A-minor Symphony. The work aroused great delight in the audience, and presented me with a whole series of interesting pleasures. The orchestration is magnificent, being both piquant and quite new.

Mendelssohn's incidental music to 'A Midsummer Night's Dream' was received with such enormous enthusiasm that it had to be performed not only at the fifth Philharmonic Concert, as had been the original intention, but also at the sixth one – this time in the presence of the Court. At the eighth concert the audience was able to enjoy a performance of the 'Walpurgisnacht', and nobody more so than Moscheles, who had already 'gone into ecstasies' when Mendelssohn had played it to him on the piano.

Between the concerts there were some cosy evenings spent with Klingemann, either at the Moscheles' house or at Chorley's house: *When we were at Chorley's, Mendelssohn really stole the show with his music, first by playing some of his 'Songs without Words', and then following these with a highly imaginative improvisation. Much to my astonishment he selected for this the theme from my G-minor Concerto, then he took a bar from the 'Pensées fugitives', which I had just played with Ernst, and finally the ballad from Benedict's opera 'The Brides of Venice'. There was ingenious interweaving throughout of contrapuntal passages and thunderous octaves with some beautifully melodic phrases which penetrated to one's very heart and soul.*

On another occasion he wrote:
After dinner at Ayrton's, Mendelssohn and I were requested to improvise together. He forced me to sit at the top end of the piano, and I followed his inspirations with the greatest of interest. The first was on a melody in the style of an English ballad, followed by one on 'See the Conquering Hero Comes'. While all this was going on, I managed to weave in the Scherzo from his A-minor Symphony.

After Mendelssohn's oratorio 'St. Paul' had been performed in the Exeter Hall, he returned to Germany on July 10th.

IN GERMANY AND VIENNA – IN SPITE OF EVERYTHING, MORE CONCERTS

In the autumn of 1844 Moscheles set off for Germany, together with his family, to visit some of his old friends, and also to return to 'good old Vienna' once again. Their journey took them via Boulogne and Aachen, and from there on to Frankfurt, where Moscheles attended a pianists' conference. Following repeated requests from his friends, Moscheles gave a concert on September 25th, at which an extremely large audience was present. Among other pieces, he played the 'Hommage à Handel' with Mendelssohn. At the time of his visit the Frankfurt Fair was in progress and, as a result, all the halls were fully booked. The only possibility was to hold the concert in Mühlens' hall, which proved to be far too small for the event. Moscheles' eldest daughter Emily wrote her own account of the proceedings:
The hall was bursting with people long before the concert had even started, and still people continued to arrive. There was also a small room adjoining the main hall which had been left open, but which was not fitted with any benches. 'What will the Frankfurters say when they find that there are no seats?',. Mendelssohn asked Rosenhain. 'I'll tell you what I think we should do. The two of us will have to go out and hire some chairs, as it is not possible for us to speak to Moscheles so soon before his concert.' Mendelssohn's good friend was quite willing to lend him a hand, but the chairs were not so easy to come by after all. Eventually, the two of them went into a small tavern and managed to find four dozen. 'They need to be sent at once', Mendelssohn told the landlord, who enquired anxiously: 'But who is going to pay?', to which Mendelssohn replied: 'A great artist by the name of Moscheles is giving a concert,

and the hall is now so full that we have run out of chairs – You will receive your money without question.' 'I've heard that some of these so-called artists run off with all the money afterwards', replied the cautious landlord. 'You'll have to make a down payment first.' Whereupon the two men emptied out their pockets, which were none too full, but the contents seemed to satisfy the landlord nonetheless. The two men then climbed aboard a carriage with Mendelssohn sitting inside holding two chairs and two more being placed at the front with the coachman. Mendelssohn called up to him: 'Drive to Mühlens' Hall, but make it fast!' Thus they arrived, with the other forty-four chairs following them, and there were finally enough places for the audience. In spite of all this, though, Madame Mendelssohn, Mother and I had to share two chairs between the three of us for the whole evening. However, there was something which excited Mendelssohn even more than the episode with the chairs. Father had added a low bass C to Mendelssohn's A-minor Etude. 'You really gave me quite a surprise', he told him afterwards. 'It really produces a most marvellous effect which shall, henceforth, never be left out, and I intend to write it down in Madame Moscheles' album immediately.' I rushed off to find the album for him and he proceeded to draw in the book a picture of the coach, himself, Rosenhain and the chairs, but only half a horse – 'I can't draw that sort of thing from memory', he told us.

Over the next few weeks, Moscheles gave other concerts in Darmstadt, Karlsruhe, Stuttgart, Augsburg and Munich.

During his stay in Munich, Moscheles became acquainted with the painter Kaulbach, and even sat for him to have his portrait painted. While he was in Kaulbach's studio, he had an unexpected encounter, as Charlotte later reported:

His studio consists of a number of different rooms. In one of these rooms, the largest of them, he is busy working on his painting of Jerusalem; it is almost complete, and it is gives us great pleasure to watch this figure clad in fur as he puts the finishing touches to his masterpiece. In an adjoining room there is a piano, and when we called on him yesterday, he asked Moscheles if he would play something. However, just as Moscheles was really finding his touch, a soft voice called Kaulbach away. We then heard loud voices, but Moscheles heard nothing, and it was only when Kaulbach and King Ludwig came to stand next to him at the piano that he realised who was there. His Majesty, of course, found just the right thing to say: 'Pleased to meet you. I wanted to go and see an artist and I find there are two'. Moscheles naturally had to continue playing. Afterwards Kaulbach explained to us that the King was very much against the idea of his working for the Prussian, and he had consequently taken him to task over the matter.

When Moscheles gave his concert, it was attended by the King, accompanied by all of his Court. In the interval the King wandered around the hall (as was his wont, according to what people said). The young girls claimed that he would then approach them and ask: 'How old are you?', and because of his deafness they would have to shout their reply, whereupon he would usually exclaim: 'And still not married!'

The Moscheles family arrived in Vienna and Charlotte wrote: We have reached St. Stephen's Square safe and sound; and the venerable old tower of the Cathedral is staring across at us through our window.

Once in Vienna, Moscheles found himself rushing around to visit all the people he had to. Among others, he met his old comrades-in-arms, Castelli and Grillparzer, and received invitations to go here, there and everywhere. One such invitation was described by Charlotte in a letter:

Of all the dinners we have attended, yesterday's one in Hietzing in Domeyer's Restaurant proved to be the most interesting. Instead of the usual entertainment, we were treated to some splendid dance music by the young Strauss, consisting of waltzes, polkas and galops. We all ended up dancing on very full stomachs!

Moscheles noted the following observation about the musical life in the city at the time:

Donizetti has now become the new sun in the Viennese musical firmament, having replaced Beethoven. This sun is unable to provide me with any warmth, nor, indeed, is it able to illuminate my path for the future.

Some time later he wrote:

I have had to bear unspeakable musical suffering. Mendelssohn's 'Lobgesang' was performed by the Society of Austrian Music-Lovers; it was an enormous pleasure for me, but it was as though I was sitting on a piece of lush green grass surrounded by a sheet of ice. Transported away from all things earthly, I was able to soar into higher spheres with the composer; there was nothing to disturb me, no applause to distract me, since the audience was sitting there absolutely serene. The chorale 'Hüter, ist die Nacht bald hin' even moved me to tears. And then Herr Hoschek, a music teacher by profession, came up to me and said: 'Do you not find that this music is thrown together in such an artificial manner?' I felt as if I had just fallen out of a hot-air balloon. I managed to swallow my fury and replied 'Take it as you please'. The Viennese folk later left the hall during the last chorus, as their Schöberlsuppe ['dumpling soup'] was calling them to the dinner table. Furthermore, the applause of those who did remain was so lukewarm that I was reminded of a fire crackling just before it finally goes out.

Moscheles gave his own concerts on November 23rd, December 3rd and December 17th. All three went off successfully, since he had chosen those of his compositions which he thought would appeal most to the Viennese public. He played the 'Pastoral Concerto', the 'Souvenirs of Ireland', and several of his characteristic Etudes. He also played his old 'Alexander Variations', which had been specially requested, even though Moscheles himself would have preferred to forget their existence. Beethoven's Concerto in E flat and Sonata in A flat were also performed. This account of the first concert was written by Emily:

It was marvellous to see the reception which the full hall gave to Father, their old favourite who had returned to them. He was called back three times altogether for encores, and a repeat performance of the 'Kindermärchen' was requested. However, just as he was about to start playing it for the second time, there was such loud applause that he was obliged to take a bow in order to receive the flood of compliments before he could continue. He finished by playing an improvisation on Beethoven's Symphony in A, after which the public burst into song for him with 'S'giebt nur a Kaiserstadt' (There's only one Imperial city) etc. It really was quite a celebration.

A little later, we read:

We attended a splendid 'fleece ceremony', in the course of which two very young knights, looking resplendent in their blue and white silk satin attire, were dubbed Knights of the Golden Fleece. Poor Emperor Ferdinand, who was both small and puny, could only lift the big and ancient sword to confer the accolade on the young men with the help of one of his senior officials. What with the Royal Family sitting in their box, the Hungarian Noble Guard adorned with precious stones and the remarkable ancient suits of armour worn by the knights with their turbans and cloaks, the whole ceremony proved to be extremely impressive.

Emperor Ferdinand later appointed Moscheles to be his Royal and Imperial virtuoso pianist and requested him to give a special concert for the Court, which Moscheles described in a letter:

The concert took place in a room which had been decorated by Emperor Leopold with the most beautiful Florentine mosaics, on which one could see the dancing reflection of the candlelight. The guests numbered somewhere in the region of 200 people, and the front row was occupied by the whole of the Royal family. They all conversed quite amicably with me, and also paid me a host of compliments. The late Kaiser's widow asked me whether she had not heard me in 1824, shortly after her illness. She had indeed. The Archduchess Sophie remembered me from my concert at the court in Munich. Both ladies had heard all about my wife and daughter and about the fine talent that the latter was already showing. Archduke Karl recalled the Serenades which had been played to him in Baden in which I had participated; indeed, Archduke Karl had heard my playing both with his brother and at his brother's residence on many occasions.

My improvisation almost turned out to be a disaster, however. I asked their Majesties to give me a theme for improvisation and they selected a piece from 'Linda di Chamounix' by Donizetti. Of course I was obliged to show my limitations and informed them that I was not acquainted with this 'most marvellous of all operas', whereupon they proposed some old-fashioned themes from Mozart's operas. I chose 'batti, batti' and the Champagne song and, finally, in view of the presence of the hero, The Archduke Karl, 'See the conquering hero comes', which prompted the Emperor to ask 'Was the last

one the March from "Vestalin"?', to which I replied: 'Something like that'. The Empress quickly butted in with another question, asking me whether I had studied in Vienna or Prague.

This concert for the court led to an amusing episode:

Count Moritz D. came up to me, cleared his throat and said: 'I am to hand you this (a roll of ducats) as a token of appreciation for your fine playing before the Court.' I took it, but told him that a memento from their Highnesses would be worth far more to me than money. He then asked: 'But what on earth can you do with little ornaments? Prume receives money for his services as well – not as much as you, mind – he gets 60 ducats.'

Eventually the Court was sufficiently convinced by Moscheles' argument, and on the next day he arrived with three diamond shirt studs which, he assured Moscheles, were 'of exactly the same value as the money.'

A few days later, Moscheles was invited to give another concert for the Court, this time for Archduchess Sophie and Archduke Franz Carl. Afterwards he made his way to Prague, from where he wrote to Charlotte, who had in the meantime returned to Hamburg:

Yesterday I visited my parent's grave with my brothers and sisters. I found that the experience soothed me rather than upset me. In fact, these peaceful days I am spending here away from all those visits to arrogant and dull people are doing me a power of good. I am always pleased to be able to go to Lemel's, as they welcome me with such affection; apart from them, though, we have avoided telling anyone that I am in the city. If I were to give a concert, it would require so much time on my part, so I am quite content instead to comfort and speak with my poor suffering brother by telling him all about my latest experiences in Vienna . . . And now a word for the children: Dear eldest daughter! I am sure that you have now told your relatives in Hamburg quite enough about your marvellous peripatetic existence and have probably just about got your breath back! I now look forward to the time when you will be able to look after yourself more and be a signpost for your brothers and sisters to guide them in their future education and training. . . . Dearest S., you will without doubt look upon the reunion with your mother as a happy turning point after the trial of being separated from her and, as a result, will enjoy her company all the more. – Dear F., If the 'optime' which your teacher writes under your work refers to your conduct in general, then you may always be assured of both my satisfaction and my love. You should make the word 'optime' your motto throughout life and adhere to it.

Towards the end of the year Moscheles travelled on to Leipzig, where he was to give a concert in the Gewandhaus on January 1st. Seeing David, Gade and all the city's other artists again cast its usual magic spell on him, as he mentioned in another letter to Charlotte.

This place has a real artistic atmosphere about it which is thoroughly conducive to music-making. My rehearsal went off very well; David conducted with his baton, and we did not need to stop once. In the evening I went to David's, although I was alone, as all the other guests he had invited this New Year's Eve had declined. Among those he has asked was the present Concert Director, young Gade, who has a very similar head to Mozart's. David played me his M. S. Variations in G minor on one of his own themes, as well as some Variations on a Scottish song. Everything was piquant. I also accompanied him from the score of Mendelssohn's new Violin Concerto, which was written for David.

On January 7th Moscheles gave a concert

in Dresden. Hiller arranged a grand matinée function in his honour, which was attended by all the leading artists and music enthusiasts in the Saxon capital. Moscheles also met Richard Wagner there, who was the Court Kapellmeister in Dresden at the time.

Upon his return to Leipzig Moscheles was asked once again whether he would be willing to accept a post at the newly opened Conservatory. One of the Ministers, von Falkenstein, explained to him that nothing would please them more than to be able to employ Mendelssohn as the Director, while appointing Moscheles as Head of the Piano Department. At that time, however, a lack of funds prevented the Conservatory from offering them both a sufficient salary. Following his discussion with Falkenstein, Moscheles commented: *I now have the opportunity of becoming a German artist once again and giving up this life of being a fashionable schoolmaster.*

The next stage of his trip took Moscheles to Berlin, where he hurried straight away to the Opera, in order to hear Meyerbeer's 'Feldlager in Schlesien':

It would not be possible to describe my surprise when I saw the magnificent Opera House. This, combined with the piquancy of the music, the costumes, the ballet and the decorations, quite took my breath away. Moreover, Jenny Lind thoroughly delighted me with her singing. She is truly unique, and one of the arias with two concertante flutes is perhaps the most unbelievable bravura piece that one could ever hope to hear. . . . Poor Meyerbeer had to rush straight from his conductor's desk to his daughter Blanca's bedside as her condition had worsened considerably during the performance itself.

Later on, he wrote:

All my friends welcomed me with open arms, and nobody would accept that my stay had to be a short one. It would, however, take up far too much time if I were to give a concert or play for the Court, as I could well see from Meyerbeer's and Count Redern's reports. In addition to this, the King has left for Strelitz (N.B. Rossi has gone, too); the Prince and Princess of Prussia are preoccupied with a series of various balls and functions lasting a week or so; the Concert Hall has undergone alterations for the French Theatre performances and is consequently not available; the Hall of the Singakademie [Singing-school] could be used, but only after a week of preparations, and the Director of the Königsstädter Theatre is out of the city, which is perhaps a blessing for me, as he is reputed to be difficult to deal with. . . .

After a short stay in Hamburg, the whole family returned to London.

There was an unpleasant sequel to Moscheles' German trip in the early part of 1845. A German provincial newspaper published an article containing a letter, allegedly written by Moscheles which, among others, mentioned the following points:

During his last stay in Germany, Moscheles lost exactly the same amount of money as he had made on his first tour, i.e. £800 sterling. Part of this sum was squandered on the journey itself, and part of it had to be paid out as a result of badly attended concerts. Moreover, he wrote to a friend in Prague: 'I am losing a great deal because of Liszt. I simply cannot believe that people have changed their opinion about piano playing so much since my own time. This is unfortunately the case though. I went to Germany, only to find that I have become rococo ever since Liszt has been playing. Fortunately I have so much money that I am not unduly bothered by the loss. What pains me most, however, is that I failed to achieve a break-through with the public in Vienna. I would never have dreamed that my popularity

would die in the very same city as it had once lived in such grand style.

As other newspapers also took the article and published it, Moscheles felt obliged to reply to the accusations:

When the enclosed article was sent to me by a friend in Germany, I had intended to pass over the matter in silence, this being in my opinion the most dignified response possible to such utter fabrication. Nevertheless, as I now learn that the article has found its way into various other publications since it first appeared, I consider it to be my duty towards all the Royal Courts in Germany, who received me with such honour last autumn and winter, as well as towards the audiences in the various cities where I was applauded so warmly, to hereby declare that the contents of the whole article are untrue. Throughout September, October, November and December of last year, I gave concerts in Aachen, Frankfurt, Darmstadt, Karlsruhe, Stuttgart, Augsburg, Munich, Vienna, Dresden and Leipzig and, in so doing, I had no more cause for complaint about the harm which my friend Liszt is supposed to have done me than I had a few years ago when we both gave concerts in London at the same time. Furthermore, as far as my alleged attack on England is concerned, I am a man of honour and could never bring myself to utter such an ungrateful statement against the country in which I have both received recognition and also been able to earn my living for the past 22 years. I therefore repeat that I deny all responsibility for the said article.

Also in the early part of that year, Moscheles' brother succumbed to a chronic illness. Moscheles described the effects this had on him in a letter:

Out of necessity, the only thing that fills my mind and my time at the moment are sad thoughts of my brother, and yet yesterday, while I was at Alsager's I felt lifted above earthly things by the power of our art. I had to play four of Beethoven's Sonatas and an improvisation, and I was pleased that my strength was not defeated in the B-minor Sonata. It was while playing the Adagio in F sharp minor, however, that my emotions were strongly aroused, but in the Fugue I regretted having to force my fingers to produce so many discordant sounds. This movement contains more dissonance than consonance, and I feel that by writing like this Beethoven is saying: 'I want to treat a theme in an erudite manner, regardless of whether it sounds good or not.'

At the same time a friend of Moscheles from Vienna, Professor Fischof, sent him the Bach G-minor Concerto, which was absolutely unknown in London at the time. Moscheles played this piece, as well as the D-minor Concerto, in one of his matinée concerts of classical piano music, which were once again being received with great acclaim. The Duke of Cambridge also expressed a special wish to hear the newly arrived Bach Concerto at Moscheles' home. Charlotte described his visit thus:

He always come to us on his horse, accompanied only by a groom. Moreover, he listens to the music with the greatest of enthusiasm and is particularly kind towards the children. It would be impossible to show more gratitude for the hour he spent listening to music than the Duke of Cambridge; he described it as one of the most enjoyable he had experienced in a long while.

During this season, Moscheles was also summoned to Buckingham Palace to give a concert, an honour which he shared on this occasion with a number of other artists.

In addition to his piano-playing though, Moscheles continued to wield the baton at the Philharmonic Concerts. Sir Henry Bishop conducted the first three, and Moscheles the remaining five. During rehearsals for these concerts he would sometimes make little speeches to the orchestra. On one occasion, the following was said:

Gentlemen! As we are appearing in this concert here together, I should like to compare your performance with that of the fingers of a hand belonging to a highly trained pianist. If you will permit me, I shall be this same hand which controls the movement of the fingers. I can attempt to bring these fingers to life using all the interpretations which the masters are constantly imparting to me, and if we are able to encounter ourselves in these interpretations, we will have achieved an enormous amount.

On another occasion, while rehearsing a Beethoven Symphony, he told the orchestra how he had heard that particular work and many other works by the master in Vienna, when they were new compositions, and how he retained the traditional tempi which Beethoven had set in his own conducting. To end with, he caused great amusement in the orchestra by imitating the gestures which Beethoven himself had used when conducting; for example, the way he would crouch lower and lower until almost disappearing to signify any pianissimo passages, then he would gradually straighten up for the crescendo, and finally stand on tiptoes and leap up whenever there was a fortissimo.

However, Moscheles did not forget to add: *Just as I could never hope to imitate the great man in his compositions, so I must also take care when imitating his actions; when he did it it was originality, but when I do it, it is merely a caricature.*

In the last concert he played the Bach D-major Concerto and afterwards expressed his delight at the pianissimos achieved by the orchestra: *It has long been my wish to train these noble and skilled people to play with even more light and shade.*

BONN MUSIC FESTIVAL 1845

At the beginning of 1845 Moscheles travelled to Bonn for the Music Festival to be held there. The Festival was to be directed by Franz Liszt and Moscheles had been invited as an honoured guest. As soon as he had reached Cologne he wrote to Charlotte:

The weather has been bleak, rather like my own mood, since being apart from you has unbalanced me somewhat. My philosophy will have to help me to overcome this . . . Meyerbeer is tearing his hair out at the moment, as he has to hold the rehearsals for the Court concerts here in Cologne starting from tomorrow. All the large-scale vocal works are to be performed without orchestra, but with just piano accompaniment instead. In between these rehearsals Meyerbeer hopes to go and hear the performances in Bonn . . .

On August 10th he arrived in Bonn:

I am writing to you from the Hotel de l'Etoile d'Or, the current residence of all the crowned heads of music – be they brown, grey or bald – and of many bewigged or lacquered skulls. This is the meeting point of all those music-mad ladies, young and old alike – of all the art critics, all the German and French reviewers and the English reporters and, finally, of Liszt himself who – by dint of his regal talent – outshines anybody else present. I had hardly arrived when I met Dr Bacher from Vienna, the envoy from the Austrian Music Society who offered to share the room he had reserved with me; an inestimable act of friendship indeed, as one would think from looking at the streets that there had been a great fire with everyone looking for lodgings. There are ladies and gentlemen – and many English people among them with their retinue of porters – moaning and groaning and begging for accommodation in the hotels or in private houses.

Friends and acquaintances are being reunited and greeting one another warmly, and there are brightly-coloured flags flying everywhere; all in all quite a hustle and bustle. I have already seen and spoken to various colleagues from all four corners of the earth, and I also went to Liszt's place, but he had his hand full with secretaries and masters of ceremony.

Liszt kissed me and said a few hurried and muddled friendly words to me, then I saw him again at the Concert Hall when he was welcoming Mme Pleyel and the other ladies. Four hundred of us then ate at the table d'hôte, and the first concert took place after six under Spohr's direction in the new Beethoven Hall, which is built of wood. Although the great D-major Mass [by Beethoven] afforded me considerable pleasure, I was somewhat saddened that the composition deviated from the true church style and, therefore, lacked the unity of colour which I appreciate so much in the master's other compositions. The performance of the Ninth Symphony which followed was almost flawless, and the soprano who sang the choral passages was not only better than I have heard in London, but better than I have ever heard anywhere. Staudigl was unsurpassable but, just as they had been in London, the timpani were not properly tuned. – Herr Jäger from the Committee gave me a seat of honour among the artists. I met Liszt while I was there and he was particularly friendly towards me. I am writing to you after the supper given for the public at the guest house to put me in a good frame of mind for the night. In the meantime, though, I remain con amore, languendo, poco a poco agitato, ma sempre giusto yours. . . .

The diary contains these accounts of the ensuing days:

August 11th: A new steamboat was christened 'Beethoven' today and then launched with tremendous ceremony. There was a great crush of people all wanting to sail on her first trip, causing considerable disorder, jostling and even danger to life and limb. To the sound of cannon salutes the ship made her way along the river, accompanied by another ship, to Nonnenwerth, where a cold breakfast was awaiting the passengers. I managed to secure an ideal place next to Spohr and Fischof, and although there were a number of pickpockets around, we were spared.

August 12th: From 8 o'clock in the morning onwards there was great activity in the streets with all the students and guild members gathering. I waited with the guests of honour at the Town Hall and at nine we went into the Minster Church, albeit with considerable laboriousness. Beethoven's Mass in C was performed, which I found uplifting and a pure delight. From the Minster we went and sat in the stands which had been erected all around the Beethoven Monument. We were then subjected to the burning rays of the sun until past twelve; most tiresome. We were finally put out of our misery by the arrival of the important guests on the balcony of the Prince's residence. These consisted of the King and Queen of Prussia, Queen Victoria and Prince Albert, and the large Royal household. There then followed a speech and chorus from Professor Breidenstein. The moment of unveiling moved me deeply inside, in particular because of the marvellous likeness to the immortalised composer that Hähnel had managed to achieve. At the table d'hôte in the Stern there was the same chaos once again; I sat next to Bacher, Fischer and Vesque, while Liszt and his entourage of ladies and gentlemen predominated. Lola Montez sat with the latter group. At 5 o'clock there was a concert in the Hall.

August 13th: Last day of the Festival. Liszt's Cantata composed for the event started the proceedings. Parts of it are well thought out, and the work is imbued with considerable feeling, such as the introduction of the Andante from the B-major Trio, for example, which is thoroughly appropriate to the work and executed with skill. The piece also contains fine instrumental effects but, on the whole, it is too fragmented. He was rewarded with thunderous applause and a congratulatory fanfare from the orchestra. The Court arrived after the Cantata had finished and were given a repeat performance . . . I must also mention that I found Liszt's performance of Beethoven's E-flat concerto to be highly satisfying, for the most part. I cannot imagine the energetic spiritual part of the work being played better, but there were other passages which I would have preferred to hear in a more relaxed manner.

Once the Court had departed, a few more pieces were performed, and some others were left out! At 2 o'clock there was a banquet at the Stern, where the jostling was even worse then before. The beginning of the toasts heralded a sequence of events which will remain in my memory and in the memories of all those present on account of both their brutality as well as on account of the lack of restraint shown by those concerned. Once the toast to the King's health was over, the improviser Wolff proposed a toast to what he called the cloverleaf; this was supposed to represent a triad. The root of the triad was Spohr; the third, which unites everything with love and harmony Liszt, and the dominant, which resolves the discord of everything was Professor Breidenstein. Everybody cheered with approval. Spohr then proposed a toast to the health of the Queen of England, Dr Wolff proposed one to the health of Professor Hähnel, the creator of the [Beethoven] monument, as well as to the health of the brass-founder in Burtscheid, while Liszt proposed a toast to Prince Albert's health.

Liszt then spoke (in a somewhat confused manner) about the object of the celebration; all nations wanted to honour the master, and long may these nations live – the Dutch, the English, the Viennese, who had all come here on their pilgrimage. At this point Chélard rose to his feet and shouted impetuously to Liszt: 'Vous avez oublié les Français'. A large number of voices then surged in like waves on the shore, some agreeing and disagreeing. Liszt eventually demanded the right to speak again and attempted to redeem himself, but seemed to become more and more entangled in a maze of words, until he finally explained to all those present that he had lived among the French for 15 years and it had certainly not been his intention to neglect them. The disputing parties then became even more impetuous. Many left their seats, the ranting and raving became deafening and some of the ladies turned quite pale. The banquet was interrupted for a whole hour, during which time Dr Wolff stood on the table and attempted to speak again but he was removed from his place three or four times before finally leaving the room and the Babel in the room to its fate. The parties were assembling in all parts of the large hall, but because of all the din no one could tell what the fuss was about. The French and English journalists then started to interfere in this battle of words with complaints about various oversights on the part of the Festival Committee. Just as the tumult was about to erupt into violence, the landlord offered the sensible suggestion of requesting the band to start playing. This drowned all the noisy troublemakers who withdrew on to the courtyard; the waiters started serving again, even though many guests, particularly the ladies, had already left the room. . . . At 6 o'clock I departed from the scene of this scandal, feeling dazed, with the noise still ringing in my ears.

There is an old humorous poem in French which says 'Vous m'envoyez le lendemain un billet daté de la veille'. A similar thing was to happen to Moscheles at the end of the Bonn Music Festival. He had not received an invitation from Meyerbeer or Liszt to attend the Court concerts in Stolzenfels and Koblenz, to which many members of the artistic fraternity had been summoned after their names had appeared on various circulating lists. As he had not received an invitation, though, he travelled on to Cologne on the 14th, where he met his family and devoted a couple of days to the beauties of the Kölner Dom and to visiting friends. It was not until the 17th, after he had already departed, that the following letter reached Cologne:

My dear friend,

When his Majesty the King learned that you were in these parts, he requested that you should receive an invitation to attend the Court concerts which the King himself is holding tomorrow evening, Sunday the 16th, at his castle in Koblenz. This order, which I am honoured to be able to execute, has just this moment been handed to me by Count von Redern on behalf of the King. It is now midnight, however, and the concert at Stolzenfels has just finished, so it will not be possible for me to send these lines to you in Cologne before Sunday morning. I sincerely hope that they do not arrive too late. Whatever the case though, they will be an indication to you of the high esteem and great affection in which the King holds your name. I bid you a fond farewell, dear friend and remain

Your humble servant,
Meyerbeer

Lefèbre from the House of Eck in Cologne

forwarded the letter to Moscheles, adding a few lines to express his regret, as he envisaged that the letter would not reach Moscheles in time. Moscheles in turn sent a copy of the same letter to his father-in-law and appended these lines:

I leave it up to your astuteness to fathom the whys and the wherefores of this whole matter. Why, one may ask, did I not receive my invitation along with the other artists while I was still in Bonn? And, likewise, why did the order from the King not reach me in time? One would have thought that a Royal messenger sent early on Sunday the 16th would have arrived in Cologne reasonably quickly. . . .

Moscheles sought compensation for this incident by taking a trip on the Rhine with his family. The Princess of Prussia was also on board the steamer, and in her honour the hills and ruins along the route were illuminated at night. Moscheles described the whole thing as a 'fairytale spectacle'. The family selected a peaceful spot in the Lichtental near Baden to spend a few days resting. Moscheles noted in his diary that: *. . . there is no end to the possibilities for walks and picnics in this charming area.*

From Baden the family proceeded to Paris, where Moscheles composed his 'Sonata symphonique' and subsequently had it performed, first with Hallé, and later with his daughter, to various friends in artistic circles. On the day before his departure his presence was requested at St-Cloud in order that he could give a public performance of his promised new compositon. The diary continues the story:

On November 23rd I went with E. to St-Cloud, and we were received most warmly there by the Royal Family. The Queen, Mme Adelaide and the Countess of Orleans were all sitting taking tea with their ladies-in waiting and their beaus; the King came out of an adjoining room in order to hear the Sonata which E. played extremely well; she also had to play a solo. I then improvised in the style of Grétry, which is the King's favourite genre. Everything went off with great success.

Thus ended the Moscheles' stay in Paris.

CALL TO LEIPZIG

In December of 1845, Moscheles received the following important letter from Mendelssohn :

Would you be prepared to allow your frequently promised idea of returning here to become a reality and come to work with me at the Leipzig Conservatory? What marvellous things could be expected, both by your friends and by our art, if you were to accept my offer. I do not doubt for one moment that life here would appeal to you, particularly as you now see life over there in a different light, if I am to believe what you tell me. I would also admit to you quite candidly that everything I hear about the hustle and bustle over in England these days, which I actually saw for myself during my visit a year and a half ago, is such that I can fully understand how your stay becomes less and less appealing every year, and how you long to get away from the whole thing. . . .

I would ask that if you do wish to mention anything concerning the matter to tell me and give me the opportunity to enter into negotiations on your behalf, and these negotiations could prove to be some of the most beneficial that have ever been carried out in the interest of music in this city . . .

Moscheles would possibly have accepted the offer immediately had this important step not required such careful consideration. He therefore asked for time to ponder his decision, and in the meantime he exchanged letters with his father-in-law, who sought to give him advice.

The formal request from the Leipzig Conservatory had already arrived in London on January 2nd. It was phrased in the most friendly terms and signed by Dr Seeburg, Dr Keil, Herr Preusser and Herr Schleinitz. Mendelssohn added his own short note: *On the day when you agree to come, I shall drink my best wine, as well as opening a bottle of champagne!*

He also included detailed notes about earning and expenditure in the job and closed by saying:

The general wish of the people here that you do come and their joy at the thought of your coming is something honourable in itself, but this bears no relation to the honour that you would do these people by moving back here. Still, a relationship showing mutual admiration such as this is both healthy and beneficial and bodes well for a happy future on both sides. In short, I shoud like you to come.

Moscheles subsequently wrote to his father-in-law on January 21st:

As you will see from the enclosed copies of these letters which I have just received, the business with the Leipzig Conservatory continues. I now feel more inclined than ever to give up my position here . . . If one wishes to be a man for the public here, a great deal of concessions need to be made, and I am neither prepared to compose music for commercial purposes, nor am I willing to teach students who, for the most part, gain no deep insight into the art, but who are obliged instead to learn whatever current fashion dictates. I do, of course, often discuss this vital issue with my wife and we are both agreed that while sacrificing so many of our creature comforts – we will never sacrifice our magnificent life together – we do not wish to look for another London in Leipzig. If

I find the artistic existence there which I expect to find, then I know for certain that we – I above all and then my Charlotte – will be fully satisfied with the decision in retrospect. If we were to move, I would leave England with the pleasant realisation that I have been able to offer my help where I could, by giving lessons, by playing, or by offering financial assistance. We would also depart, aware that we had left many friends behind, who regret to see our departure and whose affection and company we would sorely miss when so far away from them. On the other hand, we would be coming to live much closer to a large number of our relatives, and that is definitely a bonus. I have not yet announced publicly that I have been requested to go to Leipzig and, indeed, if I am to accept the post, I first have to resolve the matter of finances; after all, I do have a family to feed and clothe. Please continue to act as the President of the Family Council and inform me of the minutes of your meetings. We should not allow ourselves to go grey over this matter, however, for, whatever fate may choose to present us with, my Charlotte and I are such a happy couple that we would even be content to live in a hut. Moreover, we shall always try to bring up and educate our children well, so that they will never require great riches either. I remain today as ever, whether in London or in Leipzig, your faithful son-in-law

I. Moscheles

On January 24th a letter arrived from Mendelssohn in which he dispersed any doubts about the financial status of the post, and the following entry is to be found in the diary for January 25th: *Today I composed my letter of acceptance to the directorate of the Leipzig Conservatory. The first step has been taken.* Mendelssohn was delighted by the news and promptly announced: *I shall go and paint the town red.*

Before the news had travelled around the musical world, Moscheles received a request from Birmingham to conduct at the big music festival to be held there in September. He had been engaged to direct just one concert, Mendelssohn's 'Elijah', and could hardly have wished for a greater honour and delight than the opportunity of conducting this work at the end of his years in England.

Before that, however, he would have to prepare his farewell concert in London. Moscheles wanted to show the public in this concert that his career in England was finishing on the same note as it had begun. It was not going to be a mammoth concert with Italian singers and a grand competition for soloists. He had no desire to indulge in whatever the rest of the musical world found fashionable.

Mme Pleyel joined Moscheles for the concert and played his 'Sonata symphonique' with him; a number of other friends were also present. Moscheles was extremely pleased with the event and wrote to his father-in-law on June 19th to convey the news to him:
The audience erupted with jubilation both during and after every piece that I played; they waved scarves and cheered, all standing on their seats. I found it most touching and was unable to hold back my tears while taking my bows. After this I was surrounded by many of my friends and acquaintances for an hour. My farewell to the public here really could not have been more spectular.

After the concert the London newspapers continually bemoaned the loss which music and art in London would suffer as a result of Moscheles' departure to Leipzig. All this prompted Chorley to raise the following question at the Athenaeum:
Why did a large city like London never offer him a proper post to keep him here, in which

he would have felt secure and happy, in the same way as a little bourgeois town like Leipzig has now done? That would have put a stop to all your complaints about his loss.

The ensuing summer months were taken up with the preparations for the Birmingham Musical Festival. In the meantime, the family held a big farewell party to which over 200 people were invited. Moscheles described his hectic life at the time in a letter to Hamburg:
I usually get to bed at about one or two in the morning these days, and just thank God that I have an iron constitution which can tolerate all this work, day and night. Yesterday, or rather today, I went to bed at 4 o'clock just as the sun was rising, and I am now writing to you at 8 o'clock.

The first rehearsal of the English version of Mendelssohn's 'Elijah' took place at Moscheles' house with Mendelssohn himself conducting. This was followed by two rehearsals with orchestra in the Hanover Square Rooms, one of which is mentioned by Moscheles in the diary:
. . . but the lady singers caused Mendelssohn to create somewhat. Apparently the aria was not ideally suited to the voice and he should transpose it. He resisted most politely, but then told me his true opinion, without mincing his words, about 'such a suggestion'.

As soon as he arrived in Birmingham, Moscheles held a rehearsal, but the next day he felt so sick that Mendelssohn had to replace him in an evening rehearsal. Mendelssohn was particularly kind to Moscheles during the illness:
He showed me the same sympathy that a brother would have, while his frequent visits to me – in spite of the fact that everybody else would have liked to see him – and the attention he devoted to me were often extremely moving. When he came back from the rehearsal which he had conducted in my stead, he seemed to be absolutely exhausted.

Charlotte poured him a glass of champagne which had a magic effect on him, giving him a new lease of life.

Once he was restored to good health, Moscheles himself was able to direct the first morning production, the 'Creation'. This was followed by some pieces from Rossini's 'Stabat Mater' and, later on, by a three-hour mixed programme of English and Italian music which was, according to the diary: ...*a pure delight for the audience.*

On August 26th Mendelssohn celebrated a marvellous triumph with the first performance of 'Elijah'. Moscheles expressed his own view thus:

In my opinion, this work has even greater zest and even more dramatic variety – while still being in the purest oratorio style – than 'St. Paul', and it places Mendelssohn on an even higher level than before.

Parts of the oratorio had to be repeated as a result of the tumultuous applause, even though applause was normally very much frowned upon at such music festivals.

Over the next few days Moscheles directed such works as the 'Messiah', Beethoven's Symphony in A and the 'Missa Solemnis', as well as playing the 'Hommage à Handel' with Mendelssohn. The diary contains an account of one of these concerts:

The parts of a small recitative which was printed in the programmes could not be found anywhere. A source of great embarrassment. Mendelssohn came to the rescue, however, by sitting in one of the adjoining rooms while the first part of the concert was being given, and composing the recitative, as well as orchestrating it and copying out all the parts. The ink was still wet when it was given to the orchestra, who nevertheless played it magnificently without any rehearsal, and the audience was none the wiser! Only Mendelssohn would be capable of such a feat!

The Birmingham Music Festival finished on August 28th, and on September 15th Moscheles and his family left the house in which they had spent sixteen happy years. They wandered around all the rooms with moist eyes for one last time. Both of their two youngest children had been born here; there was the room where they had worked at their lessons every morning or where their games had been organized. It was here, too, that they, the parents, had spent nights of worry watching over their bedridden and suffering children. And it was here that they had celebrated the children's return to good health, as well as their birthdays, with both gratitude and joy. Many a composition which would continue to live on had originated downstairs in the study and had gone out into the world, bringing glory to its creator. Indeed, it was his industry and his tireless striving which had brought him the wherewithal to provide his family with such a marvellous existence in these very rooms.

On their journey to their new home, one of the places they stopped at was Frankfurt, where they were able to enjoy the pleasure of hearing the enchanting Jenny Lind.

Leipzig (1846–1870)

RETURN TO LEIPZIG

As the railway had not yet reached Leipzig in 1846, the Moscheles family arrived at the Leipzig Post Station on October 21st by coach. The diary continues the story:

When we alighted, Mendelssohn was there to meet us. Not only did he show great kindness towards us, but he had also gone to considerable trouble on our behalf. He had prepared everything for our reception, just like a courier that one sends on ahead to make all the necessary arrangements. We first had to climb into his carriage which took us to the Blumenberg, where he had rented a room for us, and as soon as we were there his wife joined us. Both of them took great pains to ensure that our temporary accommodation was as comfortable as possible.

On October 26th, Moscheles wrote a letter to his relatives:

My dearest family,

This new and probably last period of my artistic career and of my life overall is doubtless occupying your thoughts so much at the moment that I should like to take this opportunity of reporting all the latest news to you. This last stage, with God's help, has begun extremely auspiciously. And who is responsible for our great happiness at the moment? None other than Mendelssohn, Felix Mendelssohn, whom I should prefer to call my own brother or my son. You already know all about the reception he gave us at the Post House. Later that evening, three of the Directors from the Conservatory, Hofrat Keil, Stadtrat Seeburg and Herr Preusser came to welcome me with their warmest good wishes and also to express their hope that my stay

here will be a pleasant one. Moreover, they gave me their assurance that they would do everything in their power to fulfil any wishes or demands I may have at the Conservatory. The following day I paid them each a return visit. In the evening we were delighted to be able to attend one of the subscription concerts at the Gewandhaus. Our seats, which were near to the orchestra, had been sent by the directorate. Under Mendelssohn's direction the orchestra performed a Haydn Symphony and overtures by Hiller and Lachner with a precision such as I have seldom heard; the nuances in the playing were likewise a pleasure to listen to, and one of which I have been deprived for a long time.

A short while after this, Schleinitz, the Head of the Conservatory presented Moscheles with a list of the Professors:

Dr F Menselssohn-Bartholdy, Composition and Solo Performance.
Organist C. F. Becker, Organ-playing, Practice in Conducting.
David, Klengel, Sachse, Violin Teachers.
Gade, Harmony and Composition.
Hauptmann, Harmony, Counterpoint.
Moscheles, Direction of Pianoforte Studies, Training in Performance Technique and Pianoforte Composition.
Plaidy, Wenzel, Pianoforte playing.
Böhme, Solo and Choral Singing.
Brendel, Lectures on Music.
Neumann, Italian.
Richter, Harmony and Orchestration.

Moscheles learned from Schleinitz that Mendelssohn, with his customary modesty, had requested that his name should not appear at the top of the printed list, but rather that the list should be drawn up in alphabetic order.

Mendelssohn later had to make a speech at a banquet given by the Professors in honour of their new colleague Moscheles, who recorded what had been said in his diary:

He had never felt that he had the talent or the calling in him to make a speech before, but on this occasion he had to reveal his innermost thoughts. My settling in Leipzig and my employment by the Conservatory had been long cherished wishes of his, and he looked forward with great joy to seeing how much the realisation of this wish would meet with the approval of both fellow artistic colleagues, and also of the public in general. He would never forget the impression which my talent had left on him as a child, how I had stirred up the fire of the Gods within him and aroused such enthusiasm. I had constantly stood by him, giving him encouragement, and it was a source of great pride for him that he could be assured of enjoying a lasting friendship with me. He had no doubt that all those present shared his feelings and would be happy to propose a toast to my health. The three cheers I received were sung as a triad, and when it came to the clinking of the glasses for the toast, I could no longer suppress my tears. I managed to stutter a few words of gratitude in reply and apologised for being so tongue-tied on account of the awareness I had that there was a man living among us, a friend of mine who had just paid me a tribute, who far outstrips me as an artistic hero, is himself highly revered as a person, and is the epitome of high-mindedness.

After the meal Moscheles and Mendelssohn took a long walk together, in the course of which they discussed the state of music in Leipzig at great length. The discussion was, of course, recorded in the diary:

I put the question to him why someone like him, who was admired in every major European city, allowed himself to be tied to Leipzig of all places. He explained to me that there was a certain feeling here, a particular school of musical thought, as well as the artistic ambience and opinions, all of which attracted him so much. Moreover, the Conservatory itself was something very close to his heart; so much so that while he was composing his last oratorio he had not missed one single lesson.

The two friends continued to make music together, and this enjoyable pursuit became an almost daily feature of their lives, as we read in the diary:

After supper we had a most entertaining time playing on two pianos, and we closed with a competition in improvisation! It was really an intellectual exercise for me, and I had to concede defeat on a few occasions as I found myself listening to Felix with such warmth and admiration that I forgot to join in myself!

For October 26th the diary contains the following entry:

Felix had been considerate enough to go to the trouble of arranging a musical performance which was to take place at the location of my future employment (the Conservatory), and which was given by the pupils themselves, who were to perform their best piano pieces for me. Stadrat Seeburg made a speech, announcing that my appointment at the Conservatory was an event of great importance. I replied by saying that I considered myself to be just one single stone of this fine building which rested on such solid foundations. I did, however, hope to be able to contribute to the reinforcement of the structure as a whole, and if I were also able to help grace and embellish the external appearance of the place with my presence, my dearest wish would have been fulfilled.

October 27th: Entrance examination at the Conservatory in which Mendelssohn was involved. His very presence was an inspiration to teachers and pupils alike. In the evening we went to his house and talked a lot about musical matters, as well as about house furnishings; he gave me a lot of good advice. He showed me his recently composed chorus 'An die Künstler (To artists). Joachim then played the Kreutzer Sonata with him.

Evenings such as this were to be repeated and, in the course of them, Moscheles was able to admire some new Songs without Words which were, as yet, unpublished. He could hardly believe, however, that Mendelssohn still wished to make alterations to 'Elijah', ever since it had been performed in Birmingham:

'You want to make this beautiful work even more beautiful?', I asked him. He replied that he did, but an explanation of how he would do so was not forthcoming. 'Your genius demands far too much', I objected. He had already surpassed himself in his 'Elijah'. 'Why not devote your powers to new works?'. My argument failed to change his mind, however, and he remained convinced that the work needed to be altered.

They also looked at the Violin Quartet in B, which Mendelssohn claimed was not a good composition.

A short while later, the great genius showed great concern for his devoted servant Johann who was suffering from a serious illness and being nursed at home. Mendelssohn went to visit him every day and expressed his sincere regret at his ultimate death.

At the beginning of November Mendelssohn arranged a grand musical soirée for his friend. As he said at the time: One should certainly make good music for a man like Moscheles, but not for just anybody.

For November 16th we read this entry in the diary:

Early rehearsal and in the evening a concert with music by Schumann. Schumann's Symphony in C was conducted by Mendelssohn at the express request of the former, and Mme Schumann played Mendelssohn's Piano Concerto in G-minor exquisitely, with the orchestration of the piece coming to the fore brilliantly. She then played my Rondo in A with her younger sister and, to close, Songs without Words by Fanny Hensel, a piquant Barcarole by Chopin and one of her own Scherzos.

Moscheles finally started his teaching at the Leipzig Conservatory on November 27th 1846. He was required to give sixteen lessons per week, in addition to which he had to teach eight lessons to private students. What is that compared to the mad rush of London?

December 3rd: I played Beethoven's Concerto in C-minor at the Gowandhaus with my own improvised cadenzas.

December 7th: Mendelssohn came to us today for his first long visit to our new flat, where our Erard has now joined us as a beloved member of the family. He wandered round all the rooms rubbing his hands together and saying 'pretty, pretty', as was his wont when he particularly liked something. He would always use this one word, which he found to be particularly expressive, even if he was contemplating a spectacular view. By doing this on one occasion, he provoked great anger in one of his Leipzig friends who had accompanied him on the journey, and who himself launched into ecstatic phrases describing the marvellous panorama spread before them. He said that he just could not understand Mendelssohn's indifference, as he called it. . . .

In the winter of 1846, the Moscheles were able to celebrate the Christmas festivities with their relatives in Hamburg, as they were now much closer to them following their move to Leipzig. They also stayed on to spend the end of this eventful year there.

A letter written by Moscheles to his relatives in Hamburg outlined in depth his new life in Leipzig.

We have barely returned from our pleasant excursion to visit you, dear family, but we are all back safe and sound. Upon our return we came to realise that our domestic situation here is no less comfortable than it was in London. Our little flat always looks so nice and so homely that we now feel very much at ease here. I believe, too, that all our guests – be they casual callers or specially invited guests – share this feeling with us, even though some have pointed out to me that 'It's such as shame that you do not have a music room, a man like you' etc. It is my belief, though, that good music can be made everywhere, and I have always belonged to a school of pianism which seeks to put far more stress on clarity and accent rather than on loud bashing on the keys – and more stress, too, on the correct understanding of a work and being able to render this in one's playing rather than on surprising effects.

As far as the local people are concerned, we are overwhelmed with kindness, and the wining and dining we indulge in here, there and everywhere would be just as strenuous as it was in London, were it not for the earlier hours and the smaller scale parties, which are always enlivened by interesting personalities. I hardly need to tell you that our frequent meetings with the Mendelssohns, either at our place or theirs, remain a spiritual delight for us. The last time we were there, they had also invited Joachim (our darling); Felix accompanied him in his [Mendelssohn's] Violin Concerto, and both of them played the piece from memory. Then Felix allowed us to hear the Songs without Words by his sister Fanny; the style is very much an imitation of his own, but the treatment is extremely musical and interesting. After this, he played us the part of 'Elijah'

where the widow seeks help from Elijah. He has revised the work, and I must confess that Elijah in particular now comes across as a far weightier and more dignified character than he had previously done at the performance I heard in Birmingham, when I considered the whole work to be absolutely complete. The Angel Trio is also delightfully beautiful now.

I take great delight in David's company and playing as well. Yesterday evening we were at his house and heard him, together with the Müllers from Braunschweig, playing a Quartet by Haydn, one by Beethoven and Mendelssohn's Octet. I have not heard such high-quality music-making in a long while.

In spite of everything, though, we are all in good health, and that remains the finest gift that God can bestow upon us.

On another occasion Moscheles wrote:
After we had eaten at Mendelssohn's, I went with him to see the Berlin piano-builder Schönemann who had brought his new invention to Leipzig. With this invention, a pedal produces the octave of every note and, in so doing, one can dispense with the brightness of a D octave. Thus, a small keyboard, when affixed to a large one, permits a span of two octaves. However, the whole thing lacks in tone and the invention is still very much in its infancy. We amused ourselves nonetheless with this strange contraption and played some octave passages. With the device, the notes can be heard, albeit somewhat weakened, doubled eight times. No sooner was all this over with than Mendelssohn was standing at his conductor's desk at the Gewandhaus, and I took great delight in listening to his Overture to 'A Calm Sea and a Prosperous Voyage'.

The chosen people, Moscheles and Mendelssohn, continued to enjoy each other's company, and when they attended the Gewandhaus Ball Moscheles wrote this comment:

People danced briskly and there were many beautiful blossoms among the girls.

On January 14th Moscheles held a dinner at his flat to mark the start of his employment at the Conservatory. This was followed a short while later by the beginning of the Gewandhaus New Year concert season, which Moscheles described in his diary:
Mozart's G-minor Symphony was magnificent. Mendelssohn conducted this last piece with a seldom heard restraint, which enabled all the chromatic modulations to sound much more distinct than I had ever heard them in London.

In the next concert the Leonora Overture No. 3 was, according to Moscheles, 'inspiring', and had to be repeated. The diary continues the description:
The whole audience, and I in particular, warmed to Mendelssohn's A-minor Symphony.

The next concert was an historic one conducted by Gade, Moscheles was asked if he would participate, but he refused, as he had played Beethoven's C-minor Sonata and his own Septet with David in a chamber music concert only shortly beforehand.

After that came yet another historic concert, this time conducted by Mendelssohn:
Instead of hearing Johann Sebastian's music we were treated to a Symphony by Phillip Emanuel Bach in the form of a Concertino. I derived particular pleasure from Vogler's Overture to 'Samori', on account of his treatment of the three timpani themes; the Overture to 'The Magic Flute' was superb, as it was not too fast. I must say how much I am enjoying all the good music here in general.

A performance of Schumann's 'Paradies und Peri' was then put on for the benefit of the poor and needy in the Erzgebirge, which prompted this assessment in the diary: *The performance fluctuated somewhat, but I*
nonetheless enjoyed those great and beautiful moments contained in this work.

The diary continues:
All the best artists and art enthusiasts in Leipzig take great delight in meeting at Frau Frege's, in order to admire her marvellous singing. Her voice is always beautiful and her performance always of the highest quality. However, in Mendelssohn's songs she remains – in his opinion as well – unique and unsurpassed. Yesterday I attended a morning function at her place, and she, Mendelssohn, David and I all made music together.

Mendelssohn also liked to attend all the children's parties held in the Moscheles household but, as Moscheles wrote: *our discussions were always about music, while other people amused the children with silly games.*

Mendelssohn's 38th birthday was celebrated joyously on February 3rd with other members of his family. Who would have suspected at the time that it was to be his last? There was a prologue, a joke in Frankfurt dialect, as well as a charade on the word 'Gewandhaus'. Mendelssohn revelled in the whole thing. Charlotte later wrote an account of the festivities:
He rocked back and forth in his chair, choking with laughter. Who would have thought of him as being the great musician who knew how to express himself in the correct fashion before the most high God using his sublime harmonies? Who would have thought of him as being the father of a family? This was a schoolboy celebrating his birthday, and he appreciated every pun and joke that was made with gratitude. He applauded everything with the greatest enthusiasm and was backed up by a chorus of all the children. There was real jubilation on all sides.

The horrors which were to follow were still hidden behind a veil of compassion, and there were no dark shadows cast over the general merriment of the party.

The diary continues with this entry for February 17th:

I poured my heart out to Mendelssohn today about my refusal to play in Gade's historic concert. I told him that I did not wish to impose my own performances and interpretations on today's tastes too often. I had played in the Gewandhaus as a special favour for the directors, which I later proved by sending my fee back and contributing it to the pension fund. People had been able to hear me in the chamber music concert and that was sufficient. I also told my friend that today's compositions now have to contain so many inches of Italian phrases, and the playing has to include so many scores of octaves in order to please the public. I said that I found it sickening, and he agreed with me. However, I expressed my strong disapproval over his decision not to take part in the performance of 'St Paul' planned for Good Friday, and I eventually managed to persuade him to change his mind, so that he started rehearsals for the work soon afterwards. He did not want to play in the Gewandhaus either, though, and informed the directorate of his refusal to do so.

Following the second rehearsal for 'St Paul', we find this entry in the diary:

Mendelssohn's strictness with the choir, which consisted of numerous enthusiasts, was just as striking as the way that he kept the ensemble together with his piano accompaniment which was excellent.

Moscheles attended all the rehearsals and after the performance commented: *It is only by virtue of a close acquaintance with this magnificent work that I have come to appreciate it fully.*

The examinations at the Conservatory prompted a long description in the diary:

I seem to have my fair share of problems with those pupils of mine who have come over from England to receive tuition . . . I asked the beautiful young ladies to play Czerny's piece for eight hands in the main examination, but once again they arrived with white powdered faces, which causes all the Germans to whisper about them. Miss F. distinguished herself by the enormous construction of hair piled up on her head. And what else apart from that? She had forgotten her music! Mendelssohn, who was beside himself, rightly shouted at her: 'One may forget little things, but to forget your music for a public performance is really going too far! Now the audience has to sit and wait because you have forgotten your music' etc. Faced with a dilemma as to what we should do, I went to fetch the piano-tuner from his corner: 'Please tune what is necessary on both pianos and do not stop until the orchestra's errand boy whom I have just sent out has returned with Miss F's music score.' He did as I requested, so even if the pause was not pleasant, the time passed without a lot of fuss. The young ladies did not play badly after all, and were admired and applauded by the audience. It could just be that Miss J's pretty little face played its part here.

The diary continues . . .

Young G. has gone off to Paris to learn how to play the piano in the republican fashion and, what is more, from Chopin, who mourns for his nation's lost freedom in his Mazurkas and Ballads. Seriously, however, he could learn many positive things from Chopin's playing, but as far as composition is concerned, Chopin has proved that he has only solitary favourable thoughts which he does not seem to be able to work into a nicely rounded whole. In his Sonata for Cello which has just appeared, I often find passages which sound to me as though someone was experimenting on the piano and banging away at every possible key just to see if there was a melodious sound at home at all!

During a five-week stay in London, Moscheles struck up a closer acquaintance with the 'Swedish Nightingale' Jenny Lind:

I cannot find words for Jenny Lind, for how would it be possible to express in a few words impressions which are both so magnificent and so agreeable? All the epithets for her have already been exhausted and I have too high an opinion of her to degrade her with the banal words of praise now being poured on her by newspaper writers. She has made a tremendous impression here. Everyone wants to see and hear her, or everyone has already seen and heard her and wants to see and hear her again. I also wanted to meet her away from the theatre so, as she lives quite a distance from the theatre, I sent her a written request to enquire whether she would grant me an hour of her time. She was announced to me during the lunch hour of the next day and simply came up to me herself and told me that she would be pleased to receive my visit. It is extremely rare that one finds such greatness and such modesty together – if ever – and even though I had already been told about the great qualities of her character by Mendelssohn, who is better acquainted with her, I was, nevertheless, surprised by her manner. I had to play my fantasy on her Swedish songs for her. Mendelssohn had chosen the themes with me, and she paid me a string of compliments about my conception and rendition of them. We returned her visit in Old Brompton, where she lives far away from the noise of the capital and the glory of her performances.

By July, Moscheles was at home in Leipzig again, and he spent the lion's share of his time arranging Beethoven's Symphony in A, which Hummel had already arranged before him. He described this work in his diary:
Hummel takes every possible liberty in this work, and seeks to improve on Beethoven's performance instructions as well as on his notes. For example, at the beginning of the first Allegro he has changed the rhythm of the bass:
Instead of

He has written

Furthermore, towards the end of the piece on the eleventh page he has cut 10 bars !!! – and in the last piece on the thirtieth page twenty-two bars!!!?

During these summer months there were quite a few musicians travelling through who wanted to play and sing, or audition for Moscheles. He seldom enthused over their performances but, as he wrote in his diary
. . . you have to hear everything nonetheless, and then I have to show these folk that it is possible to play the piano without bashing away at it, and also that one can also play a pianissimo without using the soft pedal. The pedals are merely aids, and anyone who relies on them absolutely is automatically awarding his fingers a certificate of incompetence. Moreover, anyone who writes composition with titles such as Polka du Diable, Valse infernale and Menuet à la Demon or, by way of a contrast, Moonlight Elegies, Nocturnes of Yearning and Sonata for Aeolian Harp, is seeking to impress by the titles and not by any original thoughts. C. L.'s 'Approach of Spring' is more appropriate to

autumn, since the composition is wilted like falling leaves.

Moscheles spent part of the ensuing summer holidays in Dresden, while Mendelssohn stayed in Switzerland with his family. He was not in the best of health, having unexpectedly lost his sister Fanny, to whom he had been extremely close, a short while beforehand. He was to survive her by just a few months.

THE DEATH OF MENDELSSOHN

Mendelssohn returned from Switzerland on September 17th 1847. Mentally, he was still the same as ever, but his physical appearance seemed to have changed. He had aged and was now listless, and he walked much more slowly than before. However, if one had seen him at the piano or heard him discussing music and musicians, he was the picture of liveliness and passion. His friend Julius Rietz had just taken up a post as Kapellmeister in Leipzig, which was a great source of delight for Mendelssohn. As he said at the time:

Yet another one who takes good music seriously, who is thoroughly competent himself when making music, but who can also raise the performance of others to the highest level of perfection. This will surely give the Gewandhaus Concerts just the right degree of solemnity. And what music will we be able to make with him here? Rietz plays the cello so well that it promises to be a splendid winter!

He was so full of enthusiasm that he arranged a musical evening straight away, at which Rietz and Moscheles were to make music together at his house. In the course of the evening a lively discussion developed about the new piece for eight bands which Moscheles had written for Benedict. Moscheles wanted to call the piece 'Jadis et aujourd'hui' (Times past and times present).

He explained that the serious fugue referred back to the good old days, while the more light-hearted passages referred to the music of his own era. 'But why that?', Mendelssohn asked. 'Are there not interesting fugues being written nowadays? – Our own age is also yielding good compositions.' 'But current popular taste has deteriorated', Moscheles replied. 'People only want to hear light music and rhythms which the ear can easily assimilate.' 'Yes, that's what they want', Mendelssohn interrupted excitedly, 'but they shan't have it. Are you and I not still alive? Is it not our intention to write good music? We want to prove that this era can still produce good music, and for that reason I beg you to change the title of the piece.' Mendelssohn's plea was irresistible, and so the original title 'Jadis et aujourd'hui' was altered to 'Les contrastes', with Mendelssohn subsequently expressing his approval.

The diary continues with the events of the following weeks:

October 3rd: After the Mendelssohns had eaten with us, Felix and I amused ourselves on the piano by playing some fugues and gigues by Bach. After that, however, he produced a splendid parody of a Polka as peformed by the City Musicians in Frankfurt, to which he had been subjected on countless occasions, much to his annoyance. . . .

October 5th: I spent the whole afternoon at Mendelssohn's. He played his latest Quartet to me, all four movements being in F-minor. The passionate nature of the whole work and its mournful key seemed to me to be an expression of his deeply disturbed soul; he is still fighting the grief caused by the loss of his sister. He also showed me the manuscripts of some songs; all of them were pleasant enough, if not always particularly original.

October 8th: Examinations held at the

Conservatory. Mendelssohn wrote some bass continuo exercises on the blackboard with a piece of chalk. While the students were working them out, he sketched some charming landscapes with his pen. He is a genius who never stops creating! In the afternoon and evening we went to his house. He played his D-minor Sonata for Cello and Piano with Rietz, as well as Beethoven's Op. 102, and later on he and I played my Sonate symphonique.

On October 9th Mendelssohn went to fetch Moscheles and Charlotte to accompany them on a walk:

We watched him making his way slowly and sluggishly through the garden up to the house. When my wife, showing great concern, asked how he was, he replied: 'How am I? Dismal. That's how I am'. She comforted him, telling him that the sunny weather and the walk would do him good. And, indeed, in the course of our walk through the Rosental, he became so much fresher and livelier that we forgot all about his ill health. He told us about his last visit to London, as well as about his visit to the Queen and how she had sung to him in such a charming manner, after he had played to her and the Prince. He continued by saying that the Queen very graciously announced to him that he had given her so much pleasure, and asked how she could return the compliment there and then. He requested to see the children, so she took him to the beautifully maintained nursery, and the little princes and princes and princesses were so well brought up and so well behaved that it was a real pleasure for him indeed.

We parted company just before 1 o'clock with all of us in the most cheerful frame of mind.

However, the very next day, Mendelssohn felt extremely unwell at Frau Frege's house. He had gone there to ask this singer, whom he held in such high esteem, whether she would like to sing in the forthcoming performance of his 'Elijah'. He had previously told Moscheles:

She is afraid of appearing before the public at the moment, as she has been suffering from a bad throat. However, no one else would be able to sing it as well as she, so I shall have to encourage her.

The following description of his visits to Frau Frege on October 9th was recounted by the latter herself, and subsequently written up by Charlotte:

When he came in, he said to me: 'I have come to see you today and will return every day until you have given me your acceptance. I have brought the altered pieces (from 'Elijah') with me. I must tell you, however, that I feel particularly dejected at the moment – so much so, that I even wept during my Trio recently. But today, before we have a look at 'Elijah', I should like you to help me to collect some material together for a song book, which Härtel's are pressing me to do.' He had brought the book, Op. 71, with him, and the seventh song was to be the old German Spring song 'Der trübe Winter ist vorbei' [The gloomy winter is past], which he had composed during the summer of this year, but had only written it down on October 7th. I knew approximately in what order he would arrange them, and placed them on the piano one by one in that order. After I had sung the first one, he was deeply moved and asked for it to be repeated: 'That was to have been a birthday present for Schleinitz on October 1st – but, as I said, my mood is so depressed at the moment, and I cannot tell you how sad I felt again when I saw Fanny's room in Berlin, still just as she left it. However, I have so much to thank God for – after all, Cécile and Felix (his youngest and often sickly son) are both very well.' I had to repeat all of the songs several times and stuck with my original thought that the Spring song was less suitable for the book, to which he replied. 'That may be so. The whole book looks serious though – and it can be sold to the world like that.' Even though he now looked very pale, I had to sing the first song to him for the third time, and he made all kinds of friendly and kind remarks about it. Then he said: 'If you are not too tired, could we sing the last quartet from "Elijah" now?' I went out of the room to fetch some lamps and when I came back I found him sitting in the other room in the corner of the sofa. He felt that his hands had become very cold and stiff and, as he wanted to be sensible about it, he decided he would rather go for a walk around the town, since he felt too poorly to be able to make good music. I wanted to order a carriage for him, but he would not hear of it, and he left at half past five, after I had given him some sugared water and some lemonade powder. As soon as he went out into the fresh air he felt that it would be better to return home immediately. When he reached home he slumped into the corner of the sofa, but Cécile found him at 7 o'clock with his hands dried out once again. The next day he suffered from a terrible headache, which the physician treated with leeches. He thought it was some kind of stomach upset, and it was not until much later that he declared it to be a case of overstrained nerves. For some time now, I had noticed his pale complexion while he was conducting and playing – even before Fanny's death. Now the whole thing was beginning to affect him more than before.

Everyone was distressed by Mendelssohn's illness but, as he felt better again after a few days, it was firmly believed that he would ultimately recover.

The diary continues the story:
On October 15th he allowed me to tell him all sorts of details about Hiller's opera ('Conra-din der letzte Hohenstaufe'), and he was delighted that it had been so well received.

Numerous friends paid him visits, and Mendelssohn was in good spirits, making plans upon plans for the future. He even wanted to travel to Vienna, in order to direct a performance of 'Elijah', which he had previously promised to do. His health began to improve more and more, and on October 28th he actually went for a walk with his wife. Nevertheless, immediately after this, he collapsed, whereupon the doctors diagnosed apoplexy. Yet again he seemed to make a recovery. A short while later, however, he started speaking English in a highly agitated manner, and on November 3rd in the afternoon he suffered his third stroke, which clouded his senses completely.

November 4th arrived. Moscheles, who remained close at hand throughout, wrote these lines on the morning of that same day in the Mendelssohns' house:
Mother Nature, art thou demanding thy rights? Angels who dwell in the heavenly spheres, do you wish to reclaim your brother whom you consider as your own, and whom you deem to be too noble to keep company with us ordinary mortals? We still possess him, we still cling to him, and we hope that by God's gracious mercy he will be able to dwell longer among us; he who has always enlightened our lives as an example to us of all that is noble and all that is beautiful. Only Thou, O Creator, knowest why it is. Thou hast poured into this soul treasures of the spirit and the mind which the tender shell of his body can bear for only a limited time, and these same treasures are now threatening to shorten his very existence. May we plead to thee as a fellow brother? Thou hast achieved such a marvellous creation in him. Thou hast shown us how man can be raised towards thee and how he can even approach thee. No man has come closer to thee than this man for

whom we now stand in fear and trembling. We beseech thee to allow him to enjoy his earthly rewards, to enjoy the love of his chosen companion, the development of his children, the bonds of friendship and the adoration of the world.

November 4th – Midday – : His doctors, Dr Hammer, Hofrat Clarus and the surgeon Herr Walter took turns at watching over him. The bulletin written by Schleinitz declared that the situation was now hopeless. All the while, Herr and Frau Dr Frege, David, Rietz, Schleinitz and my wife and I waited anxiously outside the sick room. The only words of encouragement the doctors could pronounce were: 'If he does not suffer another attack of apoplexy or pulmonary apoplexy, this apparent calm state could improve and lead to his ultimate deliverance from the illness. – However, the calm state itself is the result of a decline in his physical strength.'

4th November – Evening – : From 2 o'clock onwards, when it was feared that there might be yet another apoplectic attack, he started to lose all consciousness. All his finer organs and intellectual powers were now gone, and he lay there restfully, his breathing loud and heavy. In the evening we took turns to sit around his bed, no longer fearing that we might disturb him. His angelically peaceful countenance was the mark of his immortal soul, which left such a deep and indelible impression on our own souls. His beloved Cécile bore her heavy burden of grief and pain heroically. She did not succumb to any frailness and did not utter one word to betray her inner turmoil. Felix's brother Paul sat by his bed continually, like a moveable marble statue. The tragedy of the whole scene was intensified by the fact that we were awaiting the arrival of his sister, Frau Dirichlet, or of his other brothers and sisters, and of Herr and Frau Schunck – but all in vain. Dr Härtel

had travelled up to Berlin to fetch them and also Dr Schönlein – but they all failed to appear. – From 9 o'clock in the evening the terrible conclusion drew nearer. His breaths became slow and laboured. The doctors counted them as if they were hoping to be able to enrich scientific research with new discoveries. His features were transfigured; Cécile knelt by his bed and burst into tears. Paul Mendelssohn, David, Schleinitz and I stood round the bed in deathly silence, immersed in prayer. With every breath that was wrested from him, I could feel the struggle of this great spirit, wanting to free itself from its earthly shell. I had often heard his breathing while admiring his performing, as if he were riding heavenwards on Pegasus, and now these same sounds had to ring out announcing this terrible end. I was transported to another world when I thought of the morbid sounds of the funeral march in Beethoven's 'Eroica', particularly at this point:

Indeed, it was only the suppressed sobbing of all those present and my own warm tears which united me with the present.

At 24 minutes past nine, with one last deep sigh, he exhaled his great soul from his body. The doctor led Cécile into another room and stood by her as she grieved in silence. I knelt before the bed and accompanied the soul of the departed on its journey to heaven with my own prayers. I then kissed his high forehead before it had cooled in the sweat of his death throes. We bemoaned this irreplaceable loss for several hours more, and then each of us withdrew with his own private grief. His *children had been sent to bed at 9 o'clock, and were already sleeping peacefully when God called their father to Him. However sublime and dreadfully uplifting the funeral ceremony would be, it would never match the emotions that I would retain for the rest of my life when I remembered this irreplaceable man and beloved friend. . . .*

The whole town mourned. The Gewandhaus did not put on a concert on that November 4th, as it would usually have done, since nobody would have wanted to go. Over the next few days Moscheles participated in the discussions about his friend's funeral, and orchestrated Mendelssohn's Song without Words in E-minor for the occasion.

The burial ceremony took place in St. Paul's Church in Leipzig on November 6th, after which his mortal remains were transferred to Berlin. The 'Berliner Staatszeltung' published this account of the proceedings: *Mendelssohn's body was carried into St. Paul's Church (The University Church) on November 6th, accompanied by a brass band playing Beethoven's Funeral March. The cortège was made up of the members of the Gewandhaus Orchestra and the students from the Conservatory, which the deceased himself had founded. The coffin – with the shroud being carried by Moscheles, David, Hauptmann and Gade – was followed by the Professors at the Conservatory, Mendelssohn's brother as chief mourner, and several musical societies from Leipzig and Dresden. After the address had been given by the pastor in the church, an organ prelude was played, and chorales from 'St Paul' and from one of the Bach's Passions were performed by the orchestra, under the direction of Gade and David. The coffin stood open throughout the whole of this service, and the departed, wearing a laurel wreath on his forehead, was drawn by the artists Bende-*

mann and Hübner, and Richard from Dresden. At ten o'clock in the evening the coffin was closed, and it was subsequently carried to the station of the Berlin Railway by students of the Conservatory. A torchlight procession consisting of more than 1000 people escorted the cortège through Leipzig's overcrowded streets. A similar honour was bestowed on the body, with dirges being sung, as it passed through Cöthen, Dessau and other towns on its way to Berlin. The corpse reached Berlin on November 7th at eight o'clock in the morning. Upon arrival, the coffin was adorned with oak leaves and a large laurel wreath before being transported by six heavily laden black horses to the Cemetery of the Holy Trinity. Thousands of people followed, their heads uncovered, and Beethoven's Funeral March was played once again. Two preachers and other friends of the deceased made speeches at the graveside, and a choir numbering some 600 people sang a hymn by Groeber, 'Christ und die Auferstehung' [Christ and the Resurrection]. It would be impossible to describe the feelings of sympathy expressed by all those present as the men threw earth and the women and children threw flowers on to the coffin, which had been lowered into the grave. Now Mendelssohn rests next to his sister, whose own death had such a tragic effect on him.

On November 11th a concert was held in the Gewandhaus in memory of the deceased. His oratorio 'St. Paul' was performed as well as the motet 'Herr nun lässest du deinen Diener in Frieden fahren' (Lord, now lettest thou thy servant depart in peace), his song 'Vergangen ist der lichte Tag' (The light of day is now past) and, finally, Beethoven's 'Eroica'.

The King of Prussia had sent Mendelssohn a letter, in which he expressed his great satisfaction at the first performance of 'Elijah' in Berlin. Unfortunately, however, this letter reached Leipzig on the day after the death of the great master.

The King of Saxony later attended a performance of the 'Walpurgisnacht' in the Gewandhaus; fragments of 'Die Lorelei' were also performed, causing Moscheles to express his sadness in his diary:

Oh, why must it be just fragments? Why was he not allowed to complete such promising works?

Numerous sketches appeared about Mendelssohn's life but, as Charlotte wrote . . .

. . . none of them described him as well as his own letters. Each one of his friends can attest what Mendelssohn meant to him, and what he has lost as a result of his death. The world must bemoan the fact that this creative genius was recalled to his maker before he had had the time to bring all the seeds of creativity in him to fruition. One can only read with amazement how he always showed his noble-mindedness and his devotion to all those that he loved. He never wished harm to anyone, and he considered his art to be a gift from heaven. This gift had been bestowed upon him, and he, in turn, had to lavish great care and attention on it as a wonderful possession. And while so many of his contemporaries wrote for the world, for popular taste and for the public, he strove solely to clothe his poetic or divinely sublime ideas in the most noble and delightful harmonies. His works also found their critics – which composer would not find this? However, no one can ever accuse him of ever having been untrue to himself or to whatever he deemed to be right and proper.

Charlotte was deeply depressed by Mendelssohn's death and thought that it would now be quite out of the question for them to stay on in Leipzig, as their loss was so great. Moreover, the very purpose of their being there, working in conjunction with Mendelssohn, had been shattered by this blow.

Nevertheless, Moscheles immediately convinced her to the contrary:

He requested me to come to this institute which meant so much to him; it would have been a daily delight and pleasure for me to be able to work with him, but it now remains my duty and sacred legacy to carry on the work without him. I now have to work for both of us.

Moscheles therefore resumed his lessons on Monday, November 7th, and found the best possible solace for his grief in his intensive work with the students. Meanwhile, Leipzig's musicians frequently met at Moscheles' house, and in other houses, to perform Mendelssohn's music. Thus the great man continued to live on with them throughout the winter.

REVOLUTION OF 1848

The year 1848 began with the usual lively musical activity which characterized the city of Leipzig at the time, with the brilliant musical pair of Robert and Clara Schumann really coming to the fore; he on account of his select novelties for piano and orchestra, while she was unique in her outstanding renditions of the latter. The following letter was written by Moscheles at the time:

We are still living with the memory of Mendelssohn, and maintain close contact with the bereaved family. His wife has been courageous enough to be present at all the performances which her husband's friends have arranged, as well as listening to such deeply moving compositions as the last Quartet in F-minor and the Nachtlied, performed as only Frau Frege can. On his birthday, February 3rd, 'Elijah' was performed, and I attended all of the rehearsals . . . Gade's direction showed diligent preparation and was good, apart from a few tempi which Mendelssohn had taken differently in Birmingham. There the organ had heightened the effects in many passages. The concert, which was given for the benefit of the pension fund, was, inexplicably, able to fill only two-thirds of the hall. Moreover, the reverent silence with which the work was received at the end allowed a few rustling programmes among the audience to demonstrate that the public had not been moved by it. The whole business provoked considerable indignation in us, and also in some other like-minded individuals.

The proclamation of the Second Republic in France in February 1848 marked the start of a turbulent development in Europe which was eventually to suck all the large states into its whirlpool, with the exception of England and Russia. Bloody rebellions occurred in March in Germany and Austria, and in May the Constituent National Assembly was opened in St Paul's Church in Frankfurt, which was to lead to the unification of the German Reich with a new basic political structure.

Moscheles wrote:
It is as though the countries are all suffering from a serious deformity, and a conference of all the surgeons is being held in Frankfurt. Artificial arms, legs, eyes and noses are being sewn on to the mutilated body of the states at this big assembly, and it is the tragic lot of this era in which we live to have to stand by and watch all these operations. It is a hard test for us indeed, but God has imposed it on us nonetheless! I do not feel this great urge for freedom myself, and all I desire is a just monarchy. However, I would definitely not want to live under Nicholas's rod of iron, nor would I wish to see any of my fellow men having to do so.

The Moscheles' relatives in Prague fled to Leipzig, as the situation in their home town had become too distressing.

. . . and my dear old Vienna, celebrating on account of human blood being spilt. My foolish, musical Vienna! I find it much harder to imagine Vienna in a state of turmoil than I do Berlin, where this whole tragic business is developing at an alarming rate. May God preserve us from a repetition of the events of the nineties.

On another occasion he wrote this:
When I play I forget everything, but I must admit that when I compose these days, I am unable to collect my thoughts properly. However, I also find great comfort in nature . . . Yes, there are still some beautiful spots on this earth, and I share the hopes of everyone else that we will enjoy freedom again after all the misery we have endured.

Moscheles likewise found great solace in Beethoven's music. After a performance of the Ninth Symphony conducted by Rietz, he wrote:
It was a great delight for me! This performance revealed many new glories in the work. Certain details and effects were apparent which, in spite of all my efforts and hard work, I had never been able to achieve with the orchestra in London. The instruments were somehow interwoven in a truly musical fashion, thus forming an ideal blend as a whole, which I had yearned for in England for a long, long time. If one were to compare this work with other symphonies, it would be rather like comparing the Kölner Dom [Cologne Cathedral] with other churches.

At the request of Cécile Mendelssohn, Moscheles revised the orchestral parts for Mendelssohn's Symphony in A, and a short while later he went to Berlin to visit his friend's grave.

As a result of the poverty which was rife at the time, numerous charity concerts were held, predominantly for the benefit of unemployed workers, and Moscheles often took part in these events. At one such concert, which was given by Frau Fege, with the assistance of many artists, including Moscheles, the outcome was particularly spectacular, and as Kammerrat Frege had magnanimously agreed to pay the costs of 200 Taler, they were left with a total of 640 Taler for the factory workers.

In the midst of all these dismal times, the Viennese comedian Johann Nestroy came to Leipzig to cheer the people up, and to entertain them with his play 'Freiheit in Krähwinkel' (Freedom in Backofbeyondia). Moscheles commented upon the performance afterwards:

It takes someone like Nestroy to parody state reform and freedom without boring people or even insulting them. Earlier on, he would have been locked away on the Spielberg for performing such a play – now, however, he can even portray Metternich as a comic figure on the stage with impunity.

(Metternich, the all-powerful Chancellor of Austria, had abdicated in March and had fled to England.)

The political unrest continued to spread, but before the real storm was unleashed, Moscheles managed to spend a few days in Dresden again. This short entry described part of his visit:

On Sunday morning while I was in the choir gallery of the Catholic Church, I met Wagner, who is both a republican composer, as well as a true republican.

At the time, Wagner was actively involved in politics; indeed, the following year he was forced to flee on account of seditious speeches he had made at various riots. A number of deaths occurred in the course of the riots and Wagner was held to be partly responsible.

The fourth of July approached and with it came the fall of the French Ministry. It had been announced in Leipzig that Archduke Johann, who had been elected by the Consti-

tuent National Assembly as Adminstrator of the Reich, would be travelling through the city. In view of this, a guard was formed to protect the visitor, of which Moscheles was also a member. His chosen weapon was a pike, which probably served more as part of his uniform than anything else, since he had never made any secret of his very limited skill in military matters. When he returned from his night watch one evening, he recounted how Brassin, the bass at the Leipzig Theatre, who had also been on watch duty, had chatted amicably with him about the last performance of 'Don Juan' *so that the time passed quickly and was much enjoyed by both of us.*

In September he wrote a letter to his father-in-law:

The private examinations at the Conservatory, which are shortly to be followed by the public ones, are taking up a great deal of my time at the moment, as far more new students have enrolled than one would ever have expected . . .

Mendelssohn's musical bequest, which included a number of unpublished works is now in the hands of Schleinitz, who is acting as the guardian of the children. One of these works, the 'Reformation Symphony' was rehearsed yesterday in private. It breathes a tone of sacred gravity and it pleased me a great deal, even though he himself criticised the work. Nevertheless, he was as well acquainted with the profundity and dignity of this sacred style as he was with the spirit of the dancing elves or with the light-heartedness of the songs! His genius will continue to feed my own mind as long as I live.

Things started to look even more gloomy on the political front in the late autumn of that year. In September there had been an uprising against the Constituent Assembly, causing them to seek assistance from troops. Moscheles commented on these increasingly bitter disputes:

All the reforms which are supposed to produce a new age for us, still seem to be unripe and lacking in insight, and I just wish we could lay them out in the straw, as we would with fruit, so that they could ripen. Perhaps this would prevent us from having to use human blood as a fertiliser.

'Good old Vienna' had had to bear all the devastations of the political storm, as the freedom-fighters wanted to liberate the city after its many years of oppression. Litolff, who had at one time been a pupil of Moscheles, joined the would-be liberators and wore a white band around his skilled musical arm. Robert Blum made his way to the imperial city, along with numerous other people who shared his views; however, he and his friends were seized and he was shot. On November 26th, a funeral ceremony was held for him in Leipzig, after which Moscheles noted in his diary:

I attended the service and sat in the choir gallery of St, Thomas's Church, where I became thoroughly engrossed in the score of Cherubini's Requiem in C-minor.

CRISES IN MUSICAL CIRCLES

On the 2nd January 1849 Moscheles tells of an event that appears symptomatic not only for Leipzig but in a certain sense for the whole situation in Germany at that time:

It is the death of a fifty-year-old patron of the arts. She lived in prosperity during Haydn's, Mozart's and Beethoven's times and was received abroad with honours and awards. There were times when she was a gossip, but her entertainment was frequently instructive. She never sojourned with individuals, only with music; her name – the 'Leipzig Allgemeine Zeitung für Musik'. In the last issue the editor writes, among other things: 'Productivity in art has so much deteriorated

that there is no longer sufficient material for a newspaper dedicated to music'.

This deterioration was mainly due to the political confusion in which Germany found herself at that time and which worsened in 1849. After the rejection of a liberal national constitution serious insurrections arose in May which were suppressed by the Prussian troops. In Dresden the artists too were active in the uprising, and Moscheles writes: *A Schröder-Devrient, a Richard Wagner, who harangues the people of Dresden! Where will all this lead to?* It led to, among other things, outrages in Leipzig, and a short time after, Wagner fled to Switzerland. When the seething elements quietened down, Moscheles took his family to Prague. *They must get to know everything,'* he wrote.

Their father's birthplace, the tombs of the deceased, the place on the 'Ring' where, as a small boy, I was fond of holding the sheets of music for the wind-instrumentalists, the house owned by Dionys Weber – yes, even the cornerstone where I broke the bottle of wine which I was carrying for him to his friend, the prelate. And finally, I want to introduce my children to those relatives still living and to acquaint them with the sights of Prague.

In the final issue of the 'Leipzig Allgemeine Zeitung für Musik' Schleinitz published the statutes of a Mendelssohn Foundation, which had been at the planning stage for some time. The concept of the Foundation was (together with the Leipzig Conservatorium) for the purpose of upholding the remembrance of Mendelssohn. The patron of the foundation was the King of Prussia, and Moscheles was requested to join the directorate. To this Moscheles remarks incidentally: *The King has also honoured me with a letter and a golden casket for my dedication of the 'Contrasts'; but I do not like to speak of this* otherwise it will find its way into all the newspapers.

A short time later there is a note in his diary:

Paul Mendelssohn has visited me to ask me on his sister-in-law's behalf to supervise, in collaboration with Hauptmann, David and Rietz, the posthumous publication of his brother's works – a service which I shall undertake with love and piety. . . . Already on the next evening I heard at David's some of the posthumous quartet movements. The most outstanding is the Quartet in F-minor, and an important Quintet in B-major.

Mendelssohn's 'Athalia' was also performed.

Felix played the Athalia on the piano for me in London . . . Every wind instrument, especially in the Priests' March, tooted, as he called it, and I had the most surprising modulations running through my head. At that time I liked the work. Now, after I have been working on the rehearsals and the performance, I absolutely adore it. At certain points, my heart was again and again deeply moved. How his must have been when he wrote it! But the Leipzig public, strange to say, were not moved – like 'Elias' they remained cool. What should one deduce from that?

At Mendelssohn's birthday celebration at the Conservatory, Moscheles played his posthumous Variations in E-flat major. In the following passage we read:

In the Gewandhaus we heard Schumann's C-major Symphony. It continues ingeniously in Beethoven's style, it is similar in bravado, yet not in depth of soul. His D-minor Trio in the Chamber music . . . I recognised as a composition of the most passionate character. This is moving not only because of the intensity of thought, but also because of its assured running of the most far-removed tones. The Scherzo is the most piquant of pieces and

must be repeated, the Adagio very melancholy. Frau Schumann played her husband's pieces, Mendelssohn, Chopin . . . everything masterfully . . . Schumann, with whom I would have loved to speak, remained aloof.

Family circumstances called Moscheles to London for 14 days. The first letter he wrote from there to his wife begins:

I remain your ever-loving faithful husband I. Moscheles.

I begin with the end just as jadis began my C-major Concerto, with the final cadence, because in both cases my principal thought is expressed:

. . . First now though to the local situation. Exeter Hall offered me an engagement immediately upon my arrival, but with an ease bordering on pride, I explained that I didn't wish to play in public any more. Everyone receives me with open arms. Beethoven's mass in C-major was pure ecstasy; Mendelssohn's Song of Praise too. Costa's waving about with the baton disturbed me somewhat, however, he held the 700 players superbly together, even if not always what I consider to be in the correct tempo.

In the spring a further piece from Mendelssohn's legacy was brought to light. It was the fragment of the oratorio 'Christus', and the pupils of the Leipzig Conservatory studied it with Moscheles' assistance. He wrote:

It consists of five or six choruses, recitatives and a tercet in the most exalted style worthy of the subject. A funeral chorus of Zion's daughter, one of the people's 'Crucify Him' are masterpieces that themselves as frag-

ments must be assured of an honoured place. The date of publication is not yet certain.

Later Mendelssohn's 'Oedipus' had its pre-mière, under the direction of Rietz, and Moscheles, who was enraptured of the whole piece, commented:

The pathos of the male choruses, the antique tonal colour of this delightful work enveloped my senses magically and led me back to the antique world. The public forgot to applaud, whether out of ignorance or bliss remains a moot point. I read Berlioz' feuilleton about Meyerbeer's prophet. The libretto is frightful, and there must be emotions in it that make you shudder to the bones. The music should be worthy of Meyerbeer and I look forward to it with great expectations.

In the Gewandhaus Concerts of that spring Liszt was also to be heard.

He played the first piece of a Henselt'sch Concerto and his Don Juan fantasy with his gigantic bravura and always with ingenious effects. Strangely I still think of the throwing about of his hands which appear to want to say: this is rapture. . . . Strangely though too is that the most dangerous leaps, in spite of all this tossing about, only seldom fail. His overwhelming virtuosity gained him thunderous applause. His visit to us was very interesting; he spoke amiably and frankly about his private circumstances, and who could speak better and more kindly than he?

In summer Moscheles spent a few weeks in Paris. From there he wrote to friends:

Unfortunately we have heard about Chopin's grave illness, made enquiries ourselves and found everything sadly confirmed. Since he has become so resigned, his sister remains with him. Now the days of the poor fellow are counted. His suffering is great. He has drawn a sad lot!

On 17th October 1849 Chopin died as a result of tuberculosis from which he had suffered for many years. The diary has this to say on Chopin's death:

Music has lost so much with the passing of poor Chopin, for although he was not a classical musician, and created no great artistic work, he nevertheless possessed very rare qualities: soul, feeling and character. Jules Janin writes in the 'Journal des Débats', how Chopin requested a Polish song and Mozart's Requiem to be played to him before his passing.

On his return to Leipzig in the late autumn of 1849, Moscheles experienced once more a disappointment with the public. About a Gewandhaus Concert he wrote:

The Leonore Overtures, Mendelssohn's A-major Symphony, his 42nd Psalm, everything was captivating and beautiful. However, I found that some of the tempi were not in accordance with my tradition. And the reception? – lukewarm. O clique! As if in a city where one reveres the genius of a Schumann, Mendelssohn is decried as schoolmasterly, and must be placed under him! The public loses all initiative and in its comprehension and its feelings stand under a guidance which is just as oppressed as is the uprising of the German people.

At the end of February 1850 the Moscheles family went to Hamburg and celebrated there their silver wedding anniversary. *Looking back over these 25 years of wedded bliss is like looking at a lantern-slide without any blemishes,* says Charlotte, and Moscheles:

The Almighty God has allowed me, after my recovery from sickness, to spend this beautiful day – one of the most important – within the close circle of my own dear people.

On his return to Leipzig he wrote to his father-in-law:

Two very contrasting works received great acclamation at the Gewandhaus. Schumann's second symphony, a great work, but originating from a passionate and somewhat gloomy soul, and Rossini's 'Tell' Overture; the outpouring of a blossoming genius from the south. Even Rietz was delighted with it. I have never heard it so performed; the power, the fire and the nuances of the orchestra are – and remain – unforgettable. I must say too that at a performance of the 'Prophets' neither the Hamburg nor the London Orchestra accomplished so much as this orchestra here. I treasure Meyerbeer's music because of its outstanding dramatic effects, but I know, just as well as the hyper-critics, what the weaknesses are.

A summer sojourn in the idyllic Bellevue near Kiel was soon clouded over by the chaos of war. The first encounter of the 'Bonin' with the Danish ships had had no serious consequences, and one was just beginning to breathe easily again, when suddenly, in the night of the 25th to 26th July the distant thunder of the cannons boomed against the windows of Bellevue. The battle of Idstadt was being fought. In that same fateful night the youngest daughter became ill and as all the doctors in and around Kiel were on duty on the battlefield, it was decided to seek help in Hamburg. Charlotte reported:

The journey in the train . . . the hundreds of wounded who travelled on it; the appalling heat which increased the misery of the unfortunates, as well as the temperatures of the sick, was distressing, and the agitation and overcrowding on the Kiel–Altona railway station was so great that one spent a troublesome hour trying to extricate oneself from the throng who were jostling the alighting passengers: gaping, questioning or moaning.

Among other things, this summer brought a separation from the only son, whose art studies were now to begin in Paris, following his successful 'Abitur' (school-leaving examination).

In autumn 1850 there appeared in the 'Neuen Zeitschrift für Musik' an anonymous article which sparked off intense indignation at the Leipzig Conservatory, especially among Mendelssohn's friends. Moscheles referred to this in a letter:

My colleagues are extremely irritated by an article that Brendel (also a colleague) has taken up in his musical magazine. It is entitled 'Jewry in Music' and it seeks to belittle in every way both Mendelssohn and Meyerbeer. I say seeks, for in what way can a wicked newspaper article affect an important person? Everyone is full of anger, including myself, but I retain an outwardly calm appearance. Rietz has now drafted the following letter to the Directorate: 'It cannot have escaped the notice of the honourable Directorate of the Conservatory how the so-called "Neue Zeitschrift für Musik" seems to have taken on itself for some time now to deride the local musical situation and achievements. Its reviews are opined in a highly prejudiced, and frequently contemptuous manner (and couched in thoroughly foreign tones to every true critic). It presumes to judge people too in a derogatory manner – people whose services to the whole musical world are acknowledged and whose works (anyone with clear sight can see) were composed by expert musicians and who are also dear and lovable laymen. This manner of abusing the musical critique has lately exceeded the limits of propriety. We, the undersigned, would be prepared to ignore the occurrence if it weren't for the fact that the editor of the magazine, Herr Dr Brendel, is also a teacher at the same musical education institute to which we also devote a part of our labours. As, however, our views are directly in opposition to the gentleman in question, and in time these conflicting views could only bring to bear a harmful influence on our inmates and confuse them, we deem it our solemn duty to bring to the Directorate's notice the tension. We are hopeful that the honourable Directorate will express its disapproval of these activities – through the instant dismissal of Herr Dr Brendel from the Conservatory. Signed: Becker, Böhme, David, Hauptmann, Hermann, Joachim, Klengel, Moscheles, Plaidy, J. Rietz, Wenzel.' When this letter was placed before the whole Directorate, it was decided to question Herr Brendel about his journalistic insults, but not to dismiss him from his teaching post at the Conservatory. . . . When Herr Dr Brendel was charged to name the author of the article, he had the worthiness to remain steadfast in his refusal.

Only after many years did it come to light that the author was in fact none other than Richard Wagner. The article mentioned is today listed in the official register of Wagner's writings.

The anniversary of Mendelssohn's death had become festive, at first in the Conservatory and then at the Gewandhaus Concert, where Cherubini's 'Requiem', Mozart's G-minor Symphony and the first part of 'Elijah' were performed. Shortly afterwards Moscheles wrote:

Seventh book of Songs without Words, three songs for a deep voice, six for a higher voice, from Mendelssohn's musical bequest and revised; the compositions of Goethe's text 'Ein Blick von Deinen Augen' (A Glance from your Eyes) – curiously striking in rhythm, but found to be correct in comparison with the manuscript.

In 1850 the Bach Society was formed in Leipzig with Becker, David, Härtel, Hauptmann, Jahn, Moscheles and Rietz on the Board and it was decided to perform the B-minor Mass as a first offering. In that year Moscheles wrote several Lieder and a Mazurka Appassionata, revised various works from Mendelssohn's musical bequest, arranged Chopin's Violin-cello Sonata for Four Hands and finally, towards the end of the year, took up his own cello sonata. He also played all the novelties, about which he once remarked:

I must admit that when I read these I am more and more envious of large hands. My short fingers do not reach, although they are not stiff and are quite capable of stretching, and Rietz with his colossal hands seems worthy of envy to me. He spans three octaves in one chord. He also plays octave passages with the second and fifth finger.

At Schumann's house Moscheles heard excerpts from Schumann's first opera 'Genoveva', accompanied on the piano by Clara. *The composer is still undecided,* says the diary, *whether the reconciliatory finale should take place in the wilderness or in a festive castle.*

Towards the end of 1850, when Germany's political situation was in severe upheaval once again, Moscheles wrote to his father-in-law:

I thank you for all the light which you seek to diffuse over me, over the political dilettantes, over the whole gloomy world situation. To me the everlasting friction of the government's principles in our poor Germany is like a bottle of fine old wine – one shakes it and the sediment at the bottom sours its noble contents. I always read all the newspapers possible and almost wish for the bad old days back again, when at least we had only the foreign enemy to fight. But now! German against German! Shame on them! They would do better to leave it to the diplomats or settle the matter through lawyers in wigs, so that the annals could be written in red ink instead of blood. . . . Let us end the troubled year with the wish that the new one may bring us happier times.

FINDING SOLACE IN MUSIC

In those depressing years we find again and again in Moscheles' diary and correspondence remarks that illustrate how much music meant to him. On one occasion we read: *The magnificent Eroica performed with the finest nuances, seized me and tore me from my melancholy. It transplanted me in a distant ideal world.* And on another: *The people hang their heads low here in despair as everywhere, but I cling tight to my music profession and allow myself to be uplifted by the Muse Euterpe,* and: *the art, the dear art stays by my side again as consolation. . . . In work I forget all my worries; I wanted to be merry, the music should be fresh and cheerful.*

In spring 1851 he finished his Sonata for piano and cello, but:
I do not think of the publication. I like to let my pieces be for a little while so that they finish fermenting – which means that I can still refine them a little after the first flush of their creation.

Some time afterwards he performed them with Rietz in the Chamber Music for the first time in public and they were receieved with a great ovation and curtain calls.

Someone once asked Moscheles whether Beethoven's 'Christus am Oelberg' was not somewhat profane; to which he replied:
By all means he was frequently reproached with this, and even if with some justification – who would wish to censure the great man? Who with Gottfried Weber in his 'Cecilia' attacks even Mozart's 'Requiem' as being not strict enough in style? With such superb music one should set no strict limits between the devout and the dramatic. It is altogether too difficult to determine.

In May he heard 'Lohengrin' in Weimar and wrote this in his diary:

Liszt conducted the well-instructed orchestra. From the introduction, with the high-pitched violins and gradation effects, the instrumentation struck me as astoundingly original (also originally hard). A dramatic life is characterised in this music, but that this lies mainly in the recitatives does not appeal to me. I would like to see them more often broken up into rhythmic melodic phrases or formal pieces. Wagner's treatment often tires me because it is too monotonous and too heavily served up. I could have gladly done without an accomplished main theme – a continuous feeling of many beautiful but too transient details, many striking effects. And yet the work interested me immensely. One must hear it and then hear it again in order to appraise it more accurately.

In Weimar Moscheles was called upon to write something for the Schiller Album. He thereupon composed a fantasy about Schiller's poem 'Die Erwartung' (The Expectation) about which we later read: *Cranz from Hamburg, who heard here (in Leipzig) 'Die Erwartung' sprang up and said: 'I must have this piece. Name your price for it.'* Moscheles also heard at that time two compositions by Schumann, the 'Requiem für Mignon' and the Overture to the 'Bride of Messina'. To the former he wrote: *It is less appealing to me than are his greater works. In the 'Forest Scenes', which I have been playing lately, the form is too sketchy for me. I can well understand that he wants, like a good poet, to imply something and that he wishes to leave to the listener the completion of the fantasy, but I prefer more certainty, more working out in the music – not the fanciful, apparently aimless fumbling about with feelings. He is at his best in his symphonies.*

We put forward here a few further comments that Moscheles wrote in the diary about the performances which he heard at about that time:

Beautiful theme and workmanship, but too often repeated; double the effect would have been gained with half as often. [About the C-major Symphony by Schubert]

The Hadyn symphonies were again fresh, sound, without demonic elements.

Even at the rehearsal of Antigone I was captivated and delighted (relating to the music); I find it less suitable for the concert hall.

Mendelssohn's Finale to the Lorelei Opera is delightful, beautiful, gruesome, dramatic, melodic. Everything that is noble, even the great drum is ennobled here. The general impression was electrifying and even the advocates of the new trend were enthusiastic in their ovation, where otherwise they have declared Mendelssohn and his works old-fashioned. Should this fragment not reach the stage, through its purity and sincerity it will always remain valuable for the concert hall, a credit to Mendelssohn's legacy.

The listeners were carried away by storm of passion at Beethoven's Ninth symphony. The performance aggressively met all difficulties and the battle was gloriously won. 'Joy of devine sparks' glowed in every heart. The pieces were conducted by Rietz with David as leader of the orchestra and had been studied most diligently and with the most stringent consciousness.

In November Moscheles played his Pastoral Concert to benefit an impoverished family.

To do good always maintains its right, also for retired pianists. I myself play Liszt's new solo concert, the Paganini Etudes and other modern pieces, to learn the style.

And shortly afterwards:

With Liszt's unexpected visit I had a lovely bévue. Just before his entrance I had sent for the 'Scudo' from Paris and I asked him: 'Do you know the book? The first article, I see, bears your name.' 'Yes, in order to give myself a good knocking,' he replied, laughing, and began to read out loud the author's attacks. At first I was filled with consternation because I had expected quite the opposite from this publication. Then I laughed with him. He knows me too well to believe I would do it on purpose and he can laugh at such a thing.

A letter from Moscheles dated 24th December reads:

It is 5 o'clock in the evening and the great festival, that not only all Christians but also many Jews celebrate, is soon to begin. Now that the light of our era has so spread through tolerance to mixed marriages why should not Rabbi Samuel light a little Christmas tree for his Marie? All social, moral and mercantile connections of our era come to my mind naturally before the beginning of our homely celebrations, which through the general well-being and the anticipated happiness of the youngsters is for us a heightened fascination.

At the beginning of 1852 Henrietta Sonntag made an appearance in Leipzig, *somewhat older, a little less sylphlike,* says Moscheles, *but nevertheless charming, good and undemanding, with well-tuned voice and flawless vocal dexterity.*

We have seen her at every performance; the voice suffices perfectly for our little house and she can still, as in earlier years, say about her voice, 'it must flow as liquid as a stream'. One should not make comparisons, but as delighted as I was by this tranquil cool rendering, I could not but help think of the deeply comforting performance of Lind and of the passion of Malibran. So ungrateful is man. When I hear her sing my songs, which she likes to do often, she delights me.

Later he writes:

. . . and now I must compose a bravura piece for Sonntag. I play often for her at her

request – lately my Magyar Sounds in which one of the melodies so pleased her that she said, 'I should love to sing that, make me a few variations to it, Moscheles!' Naturally her wish was my command and so I started to write a rather impossible bravura.

As she left for Dresden Moscheles wrote: *Until now she has filled the whole of Leipzig. Yes, one almost forgot to run the trains on time and to wind up the town clock.*

The composition of vocal variations evoked in Moscheles some new Lieder, which were now composed one after the other. On 18th March the diary says:

A pleasure of the most rare kind thrilled me through and through with Frau Schumann's playing of my G-minor Concerto. I had never before heard it so correctly comprehended as by this master hand. I placed Schumann's symphony again above his Sonata (A-minor with violin) and the M.S. Trio in G-minor. The former pleased me better than the latter. This carries on in a disquieting passion, in contrapunctive entanglement, rhythmic deviations and frequently suspended notes. The melodic element is thereby lost as a sunbeam in the fog. Even the humour of the last part of the Trio I could wish to be less tempestuous and rather more blithe and cheerful. The 'Pilgrimage of the Rose' has much noble ardour and happy sensitive painting. In the love greeting it is too pathetic, almost bordering on the religious.
Frau Schumann played my Cello Sonata with Grabau and I may say with love. Ssshh . . . he himself remained mono-syllabic to my remarks about art in which I wished to draw him. It brought forth only a one-syllable nod.

These remarks cast a dark shadow in advance over the dramatic events that were soon to follow: in 1853 Schumann plunged into the River Rhine in mental derangement.

He was rescued, although he was never more to regain normal consciousness. He died in 1856.

In the Bach Society Moscheles was forced to face a defeat. He moved a resolution that the first delivery of Bach's works with piano arrangements were to be published.
The village schoolmaster and the unlearned, who are unable to read a full score should get to know the master through the piano arrangements, he believed. Yet he could not put his viewpoint across. In the following year, when the arrangement of the piano pieces was taken over by Becker, he declared himself superfluous and resigned.

On Good Friday the Matthew Passion was given in Leipzig. *I am deeply moved by it,* wrote Moscheles to his father-in-law, *and I have expressed my opinion on this great work in the 'Deutsche Allgemein'. But what are mere words? This double chorus through which the exalted chorale is sustained, the moment where Peter 'bitterly weeps' over his own betrayal, the aria 'I will watch over my Jesu' and then all the other arias and choruses – and each one of them delightful! You must hear it at the first opportunity. Schneider was the most superb evangelist, all the other singers, male and female, Rietz and David – excellent. When you read all this and see me so deeply immersed in the arts, you will hardly venture to ask me my opinion on papers of state and such things. It is as if you should give your view on a certain musical score. Please therefore act on my behalf. I am happy to be in your hands. Did you already know that one of your fellow citizens Otto Goldschmidt has had the good luck to be wed to our great artiste Jenny Lind? He has won a coveted prize, she, for her part, has tied the bond with an honourable man and a skilled musician.*

From the time Moscheles went to Leipzig he spent his holidays with the family, mostly hiking. They roamed through the Harz, the landscape between Dresden and Friedland and so on. As an inveterate music enthusiast, he stopped everywhere to inspect instruments. None was too dusty or too finger-worn that it could not be restored to make a sound. It was just as though the presence of a mute keyboard expressed an unexpected furrow of possibility:

Admittedly many have only tavern keyboards, little organs out of breath, but I have to try them and everywhere there is a cantor, an organist and also a waiter or privy councillor who listens to me astonished, not to mention the beautiful, occasionally ugly, sex.

But he endured the amateurish arrangements for the piano just as little as unused keyboards. He wrote once in a letter:

Today I have a very funny story to tell and you must laugh with us, even if you are not feeling disposed to humour. We arrived at Tetschen late in the evening, hungry and dead tired and called for something to eat. But, oh dear! In the next room there was the strumming of a piano. Just think, only a thin door between me and Weber's Invitation to the Waltz played by an unpractised hand in 'slow presto' as Mendelssohn used to say. I ring. Who is that playing? I ask the waitress. Oh, it is only a young man who is out at business the whole day; in the evenings he plays for a couple of hours. What a prospect! I try to eat but the food won't go down, and suddenly I come to a decision. Without saying a word to my astounded family, I take my hat, hurry out and knock on the neighbouring door. The 'Enter!' brings me face to face with the innocent delinquent. 'Your playing has tempted me, a stranger, to pay you a visit,' I say with hypocritical friendliness, 'I play too a little and I have studied this piece. Would you care to hear my version?' With this I walk over to the piano. The young

man, completely nonplussed, moves over to make room for me. Without waiting for an answer, I race through the piece in the quickest possible tempo and bring every possible double chord in. That worked! Ah, says he with a sigh, I shall never be able to play like that! 'Why not?' I reply, 'if you practise hard, but if you'll excuse me. . . .' My purpose was done, the night-time piano player was dumb (whether for ever I don't know) but I could eat in peace – and sleep. The others had pressed their ears to the wall and had listened to the whole comic scene; I believe it will make a lasting impression.

At the invitation of his one-time pupil Litolff, Moscheles went to the Braunschweig Music Festival in the summer of 1852.

I have met Liszt and many acquaintances, heard the 'Elijah', the Ninth Symphony and others. The Aegidien Church is a delightful place and the 700 participants filled it out well, if only Litolff had shown more calm and composure when conducting! His hand is too excitable to hold the conductor's baton. His playing was superb. He persuaded me to listen to the 'Homage to Handel' with him at one of the festival concerts.

In October he visited a Tannhäuser performance in Dresden conducted by Reissiger and wrote:

I was often surprised by ingenious details, by good instrumentation, also by the originality. But on the whole it makes the same impression on me as Lohengrin does. Too much recitative, too many fragmentary and monotonous passages are produced through its formlessness. I also recall ingenious passages with a thrilling effect, but my heart and soul stayed cold at this mass of passionate music.

In spite of this lack of satisfaction he went soon afterwards to Weimar to familiarize himself with another new piece – this time by Berlioz. He had once already explained:

Weimar is always rich in new works and even if 'new' does not always mean 'good', it remains a duty to bring the new to the ear, for one should get to know everything.

About Berlioz' performance in the Goethe city we read:

B. had a warm reception at his laurel-bedecked podium; my expectations were not set very high, but he excelled them. Much of it is baroque and disconnected, much, however, hugely successful. In Faust the use of the Rakoczy March was electrifying; it was repeated, as well as the soldiers' songs and the waltzes. Queen Mab's music in Romeo and Juliette is also exciting in its effect and quite worthy to be placed alongside Mendelssohn's works of a similar nature. B.'s conducting embued the performance with life so that everyone was carried away with it, and I was pleased to have got to know him as composer and conductor. The orchestra, with two pairs of kettle drums, was exuberant and powerful; the choir superb, having studied under Herr Montag.

On another day he, together with Liszt and Berlioz, was invited to the Grand Duchess at Tafel and in the evening he heard Berlioz' 'Benvenuto Cellini' conducted by Liszt. *I was surprised by the fluidity of the melodies, says the diary, by the occasionally very discreet instrumentation; yet much of it was unclear and the finale, the 'Carnival of Rome', was totally incomprehensible. The public expressed a favourable opinion of the music, although no single piece roused enough enthusiasm for a da capo. B. was called for after every act. After the opera Liszt assembled the whole musical circle; the mood was very lively and Berlioz was the célébrité. I conversed with him for quite a while and found him extremely gifted.*

At a social meeting of the Leipzig professors of music towards the end of the year Moscheles was present with music and speech. First he played Beethoven's Sonata Op. 53 and then introduced the Solo Fantasy Op. 77, its origin and character, with the following words:

This fantasy is rhapsodic and baroque, and is, therefore, little known among admirers. It seems to me that Beethoven wanted to put a part of himself in it, while, quite unprepared, perhaps even in a bad mood, he sat at the instrument and journeyed planless around his inner thoughts. I myself have occasionally heard him play in this manner and every time I hear this fantasy I immediately recall such moments.

As always Moscheles was visited by many touring pianists in the winter of 1853. And yet the now preponderant manner of their playing did not appeal to his piano at all. *The everlasting powerful chords, trills and arpeggi gripped my Erard and was entirely too much for it.* The unavoidable happened, the tuning block was torn, and as the damage could not be repaired in Leipzig, he called Paris for advice. The Erard company generously placed at his disposal their latest concert grand as replacement. *It has organ and flute tones, tenderness and power,* wrote Moscheles full of enthusiasm,

and on top of that a feather-light touch. With such a gleaming appearance, Schiller's words went through my head; in the beautiful body there must also live a beautiful soul. Really I can influence it just as if it were an emotion; the tones spin out as from a string instrument, and without any dampening – reach a pp. without using a one-string soft pedal, carry out every contrast of touch.

Later, when the old instrument was being sent back, Moscheles was in an elegiac mood: *The true, harmonic friend, how unhappily I must part from him. It is as though a beloved person was leaving us. As I watched from my window the box roll away, it appeared to me like a coffin. But thank God (his predominantly cheerful nature supervened) we have no real loss to complain about; on the contrary there are a thousand pleasures through the newborn waiting for us.*

JOURNEY TO ITALY

The spring of 1853 was chiefly devoted to preparations for the celebration of the tenth anniversary of the Leipzig Conservatory. For this event the present and former pupils combined their accomplishments. There were overtures by Büchner and the first movement of a symphony by Grimm that Moscheles designated as 'great progress'. For the first time fragments from Mendelssohn's unfinished Oratorio 'Christus' were heard.

In the summer of 1853 Moscheles – with Charlotte, both daughters Serena and Clara, and also his son Felix – undertook a journey to the South. They travelled by way of Nurenberg and Munich, and then on to Starnberg, to the Maler Kaulbach. There, by the sunny lakeside, Moscheles composed a Canon for the party which was at once performed. These were pleasant days. And then the family travelled on to Partenkirchen and to Innsbruck. The diary captures the landscape impressions that were entirely new to Moscheles:

Behind Innsbruck the river Inn foams wild over great masses of stone, greenery-overgrown mountain summits, fir-tree slopes and the venerable snow peaks of the Tyrolean Alps in the distance . . . The evening in Mals is refreshing; mighty waterfalls hurl themselves down from the mountains, rushing and roaring like the waves of the ocean. Everything is surprising, moving.

In the Tyrolean village of Gries Moscheles was, as so many times before, seized by the irresistible urge to get the best possible out of

a musical instrument. It was Sunday morning, and in the pretty little church the country folk had gathered for Mass. The accompaniment by the organist was rather sluggish. Then, suddenly, during the Kyrie, Moscheles approached him:

I placed my fingers between his on the keyboard and I playfully climbed onto the organ seat, from which he, astonished, slipped off. I carried on the music from where he had left off. On ending the piece, he said: 'Now you must play the prelude until the ministers sing,' and then again 'now you have to accompany the schoolchildren in the Gloria.' I obeyed. He was getting more and more agitated and embarrassed, watching me questioningly. Finally he could contain himself no longer. He burst out: 'But in God's name, who are you?' I wrote my name on the music. He opened his eyes wide in astonishment, fell about my neck, kissing my hands, and carried on kissing them after I had already begun to accompany the Creed.

Finally the travelling party reached Venice. They found accommodation in the Palazzo Mocenigo, where Byron had stayed before them. Some of the rooms were occupied by the 88-year-old Contessa Mocenigo, the former matriarch of the dynasty.* Their ancestors, the Doges, are portrayed by Giambellino and others on the ceilings of the rooms. The Contessa was, however, herself an apparition from the past.

Whenever she enters her richly-gilded gondola that is decorated with coats of arms, and she, wrapped in a thick veil, sits down on her golden stool, we all rush to the balcony to observe this picture of mediaeval custom.

Musically too Moscheles was well catered for.

I have a wonderful grand piano that possibly sounds twice as good because it stands on a

*Mocenigo, Venetian aristocratic dynasty from which five Doges emerged from the 15th to the 18th centuries.

marble floor. New sensations pour forth under my fingers whenever I think of the poetry that these walls could whisper, of the lagoon with its palaces; of the moon on the Piazzetta; of the reflection in the waves, and of the whole magical lighting. Everything is a retrospection of the old times and conditions with their great historic memories, their riches and their horrors.

A few days later we read:

I played in a piano establishment on a Boisselot from Marseilles in front of a few people – among them our 88-year-old hostess, the Contessa. I have always belonged to the German school, so I tried here to Italianise myself, and there was something that she did not understand, so she called it classic. . . . It is impossible to describe all the treasures that we see here daily . . . only something that I must tell you is that I stood transfixed in front of Titian's Ascension in all its superb colouring.

Another time the diary says:

Yesterday there was a serenade. A great wooden construction, draped in red and white and lit by two pyramids hung with lanterns, floated at dusk down the canal. It was a music-boat, on which a whole orchestra, two grand pianos and the soloists had room. There was singing, playing on the violins, flutes and piano. . . . For beauty-loving eyes it was everything they could desire. Bengal lights illumimated the canal just like a scene from A Thousand and One Nights.

On the return journey, by way of Bellinzona, Gotthard and Lucerne, Moscheles stopped off in Zürich to visit the son of his old friend Nägeli.

He owns a treasure – the manuscript of Bach's B minor Mass, which his father had got hold of through Schwenke in Hamburg. I let him show it me, and I have no doubts as to its authenticity. The Leipzig Bach Society would have been pleased to buy it from him, but he steadfastly refuses. Apart from this he also owns an unpublished concerto for four pianos by Bach; it is in A minor.

After returning to Leipzig, Moscheles took up once again his regular pattern of life, the rhythm of which was chiefly governed by the curriculum of the Conservatory. At the annual pupils' concert Liszt was also present, since he was staying at the time in Leipzig.

He appears to be content with the pupils and speaks to them sometimes with sensible words, but he would not play to them; and this brought many unfulfilled wishes to light. We heard him at David's play an arrangement for the piano of his fantasy about the prophets, actually meant for the organ. Hans v. Bulow helped with the pedal bases in the lower octaves. The first and last piece raged strongly in a fugue, the middle piece was played solely on a string and had a calmer motif and appealed to me more. At my wishes to give us something more, he played a piquant waltz in A sharp major and brought many over-seasoned effects through the transposition. In this, however, there were again individual strongly marked accents.

At the end of September he wrote:

I run through many new pieces: Czerny's Op. 800, Gradus ad Parnassum with easy to reach but commonly used difficulties; Liszt's Hungarian Rhapsody – interesting because of its correctly compiled national music, and even Fumagalli's Carnevale di più I try to play as cleverly as possible. . . .

Brahms was also among the new composers at that time. And Moscheles says:

Brahms' compositions have great momentum, and Schumann, whom Brahms has chosen as model, recommends him as the 'musical Messiah'. I find him often piquant, as Schumann does, and occasionally too construed. Our school, it is said, reproached

Beethoven at the first appearance of his works, for being too contrived, and he was not understood straight away. It is true that Beethoven's spirit lured him to unprecedented territory that was not open to everybody – and yet it has been proven since then that he not only construed, but found what he wanted to express musically. Let us hope that this is also the case with this younger composer. Brahms' technique, his 'sight-reading' make him and his teacher, Eduard Marysen, well reputed. . . . Also heard a lot of Berlioz and followed it with close attention. My opinion on his pieces is as unshakable as ever; recognisable and yet frequently incomprehensible. Or should one not understand such a Witches Sabbath for example? . . . Strange! Now we listen with pleasure to the simple opera: 'Doctor and Chemist' by Dittersdorf . . . One tends to forget how Rossini in 'Tell' and Meyerbeer in his operas crammed the world with their richness in instrumentation and their scenic effects; how Wagner still surpassed both of them. Les extrêmes se touchent. . . .

At the turn of the year he wrote to his relatives:
The heaven is going about in sackcloth and ashes. Should I do it too, because world events from the Orient appear ominous – or because I have gone down with a knee complaint? No, the warring powers will see to the balance of Europe, I care for my musical nursery school, and Dr Reclam cares for my knee. I believe that he has found the philosopher's stone; for homeopathy and allopathy had no effect whatever – and his galvano-electric apparatus seems to help. With the fingers and the advice I am, by the way, as active as ever. The pupils come to me and I play a lot. The toes are still pliable, neither weak of age nor stiff, and I have no other chronic sickness that I must carry about with me. . . .

THE TEMPORAL AND THE TIMELESS

At the beginning of 1854 Moscheles played his Trio in the Music Quartette and at the express wishes of his friend Spohr, played Spohr's new Septette. A reporter described the latter as especially in the adagio one of the most beautiful and engaging compositions of the melodically rich Kassel Schwan type, (Schwan was now in his sixties) and then continued:
Moscheles, of equal seniority, has managed to maintain the spirit of youth in his wise old head – both in the playing and in the composition, and has achieved a place of honour among experts and the public.

Moscheles then added in a letter:
My dear children, note from me, as latecomer, only the remark that it is strange to me when I am called by the newspapers the 'Nestor' or the 'doyen' of the piano, because as long as I can still play with youthful spirit, I forget my age. . . .

A welcome occurrence of winter 1854 was the arrival of the couple Lind–Goldschmidt in Leipzig. The 'Swedish Nightingale' performed at pension-fund concerts and subscription concerts, and Moscheles reports:
Her voice sounds wonderfully beautiful, and she can lower the pitch to an unheard of ppp. whereby the softest tones can be audibly spun out to the most far distant corner of the concert hall. With her coloratura she has astounded everybody and through her soulful performance she moved everyone's heart, and yet she is at one and the same time naive and sings a children's song by Tauber, or the 'Sonnenschein', so that one is totally rejuvenated again. Goldschmidt also let us listen to many beautiful pieces, and was in Chopin's Concerto, in Mendelssohn's Variations sérieuses, in a Bach Prelude and in his own drawing-room pieces, the efficient, proven

artist – dignified and solid and without striving for effects. It gave me great pleasure to be able to prove how much I think of him through the loan of my Erard piano.

Later we read:

We still have pleasurable hours with the Goldschmidts; at a family dinner, at a Prussian Matinée, where his Trio with its clear melodic and wholesome music made me happy; and finally at the Conservatory. They showed real satisfaction with the efforts of the pupils – particularly with little Fritz Gernsheim, who played Mendelssohn's Serenade and Allegro splendidly, and she repeatedly expressed, 'her regard for the musical institute for which her husband thanks his musical training'; and she did this not only in words, but also in music, for she sang Mendelssohn's Hymn for Soprano and Choir beautifully. It was an accomplishment that will certainly leave a lasting impression on the whole audience.

Concerning the Conservatory pupils, however, Moscheles was not satisfied with everyone:

Unfortunately there are many who do not apply their time to the study of composition, but provide drastic articles for the musical press, whereby I always think back to Mendelssohn's words: What do they have so much to talk and write about? They should be making good music! I do not believe that he would have approved of the pieces that I occasionally have to listen to – so full as they are of weltschmerz.

To a letter from his second daughter, who had recently gone to live in Jerusalem, Moscheles once replied:

The unsophisticated Asiatic national music with its monotonous melancholy, as you describe to me, is admittedly on a completely contrasting standpoint. It may interest the natives just as Handel or Mendelssohn interests us, and they would be bored by the

Eroica. The Europeans there who are not able to grasp more than a song or a choral work are also characteristic. They will also find it difficult to reach up to Beethoven's last works, while our own German youth already regards this hero as old hat and they try to spread their wings above him . . .

We again read in the diary:

David has resigned from the Board of Directors of the Gewandhaus concerts. . . . The rough attacks on him in public newspapers are annoying and he is right when he feels he can no longer put up with them. While we were speaking about it I was able to show him an article concerning my own person; namely Schindler's recently-published article 'On the Development of Piano-playing since Clementi.' There was always that 'I' everywhere: He had dealt with Clementi, Cramer and Beethoven on the welfare of the art; piano-playing has been spoilt and lost through Hummel and Moscheles. The latter even had the presumption to metronomise the works of Beethoven, whom he has never even heard play. He, Schindler, has already given him a telling off somewhere else. Liszt, who is also brought into this violently, begged Schindler to give him three years in which to improve (a good joke of Liszt's). Schindler has given him four years – and has now given him up. . . .

As rejoinder to this article, Ferdinand Hiller had an open letter to Schindler printed, wherein he put the questions: 'Whether Schindler had ever come so far in his life to be able to play Cramer's first étude? Whether there existed anywhere a trace of a Schindler composition as evidence? Whether he has a past history as a conductor which is unknown to the world? Whether he has claims to the post of Beethoven's executor?'

The letter ended with the words:

Only scroundrels are modest, says Goethe: I am counting therefore on an honest and *immodest answer. Your – as far as possible – obedient F. Hiller.*

Moscheles himself took the whole affair more casually.

I occupy myself earnestly with Beethoven's genius, for I am writing cadenzas to his concertos which Senff are going to publish. Naturally self-creative artists do not require them for their performances; they can follow their own inspirations. I hope, nevertheless, to be useful to less-capable players. . . . Also I must now prepare a new edition of my preludes.

In the autumn of 1854 Anton Rubinstein arrived in Leipzig. Moscheles reports:
Rubinstein, whom we heard as child prodigy fourteen years ago in London, appeared as composer of a symphony that he has called 'Ocean'. The clarity of the first movement was as soothing as a mirror-calm sea for me. Then came the modern capers and roars and it became imcomprehensible and stormy, and my thoughts could no longer find anchorage in those daring harmonic shallows. Nevertheless I do recognise in him an excellent composing talent.

Later, as Moscheles listened to the young artist at the Gewandhaus, he wrote:
In his concert there were beauties with poetic momentum, here and there admittedly also frolicsome extravaganzas. His shorter pieces mostly have a praiseworthy rational form; a power and technique next to nobody's. And his features – especially his short stand-up hair – reminds one of Beethoven. As a person he is, in his simple, upright matter, very dear and worthy and he is always a pleasure to be with.

On New Year's day Moscheles wrote the following (although otherwise rejecting all superstition):
I read only of shipwrecks and floods, and as the torrential rain and gales lashed against the window last night, I thought one might almost take this thunderstorm – just visiting us on this New Year's night – as a bad omen. Came the dawn, however, and happier thoughts entered my head. I felt that the restlessness lay within me, myself. I hope today, as always, that we shall not be too sorely tried, and that peace in Europe will not have to be bought with too much spilling of blood!

We find the following remarks in the diary about the musical events of the 1955 season:
Rubinstein was acclaimed a great success through his virtuosity and composition; his pieces have a logical form.
Hiller's Symphony 'Im Freien' is the work of a dignified musician and full of good intentions. It was also well accepted, although there was some lack of warmth among the audience and I fear our friend has some bias against him. His overture to 'Phaedra' is an efficient work with poetic-pathetic content. Spohr's symphony for double orchestra, entitled 'Irdisches und Göttliches' (The Mortal and the Divine) passes through the various emotions of a lifetime in all its gradations. The subject is worthy of Beethoven; under Spohr's hands the artistic structure usurps the free outflow of feelings and the music is monotonous.
Something strange took place yesterday in the Gewandhaus. After the roaring overture to the 'Flying Dutchman' not a hand stirred, not even a hiss was to be heard. There is a lot of fervent spirit in the piece and on top of this such a mass of progressive instrumentation and such a heap of diminished septimes and dissonances of every kind that it becomes stupefying and unpalatable. Gluck also had his musical demons and Mozart his hell in Don Juan – but nobody had a headache from them. And yet in the press the opinion is frequently put forward that: 'Just as Beethoven's last works were not understood imme-

diately, so also Wagner's perception will only be fully realised in the course of time.' Every performance of Beethoven's Overture in C. Op. 115 is particularly interesting to me because it evokes the old Viennese time, when he loaned it to me in manuscript for one of my concerts. This time it was superb.

In a concert to benefit the poor, Moscheles played the A-minor concert by Mozart with his own cadenzas, and he noted the day after: *I had everything that one could wish for with regard to reception, curtain calls and such outward appearances, and concerning the Adagio I said to myself: Ah! How delightful the piece sounds, and I didn't wonder that it pleased the audience so much. It pleases me too that I can prove to myself I haven't abandoned my art, although public performances do not rouse me any more. I hope to keep the warmth and freshness of Mozart's precious works to the end of my life, for they are a very part of me.*

Moscheles composed in this year, among other pieces, a fantasy on Schiller's poem 'Die Sehnsucht' (Longing) and wrote of it in his diary:
It is not a sickening yearning, but a poetic–philosophic longing and I, as musician, must reflect in the performance the empathy that I find with the poet, and must produce an analogy between the 'you must believe, you must venture' and my music.

Some time later there is again a reference made in the diary to Wagner's music:
I place Wagner's Overture to 'Faust' higher than his other works. Everything demonic in it is well-motivated and it intimates at better sentiments through its clear-melodic thoughts. But for my taste there is still too much overloading in the instrumentation in this piece – as in every one of Wagner's works.

At the end of 1855 Moscheles wrote in a letter:

At the wishes of several orchestra members a posthumous work by Mendelssohn is to be given at a Pension-Fund Concert – the so-called 'Reformation Symphony'. He himself was dissatisfied with this composition and never wished it to be published. His brother, whom we questioned with reference to the performance, left the decision to Rietz, David, Hauptmann and myself. We arranged a rehearsal and then, in spite of the many beautiful parts the work contains, we decided after all not to perform it: the reason being that the whole piece does not reach the standard of Mendelssohn's other works, and we are afraid the critics may denounce the memory of our dear friend.

As good as the intentions were, they nevertheless led to an unpleasant newspaper polemic, as there were bitter remonstrations from England for it was thought that this work should be made available to the public.

On 1st January 1856 Rietz, as conductor, brought a predicament to Moscheles. David, he said, was hindered from cooperating in Beethoven's Triple Concerto that he was to perform with Rietz and Moscheles. He asked Moscheles whether he would appear alone as 'friend in need'. To which Moscheles replied: *I will play you something else by Beethoven instead of the Triple Concerto. You can select which piece yourself.* Rietz chose the C-major Concerto which was rehearsed a few hours later and performed in public in the evening.

Moscheles was preoccupied not so much by this improvized accomplishment as by the wish to participate in the Matinee on Mozart's birthday centennial which was to take place on 27th January at the Gewandhaus. When the programme was finally announced he was greatly disappointed to find that the piano had been passed over, which meant that it was impossible for him personally to pay homage to the master on the day. Annoyed with this 'unfair snub' as he repeatedly called it, he declined a later offer by the Gewandhaus Directorate to participate in a public concert.

As the Mozart programme is of interest on account of its historic dates, we present it here in full:

Overture to Re Pastore Romance and Duet from the same opera 1775 composed as Festival Opera in Salzburg and performed the first time to celebrate the visit of Archbishop Maximilian to Bishop Hieronymus.
Concerto for Violin and Viola composed in 1778, played by Messrs. Dreyschock and David
Overture to Idomemeo, Scene and Arias and march from the same opera
First performance in Munich, 29th January 1781
Priests' March, Arias and Choruses from the Magic Flute
First performance in Vienna, 30th September 1791
Overture to Titus
First performance in Prague 1791
Final Scene, 2nd Act Don Juan
First performance in Prague 28th October 1787
Symphony C-major with the final fugue, composed August 1788

Mozart was at that time also celebrated at the Kammermusik, in the theatre and in other places, as well as at a soirée at Moscheles' home, at which the 'Bandl Terzett' formed the lively finale.

The following story, told by Moscheles in a letter, is also lively:
In the musical world there is an anecdote making the rounds – whether true or false I do not know – that sounds rather inharmonious. Liszt, it appears, recently put on Tannhäuser in honour of Litolff and Berlioz and invited both of them to the rehearsal. There they were both bored and took consolation in a bottle of wine in the 'Erbprinzen'. When they met Liszt there ensued a harsh exchange of words, and finally the latter stated: 'You two put together do not make one Wagner.'

In the autumn Moscheles often ran through old and new compositions with David. After a performance of the Riedel Society, the diary says:
In Palestrina's Stabat Mater (16th century)

the following harmonic progression is characteristic:

As in the Old-German choral by Steurlein (also 16th century) this.

Among his own compositions in 1856 there was the great Terzen Etude in E-flat major (for the piano school of Lebert and Stark), various Lieder and towards the end of the year the 'Humoristic Variations'. As the diary reports, these came about during a sleepless night: *Unwell and sleepless as I was, spiritual activity helped me over the unpleasant physical conditions.*

He played the piece at the beginning of 1857 in the Kammermusik and a critic characterized it in a review as 'parody on the striving toward the contemporary'. *Yet I only wished to show,* answered Moscheles, *that I can be new and baroque too if I feel like it.*

In 1857, as always, numerous well-known and lesser-known artists came to Leipzig to produce works at the Gewandhaus. Ernst Pauer was one of the first in the new year, and Moscheles said of him:
An important appearance. He bears a light touch in his fingers and a conviviality on his

forehead. . . . *He unfurls in Beethoven's Concerto in G his whole technique, and it was especially interesting to me to see that Pauer, as well as I, is in possession of Beethoven's sketches to the cadenzas of this concerto. Haslinger, who never wanted to publish them, loaned them to me, and as I now see – also to Pauer – to transcribe. I found them not to be in the same rank as the great concerto and therefore I didn't use them. Pauer played one, without having made much of an effect, for nobody asked by whom it was. It does not have the Beethoven impetus.*

In the spring the diary reads:
We are now at the end of the pre-March, or better, the pre-Easter music and how much beauty we have listened to and enjoyed! The Prometheus by Beethoven that admittedly is evocative of his earliest period, in which, however, the noble spirit of the master floods through; – a posthumous overture to Hermann and Dorothea by Schumann, which breathes a touch of poetry. . . .

On the darker side, however, he remarks:
The music of the 'Signs of the Times' is annoying to me when such a migrant bird from the new school of piano alights in my nest and happily pecks at the feeding bowl of my Erard, but without requesting any morsel of food from me. The Erard must sometimes break a string because of this, as he cannot, like a person, jump out of his skin. It makes me laugh afterwards that the present artists' guild thinks I am dead, for I am still drawing partially from my own blood and partially I nourish my strength on old Bach, whose toccacatas and fugues I now play with renewed passion.

ON HERCULANEUM AND POMPEII

A Liszt week was arranged for the spring of 1857 in Leipzig. With this in view Moscheles made a thorough study of the score of Liszt's works which were to be conducted by the latter. Moscheles attended the rehearsals and concerts with great enthusiasm, and afterwards wrote in a letter:
The people of Weimar have fought a battle with the people of Leipzig. There were no fatal casualties, but a few wounded. Liszt is supposed to have said before the concert: 'They will most likely give me a beating,' but they did not. He conducted his preludes, and though they have some great effects, they have not enough clarity . . . His tempestuous mazeppa music and his pianoforte concerto was played by Bülow with utter professionalism. Everything was greeted with propriety, even if without much enthusiasm. . . . Behr gave Tannhäuser for his benefit concert under Liszt's baton and with the participation of the Weimar singers. They sought my opinion on this opera and, indeed, on the whole Liszt week, and I openly admitted that I am not altogether in favour of this direction even although I find some good points in it – and when I do then I gladly acknowledge them. May the new composers not reach beyond Beethoven, Hadyn and Mozart, nor try to overthrow them – they who till now have been our signposts. We small lights should naturally be buried under this rubble – and I for my part would deem this an honour. Who knows, in years to come, whether we shall be excavated like Herculaneum and Pompeii?

In the meantime, however, the small lights were still living – and living intensively.

In the early summer Moscheles attended lectures given by Professor Möbius on Gellert, Klopstock and Lessing, and noted in his diary:
Poetry is music too, and the logic and philosophy upon which it is based is similar to the

stringent fundamentals of a well thought out musical work.

Autumn brought Jenny Lind and Otto Goldschmidt again to Leipzig.

A letter from Moscheles says:

We have once more enjoyed the pleasure of the Goldschmidt pair. He played Beethoven's Concerto with his own cadenzas, and etudes and gigues by Bach. She sang, besides the aria from the Freischütz and Lieder, Chopin's mazurkas, accompanied by him, and sang three or four times in a row the following electrifying cadenza:

At the beginning of 1858 we read in the diary:

The year starts with a very honoured present for me. The Härtels sent me a fine steel engraving – Mozart in his youth – after a picture in Italy. I immediately put it into my album next to the autographed cadenza of the great man and my pleasure in it is heartfelt. The Gewandhaus began its concert cycle in earnest; the first part with only ecclesiastical music, the second part with Mozart's C-major symphony, played impeccably and yet to my mind the tempi of the first and last movement were too fast. Is it because I am older and my blood is circulating more slowly? Or is it that the others are following a new direction where everything is carried to extremes? I don't know – it is a question of feeling.

Evidently in this year too there were more musical rows again, initiated by Liszt's and Wagner's panegyrist. It began at first with Beethoven's last work which was pronounced as 'gloomy' by the 'Augsburg Allge-

meine', whereas the futurists in the 'Neue Zeitschrift für Musik' called it humorous. *The humour of despair known to Hamlet,* replied the former, and added: *The insignificance hangs here as everywhere on the great man's exposure, in order to motivate one's own unclarity.*

Then all the futurists' opinions on Mozart were voiced – and, going right back to Bach, they were listed and discussed – and finally the Graner Mass was sharply criticized. The article concluded with the words: *This kind of composition is really nothing much more than arithmetic.*

To this Moscheles writes:

Fortunate is he who can remain at a distance from such prejudices for they demean the very soul of artistic balance. . . . I have now studied – apart from Beethoven's Sonata Op. 106 – Mendelssohn's Variations sérieuses and Rubinstein's G-major concerto and much Liszt. At first his transcript of the 'Eroica' and then the score of his A-major concerto, but I cannot get over many places.

A little later he notes:

The antiquated and yet (by me) so much loved art has suffered two great losses – and I am robbed of two unforgettable friends. Neukomm died on the 3rd, J. B. Cramer on the 19th April. It is impossible to fill such gaps . . . and our beloved Neukomm was a dear member of the family!

In the summer the two already close families of David and Moscheles were brought even closer. In the early hours of the morning refreshing walks were taken into Rosenthal. After a hot day's work they would meet to play music together. David had an idea of arranging Moscheles' 24 Etudes for the violin and accomplished this with his usual mastery. Moscheles wrote the simple piano accompaniment to the new arrangement, worked a lot on Clementi's sonatas and also on the 'Gradus ad parnassum' for Hallberg's edition. *They should not lead me in error with their lack of finger notations or exact marking of the interpretation and the tempi,* he said. *This is the reason why I have to compare every issue that I have for advice.*

Furthermore Moscheles scored orchestrally Mendelssohn's E-major concert for two pianos. A student called Moritz, who was in possession of this, loaned it to him. A catalogue was compiled at about this time of his own works which accurately revised them and which later was published by the music dealer Kistner.

In July 1858 the Prague Conservatory celebrated its jubilee and the sister institute in Leipzig sent Moscheles and David there to bear greetings for the festival. From his native city Moscheles wrote:

The Prague Festival turned out extremely brilliantly. It began with a high mass in Jacob's Church. In the evening there was a concert in the theatre at which present-day pupils and alumnae (now masters) participated. The enthusiasm for all and everything was unrestrained. The second evening brought Spohr's 'Jessonda' which was conducted by him, and the laurel crown, the enthusiastic reception, the curtain call after each act, nothing was lacking in the homage paid to the master in a moving way. On the third evening Ward, under Kittl's baton, gave Gluck's Overture to Iphigenie, a psalm by Handel and the 9th Symphony. This was well enough as a school effort but although David and R. Dreyschock took part, there was something missing for my indulgent ears. On the fourth day a great festival banquet in Baumgarten took place with music and countless toasts. I was called on to give a speech of thanks in the name of all the guests, so I collected my wits about me, expressed admiration for the Bohemian sense of art which promulgated these established institutions. And I said how proud I was to belong to this musical country. I spoke not without emotion about how I had left my native country around fifty years previously to travel to art-appreciative foreign countries etc. Everyone seemed to be with me; every sentence was received with overwhelming joy. Everybody wanted to drink my health and it had no end, there was such a flood of heartwarming words and champagne – the last flowed so freely over my coat that the spilled quantity of wine was enough to make a soldier drunk. . . . We people of Leipzig handed over a votive tablet on behalf of our institute, and I still found time to listen to the four and eight-handed accomplishments of the pupils of the Pianoforte Institute of Proksch. I enjoyed here many family pleasures; at first I was with my loved ones in Podiebrad then I was with my own people in Prague. It is a very strange feeling to enter those same rooms wherein I acted out my youthful dreams fifty years ago. All the objects of that time attracted me so richly hued – as though in a kaleidoscope; the portrait of my beloved mother smiled down at me from the wall; my sister was her usual kind self with her open-heartedness. I had to play something for them too and they were thoroughly enchanted.

The return journey could have been very unpleasant because of torrential rain, but what does the weather matter to 'wandering virtuosities'? 'In art there is always sunshine' as the saying goes.

We were on good terms with the train conductor and had the compartment to ourselves, and David, who never left his violin, played with steam even more beautiful than ever; we heard one concert after the other in the compartment and then passages from Moscheles' études were practised. 'How does this sound? or is it better like this?' The time passed rapidly and all too soon we were in Dresden.

They had hardly been back a moment to Leipzig before preparations for the next journey were under way, this time to Antwerp and Brussels where there was to be an exchange of musicianship with Féris, Kuferrath, Léonard et al.

The subsequent journey from Namur to Dinant, with its pleasant natural surroundings, brought many joys to the little company. In the small town of Huy Moscheles wrote in the diary:
What a delightful journey! Two first class carriages connected by an open platform onto which passengers can alight during the trip. We sat there on camp-stools in fine weather and had the majestic rocky precipices on one side; on the other the beautiful Maas – and on its banks verdancy, villages and villas. When the weather was bad huge mirrors inside the carriage reflected the wonderful scenery for us. Such a train journey is, I believe, a unicum.

Unique too was the small romantic Huy on the river Maas (at that time numbering 10,000 inhabitants). *In the streets*, says one of Charlotte's letters,
one can hardly move for flowers, flags, barrel-organs and drapes. It was the septennial of 'La Vierge' the patron saint of the little town. As we read the announcements of a 'Concours de chant' and a concert by the famous royal musicians 'Guides du roi', Moscheles handed a card to the director to request tickets which, as one says, had all gone like hot cakes. Five minutes later the man himself came, and did not go until Moscheles had agreed to preside on the jury of the 'Concours de chant'. Then Mr. Godin, the President of the Festival Committee, came to invite us to be his guests. He is a very well-to-do paper manufacturer. The following day we had to move to him and his family in a magnificent castle situated in a great park

which houses the historic monument – the tomb of 'Pierre l'heremite'.

Moscheles adds:
My duty on the jury cost me many beads of perspiration as I was obliged to sit out in the burning rays of the sun for four hours in the morning and four hours in the afternoon between the President and the Mayor. We sat in full view of the public on a high platform. Round about us was the music, a surging crowd of people and the whole elegant world of the environs. The various choirs marched on in order to be heard – each one holding an embroidered velvet flag aloft. Not a single one was bad, many could even be termed good.

From Spa where, before the return journey to Leipzig, a few days of rest were spent, he wrote:
I shall be neither richer nor poorer here, for I have seen enough of the misery in this gambling den without setting any bets. The people who stand round this green baize table appear to me like flies encircling the flykiller pot. They take sips out of it until they fall down unconscious. This is apparently what happened to the famous singer T. I wished to make his acquaintance in order to hear him, but he departed suddenly. He had lost everything.

In the autumn of 1858 Spohr arrived in Leipzig:
He was invited by the concert director who wanted to hear some of his compositions again. He appeared, and was more than satisfied by the orchestra under Rietz. He even thought it had improved. It rewarded him for his praise with a mighty fanfare. The audience and his musical peers cheered in jubilant agreement. We heard his C-minor symphony and overture to Jessonda. On the following morning there was another musical performance at the Gewandhaus in honour of the famous guest. The Leonora

*Overture No. 3 electrified me as usual, and
when I heard Mendelssohn's A-minor symphony I thought: Futuristic music, what do
you think you're doing?*

As Moscheles found that during this
winter his painstaking trouble on behalf of
others had considerably mounted, it was
with particular attention that he read a letter
from the ageing Alexander von Humboldt
published in the newspapers. The great man
would not put up from henceforth with any
scientific enquiries and similar matters, 'as
their number amounts to 2000 per year, he
sees himself as an address comptoir and he is
not prepared to devote his declining strength
to such efforts . . .'. *It makes me think,* says
the diary, *that the lesser lights too should not
allow themselves to be misused. One must
make a choice.* Not much later the newspapers announced the death of the great
explorer.

In 1859 there was a reconciliation in the
disputing parties of the German music world
in which Liszt was prominently active. Moscheles reports:
*The musical world is running in a daring
race. The 'Neue Zeitschrift für Musik' cele-
brates its 25th anniversary in June and the
party whose interests it mainly represents is
to organise a great artists' festival at this
time. This will be the novelty of the year. The
Riedel Society is zealously studying the
Graner Mass.*

When Liszt arrived for a short visit to
Leipzig in May, he persuaded Moscheles to
participate in the Festival with a lecture on
his 'Homage to Handel'.
*He calls me one of the pillars of piano-
playing that must not be missing. I call
myself the essential contrast between the old
and the new school, and accept. I have my
principles, my convictions, yet I will definitely not set myself brusquely against the new
party.*

During this period an artist conclave
travelled to Weimar to hear a new one-act
opera by Rietz 'G. Neumark und die Gamba'.
He himself conducts, wrote Moscheles, who
attended,
*and the work was received with great ova-
tion and curtain calls for the composer.
Before the opera Liszt entertained us with the
most engaging piece: full of cunning, the
laying aside of cigars, and as he sat at the
piano, I heard – to my utter amazement – my
old Opus 42 Variations on the Austrian Lied*

*that I have ignored for forty years. He played
it by heart and instilled in it such spirited
effects that it caused quite a sensation. He
also let us hear his own organ fantasy on the
letters B a c h – bravely ingenious intricacies,
thunderingly performed. On the same night
we all returned to Leipzig.*

A few days later we read:
*I gave Liszt an artists' banquet, comfortably
informal. After the meal he, with cigar in his
lips, found among the music my 'Dance' and
'Humouristic Variations' – both for four
hands, and I had to play them with him
straight away. Everything cracked and fizzed
superbly; then came the old variations again
and at last my 'Sonata mélancolique' with
truly artistic enthusiasm, it was a real
delight. It is a pity that I cannot enthuse over
the direction which he adopts in his compositions. This is the veil that falls over our
artistic intimacy.*
*At David's we had a musical assembly. Liszt
played his colossal Bach Fantasy and with
Brosart his Orpheus, on two pianos. A
number of guest musicians, with Liszt at their*

head, came to me too, to hear me play. They wanted to know where I stand. However, my relationship with Liszt is cordial. We know well enough what we think and expect of one another, and when we play four handed we make, in spite of our different strain, a great team, coached without whip by the God Apollo. Liszt still plays with wondrous fervour or with idyllic caress.

The artists' festival with different matinees took place, at which Moscheles and Jaell played the former's 'Homage to Handel', as well as a concert in the theatre with compositions by Mendelssohn, Schubert, Berlioz, Schumann, Wagner and Liszt. Finally the performance of Liszt's Graner Mass was given and well received. At the end Moscheles wrote:

All the guests have reason to be satisfied and we Leipzig folk also, in that we were able to prepare this for them . . . and if the pen war of the various parties had already begun, well, it will not cause permanent mischief, since this music festival was a peace congress.

In the summer of 1859 Moscheles took his family to Thüringer Wald in a *greenery-entwined cottage at the foot of the Wartburg with a heavenly view across meadow, forest and mountains.*

Shortly upon arrival there was a comic episode. While the family were sitting down to supper in the hotel they suddenly heard in the next room Moscheles' G-major Etude in David's arrangement played masterfully on the violin. Wonder of wonders! Moscheles jumped up and rang. 'Who is living next door?' he enquired of the waiter. 'The impresario Herr Singer,' was the reply. And so the wonder was explained. The connecting door remained not a moment longer closed and everyone was delighted at the meeting.

During their stopover Moscheles composed a Wartburg Lied for four voices which was rehearsed in the great concert hall, and he wrote in his diary afterwards:

The epigram that I found on this occasion must be noted here. It goes:

> *Music is perhaps most real,*
> *When voice and heart can both so feel.*

After the summer holiday he wrote to his youngest daughter Clara who was studying singing in Paris under Pauline Viardot:

With your composition attempts I recommend you always to express a proper emotion, a serious or a merry one, a contented or an anxious one etc. If you can manage to do this in short pieces you can attempt larger ones in which the emotions can change dramatically. Always think of a scene from human life and disdain simply mechanical means in order to make an effect. The technical must only be an aid to heighten the dominant idea and to give it power or character.

In the same letter we read:

Everything you write to me about Berlioz interests me especially because he is certainly among the upcoming artists one of those who has inventiveness and does not try to distort the art intentionally. His opera 'Benvenuto Cellini (heard in Weimar) forebodes great expectations for the 'Trojan' which is soon to be performed. he has never shown me much sympathy and possibly believes me to be his opponent, but wrongfully.

About everyday life in Leipzig he further writes:

Our life is colourful; at 3 o'clock to bed and at 9 o'clock in the Conservatory. . . . We have learned a lot from the small Röntgen boy. He is truly a child prodigy. At five years old his sense of hearing is acute and he already plays beautifully. As he is unable to reach the pedal with his little short legs his three-year-old sister lies under the piano and presses it down at the right moments – which goes to show that she is also musically talented.

In October 1859 Spohr died, and at the beginning of November a concert took place at the Gewandhaus to commemorate both his and Mendelssohn's day of death. Mozart's Requiem and Mendelssohn's 42nd Psalm were played.

Later in the month Leipzig celebrated the centennial of the birth of Schiller and magnificent homage was paid to the great poet. Moscheles, as member of the Artist Society founded by Carl Werner, spent five hours in the festival parade. *The concert with the ninth symphony interested me more than this or the theatre performance,* he wrote, *I have never heard the work so played, it electrified me. The enthusiasm stretched from the conductor and leader right down to the tympanist, and everybody – audience and participants – felt that something had been accomplished that was beyond the wildest imagination. There was such rejoicing. Now the festivities are over, but the symphony is to be given once again. Rietz has written an overture for the celebration and Richter a Cantata with lyric by Dr Adolar Gerhard. I have dedicated my piece after Schiller's 'Dance', two and four handed, as a small contribution to the Schiller Foundation.*

On 2nd December the Great Hall in Leipzig celebrated the 450th anniversary of its foundation, with the attendance of the Saxon Royal Family. Moscheles remarked: *Rietz, who has been awarded with the Doctor title has done a composition in the most tasteful style for the celebration.*

At the beginning of 1860 Rietz left the Saxon capital for ever to take up an appointment in Dresden. *His resignation is a great, irreparable loss* wrote Moscheles.

In his letter to his children who were then in Paris, we read:
The Gewandhaus rehearsal was very thrilling for me because of the performance of the Melusine Overture and the Finale of the Lorelei. And when Paul Mendelssohn entered the hall I was really taken aback. The beloved traits of his immortal brother stood before me in all their loveliness, in spite of the little similarity between them.

And another time:
Our busy Leipzig has instigated another new society, this time among the Israelites. It is to be called the 'Moses and Felix Mendelssohn Society' and it has the good purpose of supporting poor students and Conservatory pupils. In the interest of the latter Schleinitz and I are offering advice.

And on the occasion of a visit by the actor Emil Devrient:
We have heard Emil Devrient talk about his performances, which was very interesting. I particularly liked the bit about him always paying the prompter so that he will keep quiet, for the less the artist relies on others, the greater he is. I also like the fact that he alone packs his six costume trunks he carries about with him – this is sympathetic to my sensitive sense of order. To end this letter on a musical note, I will tell you that I recently had some clever pupils with me, and I played much of my own work and finally Beethoven's Fantasy with the descending introductory run. I was really good on the fingering since my regular readings of the new breakneck compositions have kept me well oiled. The young people seemed surprised, moved, and appeared to want to say: 'You understand it better than we thought.' Perhaps they will believe me in future when I preach to them that more effect lies in comprehension and interpretation than in the mere victory over technical difficulties and bravura – and that these last are only the means and never the end.

In this winter of 1860 Moscheles arranged a new edition of his Etudes Op. 70. published his symphonic-heroistic march, six Lieder and four vocal duets. But to a suggestion to write progressive pieces he replied, *it is almost impossible to integrate fantasy with such works.*

Schumann's fiftieth birthday occurred during this time and was celebrated with a performance of his 'Genoveva' in the theatre. The diary says: *Schumann's opera captured my attention to such a degree that I was not tired the whole evening by following this ingenious music, and thereby I was entertained.*

MEETING WITH ROSSINI

In the summer holidays of 1860 Moscheles journeyed to Paris and wrote from there to his wife:

Everyone is hospitable to me and in the end I have to play for them. They want to know how Moscheles of the old times gets by in the new. On being praised, I think to myself: Rabattez la moité et marchandez sur le reste. . .*

A little later we read of a Rossini performance:

The performance of 'Semiramis' was tedious; the music old fashioned, the singers not to my taste, the ballet dancers ugly, and when I noticed Auber asleep in his box the whole evening, I played truant before the fourth act so that the same wouldn't happen to me.

Much more happily Moscheles met the 68-year-old maestro Rossini outside the Opera. Right at the start of his Paris stay he travelled with his son Felix to Passy, where the latter had already been a house guest for a long time:

On our arrival we were escorted to the beautiful villa and into the ground-floor salon with its richly gilded furnishings, and before

*French saying meaning approx.: Take only half, and even this not at face value.

Rossini himself appeared we saw his photograph framed in a wreath of porcelain, the leaves of which bore the names of his works. The ceiling portrayed in its paintings scenes from Palestrina's and Mozart's life; in the middle of the room there was a Pleyel. When Rossini appeared he was, with southerly enthusiasm, warmhearted in his kiss, in his pleasurable expressions at my reappearance and in his compliments about Felix. During the visit his frank views about the direction of singing and studies were full of striking truth and witty satire, particularly against the contemporary 'new' works. 'I don't want to hear any more of them,' he said, 'they screech! I only want to listen to a sonorous voice, not a shrieking singing or speaking voice; everything must sound melodic.' Then he spoke of his desire to occupy himself with the piano and, if it didn't sound too immodest, to compose for the instrument. But his fourth and fifth fingers would not perform as he wanted them to. The piano, incidentally, is now being ill treated: 'Ils enfoncent non seulement le piano, mais encore le fauteuil et même le parquet.'*

Then he naturally came to speak of various instruments and said he thought that the guitarist Sor and the mandoline player Vimercati had proved that even with limited means great artistic accomplishments could be achieved. I myself have heard the musicians he spoke about and fully agreed with him. Rossini told me how one evening he arrived in a small Italian town, and was already anticipating a pleasant night's rest when Vimercati, who was leader of the orchestra there, invited him to a performance of one of his (Rossini's) operas. Rossini, at that time not being so hard-hearted as he is now in constantly refusing to attend any performance of his own works, went along to the theatre and even replaced the missing

*They don't only strike the piano, but the chair and the floor too.

double-bass player. This brought to my mind the missing viola and the too deep bassoon in Mozart's D-major symphony under which I had to suffer in York. I showed Rossini the effect of this on the piano and he laughed heartily. He then wanted to hear something in a more serious vein. I improvised and Rossini asked 'Cela est-il gravé? C'est de la musique qui coule de source. Il y a l'eau de réservoir et l'eau de source; l'une ne coule que grand vous ouvrez le robinet, elle sent toujours la vase, l'autre, fraîche et limpide, coule toujours.'. . .* About musical thinking he said, 'Aujourd'hui, on confond le simple et le trivial; un motif de Mozart, on l'appellerait trivial si on osait!'**

When the conversation came round to the Leipzig Conservatory, he was pleased to hear that the organ playing was undertaken with such sincerity. He complained about the degeneration of church music in Italy, and thought enthusiastically of the sublime creations of a Marcello and a Palestrina. Before we parted I had to promise to visit him again – even before the dinner to which he had invited me.

Moscheles was true to his word, and at his request Rossini played for him – not without a modest introductory speech – an andante in B-major, beginning something like this:

---

and which after the first 8 bars took an interesting modulating turn:

The piece is what we in Germany would call tame, wrote Moscheles on this subject, and further said:

He then fetched two manuscript compositions, an introduction and fugue in C-major and a kind of pastoral fantasy with a brilliant rondo in A-major, which he insisted on my playing for him. When I added a missing sharp to one of the manuscripts he exclaimed that I was worth my weight in gold to him! C., who accompanied me, and had already sung for him (without any anxiety) my 'Spring-song' by Hölty and my 'Message' to his satisfaction had to repeat both Lieder for the singers Ponchard and Levasseur and I had to accompany C. again. When he said firmly that I had sufficient melodic fluidity to write an opera, I replied, 'It's a pity that I am not young enough to be one of your pupils.' I had to play his manuscripts then and that raised me to 'King of the pianists'. 'For what I am, I have the old school and the doyen Clementi to thank,' I said, and at the mention of this name Rossini went to the piano and played by heart fragments from the latter's sonatas.

In the following few weeks Moscheles played to Rossini many times. In the 'Humoristic Variations' Rossini found barriers; they appeared to go so much against the grain of the traditional. The title of the Grande Valse he found too modest. Moscheles must have danced with an angelic looking lady to create it, and that should be expressed in the title. The title must heighten the enthusiasm of the audience. *A repugnant viewpoint, adds Moscheles, but I was not going to discuss it.*

Dinner with Rossini is dedicated to the gourmet, he tells,
and he proves to be one himself, in that he helped himself generously to the selected dishes. When I showed him my album after dinner he was enthusiastic about every name it contained. Finally we became very merry and I had to perform my jests on the piano. Felix and Clara sang a duet which he accompanied with his imitations of a horn. Our jest made quite a sensation for the joyful Italian and so our merriment continued until he embraced me with a goodnight kiss.

We read about the next visit, which was to be the last before Moscheles' departure:
Rossini showed me the manuscript which he only yesterday composed – a delightful Lied without words, the well-known techniques, from which the exciting melody pleasantly pours forth. About the 'Semiramis' he says: 'You have seen the beautiful decorations in it haven't you?' and thereby he laughs mockingly. . . . Of Pasta, Lablache, Rubini and others he spoke with warmth, and he said I should not regard his newly spawned pianistic talent with jealousy but rather give him a good name as such in Leipzig. For my intimacy with Clementi he showed renewed interest. He wishes to visit me in Leipzig as Clementi's honourable successor, but he cannot abide the railway train. This was all jestingly spoken. But when the conversation turned to Chevet who wants to have the written notes marked by numbers, he says seriously and in a scholarly way that the notation as it has developed since Pope Gregor is quite sufficient for all musical requirements. He cannot deny Chevet his recognition, although, as Member of the Institute, he did not confirm judgement in his favour because he didn't believe in the practicability of this system. So the conversation never dried up and continued until 11 o'clock.

And then followed the inevitable kiss – which this time also served as blessing for the parting.

Later Felix reported to his father on further conversations with Rossini:
He brought up the subject of German music and I asked him which of the classic composers he most admired. Of Beethoven he said, 'Je le prends deux fois par semaine, Haydn quatre fois et Mozart tous les jours. Vous me direz que Beethoven est un colosse qui vous donne souvent des coups de poing dans les côtes tandis que Mozart est toujours adorable. C'est que lui a eu la chance d'aller très jeune en Italie, à une époque où l'on y chantait encore bien.'* Of Weber he said: 'Il a du talent à revendre, celui-là.'** During the conversation too it came up that Rossini's Tancred in Berlin was sung by a bass voice, and that Weber had written vehement articles against the theatre there, in which the composer's name was also mentioned. Enough – when Weber came to Paris he declined to visit Rossini because of these events. Rossini, however, let him know that he had not taken offence at the articles and that he should come.

So the two got to know each other. I asked him whether he had seen Byron in Venice? 'Only in a restaurant,' came the reply, 'where I was introduced to him, but the acquaintance remains superficial; il parait qu'il a parlé de moi, mais je ne sais pas ce qu'il dit.'***

I translated Byron's words for him in the original English, and in a somewhat milder form. They were fresh in my memory: they have been crucifying Othello in an opera. The music is good but lugubrious, and as for the words, all the real scenes with Iago are cut

---

*I play him twice a week, Haydn four times, and Mozart every day. You will say that Beethoven is a colossus who often kicks one's side. Mozart is always adorable and this is because he had the fortune in his youth to go to Italy at a time when they still knew how to sing well.
**'He has talent in abundance.'
***He is supposed to have spoken of me, but I don't know what he said.

out and the greatest nonsense put in instead. The handkerchief is turned into a billet-doux and the first singer would not blacken his face. The singing, the dresses and the music are very good. The maestro regretted his ignorance of the English language and said: 'Dans mon temps, je me suis beaucoup occupé de notre littérature italienne. C'est à Dante que je dois beaucoup; j'ai plus appris de musique en lisant Dante que dans toutes mes leçons de musique. Aussi j'ai absolument voulu introduire des vers de Dante dans mon Othello – vous savez les vers du gondolier. Mon poête a eu beau me dire, que les gondoliers ne chantaient jamais le Dante, tout au plus le Tasse. Je lui ai répondu, je sais cela mieux que toi, car j'ai habité Venise et tu ne l'as pas habite – il me faut de Dante.'*

He composed for me with great generosity a piece for my mouth horn and wrote it in the album. At the top it says 'Thème de Rossini suivi de deux variations et Coda par Moscheles père,' and underneath he wrote: 'Offert à mon jeune ami Felix Moscheles. G. Rossini, Passy, ce 20 Août 1860.'**

Moscheles immediately wrote down the two 'commissioned variations and coda' and asked the maestro whether the small piece could be dedicated on publication to him. He received the following answer:

Paris-Passy, 1861

Mon Maître (de Piano) et Ami!

Permettez moi de vous remercier de votre aimable lettre. Rien ne pouvait ni ne devait m'être plus agréable, plus flatteur

*In my time I was occupied with Italian literature. I owe much to Dante. I have learned more about music from him than in all my music lessons. This is the reason why I wanted particularly to have a Dante verse in my Othello. My librettist told me that the gondoliers have never sung Dante, at the most Tasso. I answered him, I know better than you for I lived in Venice and you didn't – I must have Dante in it.

**Theme by Rossini, followed by two variations and coda by Moscheles senior. For my young friend Felix Moscheles, G. Rossini, Passy, 20th August 1860.

qu'une dédicace de vous. Ce témoignage de votre affection est d'un priz inestimable à mes yeux, je vous en remercie avec toute la chaleur qui me reste, et qui n'a point encore glacé mon vieux coeur. Vous me demandez l'autorisation de faire graver le petit thème que j'ai noté pour votre cher fils; – elle vous est accordée. Rien de plus honorable cher ami, que d'associer mon nom au vôtre dans cette petite publication, mais hélas! quel est le rôle que vous me fai es jouer en si glorieux mariage? Celui du compositeur vous octroyant à vous le grand patriarche, l'exclusif du pianiste. Pourquoi ne voulex vous donc pas m'admettre dans la grande famille un de plus hein! quoique je me sois placé très modestement (mais non sans vive peine) dans la catégorie de pianiste de 4ème classe. Voulez-vous donc, cher Moscheles, me faire mourir de chagrin?

Vous y réussirez, vous autres grands pianistes, en me traitant en Paria, oui vous serez responsables devant Dieu et devant les hommes de ma mort.

Veuillez me rappeler au souvenir de Mme et des chers enfants, en agréant pour vous l'affection sincère de votre ami de coeur,

G. Rossini

[My dear (piano) master and friend! Let me thank you for your kind letter. Nothing could be more pleasant and flattering to me than a dedication from you. This evidence of your intention has inestimable value, and I thank you for it with all the warmth my old heart is capable of.
You request permission to print the small theme that I wrote down for your dear son Felix. Nothing could honour me more, my dear friend than to see my name on this little publication alongside your own. But oh, what role you let me play at such a richly famous marriage! That of the composer, the great patriarch who leaves you the exclusi-

vity of piano playing. Why don't you want to take me in the great family? and this although I have placed myself modestly (even if not without pain) in the category of pianists of the fourth class. Do you want, my dear Moscheles to let me die in distress? You will be successful in this, you great pianists, if you treat me as a pariah; yes, you will be responsible to God and mankind for my death.
Give my regards to your wife and to the dear children and accept the honest affection of your bosom friend, G. Rossini.]

And here an excerpt from Moscheles' reply:

Mon cher Maître!
Savez vous, quel est mon numéro favori? C'est le numéro quatre nous lui devons l'harmonie la plus parfaite; quatre voix humaines, les quatre instruments du Quatuor, le pianiste enfin de quatrième classe qui en lui seul représente l'harmonie de toutes les voix et de tous les instruments. N'allez pas me dire, cher Maître, que vous détestez le même Nr. quatre, puisque c'est à quatrième lettre que je vous écris depuis peu, puisque c'est le quatrième protégé que j'autorise de frapper à votre porte hospitalière . . .
[My dear maestro!
Do you know my favourite number? It is number four. We have to thank it for complete harmony: the four human voices, the four instruments of the quartette and finally the pianists of the fourth rank, who alone embody the harmony of all voices and instruments. Don't tell me, dear maestro, that you detest this number four. This is the fourth letter that I have written to you in a short while and is it not the fourth protégé that I allow to knock on your hospitable door? . . .]

Towards the end of 1860 Moscheles was appointed Honorary Member of the Musical Society of London. At the same time he composed a Toccata in F-sharp minor for the Mozart Album as well as a two-voice Christmas Carol, and he wrote:
I would write bigger pieces for my instrument if I were not convinced that they would not be accepted in the current programmes. Only Beethoven's, Mendelssohn's, Schumann's and Chopin's Concertos are played. Mozart and Hummel are totally left out, and from my eight concertos, the G-minor is revived less frequently in performances. I dream that my characteristic Etudes, my Grande Valse and some of my other solo pieces electrify with bravura, my children's fairytales and my A-sharp major etude could sing in competition with the modern nocturnes. And yet none of my colleagues attempt to let them be heard in public – I myself play no more in concerts, and, to put it in Byron's words, 'for the sexton authorship, the trunk-maker'– to be buried inside – I believe I am still too good. If the rats and mice want to nibble on such food, they shall not have my music while I'm still alive. So I do among other things: a piece for a mild foundation or I write Lieder and small pieces for the household, for my grandchildren. I limit myself – not because of lack of power – but because of pride. This, my musical oral confession for you at the year's end.

In 1861 Leipzig celebrated the 25th anniversary of its impresario David *When I congratulated him*, says Moscheles, *he showed me the letter in which Felix Mendelssohn assigned to him the position of Concert leader; he is as good and cordial as everything that he wrote. He is equally as great of soul in his letters as he is in his works, and how happily the youthful artistic temperament is expressed on his first excursion in the South! Thereby he enjoys everything twice as much, because he has received it in the warm filial love of his parents. Imagine the sensation this travel letter will cause! I should*

should like to give you the title: School for the Artist and Mankind.

A little later it says:

With the embellishments in Liszt's arrangement of Mendelssohn's Midsummernight's Dream I was again not satisfied for it fits it as badly as would a crinoline the Venus of Milo.

In the winter of 1861 at David's, Moscheles saw six or eight manuscript quartettes and quintettes by Beethoven:

They belong to Paul Mendelssohn and were lent to him in order to edit a new edition for Breitkopf and Härtel. They contain a treasury of learning even in the crossed-out passages or the single notes.

Just how very precisely Moscheles was acquainted with almost all of Beethoven's compositions is shown in the following entry in the diary:

In the quintette by Beethoven I recently attended at the Gewandhaus, I heard at the place

a between note that was foreign to me; so:

I had the score shown to me and found that Beethoven added this quarter for the violoncello.

He continued to occupy himself also with Bach. He did not only play him, but allowed himself through Gounod's addition of a cello part to the first prelude of the 'Well-Tempered Piano' to be inspired to write a similar work. There evolved a series of ten melodies for cello, and these accompany ten of Bach's preludes. Later he transposed these melodies with heightened effect for a second piano. He himself loved this work, but they were harshly criticized by others. Why should he want to improve the unimprovable Bach by adding these accompaniments? asked his critics. Why didn't he write them himself if he was so inclined? The majority of experts and art authorities were pleased however about the orchestral effects and the counterpointal work in this composition and labelled it 'stylish and well sounding'.

Moscheles himself says of it:

I will be famed or gravely reprimanded on account of these preludes, but perhaps they will become well known through my melodies to some persons who would never have played the preludes on their own because they considered them too dry, and then I shall be content. A more precise knowledge of Bach's works can only be an advancement for the art. With this arrangement I appear like our fiction writers, they can put an important question of the day much easier into romantic language than into a dry discourse.

In the spring of 1861 Moscheles found himself on the way via Amsterdam to London and a little later wrote from there:

Yes, such a London season is very exhausting. I enjoy little rest at night and yet I start to write even at 7 o'clock in the morning . . . . A day at Otto Goldschmidt's was rich in pleasures. Nowhere did there appear opulent luxury and yet it was elegant; nowhere extreme pomp but therefore all the more inward comfort. And now first of all the music. With Otto Goldschmidt I had the joy of playing my 'Hommage à Handel' and it was without concession to my better judgement, much more in complete consent. We also played the Bach preludes and he showed satisfaction about the idea and performance. To hear his wife singing Lieder in her own house is an indescribable pleasure; her voice still sounds as beautiful as ever, she sent us into raptures . . .

An enquiry by the Old Philharmonic – whether he would play at one of their concerts, evoked once again the old thoughts about no more public appearances, and yet the wish to be agreeable to his old friends and colleagues weighed heavily on him, so that he wrote: *I have, in spite of everything, agreed – but with the remark that I do it only out of old friendship's sake, not to play for a fee.* At this performance, the first in England after a fifteen-year pause, Moscheles reaped an overwhelming ovation.

In London he got to know at the same time the Italian freedom fighter Mazzini:

I never imagined the notorious conspirator like this, for he seemed so pleasant and undemanding. He spoke calmly about politics and appeared quite harmless. He has a lively interest in music. His guitar accompanies him to all his political hideouts, and Meyerbeer is his favourite composer. Cavour's death, Garibaldi's ill health and the quasi imprisonment of the Pope – he discussed everything, but always added at the conclusion: 'Providence will see to it that everything turns out for the best.'

Back again in Leipzig Moscheles reported on the following musical news:

Gounod's 'Faust' was given here and in Dresden and I heard the fine, piquant music in both towns with great delight. It is a popular opera even though the critics are against the crippling of Goethe's masterpiece, for it is a fresh and interesting work that has melodic fluidity and beautiful instrumentation. . . . 25 Brahms' variations on a theme by Handel, very interesting; the new Michaelangelo overture by Gade, appealing. Schumann's Festival Overture on the Rheinweinlied, a particularly clear and friendly work that I must hear again. But as contrast there was also a new tone mosaic by another author that I should like to describe more exactly in the following words: mystique, shroud, damnation, eardrums tickled with glowing tongs, apparent death! I was in a state of feverishness when I heard it.

The tragic desperation was, however, foreign to Moscheles' nature. This is especially evident in the following excerpt from a letter to his children:

I am an optimist and I have never yet been deceived. The worst that has happened to me has always ended well, and so my blessed happiness will be propagated in you. We will live off our desires and draw on our hopes until we can congratulate each other on our perseverance.

On another occasion he wrote to his daughter:

It makes me happy when I see how you take such an interest in my artistically renowned name, and do not like to see that I am labelled <u>cold</u> by a musical writer just because I do not happen to share his own views. I myself feel only mildly treated by him, for I know too that the art and its great creations (as well as the hero of the art, Beethoven) have always warmed me. Praise God, it still continues to glow in me – right down to the fingertips. And yet I do not allow the inner flame to reach to the roof. I have far too much respect for classical works to subject them to a scorching performance. When I was at a Schiller Festival recently and I was improvising on the Lied 'an die Freude', I must have seemed very warm, for I was afforded public and private praise. . . . I promised to play at the orchestra's Pension Fund Concert, with Frau Schumann and Reinecke, a posthumous Triple Concerto by Mozart. As this appeared to be an early work, however, which proved *on examination to be small and unimportant, we decided to play instead Bach's Triple Concerto (C-major) which has never been heard in Leipzig. It was an elevating feeling when I was received by the audience – as a father by his children – as we performed our piece as though cast from a mould – and I led Frau Schumann on my arm out to the front for the ovation.*

THE FINAL YEARS 1862–1870

We find Moscheles in the sixties still in full control of his intellectual and physical faculties, untiring in teaching as in listening and therefore twice as sensitive to the few grievances that befell him during this period of change. As a youth he had avoided being disloyal to his teacher Dionys Weber in that he abstained from all other instruction. But now, with his favourite pupils, he was frequently forced to witness them turning to other masters under which his own legato, his softness of touch was exchanged for a modern martellato. Instead of his reserve they tested the force of the flamboyance, instead of his moderation in the use of both pedals, they learned to apply them almost continually. This saddened him just as much as the predominate direction of taste in modern music. He often complained about the harsh contrasts: *Too much weltschmerz and too many roaring effects* with which to entice and arouse the audience. He can call it nothing other than a *conscience purging, when in a concert of bravura solo pieces one begins with one of Bach's greatest fugues and this in prestissimo.* On the other hand he was immensely pleased when Hadyn's humour, Mozart's cantilene and Beethoven's generosity found fitting recognition, *if only our friend Mendelsssohn lived on. . . .* He had

only sometimes to blame the tempi, missing everywhere the traditions of his youth.
The racing speed that swallows many notes, the spinning out of an Andante until it becomes an Adagio, an Andante Con Moto in which the Moto is missing, an Allegro Comodo which makes itself no longer comfortable.

This all disturbed his enjoyment. At the beginning he ventured to impart his views to young artistic peers, but his good intentions went unheeded and as it was not within his good taste to resist the current movement: he nourished himself on the music that he loved best and in the manner to which he was devoted – and remained silent. He had lived and written calmly – a softly gliding stream in whose refreshing coolness much had thrived, and on whose banks many lively blossoms had sprung up.

The most grateful listeners to his music and to his words were, as always, his children, with whom he kept up a lively correspondence outside the visiting periods, year after year. To them he imparted many of his views and much of his knowledge. In 1862 he wrote to his son in reply to some questions:
Beethoven wrote no less than three overtures in C-major to his opera Leonora which was first performed in 1805, but when the opera was totally reworked in 1814 and reissued under the name Fidelio, he composed another – in E-major. This could be called 'richness of thought'. . . . I love Rossini's 'Tell' as much as you do. He has employed his genius to German thoroughness, and he has left out the so called coloratura high spots. Admittedly this diminishes his popularity, but it raises him as musician.

With special devotion Moscheles dedicated himself in his last years to an old hobby – the collection and studying of interesting autographs and scores:
In the collection of a friend, Gen. Consul

Clauss, a letter was found written by Beethoven to a Herr von Warena in Gratz, that again proves his nobility of mind. Apart from this, nothing less than his own written score for voices set to the Pianoforte Fantasy with his own strange manner of splitting the syllables, e.g. . . . . Gö-tter. gu-nst, etc., and interesting Bach autographs. Again at Breitkopf and Härtel two posthumous string quartets by Cherubini which his widow sent for publishing, and at Peter's a manuscript organ fugue, and the piano score of the B-major Concerto – both by Bach. How I love to hold in my hands such embodiments of the most noble thoughts!

In July he reported:

A few days ago the Saxon Majesties honoured us at our Conservatory. We presented our best pupils to them and they showed their satisfaction – that will be a new motivation for the young people. The Queen reminded me in friendly tones of my playing before her father, King Max, in 1819. Yesterday we saw the King on his journey through Abtnaundorf, where we have been staying for a few days. In their honour Frege's had a gateway made of entwined flowers under which the royal carriage halted. Our good hostess handed over a magnificent bouquet – all orchids – and later the clear sky allowed a wonderful countrified celebration at which all the schoolchildren of the area were permitted to take part. We old town children enjoyed the time in the great park, with its fragrant hay fields and revelled in the moonlight. I revelled too about our entertainment on the piano. Nature without music would only be half an existence and good music in beautiful nature is a double delight.

From Loschwitz, where he spent the summer with the family, he wrote:

The leader of the orchestra, Dorn, who is here with his family, recently gave me a great pleasure: leafing through Mozart's own score of Figaro. He learned that the music teacher, Schurig, in Dresden, had inherited it from his father, who had bought it for a nominal sum from a touring opera company. Now I had the immortal strokes in front of me, on simple 14-line paper, very casually written – the Italian text and recitative by Mozart, the German text written in by another hand. Why am I not rich enough to pay the high price the present owner asks for this treasure? The piano score (at Simrock) deviates from the original as for example in the cavatine of the page: Non so più. *

And shortly afterwards:

Once again I supped at heavenly musical delight. Count Baudissin sent me Mozart's own score of the Magic Flute to attest and confirm its authenticity for Count Rantzau who wishes to purchase it. I had it in my hands forty years ago at André's in Offenbach. Everything in it points to divine inspiration and authenticity. The changes are interesting. Two solo bars in the overture have been crossed out. In the duet 'Bei Männern' ('We men, who know the feeling of love') the tempo has been altered from 6/8 to 3/8.

Still in Loschwitz, he writes in a letter:

There are walks with Dorn in which I am so deeply engrossed in our musical conversations that I even find myself mountain-climbing which is not my practice. . . . The main work of this stay in the country is to undertake the revision of my earliest diaries. Charlotte devotes the mornings to this, and in the evenings she reads me excerpts from them. This way I am reliving my youth – God be praised – without any regrets, for the little that I have achieved in my art, I undertook honestly and industriously.

In the Loschwitz church a concert was organized at which the Queen was present.

---

*As the house of Simrock later bought this original score for 800 Taler these deviations have long since been corrected.

Moscheles played the organ and also contributed the psalm 'Lobe den Herrn, mein Seele' (Praise the Lord, my Soul) composed as a terzette.

In 1863 he wrote his 'Variationen im Volkston' (Variations in Popular Style) and arranged the Symphonic Sonata for eight hands. He rejected repeated offers from Vienna to participate in a cycle of historic concerts. He wished to keep steadfast to his principle 'no public playing'. About a music theoretical pamphlet he said:

How can a discourse on surgery of the arm, hand and finger joints pave the way to the art of piano playing as the recently published pamphlet implies? At this price I would never have become a pianist. The soul must talk to the heart through the fingers, that is the main thing. But I do not spurn to play technically difficult passages as gymnastic exercises for my fingers and I keep to Riehl's words: 'A 50-year old man who lets his physique and his intellect hang flabby is aged seventy within two years. A seventy-year-old who wants to stay young in strength and work is a man in his best years!' Although I am not altogether in agreement with him concerning his other letters on musical education of the people – that he wants to have the violin taught before the piano. Organ and piano offer the best opportunity to grasp the tone relationships and the harmonic perfection. This must be studied first.

What Moscheles wanted to impart to his pupils went much deeper than technique, although it was occasionally not straightforward:

However hard I try to enthuse my pupils for a piece – say Beethoven's Sonata Pathetique – there are cases where I do not succeed. They master the technique, but there is no divine spark firing their spirit. Then I apply my last resource. I try to find an appropriate sentence to something in the music and then with shrill emphasis I bellow out for example 'Do you know the Gods in their rage? Implore them to help you.' I say: 'If you can say that after me, the feeling is likewise expressed in the touch' I myself have always preferred to reflect my feelings in tone. Incidentally, my wife is unflagging in her work in arranging all my ideas about music and all the advice for young artists which I discussed in the diary, and how it would please me if the youth could make some use of it! Today I helped her to arrange the memoranda on the great music festival in Westminster Abbey which I so carefully collected at that time.

In 1864 Schlesinger of Berlin published new editions of the Sonate Mélancolique, the Allegro di Bravura in C-minor and the Charmes de Paris, which prompted Moscheles to make the following observation:

These compositions that have recently seen the light of day might well be termed by many as 'antiquated', and yet they are not so antiquated as a transcription that I heard yesterday and which I classify as the veteran of the antiquated.

The family spent the summer of 1864 near Baden, where numerous artists had gathered, among them Clara Schumann, Pauline Viardot, Joachim, Vieuxtemps, Rubinstein, Brahms, Max Bruch and Jaell.

It goes without saying that we meet each other and hear each other's music, and particularly pleasurable were two musical evenings in Frau Schumann's villa in which the artist phalanx was strongly represented. I requested of our congenial hostess the novelettes by her husband, especially my favourite in E-sharp major. She played with me my 'Variations im Volkston' and decorated it with her spirit. Where a Schumann, a Rubinstein, a Viardot and the married couple Joachim make music there is a wonderful sound. These are artist and friendship reminiscences that make old age beautiful. And we still heard something old and good: the Alceste by Gluck. His greatness lay in the declamatory expression, in the soul of his music; beautiful melodic form though was missing.

Moscheles also met the pianist Pixis in Baden again:

When I visited my good old Pixis he showed me a rather well preserved piano by Clementi. Meyerbeer had inscribed in it that he composed the greater part of his Hugenots on it when Pixis lent him this instrument. As a relic of Mozart Pixis preserves a billet in his handwriting in which he begs his friend for some gulden to help him in need . . . Mozart's letters, published by Ludwig Nohl, are an unending source of interest to me. I copy many passages out of them.

A new society of artists was formed in Leipzig in 1866. Its purpose was to offer serious good music and light performances on various informal evenings. It was named 'Klapperkasten' (approximately, 'Rattleboxes'). After a Hauptmann evening there followed a Moscheles evening:

Dörffel drew out my Alexander Variations from their stale old cover and played them superbly, then I was needed at the piano as living relic, and I fantasied on Bach, Handel, and the Song of Joy from Beethoven's Ninth Symphony.

It is a pity that there is no more agreement among these musical potentates than there is now among men of state, wrote Moscheles later.

In the same year of 1866 war broke out between Prussia and Austria, and Moscheles, always an advocate of united thought, exclaimed:

I can not believe that German wants to fight in battle against German!

In London, where he spent this year's summer, he organized with others a concert to benefit the war wounded:

I am happy to play to the public once again when it is such a good cause . . . and I allow myself to be called old-fashioned when it enables me – an antiquated curiosity – to collect good guineas. That which I can give personally is too small for this mass of unhappiness. So it is the art against war, and we will see whether the peaceful can challenge the destroyer. A concert instead of the battle cry!

This concert took place in the overcrowded St James' Hall and brought, apart from Moscheles and Jenny Lind-Goldschmidt, many other artists to the stage. At the end Moscheles was able to offer that half of the net profit of 1400 Taler which he raised, to the war victims.

The London stay, as in previous years, was spent in a round of commitments – a programme of concerts, theatres, and exhibitions, receptions and talent adjudications and so on. *Yesterday I wondered,* we read in a letter,

how I could endure the piece by Boucicault 'The Strike' after such a morning. It is given every evening and everyone must see it – so, of course, Moscheles as well. It deals with the difficult worker problems and runs through the whole gamut of horrors: innocent poverty, need, revenge, and finally murder! A hair-raising story, played by Eugène Sue in flesh and blood. But – it is the old evil – only this *fills the theatre.*

On the British coast where he spent a few weeks with his English grandchildren, he wrote one of his last compositions, the Opus 140 'Family Life'.

The small pieces are meant as a keepsake for grandchildren; at first for my own and then for all my grandchildren in the art, and I hope that they will find entertainment in them. Each piece contains a tale – one which the little ones have lived through or of a situation appealing to children. In this way they can use their imagination, and feel sympathy, and if they do that then it follows that they will play well.

At that time his son Felix painted the aged Moscheles' portrait. Charlotte writes later how this came about:

It may well have been an opportune moment. Intellectually raised through artistic recognition, physically strengthened by the visit to the seaside, he looked merry and full of life. The sittings were ideal for deep talks on art with our long-missed son – a comparison between music and painting, as Moscheles constantly loved to make. And so this canvas reflects the soul of the painter and the congenial, merry glance of his father.

On Moscheles' 73rd birthday it says in the diary:

How can I count this great number of years without thanking our dear God for leading me so far, under his care, and that at the side of a loving and loved wife! To become old is something normal, but to become old and to be young and receptive to all the pleasures of life – that is a consciousness of rarity!

At Whitsun in 1867 Moscheles visited the Aachen Music Festival and wrote to his wife:

We had a great banquet with toasts and speeches, and I also spoke. At about 1 o'clock in the morning I withdrew from the flowing champagne and speeches, and was pleased that I had the strength to take part in the diverse pleasures, and in between to make music in private with a few friends. In the hotel I packed quickly and had a very short night's rest as the turkey of the house woke me with his

hu - de hu - de   hi

at the first light of dawn.

In the same year he travelled to Cologne, to Hiller, then with his family to Austria on holiday. By *an astonishing, almost superhuman railway* they went over the Semmering, *so high that we landed in the region of the Edelweiss that was offered for sale to us right inside the carriage, like the beer and sandwiches and the Gnadauer pretzels at Magdeburg.*

In 1868 the Leipzig Conservatory celebrated its 25-year anniversary, and to mark this occasion Moscheles composed a piece for eight hands. He and his wife spent the following summer again with their children and grandchildren in London.

In the winter of 1869, for the first time, there was a distinct deterioration in Moscheles' health, but his art was still the best therapy, and his teaching duties were hardly interrupted.

In the spring Moscheles was his old self again at the 150th anniversary celebrations of Breitkopf and Härtel in concerts at the Opera. In Dresden he heard Wagner's 'Meistersinger', and wrote:

I found more unity in this opera than in his earlier works. The relationship of the orchestra to the singers is, and remains, a characteristic. The first strides ahead with luscious modulation and instrumentation effects and the latter follows reciting, often parlando. I found some similarity with Don Juan, especially in the part where Leporello invites the 'maschere' in the minuet rhythm to the ball.

The day following, we read:

I spoke a lot with Rietz about the characteristics as well as the recognisable values of the 'Meistersinger' and we took the printed score to hand and admired the well-calculated instrumental effects.

From Dresden they went via Vienna to

Belgrade to stay for a few weeks with their children who were living there.

We move about, however, in European society, we make European music, and yet there is also much that is new and foreign to the eyes. The Park of the Topschidere where Count Michael was treacherously shot, the young Princes in their castle, the market with its nationalities and its costumes, the Turkish quarter with the half decayed Prince Eugene's Palace, and the Zigeunerstrasse (Gypsy Street) with its dishevelled, sparsely-clothed and begging inhabitants. Serbian tailors, weavers and shoemakers carrying on their crafts in open booths, the jumble flourishes. Slivovitch is consumed at green tables behind stunted oleanders, fruit and vegetables and hot pieces of animal skin are sold and eaten. How foreign – how original! . . . Now we have also seen a Serbian wedding, I counted 20 open caleschen, everybody took part in the most colourful costumes, even the horses were adorned with floral shawls.

At the end of July the return journey by way of Hungary was arranged, where they visited old friends and heard a gypsy group. *Their eyes sparkled, their long hair swung in rhythm and the violin bows struck with vehemence while the fingers of the left hand gripped the strings frantically. . . . At a festival ball on Margaretheninsel (The Isle of Margareth) we saw the csardas – this most exciting of all national dances, danced with much grace. The music is alternately pathetic and stormy and full of originality.*

The next stop of the travelling party was in Podiebrad – *again a beautifully-spent week in the most intimate family circle* – and then followed a halt in the countryside near Hamburg. Von Bernuth, a former pupil of the Conservatory, now Director of the Philharmonic Concert in Hamburg, and his friend Gültzow, took Moscheles to the city library. He wrote: *There, I was able to leaf through the recently acquired conductor's score of Handel – a wonderful acquisition for the people of Hamburg.*

When Moscheles was playing through Handel's Organ Concerto he noticed that in the Andante (B-major) there was a great similarity to the Gigue (G-minor) from Handel's Suites and this was later repeated. *I wonder whether Handel did it intentionally or unintentionally?* he mused.

Back again in Leipzig, Moscheles wrote: *How thankful I can be to look back on this very successful journey! We visited dear relations, near and far, enjoyed music and nature with them and got to know a foreign country.*

But at a visit of his children in October they found him often weary and strained. The late autumn of 1869 brought pain and sleepless nights, and on the 6th December there are the following lines in the diary: *Disintegration is the aim of our earthly life.*

Two days later it says:
In my feverish, excitable nightly suffering Mendelssohn's Capriccio (A-minor) Opus 33 No. 1 would not go out of my mind, from the first to the last note expressing my condition.

This immaculate piece has, however, a stumbling passage with relation to the harmonic orthodoxy that disturbs me. It is the following on from the 263rd bar to the next:

On Tuesday, 20th December, Moscheles wrote in his diary:

After a disturbed, almost sleepless night I had a highly exciting dream towards morning: it came to my ear (where from?), that since Beethoven's day of death in Vienna an old servant couple who had always preserved the holy place of his departure, claimed that every year on Beethoven's birthday his figure can be evoked – but only for those who knew Beethoven personally in his lifetime. The conservators had a description of his last moments printed and sold it for a small fee or tip. I must go there (I said to myself) and told this to Charlotte. She, full of irresistible urge to participate, called out: 'You will take me

with you?' I was moved and explained to her how difficult this would be as she had never known Beethoven personally. She begged and pleaded with me to take her so that she could at least see the shadow of this great departed hero, and she insisted that I should make him understand that my wife must be allowed this indiscretion. After much hesitation I gave in! We arrived on the day in Vienna and requested entry. We sat at the bed in which Beethoven spoke his last words: 'plaudite amici, comoedia finita est'. The conservators made a few mysterious movements with their hands – and all at once Beethoven's figure rose up, lifesize, like a white marble statue; the body was clothed in a Greek robe. The apparition approached me, stretched out his cold hands – which I immediately took and kissed. Beethoven leant towards me as though he wanted to ask me some questions! I gave him to understand through signs that he would not be able to hear my answers! He shook his head in thought, drew his hands from mine and disappeared above – and then I awoke.

On 31st December we read:
My thoughts were directed towards the Creator, who has led me through fruitful and full years to the winter of my life. Loved and cared for by my faithful Charlotte, linked by love to my whole family, I find that even as an invalid there is much comfort. With this: departure from the year 1869.

In January and February of 1870 he was able to enjoy again the fresh open air – and the spiritual air of music. The youthful talent of Emma Brandes pleased him. He let her study his Children's Fairytales, played them to her, lavished praises on her true artistic simplicity, and encouraged her to steer clear of all fashionable tendencies. He prophesied a brilliant future for her.

He had to hear one of his favourite operas, the 'Medea' by Cherubini, as well as the

Gewandhaus rehearsal of Grimms Suite. He also played a piece for eight hands with an acquainted couple and his youngest daughter. This occurred on 1st March, and then came a relapse – the last!

Full of trust, just as he had been in the year 1825 on the high seas when he had had visions of his decline, he bore his illness well. He had dealt candidly with God's gift which had been entrusted to him. His love of the art had accompanied him to his last days and his spirit still wished to hear, even when his wearisome body was lacking in strength. *He was the best son, husband, father, and friend,* wrote Charlotte in her book. *He devoted every minute of his life to good purpose, to the good of his family and his pupils. Now he can leave without regret.*

He maintained too the warmth of his person right until the end. On 10th March 1870 when death hovered in the room, he still had a loving smile for his surroundings. The soul did not tear itself away, but simply floated upwards with a deep sigh – under the kiss of the Angel of Death. He died as he had lived: peaceful and resigned to God's will!

COMPLETE CATALOGUE OF COMPOSITIONS BY I. MOSCHELES

This catalogue has been taken as it stood in the 1872/73 Diaries. It served as basis for Kistner's 'Thematic Index of Printed and Published Compositions by I. Moscheles', Leipzig.

Op. 1. Variations sur un Thème de l'Opéra 'Une folie' de Méhul, pour le Piano. Leipzig, Kistner.

Op. 2. Dix Variations sur un Air favori de l'Opéra 'Der Dorfbarbier', pour le Piano. Wien, Haslinger.

Op. 3. Polonaise pour le Piano. Leipzig, Hofmeister.

Op. 4. Nouvelle Sonatine facile et agréable pour le Piano. Wien, Artaria & Co.

Op. 5. Air favori de Weigl: 'Wer hörte wohl' etc. varié p. le Piano. Wien, Spina.

Op. 6. Variations pour le Piano sur un Air national Autrichien. Wien, Artaria & Co.

Op. 7. Variazioni sopra una Cavatina dell' Opera 'Trajano in Dacia'. Ebend.

Op. 8. Dix Valses pour le Pianoforte. Ebend.

Op. 9. Fünf deutsche Tänze f. d. Pianof. Wien, Spina.

Op. 10. Triumphmarsch nebst 2 Trios für das Pianoforte zu 4 Händen. Ebend.

Op. 11. Deux Rondeaux pour le Piano sur des Motifs introduits dans le Ballet 'Les portraits'. Leipzig, Kistner.

Op. 12. Introduction et Rondeau pour le Piano sur une barcarole vénitienne. Wien, Haslinger.

Op. 13. Fantaisie héroique pour le Piano. Wien, Spina – Nouvelle Edit. Leipzig, Hofmeister.

Op. 14. Rondo brillante pour le Piano. Wien, Artaria & Co.

Op. 15. Variations pour le Piano sur un thème de l'Opéra 'der Augenarzt'. Wien, Spina.

Op. 16. Drei erotische Lieder von. E. Ludwig, mit Begleitung des Pfte. (Traum und Wahrheit – der Kuss – das Unvergängliche). Leipzig, Hofmeister.

Op. 17. Introd. et variations concertantes pour Piano, Violon et Violoncello. Wien, Haslinger.

Op. 18. Trois Rondeaux p. l. P. Wien, Spina.,

Op. 19. Polonaise précedée d'une introd. p. l. P. Ebd.

Op. 20. Grand Duo concertant pour Piano et Guitarre. Wien, Artaria & Co.

Op. 21. Six Variations pour Piano et Flûte ou Violon. Wien, Haslinger.

Op. 22. Sonate p. l. P. Wien, Spina.

Op. 23. Variations p. l. P. sur un thème russe. Wien, Artaria & Co.

Op. 24. Rondo espagnol p. l. P. Wien, Spina.

Op. 25. Caprice p. l. P. Ebd.

Op. 26. Triumpheinzug der verbündeten Mächte in Paris, ein character. Tongemälde f. d. P. Wien, Artaria & Co.

Op. 27. Sonate (caractéristique) p. l. P. Ebd.

Op. 28. Six divertissements p. l. P. Wien, Spina.

Op. 29. Variations p. l. P. sur un thème de Händel. Ebd.

Op. 30. Rondo brillant p. l. P. à 4 ms. Ebd.

Op. 31. Trois Marches héroiques p. l. P. à 4 ms. Ebd.

Op. 32. L Marche d'Alexandre, variée p. l. P. avec accomp. de l'Orchestre. Wien, Artaria & Co.
Arrang. mit Quartett; Piano solo; Piano à 4 ms. (Leipzig, Breitkopf & Härtel)

Op. 33. Six Valses avec Trios p. l. P. à 4 ms. Wien, Artaria & Co.

Op. 34. Grand Duo concertant p. l. P. et Violoncelle ou Basson. Ebd.

Op. 35. Grand Sextuor p. P., Viol., Fl., 2 Cors et Violoncelle. Leipzig, Hofmeister. Arrang. en Sonate p. P.; p. 2 Pftes.; p. P. à 4 ms.

Op. 36. Variationen über einen österr. Walzer f. Pianof. und Violine. Wien, Haslinger.

Op. 37. Grand Caprice d'un Potp. suivi p. P. et Violl. ou Violon, concertants. Wien, Spina.

Op. 38. Fantasie (im italien. Style), verbunden mit einem grossen Rondo f. d. P. Wien, Haslinger.

Op. 39. Einleitung und Variationen f. d. P. über ein österr. Nationallied. Wien, Haslinger.

Op. 40. Les portraits. Ballet champêtre et comique, arr. p. l. P. Wien. Artaria & Co.
Ouverture p. P. seul – p. P. à 4 ms.

– Trois Divertissements p. l. P. Les motifs tirés du Ballet: Les portraits. Leipzig, Hofmeister.

Op. 41. Grosse Sonate für das Pianoforte (Beethoven gewidmet). Wien, Haslinger.

Op. 42. Grandes Variations sur une mélodie nationale autrichienne p. l. P. avet 2 Violons, Alto, Violoncelle et Contrebasse ou sans accompagnement. Wien, Artaria & Co.

Op. 43. Grand Rondeau brillant p. l. P. avec Accomp. de 2 Violons, Alto, Violle. et Contrebasse (ad lib.) Wien, Artaria & Co.
Pour le P. seul – à 4 ms. Leipzig, Hofmeister.

Op. 44. Grande Sonate concertante pour Piano et Flûte. Wien, Artaria & Co.

Op. 45. Concert de société p. l. Piano m. Begleitung eines kleinen Orchesters. Wien, Spina.
Für Piano solo. – Rondo daraus f. 4 Hde. Leipzig, Hofmeister.

Op. 46. Fantasie, Variationen und Finale über das böhmische Volkslied: 'To gsau kône' concertirend für Piano, Violine, Clarinette und Violoncell. Wien, Haslinger.

Op. 47. Grande Sonate p. l. P. à ms. (Es-dur-Sonate.) Wien, Artaria & Co.
Spätere Aufl. Hamburg, Cranz.

Op. 48. Französisches Rondo concertirend für Piano und Violine mit kleinem oder ohne Orchester. Wien, Haslinger.

Op. 49. Sonate mélancolique p. l. P. Wien, Artaria & Co. Berlin, Schlesinger.

Op. 50. Fantaisie et Variations sur l'air favori 'Au clair de la lune' p. l. P. avec acc. de l'Orchestre. Berlin, Schlesinger. Mit Quartett. Für Piano solo.

Op. 51 Allegri di Bravura (la forza – la leggerezza – il capriccio). Leipzig, Peters.

Op. 52. La Tenerezza. Rondoletto p. l. P. Wien, Spina.
Nouv. édit. Hamburg, Cranz.

Op. 53. Polonaise brillante p. l. P. Leipzig, Hofmeister.

Op. 54. Les Charmes de Paris. Rondo brill. pour le Piano. Berlin, Schlesinger. Für P. zu 4 Hdn. arrangirt.

Op. 55. Bonbonnière musicale. Suite de morceaux faciles p. l. Piano, Paris, Schlesinger.

Op. 56. Grosses Concert (Nr. 2 Es-dur) p. l. P. m. Begl. d. Orchesters. Leipzig, Klemm.
Mit Quartett. – f. Piano solo. – Rondo brill. alla Polacca p. P. à 4 ms. Leipzig, Hofmeister.

Op. 57. Fantaisie p. l. P sur trois airs favoris écossais. Leipzig, Breitkopf & Härtel.

Op. 58. Jadis et aujourd'hui. Un Gigue et

un Quadrille-Rondeau pour le Piano. Hamburg, Cranz.

Op. 59. Grand Potpourri concertant p. Piano et Violon ou Flûte (par Moscheles et Lafont). Berlin, Schlesinger.

Op. 60. Drittes Concert (G-moll) für das Piano mit Orchester. Leipzig, Klemm.
Mit Quartett, – Für Piano solo.

Op. 61. Rondoletto sur un Nocturne favori de Paër p. l. P. Wien, Artaria & Co.

Op. 62. Impromptu p. l. P. Leipzig, Kistner.

Op. 63. Introduction et Rondeau écossais concertants p. P. et Cor (ou Violon et Violle). Leipzig, Kistner.
Für. à 4 ms. arrangirt.

Op. 64. Viertes Concert für das Piano mit Orchesterbegleitung. Wien, Steiner & Co.

Op. 65. Impromptu martial sur l'air anglais 'Revenge he gries' p. l. P. Leipzig, Kistner.

Op. 66. La petite Babillarde. Rondeau pour le Piano. Leipzig, Kistner.

Op. 67. Trois Rondeaux brillants p. l. P. sur des Motifs favoris du Vaudeville: 'Les Viennois à Berlin'. Berlin, Schlesinger.

Op. 68. Fantaisie et Rondeau sur une marche autrichienne p. l. Piano. Leipzig, Kistner.

Op. 69. Souvenirs d'Irlande. Grande Fantaisie p. l. P. avec Accomp. d'Orchestre ou Quatuor, Leipzig, Hofmeister.
Pour P. solo – p. P. à 4 ms.

Op. 70. Studien für das Pianoforte, zur höheren Vollendung bereits ausgebildeter Clavierspieler, bestehend aus 24 charact. Tonstücken. 2 Hefte. Leipzig, Kistner.

Op. 71. Rondeau expressif sur un Thême favori de Gallenberg p. l. P. Leipzig, Kistner.

Op. 72. Nr. l. Fantaisie dramatique dans le Style italien sur des Airs favoris chantés par Mme. Pasta, p. l. P. Leipzig, Kistner.

Op. 72. Nr. 2. Bijoux à la Sontag. Fantaisie dramatique p. l. Piano. Ebend.

Op. 72. Nr. 3. Bijoux à la Malibran. Fantaisie dramatique. 2 Hefte. Ebend.

Op. 73. Fünfzig Praeludien in den verschiedenen Durund Molltonarten f. d. P. Ebend.

Op. 74. Les Charmes de Londres. Rondeau brillant pour le Piano. Ebend.

Op. 75. Anklänge aus Schottland. Fantaisie über schottische Nationallieder für das Pianoforte mit Orchester oder Quartett. Leipzig, Hofmeister.
Für P. solo arrangirt.

Op. 76. La belle Union. Rondeau brill. préc. d'une introd. p. l. P. à 4 ms. Leipzig, Kistner.

Op. 77. Allegro di Bravura p. l. P. (Mendelssohn gewidmet). Berlin, Schlesinger.

Op. 78. Divertissements à la Savoyarde p. Piano et Flûte ou Violon. Leipzig, Hofmeister.

Op. 79. Sonate concertante pour Piano et Flûte (ou Violon). Leipzig, Kistner.

Op. 80. Fantaisie sur des airs des Bardes écossais, p. l. P. avec Orchestre (ad lib.). Leipzig, Kistner.
Für Piano allein arrangirt.

Op. 81. Erste Sinfonie (in C-dur) für grosses Orchester. Leipzig, Kistner.

Op. 82 a. Rondeau sentimental p. l. P. Ebd.

Op. 82 b. Quatre Divertissements p. P. et Flûte. Ebd.

Op. 83. Souvenirs de Danemarc. Fantaisie sur des Airs nationaux danois p. l. P. avec Orchestre. Ebd. Für Piano solo arrangirt.

Op. 84. Grand Trio pour Piano, Violon et Violle., dedieé à Cherubini. Ebend.

Op. 85. La Gaieté. Rondeau brill. p. l. P. Ebd.

Op. 86 a.   Marche facile avec Trio p. l. P. à 4 ms. Ebd.

Op. 86 b.   Souvenir de Rubini. Fantaisie dramatique p. l. P. sur une Cavatine de l'Opéra 'Anna Bolena' Ebd.

Op. 87.   Fünftes Concert (C-dur) für das Piano mit Orchesterbegleitung. Wien, Haslinger.
Mit Quartett – für Piano solo.

Op. 87 a.   Souvenir de l'Opéra. Fantaisie dramatique pour le Piano sur des airs favoris chantés à Londres par Mme. Pasta. Leipzif, Kistner.

Op. 87 b.   Duo concertant pour deux Pianos avec acc. d'Orchestre en variations brillantes sur la marche Bohémienne tirée du Mélodrame Preciosa, comp. par F. Mendelssohn et I. Moscheles. Ebd.
Für 2 P. ohne Begleitg. – Für P. zu 4 Hdn.

Op. 88.   Grand Septuor p. P., Violon, Alto, Clarinette, Cor, Vlle. et Contrebasse. Ebd.
Für P. solo – für P. zu 4 Hdn.

Op. 89.   Impromptu p. l. P. Ebd.

Op. 90.   Concerto fantastique (Nr.6) p. Piano avec Orchestre. Wien, Haslinger.
Avec quatuor. – Pour l. P. seul

Op. 91.   Ouverture à grand Orchestre, de 'Jeanne d'Arc', Tragédie de Schiller. Leipzig, Kistner.
Für P. zu 4 Hdn. arrangirt.

Op. 92.   Hommage à Händel. Grand Duo pour deux Pianofortes. Ebend.
Für P. zu 4 Hdn. arrangirt.

Op. 93.   Concerto pathétique p. l. P. avec Orchestre (Nr.7.). Wien, Haslinger.
Avec quatuor. – Pour l. P. seul.

Op. 94 a.   Rondeau brill. sur la romance favor. de Dessauer 'le retour des Promis'. Leipzig, Kistner.

Op. 94 b.   Hommage caractéristique à la Mémoire de Mme. Malibran de Bériot en forme de Fantaisie p. l. P. Ebd.

Op. 95.   Characteristische Studien f. d. P. zur höheren Entwicklung des Vortrags und der Bravour. Ebend.
(Zorn – Versöhnung – Widerspruch – Juno – Kindermärchen – Bacchanal – Zärtlichkeit – Volksfest-Scenen – Mondnacht am Seegestade – Terpsichore – Traum – Angst)

Op. 96.   Concerto pastorale (Nr.8) p. l. Piano avec acc. d'Orchestre. Wien, Haslinger.

Op. 97.   Sechs Lieder für eine Singstimme mit Begleitung des Piano. Leipzig, Kistner. (Stumme Liebe – Der Schmied – Zuversicht – Das Reh – Im Herbste – Sakontala)

Op. 98.   Deux Etudes: L'ambition – l'enjouement, tirées de la Méthode des méthodes. Berlin, Schlesinger.

Op. 99.   Tutti frutti. Six nouvelles mélodies pour le Piano. Paris, Pacini.

Op. 100.   Ballade p. l. P. Braunschweig, Spehr.
Für P. zu 4 Hdn. arrangirt.

Op. 101.   Romance et Tarantelle brillante pour le Piano. Leipzig, Hofmeister.

Op. 102.   Hommage à Weber. Grand Duo p. l. P. à 4 ms. sur des motifs d'Euryanthe et d'Oberon. Leipzig, Kistner.

Op. 103.   Sérénade p. l. P. Ebd.

Op. 104.   Romanesca p. l. P. Ebd

Op. 105.   Deux Etudes p. l. P., écrites pour l'Album de Beethoven. Wien, Spina

Op. 106.   Fantaisie brill. pour le Piano sur une Cavatine de l'Opéra 'Zelmire' de Rossini et une Ballade de 'l'Enlèvement du Serail' de Mozart. Leipzig, Kistner.

Op. 107.   Tägliche Studien über die harmonischen Scalen zur Uebung in den verschiedenen Rhythmen. Ein Cyclus von 59 vierh. Clavierstücken. 2 Hefte. Ebd.

Op. 108.   Deux Fantaisies brillantes pour le Piano sur des Airs favoris de l'Opéra 'la Bohémienne' de Balfe. 2 Hfte. Ebd.

Op. 109 a. Fantaisie brillante sur des thèmes favoris de l'Opera 'Don Pasquale' p. l. P. Leipzig, Hofmeister.

Op. 109 b. Mélange p. l. P. sur la Sérénade et d'autres airs favoris de l'Opéra 'Don Pasquale'. Ebd.

Op. 110. Gondoliers Lied f. d. P. Rotterdam.

Op. 111. Quatre grandes Etudes de Concert p. l. P. Leipzig, Kistner. (Réverie et Allégresse. – Le Carillon. – Tendresse et exaltation. – La Fougue).

Op. 112. Grande Sonate symphonique Nr. 2 à 4 ms. p. l. P. Berlin, Friedländer.

Op. 113. Album des chants favoris de Pischek transcr. p. l. P. en forme de fantaisie brillante. Leipzig, Kistner.

Op. 114. Souvenirs de Jenny Lind. Fantaisie brill. p. l. P. sur des airs Suédois. Ebd.

Op. 115. Les Contrastes. Grand Duo p. deux Pianos à 8 ms. Ebd.
Füs d. P. zu 4 Hdn. arrangirt.

Op. 116. Freie Kunst. Gedicht von Uhland für eine Bassoder Altstimme mit Begl. des Pianoforte. Ebd.

Op. 117. Sechs Lieder für eine Singstimme mit Begleitung des Piano. Ebend. (Liebeslauschen – Dem Liebesänger – Warum so stumm – Botschaft – Schäfers Sonntagslied – Frühlingslied).

Op. 118. Grande Valse p. l. P. Ebd.

Op. 119. Sechs Gesänge für eine Singstimme mit Begleitung des Piano. Ebend. (Abends – Die Zigeunerin – Strenge – Jemand – Der Liebeswürdigen – Der dreifache Schnee).

Op. 120. Mazurka appassionata p. l. P. Ebd.

Op. 121. Sonate f. P. und Violoncello. Ebd.
Für P. und Violine – Für P. zu 4 Hdn.

Op. 122. Die Erwartung (nach Schiller). Fantasie p. l. P. Hamburg, Cranz.

Op. 123. Magyarenklänge. Original-Fantasie für das Pianoforte. Braunschweig, Litolff.

Op. 124. Sehnsucht (nach Schiller), Fantasie f. d. Pfte. Leipzig, Siegel.

Op. 125. Frühlingslied für eine Sopran- oder Tenorstimme mit Pianof.-Begl. Cöln, Schloss.

Op. 126. Grosse Concert-Etude f. P. Leipzig, Kistner.

Op. 127. Scherzo f. d. P. Leipzig, Payne.

Op. 128. Humoristische Variationen. Scherzo und Variationen f. d. P. Leipzig, Kistner.

Op. 129. Der Tanz. Characterstück (nach Schiller), f. d. P. Leipzig, Breitkopf & Härtel.

Op. 130. Symphonisch-heroischer Marsch über deutsche Volkslieder für d. P. zu 4 Hdn. Leipzig, Kistner. Für 2 Pianos arrangirt.

Op. 131. Sechs Lieder für eine Singstimme mit Begleitung des Pianoforte. Ebd. (Gieb uns täglich Brod – Frühlingsliebe – Schmetterling und Liebchen – Am Meere – Inniges Verständnis – Tanz-Reigen der donischen Kosaken.

Op. 132. Vier Duette für Sopran und Alt mit Begleitung des Pianoforte. Ebd. (Des Lilien-Mädchens Wiegenlied – Am Bache – Winter und Frühling – Unter den Bäumen).

Op. 133. Réverie mélodique für das Pianof. Stuttgart, E. Hallberger.

Op. 134. Toccate f. d. P. (Im Mozart-Album.)

Op. 135. Pastorale im Orgel-Style. Erfurt, Bartholomäus.

Op. 136. An G. Rossini. 'Am Bache'. Lied mit oblig. Begl. f. Horn (Violl.) u. P. Leipzig, Kistner.

Op. 137. Melodisch-contrapunktische Studien. Eine Auswahl von 10 Präludien aus Johann Sebastian Bach's wohltemperirtem Clavier mit einer hinzucomponir-

ten obligaten Violoncell-Stimme. Leipzig, Kistner.
Auch für ein zweites Clavier statt des Violle. arrangirt.

Op. 138. Feuillet d'Album de Rossini. Thème original pour Piano et Cor. Ebd. Für P. und Violle. – Für 2 Pianos.

Op. 139. Lied im Volkston mit Variationen üb. e. Original-Thema. Leipzig, Klemm.

Op. 140. Familienleben, 12 progress. Clavierstücke f. d. P. zu 4 Hdn. 2 Hefte, Leipzig, Kistner.

Op. 141. Marsch und Scherzo als rhythmische Uebungen (in den 5 Fingerlagen f. den Schüler) Nr. 1. Marsch. Nr. 2. Scherzo. Hamburg, Cranz.

Op. 142. Drei Charakterstücke f. d. P. zu 4 Händen. Leipzig, Kistner.

---

1. Souvenir de Bélisaire. Deux Fantaisies pour le Piano. Leipzig, Kistner.
2. Fantaisie p. l. P. sur des motifs de 'Falstaff' de Balfe. Mainz, Schott's Söhne.
3. Fantaisie sur des Thèmes favoris de l'Opéra 'Obéron' p. l. P. Berlin, Schlesinger.
4. Fantaisie à la Paganini p. l. P. seul. Leipzig, Kistner.
5. Fantaisie sur des motifs de l'Opéra 'Le Siège de Rochelle' de Balfe p. l. P. Wien, Spina.
6. Bouquet des Mélodies. Petite Fantaisie sur des airs favoris. Hamburg, Cranz.
7. The popular Barcarolle 'Or che in cielo' sung by Sign. Ivanoft in Donizetti's Opera 'Marino Faliero' arrang. as a Fantaisie with Variations for the Pianoforte. London, Addison & Hodson.
8. Pensées fugitives p. l. P. Wien, Spina. (Romance – Impromptu – Nocturne – Rhapsodie).
9. Andante et Rondeau sur un Thème allemand p. l. P. Leipzig, Kistner.
10. Echo des Alpes. Divertissement p. l. P. sur trois Airs past. de la Suisse. Ebd.
11. Die Tyrolerfamilie, 3me Divertissement p. l. P. Leipzig, Hofmeister.
12. Divertissement sur des airs tiroliens chantés par la famille Rainer, p. l. P. Leipzig, Peters.
13. Divertissement sur des airs suisses nationaux p. l. P. Leipzig, Kistner.
14. Rondo üb. eine bel. schottische Melodie f. d. P. Wien, Haslinger.
15. Rondeau militaire p. l. P. sur le Duo favori 'Entendez-vous' de la Fiancée d'Auber. Leipzig, Kistner.
16. Abschiedsmarsch des Infant.-Reg. Kaiser Alexander. Wien. Spina.
17. Zwei grosse Märsche f. d. Reg. Kaiser Alexander f. d. P. Ebd.
19. Favoritmarsch mit Trio (d. Regiments Kutschera und Max Joseph) f. d. P. auf 4 Hde. Ebd.
20. Rhapsodie champètre p. l. P. Berlin, Schlesinger.
21. Der Abschied der Troubadours. Romanze mit deutschem und italienischem Texte. Unterhaltungsstück für Gesang, Pianof., Guitarre and Violine mit abwechselnden Variationen von Moscheles, Giuliani und Mayseder. Wien, Spina.
Für 2 Pfte. arr. v. Czerny. – Für P. à 4 ms. v. Lickl.
22. Musik bei der bei Anwesenheit der hohen Alliirten gehaltnen Schlittenfahrt, f. d. P. arr. Wien, Artaria & Co.
23. Drei Modewalzer f. d. P. Ebd.
24. Zwölf deutsche Tänze sammt Trios und Coda f. d. P. Wien, k. k. Hoftheater-Musikverlag.
25. Six Valses p. l. P. Wien, Spina.
26. Six Ecossaises p. l. P. Wien, Artaria & Co.

27. Six Valses p. l. P. Leipzig, Peters.
28. Verständniss. Ged. v. Prodald, f. e. Singst. m. P. Leipzig, Payne.
29. Fantaisie p. l. P. sur des airs de Neukomm. London, Cramer & Co.
30. L'Elegante. Rondeau p. l. P. London, Chappell.
31. Variationen über G. F. Händel's Harmonious' Blacksmith f. d. P. z. 4 Hdn. Leipzig, Kistner.

The composition 'Concertante for Flute and Oboe, with orchestral accompaniment, in F–Major' (1868) of which there are at least two handwritten editions – one each in London and Stuttgart – is not listed in the index of the diaries.

In this index of biographies all those personalities have been included who were mentioned by Moscheles in his diary who were significant in his life and who bore a lasting influence on his artistic development, but whose biographic details are perhaps not so widely known.

ALBRECHTSBERGER, Johann Georg, composer, *Klosterneuburg 3.2.1736, +Vienna 7.3.1809. From 1772 he was court organist in Vienna, from 1792 Director of Music at St Stephens Cathedral; Ludwig van Beethoven's teacher (1792), also of C. Czerny, F. Fries, J. Eybler, and J. N. Hummel.

ANDRÉ, Johann Anton, music publisher and composer, *Offenbach 6.10.1775, +do. 6.4.1842. Built up the publishing business founded by his father; he was mainly engaged in promoting the works of W. A. Mozart (cataloguing them). He wrote operas, works for orchestras and choirs, as well as chamber music.

ANSCHUTZ, Heinrich Johann Imanuel, actor, *Luckan, +Nieder-Lausitz 8.2.1785, +Vienna 29.12.1865. He made his debut in Nurenberg, visited Leipzig, Danzig and Breslau and then to Vienna, where he joined the company of the Hofburgtheater. He was in close contact with the 'Schubert devotees' and was a friend of L. van Beethoven's, for whom he gave a funeral oration composed by F. Grillparzer.

ARNOLD, Samuel, composer, musicologist and organist, *London 10.8.1740, +do. 22.10.1802. In 1789 he became principal of The Academy of Ancient Music, 1793 organist at Westminster Abbey. He wrote 68 operas and nine oratorios and started the first complete edition of G. F. Handel (36 volumes, 1787–97). Important is his edition of Cathedral Music (4 volumes, 1790; Church Music of the 16th to 18th century in England).

AUBER, Daniel-François-Esprit, composer, *Caen 29.1.1782, +Paris 12./13.5.1871. Besides Boieldieu he was one of the main exponents of opera comic; writing about 50 operas, among them 'La muette de Portici' and 'Fra Diavolo'. 1842 was principal of the Paris Conservatory, 1857 Director of Music at the Imperial Court.

AYRTON, William, conductor, *24.2.1777, +8.3.1858 in London. Much credit is given to him for performing Mozart operas at the Royal Theatre in London.

BÉRIOT, Charles-Auguste de, Belgian violinist, *Löwen 20.2.1802, +Brussels 8.4.1870. Partly autodidactic, he was for a short time a pupil of F. Baillot and G. B. Viotti. From 1843–52 he was teacher at the Conservatory in Brussels. He wrote ten violin concertos, sonatas for piano and violin as well as five collections of violin études which became famous for their virtuoso technique. He was married to the singer Maria Malibran.

BERLIOZ, Louis Hector, French composer, *La Côte-St-André, Isère 11.12.1803, +Paris 8.3.1869. He studied with J. F. Le Sueur and A. Reicha. He composed symphonies, choral works and operas. ('Symphonie fantastique', 'Damnation of Faust', 'Benvenuto Cellini', etc.)

BISHOP, Sir (since 1842) Henry Rowley, composer, *London 18.11.1786, +do. 30.4.1855. In 1860 he became conductor at Convent Garden in London and 1817–18 at the King's Theatre. He was professor at Edinburgh (1841–43) and Oxford (1848–53). He wrote 110 works for the stage (operas, singspiel, ballets) and arranged operas by other composers (W. A. Mozart, F. -A. Boieldieu and others).

BÖHM, Theobald, flautist, *Munich 9.4.1794, +do. 25.11.1881. He built woodwind instruments, especially flutes (Böhm flutes) to rigorous acoustic rules and invented an easy-to-handle key mechanism. He wrote books ('On the Building of Flutes', 1847; 'The Flute and the Playing of the Flute', 1871).

BÖHME, Franz Magnus, musician, *Willerstgedt near Weimar 11.3.1827, +Dresden 18.10.1898. Pupil of Hauptmann and Rietz among others. He was music teacher in Leipzig, Dresden and Frankfurt and was known for his collection of German folk songs.

BORDOGNI Giovanni Marco, tenor, *Gazzaniga near Bergamo 23.1.1789, +Paris 31.7.1856. From 1820 he was singing teacher at the Paris Conservatory, and taught Henriette Sonntag.

BRAHAM John, (actually J. Abraham), composer and singer on various opera stages in London, *20.3.1777, +do. 17.2.1856. 1798 he appeared in Florence, 1799–1801 in Milan. He wrote a number of stage works as well as lieder and a collection of Hebrew melodies. In 1831 he became a theatrical impresario.

BREITKOPF & HARTEL, music publishers, founded 1719 in Leipzig by Bernhard Christoph Breitkopf (1695–1777). Their head office is now in Wiesbaden. The son Johann Gottlob Immanuel Breitkopf (1719—94) was one of the leading printers and publishers of his time and invented printing with moveable type. In 1795 Gottfried Härtel (1719–1827) became partner, in 1796 sole proprietor of the company. Publishers of (among others) complete editions of works by Bach, Beethoven, Palestrina, Brahms etc. as well as the Köchel index of Mozart's works.

BREIDENSTEIN, Heinrich Carl, music historian, *Steinau (Hessen) 28.2.1796, +Bonn 13.7.1876. In 1822 he was Director of Music at the University of Bonn; becoming Professor of Music there in 1826. From 1828 he supported the erection of a Beethoven monument in Bonn and composed a celebration cantata at its unveiling.

BRENDEL, Karl Franz, *Stalberg (Hartz) 26.11.1811, +Leipzig 25.11.1868. Music author, studied philosophy in Leipzig and piano with Fr. Wieck; he took over the editorship of the 'Neue Zeitschrift für Musik', founded in 1834 by Schumann, which he continued in the spirit of the neo-German school. Later he was also teacher at the Leipzig Conservatory. Founder-member and first president of the Allgemeine Deutsche Musikverein (German Music Society). Author of many works on the history of music.

BREUNING, Stephen von, War Minister at the court, *Bonn 17.8.1774, +Vienna 4.6.1827. From his youth he was a friend of Beethoven. His son, Moritz Gerhard, published the book 'Aus dem Schwarzspanierhause' which became an important source for Beethoven's last years.

BROADWOOD, B. & Sons Ltd, cembalo and piano factory in London founded

(1728) by the Swiss Burkhard Tschudi (1702–73). John Broadwood, a carpenter, was Tschudis' partner and beneficiary. The so-called English construction, built in 1770 by Americus Backens and in 1781 recommended by Broadwood, was a continued development of the Christofori's and Silbermann's construction. Henry John Tschudi B. (+1911) made the firm into a limited company and it is still a leading piano manufacturer.

BRONSART VON SCHELLENDORF, Hans August Alexander, pianist and composer, *Berlin 11.2.1830, +Munich 3.11.1913. He was a pupil of Liszt in Weimar, 1865–66 successor of H. von Bülow in Berlin, from 1867 Director of the Royal Theatre at Hanover. In 1887 he was appointed General Director of the Court Theatre in Weimar. He wrote mainly works for the piano.

BRUCH, Max Karl August, composer, *Cologne 6.1.1838, +Berlin-Friedenau 2.10.1920. He studied with, among others, F. Hiller. He was music teacher in Cologne, Music Director in Koblenz, Hofkapellmeister in Sondershausen, Conductor of the Stern Choir Society in Berlin, the Philharmonic Society in Liverpool, Director of the Orchestral Society of Breslau, and finally (until 1910) was Professor at the Academy of the Arts in Berlin. He composed symphonies, chamber music and choral works in the style of Mendelssohn.

BÜLOW, Hans Guido Freiherr von, conductor and pianist, *Dresden 8.1.1830, +Cairo 12.2.1894. He studied with, among others, F. Wieck and F. Liszt. He became Hofkapellmeister in 1867 and Director of the Royal School of Music in Munich. From 1877–79 he was Kapellmeister of the Hoftheater Hanover; 1880–85 was music impresario to the Duke of Meiningen and after

1887 was Director of Concerts in Hamburg and Conductor of the Berlin Philharmonic. He conducted the first performance of Wagner's 'Tristan and Isolde' (1865) and 'Die Meistersinger' (1868). He was married to Cosima, Liszt's daughter, who left him for Wagner in 1870.

CASTELLI, Ignaz Franz, Austrian librettist, *Vienna 6.3.1781, +do. 5.2.1862. Friend of Beethoven and C. M. von Weber. Author of Weigl's 'Schweizerfamilie' (Swiss Family) and other popular operas. He also translated many foreign operas into German. In 1811 he was appointed Court Playwright for the Kärntnertor Theatre.

CHERUBINI, Maria Luigi Zenobio Carlo Salvatore, composer, *Florence 14.9.1760, +Paris 13.3.1842. At 13 he composed his first great works and studied 1778–82 with G. Sarti. From 1788 he lived in Paris as Director of the Paris Conservatory. He wrote 15 Italian and 14 French operas ('Démophon', 'Medée' etc), and chamber music, later mainly church music. He is counted as one of the greatest masters in the development of the accompaniment obbligato. Beethoven was one of his admirers.

CHEVE, Emile-Joseph-Maurice, *Douarnenez (Finistère) 1804, +Paris 26.8.1864. Originally a physician he became a teacher of singing. He wrote several books on elementary music instruction. His method consisted mainly of the use of numbers instead of notes.

CHOPIN Fryderyk Franciszek, (French: Fréderic François), Polish composer and pianist, *Zelaowa-Wola (near Warsaw) 22.2.1810, +Paris 17.10.1849. He was the son of an emigré French citizen and a Polish lady. He studied with J. Elsner and from 1830 was a popular pianist and sought-after teacher in Paris. His many friends included Liszt, Berliot, Balzac, Heine and Meyerbeer. Lived for some time with the writer George Sand on Majorca. Was the founder of a modern piano style in which great virtuosity was completely subject to intensive poetic expression. He wrote works exclusively for the piano (nocturnes, preludes, impromptus, études, mazurkas) and works in which the piano is of major prominence.

CHORLEY Henry Fothergill, English music critic, *Blackley Hurst, Lancs. 15.12.1808, +London 16.2.1872. From 1830 to 1868 he was Director of the London Athenaeum. Author of various books on contemporary music as well as an autobiography.

CLEMENTI Muzio, composer and pianist, *Rome 23. (or 24.?)1.1752, +Evesham, Worcs., 10.3.1832. 1777–80 Cembalist and Director of Music at the Italian Opera in London, toured the continent many times. He worked in London as soloist, conductor and teacher (among his pupils were J. B. Cramer, J. Fields, I. Moscheles and F. Kalkbrenner). He was also engaged as piano builder and publisher. As pianist and teacher he developed a new and effective style of piano playing. His main works include 106 piano sonatas, a piano concerto, four symphonies and the etude collection 'Gradus ad Parnassum', which is still used in piano tuition.

COLLARD, London-based piano factory, originally Longman & Broderip (founded 1767). In 1798 Clementi joined as partner, but in 1801 he associated with W. F. C. and others in a new enterprise. In 1830 Clementi resigned from the company.

CORELLI, Arcangelo, Italian composer and violinist, *Fusignono near Ravenna 17.2.1653, +Rome 8.1.1713. He was a pupil of Benvenuti and Brugnoli in Bologna. In 1670 he went to Rome in the service of Queen Christine of Sweden, later the cardinals Pamphilj and Ottoboni. He is credited with creating the concerto grosso which served as model for Bach, Telemann, Handel and others. He wrote 12 of these concertos, 48 trio sonatas, 12 violin sonatas, etc.

COSTA, Sir Michele Andrea Agnus, conductor and composer, *Naples 4.2.1808, +Hove, Sussex 29.4.1884. From 1829 he was working as Opera Conductor and then Leader of the Philharmonic Orchestra in London, from 1847 Director of Music at the Royal Italian Opera at Covent Garden. Later he was Choral Conductor in London and of the Music Festival of Birmingham. He wrote numerous operas, symphonies and ballets.

CRAMER, Johann Baptist, pianist and conductor, *Mannheim 24.2.1771, +London 16.4.1858. He studied under Clementi and others and became internationally famous after 1788 through many concert tours. In 1824 he founded, together with R. Addison and T. F. Beale, a music-publishing company in London, which is known today as J. B. Cramer & Co. His 'Great Piano Tutorial', edited by H. v. Bülow, is still in use. He wrote 105 piano sonatas and eight piano concertos.

CRANZ, August Heinrich C. *1789, +1870. Founder of the music-publishing company which today has its head office in Wiesbaden and branches in Brussels and London.

CZERNY, Carl (Karl), piano pedagogue and composer, *Vienna 20.2.1791, +do. 15.7.1857. From 1800 to 1803 he was a pupil of Beethoven and was soon renowned as a piano teacher, his pupils including F. Liszt,

Th. Leschetizky and Th. Kullak. He wrote more than 1000 works (church, orchestral and chamber music) of which only those survived which had a pedagogic value ('Tutorial of Fluency' Opus 299, '40 Daily Exercises' Opus 337, 'Tutorial for the Left Hand' Opus 399). Publications: 'On the Important Performance of all Beethoven's Piano Pieces', 'Memoires of Beethoven', etc.

DAVID, Ferdinand, violinist and composer, *Hamburg 20.1.1810, +Klosters CH 19.7.1873. Pupil of L. Spohr and M. Hauptmann. From 1835 he was Music Director of the Gewandhaus in Leipzig, from 1843 violin teacher at the newly-founded conservatory. Of importance were his arrangements and editions (among others, the works by J. S. Bach) as well as his tutors (among them 'Die hohe Schule des Violinspiels', 1867–72).

DEVRIENT, Ludwig, actor, *Berlin 15.12.1784, +do. 30.12.1832. He was an outstanding actor at the Berlin Hoftheater (King Lear, Shylock, Falstaff, Franz Moor) and was befriended by E. T. A. Hoffmann. His nephews too were actors: Emil, *Berlin 4.9.1803, +Dresden 7.8.1872, and Eduard, *Berlin 11.8.1801, +Karlsruhe 4.10.1877, 1852–70 Director of the Karlsruhe Hoftheater, wrote the libretto for the opera 'Hans Heiling' (composed by H. Marschner) and a 'History of German Acting' (5 vol. 1848–74).

DIABELLI, Anton, Austrian music publisher amd composer, *Mattsee, near Salzburg 6.9.1781, +Vienna 7.4.1858. From 1803 he lived in Vienna and was associated with music publisher Cappi. In 1824 he formed his own publishing firm and sold it in 1852 to C. A. Spina. He wrote numerous works, from which only a few piano pieces and a pastoral mass survived. He was Schubert's principal publisher, and had also contact with Beethoven.

DITTERSDORF, Karl Ditters von, Austrian composer, *Vienna 2.11.1739, +Neuhof, Bohemia 24.10.1799. One of the founders of the new German comic opera. His 'Doctor and Pharmacist' (Arzt und Apotheker) has survived to date.

DOEHLER, Theodor von, Austrian pianist and composer, *Naples 20.4.1814, +Florence 21.2.1856. Pupil of Benedict and Czerny. From 1829 to 1834 he lived in Naples, 1837–45 touring, he was then composer in St. Petersberg, Moscow, and finally Florence. He wrote the opera 'Tancreda' and many piano pieces.

DONIZETTI, Gaetano Domenico Maria, Italian composer, *Bergamo 29.11.1797, +do. 8.4.1848. He continued the Italian opera tradition of Rossini, writing a total of 74 operas (the most famous being 'Lucia di Lammermoor'), also symphonies, church music, cantatas etc. He went to Paris in 1839; from 1842 he was Imperial Court Composer and Kapellmeister in Vienna.

DORN, Heinrich Ludwig Egmont, conductor, musical author and composer, *Knigsberg 14.11.1800, +Berlin 10.1.1892. He studied with Zelter, from 1849 to 1869 he was Court Opera Kapellmeister in Berlin. Composed operas, but mainly Lieder. Wrote critiques for the 'Neue Berliner Musikzeitung'. Pronounced opponent of Wagner.

DRAGONETTI, Domenico, Italian contrabassist and composer, *Venice 7.4.1763, +London 16.4.1846. From 1787 to 1794 he played in the Orchestra of San Marco in Venice, then went to London where he worked at the Opera House and in concerts by the Philharmonic Society. He wrote works for the contrabass and transposed organ pieces by J. S. Bach for contrabass and piano. He was known as the 'Paganini of the Contrabass'.

DREYSCHOCK, Alexander, Bohemian pianist and composer, *Zak, Bohemia 15.10.1818, +Venice 1.4.1869. He was a pupil of Thomaschek in Prague, from where he travelled for many years with great success throughout Europe. In 1862 he became Professor at the Petersburg Conservatory founded by A. Rubinstein, and Director of the Theatre Music School. His numerous compositions for piano (Concert in D-minor opus 137) are brilliant salon music. His brother was Raimund, violinist, *Zak 30.8.1824, +Leipzig 6.2.1869. He was a pupil of Pixis in Prague, from 1850 second Konzertmeister at the Gewandhaus at Leipzig and violin teacher at the Leipzig Conservatory.

EBERL, Anton Franz Josef, Austrian pianist and composer, *Vienna 13.6.1765, +do. 11.3.1807. Probably a friend of Mozart, under whose name some of his variations and some piano sonatas were published. He wrote operas, orchestral and chamber music.

ÉRARD, Sébastian, French piano builder, *Strasbourg 5.4.1752, +La Muette (near Passy) 5.8.1831. Much acclaimed for his Clavecin mécanique, which could transpose into a higher octave. In 1777 he built the first piano in France and founded with his brother Jean-Baptiste (*1745, +1826) a company in Paris and in 1786 a subsidiary in London. In 1810 he constructed the double-pedal harp and invented the repetition mechanism (double échappement) for the piano. In 1856 the firm amalgamated with Gaveau (Gaveau-Erard Ltd) producing pianos, cembalos and harps.

ERNST, Heinrich Wilhelm, violinist, *Brünn 6.5.1814, +Nice 8.10.1865. He studied with J. Mayseder and others, and at the age of 16 he made a concert tour, being a rival of Paganini, whose double stop technique he extended. He wrote pieces for the violin, among them a violin concerto.

EYBLER, Joseph Leopold, Edler von, Austrian composer, *Schwechat (near Vienna) 8.2.1765, +Vienna 24.7.1846. He was a pupil of G. Albrechtsberger, related to Haydn, and befriended by Mozart, for whose 'Requiem' he wrote a first supplement ('Dies irae' to 'Lacrimosa'). From 1794 to 1824 he was Choir Master at the Schottenhof, from 1891 Music Teacher at the Imperial Court and from 1829 to 1833 Hofkapellmeister.

FASCH, Johann Friedrich, composer, *Büttenstedt near Weimar 15.4.1688, +Zerbst 5.12.1758. One of the most prominent contemporaries of Bach, specifically as instrumental composer. He wrote several church cantatas, 12 masses, 69 overtures, 21 instrumental concerts, trio sonatas, symphonies and motettes. His son and pupil Carl Friedrich (1736–1800) founded (in 1791) the Berlin Singakademie and was its director until his death. Only a few of his compositions are now played.

FÉTIS, François-Joseph, Belgian musicologist and composer, *Mons (Hennegau) 25.3.1784, +Brussels 26.3.1871. From 1833 he was Director of the Conservatory and Court Kapellmeister at Brussels. He was a founder of modern historical musical science, and at the same time a prominent theorist and influential critic. He composed piano, organ, chamber and orchestral music, and wrote operas.

FISCHHOF, Joseph, Austrian pianist, *Butschowitz 4.4.1804, +Vienna 28.6.1857. From 1833 he was Professor at the Conservatory of the Gesellschaft der Musikfreunde in Vienna. He wrote many piano and ensemble pieces as well as 'Attempt at a History of Piano Playing', and published 'Classical Studies for the Piano'. The documentation on the life of Beethoven which was in his possession has become known as the Fischhof Manuscript (Berlin State Library).

FREGE, Livia, née Gerhard, German soprano, *Gera 13.6.1818, +Leipzig 22.8.1891. Pupil of Pohlenz, she made her debut in a concert by Clara Wieck(-Schumann). She married Dr W. Frege, a lawyer, in Leipzig. Her house became a centre for music lovers and for the cultivation of music. She was a close friend of Mendelssohn and David.

FAMAGALLI 1) Disma, Italian pianist, *Inzago (Milan) 8.9.1826, +Milan 9.3.1893. He studied at the Milan Conservatory and was appointed piano teacher there in 1857. He wrote over 300 piano works, mostly études, and a Grande Concerto A flat-major with string orchestra (Opus 83), and piano arrangements. – 2) Adolfo, Italian pianist, *Inzago 19.10.1828, +Florence 3.5.1856. Brother of Disma, he studied from 1837 to 1847 with Angeleri and Ray at the Milan Conservatory and soon became renowned as a virtuoso. He wrote more than 100 piano pieces, among them transcriptions of opera arias. – 3) Polibio, Italian organist, *Inzago 26.10.1830, +Milan 21.6.1900. Brother of 1) and 2), he studied at the Milan Conservatory and was appointed organ teacher at this institution. He wrote piano and organ pieces and chamber music. – 4) Lucca, Italian pianist, *Inzago 29.5.1837, +Milan 5.6.1908. Brother of 1),2) and 3), he worked for some time at the Conservatory of Philadelphia, later at Milan. Besides various piano pieces he wrote an opera ('Luigi XI', Florence 1875), and a symphonia marinaresca. Another brother, Vicenzo F., was teacher of composition at the Milan Conservatory.

FUERSTENAU, Anton Bernhard, chamber musician, *Münster 20.10.1792, +Dresden 18.11.1852. Son of Caspar F., he was one of the most influential flute virtuosi and he composed a large number of compositions for this instrument.

GADE, Niels Wilhelm, Danish composer, *Copenhagen 22.1.1817, +do. 21.12.1890. He studied with, among others, Chr. E. F. Weyse. In 1847 he succeeded F. Mendelssohn-Bartholdy as Director of the Gewandhaus Concerts in Leipzig, and in 1848 he returned to Copenhagen, where he conducted the concerts of the Copenhagen Music Society and where he was organist. As Director of the Conservatory (from 1866) he had great influence on Denmark's musical scene. He was a principal representative of Danish romanticism.

GARCIA, Manuel del Popolo Vicente, Spanish tenor and singing teacher, *Seville 21.1.1775, +Paris 9.6.1832. He made appearances at the Théatre Italien in Paris, in Italy and London. From 1828 he worked as teacher and composer, with 22 Spanish, 21 Italian and 8 French operas to his credit. His most important pupils were his daughters Maria Malibran and Pauline Viardot-Garcia and his son Manuel Patricio Rodriguez, singer and singing teacher at first in Paris then in London. He was Jenny Lind's teacher.

GASSMANN, Florian Leopold, Bohemian composer, *Brüx (Bohemia) 3.5.1729, +Vienna 20.1.1774. From 1763 he was composer of ballet music in Vienna; in 1772 Hofkapellmeister. A. Salieri was numbered among his pupils. He composed 20 operas and about 50 church and concert works, from the baroque counterpoint to the lieder-like melody of the pre-classic.

GOLDSCHMIDT, Otto, conductor,

*Hamburg 21.8.1829, +London 24.2.1907. In Leipzig he was a pupil of Mendelssohn, then of Chopin in Paris. In 1852 he married Jenny Lind. Later he became conductor in Dresden (from 1858 in London). From 1863 he was Deputy Director of the Royal Academy of Music; in 1875 Founder of the London Bach Choir which he made very famous.

GOUNOD, Charles François, French composer, *Paris 17.6.1818, +do. 18.10.1893. He mainly composed operas ('Faust', 'Romeo and Juliette' etc.) also masses, oratorios, cantatas, and orchestral works.

GRAF, Conrad (Graff), Austrian piano builder, *Riedlingen, Swabia, 17.11.1783, +Vienna 18.3.1851. In 1799 he went to Jacob Schelke in Vienna. After the death of his work-master he married the latter's widow and took charge of the factory. In his name it became the 'largest and most reputed piano factory of Vienna and the Empire'. Beethoven and Schubert were delighted with his pianos – both of them owned one.

GRETRY, André-Ernest-Modeste, Belgian composer, *Lüttich 11.2.1741, +Mortmorency near Paris 24.9.1813. In his operas the French genre of the comic opera reached its pinnacle. His main works are: 'Le Huron', 'Lucile', 'Le tableau parlant', 'Zémire et Wazor', 'Andromaque' etc.

GRIMM, Julius Otto, Choir conductor and composer, *Pernau (Livland) 6.3.1827, +Münster (Westphalia). 7.12.1903. He studied music at the Leipzig Conservatory, and he was friendly with Brahms, Joachim, Clara Schumann etc. He was choir conductor in Göttingen, later Münster – where he was Royal Director of Music (1877). In 1885 he was appointed Professor at the university there. He composed, among other works:

three orchestral suites, a symphony, a violin sonata, piano pieces, choir music and Lieder.

GYROWETZ Adalbert Mathias, Bohemian composer, *Budweis 20.(?)2. 1763, +Vienna 19.3.1850. He was Hoftheaterkapellmeister in Vienna from 1804 to 1831. His meticulous style influenced by Mozart and Haydn (the latter knew him personally), won great popularity for his compositions. His works include the operas 'The Optician', 'Robert, or The Test', 40 symphonies, piano concertos, string quartettes, masses, etc.

HALÉVY, Jacques Francois Fromental Elie (actually Elias Lévy), French composer, *Paris 27.5.1799, +Nice 17.3.1862. He studied at the Paris Conservatory under (among others) L. Cherubini, and he became professor in 1833 at that institute. He was teacher of Bizet and Gounod. He composed serious and comic operas ('The Jewess', 'The Queen of Cyprus', 'L'éclair', etc.) His nephew Ludovic became famous as librettist for Offenbach, J. Strauss and Bizet.

HALLÉ Sir Charles, (actually Karl Halle), British pianist and conductor of German descent. *Hagen (Westphalia) 11.4.1819, +Manchester 25.10.1895. 1836 in Paris; 1858 founded his own orchestra for subscription concerts in Manchester (Charles Hallé's Orchestra). From 1883 he was conductor of the Liverpool Philharmonic Orchestra.

HÄRTEL, Gottfried, music publisher, *1763, +1827. In 1795 he became partner of the publishing house of Breitkopf & Härtel in Leipzig, in 1796 he became sole proprietor of the firm.

HASLINGER, Tobias, Austrian music publisher, *Kleinzell 1.3.1787, +Vienna 18.6.1842. From 1814 he was an associate of the Steiner Music Dealers, in 1826 he became sole proprietor, trading under his own name. In 1875 the business transferred to Schlesinger in Berlin. He was a friend of Beethoven, for whom he published five symphonies, three piano concertos and the violin concerto.

HAUPTMANN, Moritz, composer, *Dresden 13.10.1792, +Leipzig 3.1.1868. He was a pupil of L. Spohr. From 1842 Cantor of the Thomas School and Music Director of both main churches in Leipzig. Later he taught at the Conservatory (teaching among others F. David, J. Joachim). Co-founder and lifelong Chairman of the Bach Society. He mainly composed choral works, but also pieces for the violin, strings and piano, as well as an opera. he authored numerous theoretical works such as 'Die Natur der Harmonik und Metric' (The Nature of Harmonics and Metrics).

HAUSER, Franz, Bass-baritone and music pedagogue, *Krasowitz near Prague 12.1.1794, +Freiburg i.Br. 14.8.1870. He was a pupil of Tomasek in Prague. He appeared as opera singer in Prague, Kassel, Dresden, Vienna, Leipzig, Berlin and Breslau. From 1846 to 1864 he was principal director and teacher of singing at the Munich Conservatory.

HELLER, Stephen, Hungarian pianist and composer, *Budapest 15.5.1813, +Paris 14.1.1888. He studied in Vienna under A. Halm and later moved to Paris where he was concert pianist and teacher. His over 150 piano pieces have a prominent position in the romantic piano genre and are acclaimed for their originality and characterization of ideas.

HENSEL, Fanny Cecilia, *Hamburg 14.11.1805, +Berlin 14.5.1847. She was the sister of Felix Mendelssohn-Bartholdy. In 1829 she married the painter Hensel. An excellent pianist and talent composer ('Lieder ohne Worte', and a trio, she was always in contact with her brother and her sudden death greatly grieved him. He was to follow her to the grave only six months later. In his own Lieder he included six of hers: Opus 8, nos. 2,3,12 and Opus 9, nos. 7, 10, 12.

HENSELT, Georg Martin Adolf von, pianist, *Schwabach (Bavaria) 9.5.1814, +Warmbrunn (Slezko) 10.10.1889. He studied with J. N. Hummel and S. Sechter, and was chamber virtuoso at the Russian Court in St. Petersburg. He wrote, among other works, one piano concerto and several concert études.

HERMANN, Friedrich, German violinist, *Frankfurt 1.2.1828, +Leipzig 27.9.1907. From 1843 to 1846 he was a pupil at the Leipzig Conservatory. In 1846 he joined the Gewandhaus orchestra and became teacher at the Conservatory in 1847. After 1847 he devoted his time exclusively to teaching, composing and publishing. An outstanding teacher, his violin textbooks, scales and bow tutors, as well as his publications of classical works for stringed instruments were all famous at the time.

HERZ, Henri (Heinrich), pianist and composer, *Vienna 6.1.1803, +Paris 5.1.1888. He studied with, among others, A. Reicha, and was Professor for Piano at the Paris Conservatory. He became famous mainly for his virtuoso piano technique which distinguished his compositions (8 piano concertos, etudes, variations, nocturnes, fantasies, sonatas and ronds) and a 'Méthode complète de piano'. He also constructed pianos with a repetition mechanism which he himself developed.

HILLER, Ferdinand von, conductor and

composer, *Frankfurt 24.10.1811, +Cologne 11.5.1885. He studied in Weimar with Hummel. From his earliest years he was a friend of Cherubini, Reicha, Berlioz, Rossini and Mendelssohn. In 1843 he took over the direction of the Gewandhaus Concerts in Leipzig for Mendelssohn. Later he conducted the 'Liedertafel' in Dresden and finally he built up the Cologne Conservatory. In 1851–52 he was Director of the Italian Opera in Paris. He composed 200 works (operas, oratorios, chamber music and piano pieces) borrowing from the style of Schumann and Mendelssohn.

HUMMEL, Johann Nepomuk, Austrian composer and pianist, *Pressburg 14.11.1778, +Weimar 17.10.1837. He studied with Mozart, Albrechtsberger and Salieri, and undertook various concert tours. 1804–11 he succeeded Haydn as Prince Esterhazy's conductor. In 1816–19 he was court conductor in Stuttgart and later in Weimar. Appeared as pianist in England and Russia. He developed his own style of composing which, in part, led to the future romantic piano music of Chopin and Liszt. His piano tutor 'Ausführliche Anweisung zum Pianofortespiel', (1828), ('Complete Instructions for Piano Playing') was widely known.

ISABEY, Jean-Baptiste, French miniature painter and lithographer, *Nancy 11.4.1767, +Prague 18.4.1855. Pupil of J. L. David, he reflected in his works an elegant and pleasant classicism.

JAËLL, Alfred, Austrian pianist, *Trieste 5.3.1832, +Paris 27.2.1882. He received instructions in piano and violin from his father, the violinist Eduard J. He made his début at the Theatre San Benedetto in Venice. In 1844 he became one of Moscheles' pupils. From 1845–46 he lived in Brussels, 1848–54 in the USA and thereafter in Paris. He paraphrased concert pieces and composed brilliant piano pieces.

JOACHIM, Joseph, German violinist, conductor and composer, *Kittsee near Pressburg 28.6.1831, +Berlin 15.8.1907. He played in a concert at the early age of seven. He was a pupil of J. Böhm in Vienna and M. Hauptmann of Leipzig, continuing his studies under the influence of Mendelssohn. He was a teacher at the Leipzig Conservatory; in 1849 he became conductor in Weimar; in 1853 royal conductor of Hanover. From 1868 he was director of the newly-founded Berlin Music Academy. A prominent patron of the Beethoven festival in Bonn, he composed several works for the violin, overtures etc.

KALKBRENNER, Friedrich Wilhelm Michael, pianist and piano pedagogue, *during a journey from Kassel to Berlin between 2 and 8.11.1785, +Enghien-les-Bains, near Paris 10.6.1849. He studied in Paris where he later became partner in the piano factory of I. Pleyel. His compositions (four piano concertos, one concerto for two pianos and orchestra, chamber music with piano, ten piano sonatas, études, 24 préludes) are in a virtuoso style. As piano teacher he put great value on fluency, whereby he attempted to develop finger deftness independent of the wrists. Further aims of his teaching were the playful independence of the left hand and the technique of the pedal.

KAULBACH, Wilhelm von, painter, *Arolsen near Kassel 15.10.1804, +Munich 7.4.1874. He was a pupil of P. von Cornelius in Düsseldorf. From 1862 he lived in Munich where he painted effective theatrical ceiling and wall paintings with historic, allegoric and mythological subjects, as well as book illustrations, including Goethe's 'Reineke Fuchs'.

KIESEWETTER, Chr. K. Karl, German

violinist, *Augsburg 1777, +London 27.9.1827. He was conductor in Oldenburg, and from 1814 to 1822 was conductor in Hanover, where he reformed the concert manner in that he performed (contrary to common practice at that time) symphonies in full. In 1821 he went to London where he appeared as violinist in the Philharmonic Concerts.

KIND Johann Friedrich, writer, *Leipzig 4.3.1768, +Dresden 25.6.1843. He wrote the libretto to C. M. von Weber's 'Freischütz' (1821) and to C. Kreutzer's 'Nachtlager von Granada' (1834).

KISTNER, Friedrich, German publisher, *Leipzig 3.3.1797, +do. 21.12.1844. In 1831 he took over the music-publishing business founded by Heinrich Albert Probst on 1.5.1831 and from 1836 traded under his own name. The firm of Kistner and Siegel is still in existence. In 1948 the firm of Kistner & Siegel & Co. was founded in Lippstadt (Westphalia).

KLENGEL, August Stephan Alexander, pianist, organist and composer, *Dresden 29.6.1783, +do. 22.11.1852. He studied under M. Clementi and after visits to Petersburg and Paris he became court organist in Dresden. He was famous for his canons and fugues (24 of each in every major and minor key).

KLINGEMANN, Karl, *Limmer an der Leine 2.12.1798. +London 25.9.1862. From 1827 he was in the Hanoverian diplomatic service in London. He composed several Lieder. His friendship with Felix Mendelssohn-Bartholdy gave rise to the text of the Liederspiel 'Die Heimkehr aus der Fremde', poems by Klingemann set to music by Mendelssohn, and an extensive exchange of correspondence.

KOŽELUCH, KOTZELUCH, Leopold Anton, Bohemian composer, *Welwarn (Central Bohemia) 26.6.1747, +Vienna 7.5.1818. From 1778 court music teacher in Vienna, and from 1792 court and chamber composer. Some of his works were for a long time attributed to Beethoven.

KREUTZER, Rodolphe, French violinist and composer, *Versailles 16.11.1766, +Geneva 6.1.1831. From 1795 he was Professor at the Paris Conservatory. He made many concert tours. From 1802 he was Napoleon's chamber virtuoso, later Louis XVIII's. He wrote operas, chamber music and numerous violin pieces. Together with Rode and Baillot he published the Great Violin Tutor of the Paris Conservatory. Beethoven dedicated (1805) his Violin Sonata Opus No. 47 to him (Kreutzer-Sonata).

KUFFERATH, Hubert Ferdinand, composer, *Mülheim 10.6.1818, +Brussels 23.6.1896. He studied with Mendelssohn and David, among others, in Leipzig, settling in 1844 in Brussels to become professor of composition (1871) at the Conservatory. He published vocal and instrumental pieces as well as pedagogic works.

KUHLAU, Daniel Friedrich Rudolph, Danish composer of German descent, *Uelzen 11.9.1786, +Lyngbye near Copenhagen 12.3.1832. In 1818 he became Danish court composer. He was a member of the Danish National Opera. He became famous for his piano sonatas and sonatinas (for two and four hands) which are still used in piano lessons, and also for his numerous flute pieces.

LABLACHE, Luigi, Italian opera singer (bass), *Naples 6.12.1794, +do. 23.1.1858. He reached the summit of his fame when he went to Paris in 1830. He sang in Paris,

London and St. Petersburg until 1857. He documented his experiences as singer in a 'Méthode de chant' (exercises and vocals).

LACHNER, Franz, composer, *Rain (Bavaria) 2.4.1803, +Munich 20.1.1890. He was intimately friendly with Schubert, from 1828 conductor at the Viennese Kärntnertor Theatre; 1836 court conductor in Munich, 1852 General Music Director. He published about 200 compositions (orchestral suites, symphonies, church music, chamber music, Lieder etc.).

LAFONT, Charles Phillipe, French violinist, *Paris 1.12.1781, +Tarbes 14.(23.?)8.1839. Pupil of Berthaume, Berton, Kreutzer and Rode. Chamber virtuoso in St. Petersburg until 1815 when Louis XVIII called him back to take up the same position in Paris. He composed violin concertos, fantasies, rondos, variations and almost 200 Lieder (romances) and the opera 'La rivalite villageoise'.

LEBERT, Sigmund, German piano pedagogue, *Ludwigsburg (Wurtemberg) 9.12.1823, +Stuttgart 8.12.1884. He was co-founder of the Stuttgart Conservatory (1857). In 1858 he published (jointly with L. Stark) the three volume 'Grosse theoretisch-praktische Elementar Klavierschule' (Great theoretical/practical Elementary Piano Tutor), and also with Stark a 'Systematisch-praktische Elementar-Singschule' (Systematic Elementary Singing Tutor).

LÉONARD, Hubert, Belgian violinist and violin pedagogue, *Bellaire near Lüttich 7.4.1819, +Paris 6.5.1890. From 1853 to 1867 he was violin professor at the Brussels Conservatory (as successor to the blind Bériot). He published tutors and several compositions for the violin.

LEVASSEUR, Rosalie, French soprano,

*8.10.1749 Valenciennes, +6.5.1826, Neuwied am Rhein. Had an extraordinary success from 1766 to 1786 at the Grand Parisian Opera and was an extremely valued interpreter of the leading role in Gluck's operas ('Armida', 'Alceste').

LIND, Jenny (Johanna), Swedish soprano, *Stockholm 6.10.1820, +Malvern Hills (Hereford/Worcester), 2.11.1887. Debut 1838 in Stockholm as Agathe (in 'Der Freischutz' by C. M. v.Weber) and went to Paris in 1841 where she studied with M. Garcia. She entered the Berlin Court opera in 1844 and from 1847 was mainly in London and Stockholm. In 1849 she ended her theatre career and became a concert singer and singing pedagogue (1883–86 in London). She is known as the best coloratura soprano of her time ('the Swedish Nightingale').

LINDLEY, Robert, Cello virtuoso, *4.3.1766 in Rotherham (Yorks, +13.6.55 in London. Pupil of Cervetto. He first played in the Brighton Theatre Orchestra, and in 1794 succeeded Speratis at the London Opera. He was teacher at the Royal Academy of Music at its foundation in 1822.

LIPINSKI, Karol Josef, *30.10 (or 4.11) 1790 Radzyn near Lublin, +16.12.1861. Was self taught. By 1810 he was already concert master. After a brilliant concert tour around Europe in 1839 he became concert master in Dresden until 1861. L. was a player with a great tone and was particularly accomplished in double stopping. His works include four violin concertos, caprices, rondos, polonaises, variations, fantasias and songs.

LISZT, Franz von, composer and pianist *Raiding (Hungary) 12.10.1811, +Bayreuth 31.7.1886. Knighted 1859. He studied in Vienna with Czerny and Salieri, later in Paris with Paer and Reicha. From 1835 he lived with the Duchesse d'Agoult in Geneva and Italy. Father of three children (one of whom, Cosina, later married R. Wagner). 1839–47 Liszt made a celebrated concert tour of Europe. From 1842 he was the Court Kapellmeister at Weimar. In 1861 he went to Rome, where in 1865 he was ordained to the lower order of the priesthood. From 1875 he was piano pedagogue in Weimar, Rome and Budapest. F. L. wrote a great many orchestral works (symphonic poems). His piano works were extremely important in the development of keyboard music. Later he mainly composed church music. He is also recognized as a reformer of the music world. Promoter of, among others, R. Schumann, H, Berlioz, R. Wagner.

LITOLFF, Henry Charles, French pianist, composer and music publisher, *London 6.2.1818, +Colombes (Hauts de Seine) 6.8.1891. From 1840 he undertook concert tours throughout Europe. he composed operas, orchestral and piano works. After his marriage to Julie Meyer he took over her music-publishing firm's name and renamed it Litolff's Verlag.

MALIBRAN, Maria Felicità (Felicia), Spanish soprano, *Paris 24.3.1808 +Manchester 23.9.1836. Sister of Pauline Viardot-Garcia and daughter of M. del Popolo Vincente Garcia. She studied with her father, made her debut in 1825 and appeared with the King's Theatre, Covent Garden Opera and the Italian Opera in London, as well as at the Paris Opera and the Paris Italian Theatre. She also took part in her father's troupe in New York. She was one of the most important singers of her time. She married the violinist de Bériot.

MÄLZEL (Mälzl), Johann Nepomuk, German musical – instrument maker, *Regensberg 15.8.1772, during the journey from la Guaira to Philadelphia +21.7.1838. He developed mechanical musical apparatus (panharmonium etc.) as well as hearing aids (e.g. for Beethoven). The patent of his invention of the metronome was taken from him by a lawsuit. He founded a metronome factory in Paris in 1816, and today the tempo is still set by the M. M. (Mälzl metronome).

MARXSEN, Eduard, pianist and music teacher in Hamburg, *Nienstadten near Altona 23.7.1806, +Altona 18.11.1887. He gave piano and composition tuition to J. Brahms.

MAYSEDER, Joseph, Austrian violinist, *Vienna 26.10.1789, +21.11.1863. He studied with I. Schuppanzigii (in whose quartette he played second violin) and in 1836 he became Leader of violins at the Viennese Hofkappele. He was an outstanding master of his instrument and won acclaim from Paganini.

MENDELSSOHN BARTHOLDY, Jakob Ludwig Felix, composer, *Hamburg 3.2.1809, +Leipzig 4.11.1847. He studied with Hummel (piano), Rietz (violin) and Zelter (composition). At the age of nine he was already making public appearances with his sister Fanny (married to Hensel). In 1829 he led a renaissance of Bach' works with a performance of the St. Matthew's Passion. In 1833 he became Musical Director in Düsseldorf, from 1835 he was Leader of the Gewandhauskonzert in Leipzig. In 1843 he co-founded the Leipzig Conservatory, the first institute of its kind in Germany. As well as being a pianist and conductor Mendelssohn was one of the most brilliant performers of his time. He developed Leipzig into one of the most important musical centres of Europe. Compositions: six concert overtures, five symphonies for large orchestra, instrumental concertos, chamber music, oratorios, organ works, Lieder etc.

MENDELSSOHN, Moses, Grandfather of F. Mendelssohn Bartholdy, *Dessau 6.9.1729, +Berlin 4.1.1786. He was a Jewish philosopher and publisher of philosophical works together with Lessing (1754). Mendelssohn was one of the most important popular philosophers of the Chr. Wolff school of thought. He represented the promotion of tolerance dealt with questions about everlasting life and the presence of God. For his Phaedo, modelled on the Platonic original, he became known as the 'German Plato'. A translator of the Bible, he was also dedicated to Jewish emancipation. The state, he argued, could survive a plurality of religious beliefs.

MEYERBEER, Giacomo, actually Jakob Liebmann Meyer Beer (Meyer being a first name). *Tasdorf, Berlin 5.9.1791 +Paris 2.5.1864. He studied under C. F. Zelter in Berlin and under Abbé J. G. Vogler in Darmstadt. Originally a pianist he lived in Paris and London and travelled to Venice to study Italian melodics. From 1831 to 1842 he lived chiefly in Paris, in 1842 he succeeded G. Spontini as Prussian GMD in Berlin. Meyerbeer was one of the main representatives of the Great French Opera of the 19th century. His main works: 'Robert the Devil', 'The Hugenotts', 'Ein Feldlager in Schlesien', 'The Prophet' and 'The African Girl'.

MILDER-HAUPTMANN, Pauline Anny. *Constantinople 13.12.1785, +Berlin 29.5.1838. She studied under A. Salieri and J. M. Vogel and made her debut in 1803. She appeared at the Viennese Court Theatre and at the Berlin Royal Opera (interpreter of Operas by Gluck). L. van Beethoven created a part in Fidelio for her. She was one of the participants in Bach's St. Matthew's Passion led by F. Mendelssohn Bartholdy (1829). She was famous as a Spontini interpreter and had a remarkable acting ability.

MIRLITON, a pseudomusical instrument or device in which sound waves produced by the player's voice or by an instrument vibrate a membrane, thereby imparting a buzzing quality to the vocal or instrumental sound. A common mirliton is the kazoo, in which the membrane is set in the wall of a short tube into which the player vocalizes. Tissue paper and a comb constitute a homemade mirliton. Mirlitons are also set in the walls of some flutes (e.g. the Chinese ti) and xylophone resonators to colour the tone. The mirliton is one of the few membranophones not sounded by percussion.

MONTEZ, Lola, Irish adventuress and 'Spanish' dancer, *Limerick, Ireland 1818, +New York 16.1.1861. The daughter of a Scottish officer and a creole, she achieved international notoriety through her liaison with King Louis I of Bavaria. She was raised to the rank of Countess of Landsfeld and became the King's mistress, influencing him toward liberal and anti-Jesuit policies.

MÜLLER, brothers, string quartette made up by four brothers from Braunschweig who played together from 1831 to 1855. Karl Friedrich, Theodor Heinrich Gustav, August Theodor and Franz Ferdinand Georg. Four sons of Karl Friedrich later formed the junior Müller quartette (up to 1873).

NAEGELI, Hans Georg, music pedagogue and publisher. *Wetzikon 26.5.1773, +Zurich 26.12.1836. He founded the Zürich Singing Institute in 1805. In 1819 he established a musical business and publishing house, later several singing societies. From 1815 he was singing professor in Zürich. He lectured and wrote on behalf of the reform of singing tuition. He was well-known as publisher through his publications on piano and organ works by Bach and Handel. He composed choruses, Lieder and piano pieces.

NAUMANN Johann Gottlieb, composer, *Blasewitz near Dresden 17.4.1741, +Dresden 23.10.1801. He was one of the most renowned personalities of the European music scene in the late 18th century. He studied in Italy and worked in Dresden. In 1777 he was called to Sweden by Gustav II and there wrote the opera 'Gustaf Wasa' based on Gluck's work. It was considered as the Swedish national opera until well into the 19th century. He returned to Dresden in 1786. He composed 23 operas, ten oratorios and chamber music.

NEATE, Charles, violoncellist, *London 28.3.1784, +Brighton 30.3.1877. He was a piano pupil of W. Sharp and J. Field and one of the founders of the Philharmonic Society (1813). He lived for 8 months in Vienna in 1815 in order to enjoy the company of Beethoven and worked eagerly for the dissemination of Beethoven's works in London.

NEUKOMM, Sigismund, Austrian knight, conductor, pianist and composer, *Salzburg 10.7.1778, +Paris 3.4.1858. He studied under M. Haydn in Salzburg and under J. Haydn in Vienna. He was Kapellmeister at the German Theatre in St. Petersburg, pianist to C. M. de Talleyrand and he lived for a few years in Brazil. His works (operas, orchestral works, chamber music, vocal pieces) manifest in parts characteristics of Brazilian folklore.

OHLENSCHLÄGER, Adam Gottlob, Danish poet, *Copenhagen 14.11.1779, +Copenhagen 20.1.1850. As a lyricist he was one of the greatest speech artists in Denmark. From 1809 he was Professor of aesthetics in Copenhagen. He wrote poems and tragedies.

PAER, Ferdinando, Italian composer, *Parma 1.6.1771, +Paris 3.4.1839. At first he was Kapellmeister in Venice, then in Vienna and Dresden. From 1807 he lived in Paris and succeeded Spontini's Kapellmeister at the Théâtre Italien (1812–27). He wrote 42 operas which at first enjoyed great success, but which were later usurped by Rossini's operas. He also composed church music, orchestral and instrumental works.

PAGANINI, Niccolo, Italian violinist and composer, *Genoa 27.10.1782, +Nice 27.5.1840. A child prodigy, he taught himself and became one of the most brilliant violin virtuosi. He appeared in public from 1793, was solo violinist in Lucca from 1805 to 1810 and then undertook concert tours throughout Europe until 1827. In 1828 he received the title of Imperial Chamber Virtuoso. His somewhat demonic appearance, wild amours and virtuosity on a single string fostered a reputation of his being in league with the devil. His virtuoso playing was a great influence on composers. From his own compositions there are many violin concertos, 24 capricci, and works for the guitar in existence.

PALESTRINA, Giovanni Pierluigi, Italian composer, *Palestrina 1525, +Rome 2.2.1594. From 1551 he was Kapellmeister in Rome and later in various churches as well as the Court of Cardinal Ippolito d'Este in Rome and Tivoli. He was composer for the Sistine Chapel to his life's end. He wrote over 100 masses, approximately 320 motettes, hymns, offertories, laments, madrigals etc. In the 19th century there was a Palestrina renaissance, known as Caecilianismus.

PAPE, Jean-Henri (actually Johann Heinrich), German piano builder, *Sarstedt near Hanover 1.7.1789, + Asnirès near Paris 2.2.1875. He went to Paris in 1811 and worked for a time with Pleyel; from 1815 under his own name. His method of felting the hammers (1826) and cross stringing were soon generally adopted. His firm was dissolved in 1885.

PARRY, John, Welsh Bard, *Denbigh, N. Wales 18.2.1776, +London 8.4.1851 Conductor of a military band, and settled in London in 1809 as teacher of the then popular flageolet. His main work is 'The Welsh Harper' (London 1839–48), a two-volume collection of Welsh melodies.

PASTA, Giudetta Maria Costanza, Italian soprano, *Saronno, Varese 28.10.1797, +Blavio, Como, 1.4.1865. She made her début in 1815 and appeared on various European stages (among them the Théâtre Italien in Paris). Donizetti composed his opera 'Anna Bolena' for her, and Bellini his 'La sonnambula' and 'Norma'. Her singing style was distinguished for its dramatic expression.

PAUER, Ernst, *Vienna 21.12.1826, +Jugenheim, Bergstrasse 9.5.1905. He was professor at the Royal Academy of Music in London and the Imperial Austrian Court pianist. He published popular editions for the piano, and piano pedagogic works. He organized piano concerts with historic instruments from 1861 to 1863 and also in 1867.

PIATTI, Alfredo Carlo, Italian violoncellist, *near Bergamo 8.1.1822, +do. 18.7.1901. He made his debut in Milan in 1834, played with Liszt in Munich in 1843, in Paris and London in 1844 and was one of the principal soloists of the popular Saturday and Monday concerts in London from 1859 to 1898. He composed two cello concertos, a concertino, six cello sonatas, Lieder and solo pieces.

PISARONI, Benedetta Rosamonda. Italian opera singer (contralto), *Piacenza 6.2.1793, +do. 6.8.1872. She first appeared in Bergamo in 1811, and sang soprano until 1813. On the advice of Rossini she changed to contralto and was a great success in Italy and Paris, although her face, scarred by the pox, is said to have been extremely ugly.

PIXIS, Johann Peter, pianist, *Mannheim 10.2.1788, +Baden-Baden 22.12.1874. He accompanied his brother, the violinist Fr. Wilhelm P. on concert tours before settling in Paris in 1825. From 1845 he was teacher in Baden-Baden. He wrote chamber music, three romantic operas and a musical comedy.

PLEYEL, Ignaz Joseph, Austrian composer, *Ruppertsthal 18.6.1757, + near Paris 14.11.1831. He studied under Haydn, was Kapellmesiter to Count Erdödy in 1777, and in 1789 Kapellmeister at Strasbourg Minster. He conducted the 'Professional Concerts' in 1792 in London. He lived in Paris from 1795 where he founded a music business and later a piano company which still exists. Works include: 60 symphonies, 60 string quartettes (in Haydn's style), two operas etc. His son Camille (*1788, +1855) brought the piano company to great fame and in 1838 he opened a concert hall (Salle Pleyel).

PLEYEL, Marie Félicité Denise (known as Camilla Pl.), French pianist, *Paris 4.9.1811, +Brussels 30.3.1875. Married to the composer Camille Pleyel, she was already an accomplished pianist at the age of 15 (pupil of H. Herz, Moscheles and Fr. Kalkbrenner). She enjoyed international success.

REICHA, Anton (Antonin, Antoine),

French composer and music theoretist of Bohemian ancestry, *Prague 26.2.1770, +Paris 28.5.1836. He played for many years with the young Beethoven in the Bonn Electoral Orchestra before becoming music teacher in Hamburg. He lived from 1802 to 1808 in Vienna where he was friendly with Beethoven, Haydn, Albrechtsberger and Salieri. From 1818 he was Professor for Composition at the Paris Conservatory (teacher of Liszt, Gounod, Berlioz, C. Franck). From his compositions the Wind Quintette in the best known.

REINECKE, Carl Heinrich Carsten, *23.6.1824, +Leipzig 10.3.1910. He was Court Pianist for Christian III of Denmark from 1846 to 1848 from 1851 teacher in Cologne, then Music Director in Barmen. From 1860 he was Kapellmeister at the Gewandhauskonzerte in Leipzig and also piano and composition teacher at the Conservatory there. His numerous compositions are based on Schumann and Mendelssohn's styles.

RICHTER, Ernst Friedrich Eduard, Music pedagogue and composer, *Lausitz 24.10.1808, +9.4.1879. At the foundation of the Leipzig Conservatory in 1843 he was teacher of theory with M. Hauptmann. In 1847 he directed the Sing Academy, and was later organist at several Leipzig churches. He succeeded Hauptmann as Music Director of the Leipzig principal churches. He composed an oratorio, masses, motettes, psalms, chamber music and organ pieces. His tutors on harmony and the fugue were much sought after.

RIES, Ferdinand, German pianist and composer, *Bonn 28.1784, +Frankfurt 13.1.1838. The son of violinist Franz Anton R. and brother of the violinist and music pedagogue Hubert R. He studied under L. van Beethoven and J. G. Albrechtsberger,

and was conductor at the concerts of the Philharmonic Society in London. His compositions include the operas 'The Robber Bride' (1828), 'Liska' (1831) and the oratorios 'The Victory of Faith' (1831) and 'The King of Israel' (1837), also symphonies, piano concertos and sonatas – in Beethoven's style.

RIETZ, August Wilhelm Julius, German violoncellist, conductor and composer, *Berlin 28.12.1812, +Dresden 12.9.1877. He studied under C. F. Zelter and succeeded Mendelssohn as Music Director in Düsseldorf in 1835. From 1847 to 1854 he was theatre Kepellmeister in Leipzig (1848–51 also director of the Sing Academy there) and in 1848, as successor to N. Gade, was conductor of the Gewandhauskonzerte and teacher of composition at the Conservatory. In 1860 he was Court Kapellmeister in Dresden and took over as Artistic Director of the Conservatory there in 1870. His works are stylistically influenced by the Viennese classics and Mendelssohn. He wrote operas, symphonies, concertos, chamber music, choir pieces, Lieder, and the music to Goethe's Liederspiel 'Jery und Bätely' (1840).

ROMBERG, Andreas Jacon, violinist and composer, *Vechta 27.4.1767, +Gotha 10.11.1821. Cousin of the violoncellist Bernhard Heinrich R. He succeeded L. Spohr as Court Kapellmeister in Gotha. His compositions are stylistically influenced by J. Haydn and W. A. Mozart. He wrote operas and 'The Song of the Bells' (1808, for choir and orchestra), church vocal pieces, symphonies, violin concertos and chamber music.

ROSSINI, Gioachini (Gioacchino, Giovacchino) Antonio, Italian composer, *Pesaro 29.2.1792, +Passey, near Paris 13.11.1868. From 1810 he was famous in Italy as an opera composer and from 1823 he lived in Paris where for two years he directed the Opéra Italien. From 1836 to 1848 he was in Bologna as Director of the Music School, and returned to Paris in 1855. He is known as one of the last of the great masters of the old 'opera buffa' ('The Barber of Seville', 'The Thieving Magpie', 'The Califf of Baghdad' etc.) He also wrote serious operas: 'William Tell', 'Othello', and church music and instrumental works.

RUBINI, Giovanni Battista, *Romano, Bergano 7.4.1794, +do. 3.3.1854. From modest beginnings, he rose to become the 'King of the Tenors'; 1831–43 he alternated between Paris and London. In 1843 he undertook a tour with F. Liszt to Holland and Germany, and later sang in St Petersburg, and at the most important European cities, specializing in operas by Rossini, Bellini and Donizetti.

RUBINSTEIN, Anton Grigorjewitsch, pianist and composer, *Wychwatinez, near Balta 16 (28).11.1829, +Peterhof, St Petersburg 8.(20.)11.1894. He studied in Moscow, Paris and Berlin and was Court Pianist and Conductor of the Court Kapelle in St. Petersburg in 1858. In 1859 he took over the direction of the Russian Music Society and founded (in 1862) the Imperial Conservatory in St Petersburg. He wrote numerous stage works, six symphonies, five piano concertos, ten string quartettes and oratorios etc.

SALIERI, Antonio, Italian composer, *Legnago, Verona 18.8.1750, +Vienna 7.5.1825. He was Chamber composer and Kapellmeister of the Italian Opera. From 1788 to 1790 he was Court Kapellmeister, and Director of the Court Choir Orchestra. Until 1824. In his compositions there are influences of the Neapolitan school and the works of Gluck. Among his pupils were L.van. Beethoven, J. H, Hummel, F. Liszt, G. Meyerbeer, W. A. Mozart and F. Schubert.

SCARLATTI, Giuseppe Domenico (known as Mimmo), Italian composer, *Naples 26.10.1685, +Madrid 23.7.1757. He was Kapellmeister at the private theatre of the Polish Queen Maria Casimira in Rome (1709), for whom he wrote seven operas. In 1714 he was Kapellmeister of the Giulia Chapel in St Peter, and also for the Portuguese Embassy. In 1720 he lived at the Court of Joao V. of Portugal in Lisbon where he taught the infant Maria Barbara. In 1729 he went to Seville, and in 1733 to Madrid. During his Spanish years he wrote most of his sonatas (mainly for the cembalo) which through their stylistic innovations, were of great importance to piano music. He also composed masses and cantatas.

SCHALL, Claus, Danish composer, *Copenhagen 28.4.1757, +Kongens Lyngby 10.8.1835. From 1792 he was Concert Master at the Royal Theatre, Copenhagen, from 1817 Music Director. He wrote about 20 ballets, including 'Lagertha', 'Rolf Blaaskjäg', 'Romeo and Juliette', 'Macbeth' and various violin pieces.

SCHICHT, Johann Gottfried, *Reichenau near Zittau 29.9.1754, +Leipzig 16.2.1823. He was conductor of the Gewandhauskonzerte in 1785. He composed church music (oratorios, masses, motettes, cantatas) and also a piano concerto and sonatas. His choral book with 1285 melodies is of great historical value.

SCHILLING, Gustav, German music author, *Hanover 3.11.1803, +Nebraska ?.3.1881. He was Director of the Stöpelschen Music School in Stuttgart; 1839–42 he edited the annuals of the German National Society for Music. For political reasons he fled to

New York in 1857 and from there travelled to Montreal – and finally to Nebraska. He wrote numerous musical, scientific, philosophical, historical and pedagogic publications.

SCHINDLER, Anton, German conductor and music author, *Meedl (Neustadt) 13.6.1798, +Bockenheim, Frankfurt-on-Main 16.1.1864. He was violinist and orchestra director at the Josefstädt Theatre in Vienna, and in 1825 at the Kärntnertortheater. From 1823 to 1824 he conducted all of Beethoven's symphonies. His friendship with Beethoven goes back to 1814. In 1816 he was Beethoven's 'unpaid privy secretary'. From 1831 to 1835 he was Music Director and cathedral Kapellmeister in Münster, then until 1837 in Aachen. From 1840 he was mostly on tour. He settled in Frankfurt in 1848 where he devoted his time to writing and teaching. His main work was the 'Biography of Ludwig van Beethoven' (translated into English by Moscheles), which forms the basis for all subsequent works about Beethoven. His work on Beethoven remains the most valuable source for Beethoven research.

SCHLESINGER, Maurice, (actually Moritz), son of the Berlin Music Publisher Adolph Martin Schl. He founded in 1821 a publishing house in Paris and later the newspaper 'Gazette musicale', in which Wagner, among others, wrote. In 1846 the firm transferred to the Brandus Publishers.

SCHROEDER-DEVRIENT, Wilhelmine, German soprano, *Hamburg 6.12.1804, +Coburg 26.1.1860. She made her début in 1821 and sang from 1823 to 1847 at the Dresden Court Theatre. Because of her participation in the May uprising of 1849 she was expelled from Dresden. In 1856 she worked as Lieder singer in Berlin. She appeared in the roles of Leonore in 'Fidelio' by L. van Beethoven, Adriano in 'Rienzi' by R. Wagner and Venus in 'Tannhäuser' by Wagner, and was also a talented actress.

SCHUMANN, Clara Josefine, pianist and composer, daughter of F. Wieck, *Leipzig 13.9.1819, +Frankfurt 20.5.1896. She studied under her father, had already appeared in public in 1828 and undertook extensive concert tours from 1832 on. She married R. Schumann in 1840. From 1878 to 1892 she was piano teacher at the High Conservatory in Frankfurt. As pianist she was famous mainly as an interpreter of the works of Beethoven, Chopin and Schumann, and later also of Brahms. Her early compositions are in the virtuoso style of the time, her later ones (from 1840) show the influence of Schumann.

SCHUMANN, Robert Alexander, composer, *Zwikkau 8.6.1810, +Endenich, Bonn 29.7.1856. He initially studied law simultaneously with the piano, under F. Wieck in Leipzig. He founded the 'Neue Zeitschift für Musik' (New Magazine for Music) in 1834 which was to promote romantic music. He married Clara Wieck in 1840, against her father's will. At the request of Mendelssohn in 1843–44 he became teacher of composition at the Leipzig Conservatory, then he settled in Dresden where he directed the Liedertafel. In 1850 he became Music Director in Düsseldorf, but had to retire from this position in 1853 because of ill health. In 1853 in disturbed mental state he fell into the Rhine, was rescued and interred in the Endenich Clinic. He is recognized as the main representative of the 'musical high romantic' in Germany. His piano works and Lieder are the most important of all his works.

SCHUPPANZIGH, Ignaz, *Vienna 20.11.1776, +do. 2.3.1830. He was violinist in the Viennese Court Orchestra and Music Director of the Viennese Kärntnertortheater. With the Schuppanzigh String Quartette he performed L. van Beethoven's string quartettes. He arranged the first public quartette evenings (i.e. outside the stately homes) and with them contributed much to the forming of a provincial music culture.

SCOTT, Sir (1820) Walter, author, *Edinburgh 15.8.1771, +Castle Abbotsford, Roxburgshire 21.9.1832. He came from one of the four Scottish clans, was a lawyer, sheriff of the county Selkirk, and a judge in Edinburgh. He published several epic romances in verse, mostly from Scottish history, and also wrote 27 novels in quick succession (the Waverley novels), mostly with a 17th and 18th century Scottish background. Scott was founder of the European historical novel.

SEYFRIED, Ignaz Xaver, Austrian composer and music author, *Vienna 15.8.1776, +do. 27.8.1841. He was a piano pupil of Mozart and L. Koželuch, and of J. G. Albrechtsberger and P.v.Winter in composition. From 1797 to 1828 he was Kapellmeister at the E. Schikaneders Theatre in Vienna. He wrote over 100 plays, orchestral and chamber music, as well as spiritual vocal music. He published Albrechtsberger's theoretical works in total (1826) and published 'L.van Beethoven's Studies in Basso Continuo, Counterpoint and Composition'.

SOR (also Sors) Joseph Fernando Macari, Spanish guitarist and composer, baptized Barcelona 14.2.1778, +Paris 10.7.1839. His compositions are distinguished by differentiated harmonics and his particular treatment of the main melodic theme. He also wrote a guitar tutor.

SMART, Sir George Thomas, British conductor, organist and composer, *London 10.5.1776, +do. 23.2.1876. He was founder of the Philharmonic Society in London and conducted there between 1813 and 1844. He was acquainted with L. van Beethoven and R. Schumann, and conducted many music festivals.

SONTAG, Henriette Gertrude Walpurgis, (actually Sonntag, Countess Rossi S. of Lauenstein), soprano, *Koblenz 3.1.1806, +Mexico 17.6.1854. She made her début in 1821 and appeared at the Italian and German Operas in Vienna (where she sang the role of Euryanthe at the premiere), and at the Königstadt Theatre in Berlin as well as at the Opéra Italien in Paris. She was famous for her role as Rosina in the 'Barber of Seville' by Rossini. She was also famous for her wide vocal range and her coloratura.

SPOHR, Louis (Ludewig), German violinist and conductor, *Braunschweig 5.4.1784, +Kassel 22.10.1859. He was, with Paganini, the most important violinist of his time, famous for his expressive adagio play. At first he was Kapellmeister at the Theater an der Wien, and later at the Municipal Theatre in Frankfurt. From 1822 he was Court Kapellmeister in Kassel. He wrote operas ('Faust', 'Jessonda', 'Berggeist'), ten symphonies, 15 violin concertos, clarinette concertos, chamber music, oratorios etc., and also a violin tutor.

SPONTINI, Gaspare Luigi Pacifico, Italian composer, *Majolati 14.11.1774, +do. 24.1.1851. He went to Paris in 1803 where the Empress Joséphine appointed him Court Composer and Kapellmeister (1805). From 1810 to 1812 he was Director of the Théâtre Italien. From 1819 he was General Music Director in Berlin. With his early works Spontini belongs to the Neapolitan school, while the tragic, lyrical compositions which he wrote for Paris are reminiscent of Gluck's operas. His principal works: 'La vestale', 'Fernando Cortez', 'Olympie'.

STARK, Ludwig, German music pedagogue, *19.6.1831, +Stuttgart 22.3.1884. He founded, with Faisst, Lebert and others, the Stuttgart Conservatory, at which he taught singing, harmony, score-reading and music history until his death. He published (with S. Lebert) the famous 'Grosse Klavierschule' (Great Piano Tutor) and with A. and C. Kissner a collection of Celtic folksongs (Burns Album) as well as several albums of arrangements of classical music. He wrote tutors, instrumental and piano pieces, Lieder and choral works.

STOCKHAUSEN, Julius, baritone and singing teacher, *Paris 22.7.1826, +Frankfurt-on-Main 22.9.1906. He studied at the Paris Conservatory and with M. Garcia in London. He was a well-known concert singer and also sang in oratorios and appeared as Brahms' interpreter. He was Director of the Philharmonic Concerts and the Sing Academy in Hamburg (1862–67), also of the Stern Singing Society in Berlin (1874–78). He wrote a 'Singing Method Tutor'.

STREICHER, Johann Andreas, pianist, composer and piano maker, *13.12.1761, +Vienna 25.5.1833. On his marriage to the pianist Nannette (Anna Maria) Stein (*1769, +1833) he worked at the piano company owned by her and her brother Matthäus Stein in Vienna. The pianos made by the Streichers were very popular with Mozart and L. van Beethoven because of their full tone and their balanced playing mode.

THALBERG, Sigismund, Austrian pianist and composer, *Geneva 7.1.1812, +Naples 24.7.1871. He studied under J. N. Hummel in Vienna and appeared in Viennese private circles at the age of 15. His début in Paris in 1836 started a controversy between the Liszt and the Thalberg supporters. In 1837 it came to a contest, at which Liszt proved himself the superior. In 1855–1856 he toured America, and from 1858 retired to Naples. His compositions are counted as salon music (phantasies on operatic themes, études, caprices, nocturnes etc).

TOMASEK, TOMASCHEK, Vaclav Jan (Wenzel Johann), Bohemian composer, *Skutsch, Bohemia 17.4.1774, +Prague 3.4.1850. He was self taught; directed his own music school (1820). His pupils included A. Dreyschock, E. Hanslick. He composed numerous Lieder and instrumental works (symphonies, piano concertos, piano trios, piano quartettes, piano sonatas).

VESQUE VON PUETTLINGEN, Johann, Austrian composer, *Opole, Poland 23.7.1803, +Vienna 29.10.1883. He was engaged as diplomat in the Austrian service until 1872. He was instructed by Leidesdorf, Moscheles and Votisek in the piano, and by Lannoy and Sechter in composition. He was a famous exponent in music-loving circles in pre-march Vienna. His compositions are mostly written under the pseudonym J. Hoven. They are: nine operas, two masses, string quartettes, piano pieces and about 300 Lieder.

VIARDOT-GARCIA, Pauline Michelle -Ferdinande, French mezzo-soprano of Spanish ancestry, *Paris 18.7.1821, +do. 18.5.1910. She was the sister of Maria Malibran, daughter and pupil of M. del Polo Vicente Garcia. She also studied under A. Reicha (piano and composition), made her début in 1839 as Desdemona (in 'Otello' by Rossini) and appeared at the Théâtre Italien, Paris. She was best known for her extraordinary vocal range of over three octaves.

The following belonged to her repertoire: Lieder by B. Marcello, F. Schubert, N. Rimski-Korsakov and P. Tchaikovsky. She also composed operettas, Lieder and songs.

VIEUXTEMPS, Henri Joseph Francois, Belgian violinist and composer, *Verviers 17.2.1820, +Mustapha, Algiers 6.6.1881. He studied under Bériot, Sechter and Reicha and was Professor at the Brussels Conservatory from 1871 to 1873 (until his left hand became paralysed). He is known as one of the main exponents of the French school of violinists. He composed several violin pieces and chamber music.

VOGLER, Georg Joseph, (also called Abbé Vogler), composer and music theorist, *Würzburg-Pleichach 15.6.1749, +Darmstadt 6.5.1814. He studied as stipendiate of the Kurfürsten Karl Theodor in Italy, was ordained there as priest and returned in 1775 to Mannheim, where he founded the Mannheim Tonal School. From 1784 he was Court Kapellmeister in Munich. From 1786–1799 he was Kappellmeister and teacher to the Swedish Crown Princes in Stockholm. From 1807 he was Court Kappellmeister and director of a tonal school in Darmstadt (he taught C. M. von Weber and Meyerbeer). He composed operas and church music.

WALSH, John, instrument maker, *1665, +London 13.3.1736. As one of Europe's leading music publishers, he published numerous composers' works: Purcell, Corelli and Handel, among others. His business was carried on by his son.

WEBER, Friedrich Dionys, Bohemian composer and music author, *Welchau 9.10.1766, +Prague 25.12.1842. He was a pupil of Abbé Vogler, was co-founder and first Director of the Prague Conservatory (1811) and a renowned teacher. Among his pupils can be counted Moscheles and Kalliwoda. He wrote several operas, military marches, sextettes for horns, dances and variations for piano, 18 cantatas etc. He also published several tutors.

WEBER, Gottfried, music theoretist, *Freinsheim 1.3.1779, +Kreuznach 21.9.1839. He was lawyer and judge in Wetzlar, Mannheim, Mainz and Darmstadt. Along with his juristic main occupation, he was actively engaged as composer, theorist, conductor and critic. He introduced a system of lettering for chord notation – capitals for major chords and lower case for minor. He also wrote 'Attempt at an order theory on the art of tonal laws' (1817–21).

WEGELER, Franz Gerhard, German music author, *Bonn 22.8.1765, +Koblenz 7.5.1848. At 19 years of age he was Professor of Medicine and until 1807 worked as a doctor in Koblenz. He was a childhood friend of Beethoven, and was the husband of Elenore von Breuning. Together with F. Ries he published an important source work on the youth of Beethoven, 'Biographic notes about L. v. Beethoven'.

WEIGL, Joseph, composer and conductor, *Eisenstadt 28.3.1766, +Vienna 3.2.1846. He studied under J. G. Albrechtsberger and A. Salieri and from 1791 to 1823 was conductor of the Vienna Court Opera. He is best known for his operas and church music in the style of the Viennese classics.

WESTMORLAND, John Fane, Earl of (until 1841 Lord Burghersh), English composer, *London 3.2.1784, +his castle, Apthorpe House 16.10.1859. His main occupation was as soldier and diplomat. He studied music from 1809 to 1812 in Lisbon under M. A. Portugal, as well as in Vienna under J. Mayseder. In 1822 at his instigation, the

Royal Academy of Music was founded. He wrote six operas, dramatic cantata, 'Il ratto di Proserpina', symphonies and folk music.

WEYSE, Christopher Ernst Friedrich, Danish composer, *Altona, Hamburg 5.3.1774, +Copenhagen 8.10.1842. He studied in Copenhagen under J. A. P. Schulz and was organist there from 1794 (his pupils were: J. P. E. Hartmann and N. Gade). He composed instrumental pieces at first (seven symphonies in Haydn style) and later turned to popular dramatic works (Singspielen). His comprehensive romance pieces are accepted as an expression of Danish feeling for nature. As church musician he was the first Dane to write choral works for four voices.

WIECK, Johann Gottlob Friedrich, music pedagogue, *Pretzsch, Wittenberg 18.8.1785, +Loschwitz, Dresden. 6.10.1873. He founded a piano factory and musical lending institute in Leipzig (which was not long in existence, however) and then devoted himself exclusively to piano teach-ing. He taught according to his own method on the basis of the Johann Bernhard Logier system (*1777, +1846). Among his pupils were his daughters Clara and Marie and also R. Schumann and H. v. Bülow.

ZELTER, Carl Friedrich, composer and music pedagogue, *Berlin 11.12.1758, +do. 15.5.1832. Originally in the building trade, he studied under C. F, Fasch and enrolled in his Sing Academy in 1791, taking over its direction in 1800. In 1809 he contributed a Liedertafel. In 1822 he founded the Royal Institute of Church Music (later, State Academy for Church and School Music) which he directed until his death. As composer he is known for his folklore solo and choir pieces (especially Lieder for male voice choirs). He was friendly with J.W. V. Goethe whose ballads Zalter set to music (e.g. 'Der König von Thule). Among his pupils were F. Mendelssohn Bartholdy, O. Nicolai, C. Loewe and G. Meyerbeer.